INVENTING EQUAL OPPORTUNITY

■ ■ ■ ■

INVENTING EQUAL OPPORTUNITY

■ ■ ■ ■

Frank Dobbin

Princeton University Press
Princeton and Oxford

Published by Princeton University Press, 41 William Street, Princeton, New Jersey 08540
In the United Kingdom: Princeton University Press,
6 Oxford Street, Woodstock, Oxfordshire OX20 1TW
press.princeton.edu

Second printing, and first paperback printing, 2011
Paperback ISBN: 978-0-691-14995-0

The Library of Congress has cataloged the cloth edition of this book as follows

Dobbin, Frank.
Inventing equal opportunity / Frank Dobbin.
p. cm.
Includes bibliographical references and index.
ISBN 978-0-691-13743-8 (hardcover : alk. paper) 1. Discrimination in employment—
United States. 2. Affirmative action programs—United States. 3. Diversity in the
workplace—United States. 4. Sexual harassment of women—United States. 5. Civil
rights—United States. 6. Personnel management—United States. I. Title.
HD4903.5.U58D63 2009
331.13'30973—dc22
2008039007

British Library Cataloging-in-Publication Data is available
This book has been composed in Palatino and Copperplate Gothic

Printed on acid-free paper. ∞
Printed in the United States of America

3 5 7 9 10 8 6 4 2

For Michèle

CONTENTS

ACKNOWLEDGMENTS

My generation grew up with the civil rights movement and civil unrest, with demonstrations against the Vietnam War, and with the women's movement. My parents demonstrated for civil rights in the South and the North when I was small, and dinner table conversation revolved around Martin Luther King Jr. and Malcolm X as much as around the Kennedy boys. Soon it revolved around Lyndon Johnson and Richard Nixon and Daniel Ellsberg and the Vietnam War, and around Betty Friedan and Gloria Steinem and the women's movement.

Civil rights and women's movement protesters took to the streets, but before long the energy of the demonstrations was absorbed. Absorbed in school desegregation actions. Absorbed in college open admissions programs and gender integration in the Ivy League. Absorbed in affirmative action at work. What happened to the civil rights and women's movements when they were absorbed has been a driving question for my generation. Did the movements change the world?

My interest in what employers were doing began when my graduate school mentors John Meyer, Dick Scott, and Ann Swidler asked me and my colleague Lauren Edelman to collaborate on a study of due process mechanisms in workplaces, mechanisms that we soon learned had been boosted by the Civil Rights Act. We saw that the civil rights movement had been institutionalized in personnel departments, under personnel executives who went willingly or sometimes kicking and screaming down the path of equal employment opportunity. The grievance procedures we studied were an unexpected result of the movement, and it is that early insight—that civil rights law had unanticipated and unrecognized consequences—that drives this book.

Much of the story in this book is drawn from surveys and in-depth interviews with managers I conducted, along with several collaborators, between 1983 and 2007. I owe collaborators, research assistants, and foundations thanks for their roles in employer surveys in 1983, 1986, 1997, and 2002. Each survey traced the history of employment practices in hundreds of American workplaces, over time. My collaborators in 1983 were Lauren Edelman, John Meyer, Dick Scott, and Ann Swidler.

My collaborators in 1986 were John Meyer, Dick Scott, and John Sutton, and assistants in conducting the survey were Jessica Torres and Roberta Stich. My collaborator in 1997 was Erin Kelly, and the survey was conducted by the Maryland Survey Research Center, where Johnny Blair and Elena Tracy carried the project through. My collaborator in 2002 was Alexandra Kalev, and the survey was conducted by the Princeton Survey Research Center under the direction of Edward Freeland. Nicole Esparza and Leslie Hinkson helped with that survey.

These surveys, and research reports stemming from them, were generously supported by foundations and sabbatical fellowships over the years. Thanks to the University Committee at Princeton for providing several seed grants to fund different parts of the project. Thanks to the Russell Sage Foundation for a residential fellowship leave, and particularly to Eric Wanner, Madge Spitaleri, and Auri Martinez. For research assistance at the Russell Sage Foundation, thanks to Lisa Kahraman and John Smelcer. Special thanks to Reynolds Farley for advice. Thanks to the Center for Advanced Study in the Behavioral Sciences for a sabbatical leave. Thanks to the Russell Sage Foundation for supporting the 1983 survey and the 2002 survey, to the National Science Foundation for supporting the 1985 and 2002 surveys, and to the Alfred P. Sloan Foundation for supporting the 1997 survey. Thanks to Kathleen Christensen at the Sloan Foundation for her input and support. Thanks to the Radcliffe Institute and the John Simon Guggenheim Foundation for the sabbatical leave that allowed me to complete this book. Thousands of personnel specialists have generously participated in interviews over the years. I'm particularly grateful for their time and wisdom.

Thanks go to several people who read the manuscript and offered comments: Anthony Chen, Erin Kelly, Michèle Lamont, Daniel Sabbagh, John Skrentny.

I owe my various collaborators gratitude, as well, for ideas presented here that we worked out together. The seeds of many ideas can be found in studies I worked on with James Baron, Lauren Edelman, P. Devereaux Jennings, Alexandra Kalev, Erin Kelly, John Meyer, W. Richard Scott, John Sutton, and Ann Swidler over the years.[1] I thank them for helping me to grasp the big picture, piece by piece. Thanks also to Laura Thomas and Melissa Rico, who helped with notes and manuscript preparation and made the book readable. Tim Sullivan at Princeton University Press gave me very useful suggestions about structure and substance, and the book is better for his input. Richard Isomaki and Jessica Matteson repaired my stylistic gaffes and smoothed out the prose.

I dedicate this book to Michèle Lamont, who for more than twenty years has shared my life, and for twenty years has been my colleague as well. For being my intellectual heroine, as well as my partner in life.

REGULATING DISCRIMINATION
The Paradox of a Weak State

IN 1961, JOHN F. KENNEDY DECREED that companies wanting to do business with the federal government would have to take affirmative action to end discrimination. The year after Kennedy's assassination, Lyndon Johnson signed the Civil Rights Act of 1964, outlawing discrimination in education, housing, public accommodations, and employment. No one could have anticipated the effects of these mandates on the workplace. Not a single sentence remains from the corporate personnel manual of 1960. Firms have changed how they recruit, hire, discipline, evaluate, compensate, and fire workers.

The agents of change were civil rights activists and then politicians, but the people who invented equal opportunity—decided what it would mean on the ground—were personnel managers. After the Civil Rights Act was passed, social movement activists played bit roles. Members of Congress, judges, federal officials, and presidents had parts in the drama, but it was personnel experts who concocted equal opportunity programs, and later diversity management programs, in the context of changing ideas about discrimination. Public officials approved some new programs and rejected others, but it was personnel experts who put the programs together. Some of the changes were visible and dramatic, as when firms struck rules reserving good jobs for white men or wrote rules against trading jobs for sex. But many of the changes were subtle, as when firms began advertising every open job or set up written performance evaluation systems, and their origins in civil rights law were soon forgotten.

If the Civil Rights Act of 1964 had read, "It shall be unlawful for employers to operate without written job descriptions, diversity training programs, and sexual harassment grievance procedures," firms would have seen the revolution coming. Instead, the act outlawed discrimination in broad strokes. Most managers never imagined that the law applied to their companies. Yet once enforcement was expanded in the early 1970s, personnel experts were able to sketch equal opportunity programs with a free hand precisely because Congress had presented employers with a tabula rasa rather than setting out precise rules and regulations. Personnel managers tried one thing after another, waiting to see if the courts would wipe the slate clean again. Mostly the courts let the changes stand.

This is the story of a professional network that changed course dramatically in the 1960s and 1970s. Circa 1960, personnel managers were negotiating with unions in some firms, trying to keep them at bay in others, and managing new hires and benefits everywhere. A decade later a group of personnel experts at military contractors such as Lockheed and General Electric had redefined the job of personnel. They invented the first wave of compliance measures and created a national network, tied together by military contractors worried about losing contracts and later by professional associations and business groups such as the Society for Human Resource Management and the Conference Board. This network of personnel specialists, some of whom now styled themselves as equal opportunity consultants, created wave after wave of equal opportunity innovations, linking each to ideas about discrimination put forth by activists and academics. In response to law professor Catharine MacKinnon's campaign to define sexual harassment as job discrimination, they built harassment grievance procedures and training programs. In response to new ideas about cognition and stereotyping from the social sciences, they devised diversity training programs that would make managers sensitive to their own unconscious biases. Now these privately concocted remedies are everywhere. Job hunters and judges are suspicious of firms that don't have them.

Personnel managers had created a legal code internal to the corporation—equal opportunity rules and pledges inscribed not in federal statutes but in corporate human resources manuals. Every new employee gets diversity training; job prerequisites are spelled out in writing; workers can only be disciplined by a committee; harassment claims go to a grievance panel. Firms have become states unto themselves.

This revolution has not been silent, but the public debate over equal opportunity has largely missed the point. Pundits decried quotas and reverse discrimination, which never became commonplace, but neglected the widespread adoption of performance evaluations and job descriptions, grievance procedures and training programs.[1] Many of these things were folded smoothly into the human resources manual, and so even human resources managers forgot that they became popular as equal opportunity measures. Then when affirmative action came under attack in the early 1980s, human resources experts pointedly argued that diversity training and work-family programs were not affirmative action measures at all, but were there to increase productivity.

Why Personnel Defined Equal Opportunity

There is a rich trove of books on each of the first three acts in the equal opportunity drama: the civil rights movement, passage of equal opportunity laws, and federal enforcement of those laws. Those books neglect the long fourth act, in which the personnel profession's compliance efforts translated the law into practice. The drama only had a fourth act because, rather than spelling out precisely what equal opportunity meant, Congress left it to judges and bureaucrats to decide, and judges and bureaucrats heard constant appeals from citizens to rethink the definition of discrimination. Public officials came to define fair employment by looking at the "best practices" of leading firms, and so in the end the personnel profession defined equal opportunity through its compliance initiatives.

In the first act of the equal opportunity story, the civil rights movement called for Congress to outlaw discrimination in employment, education, housing, and public accommodations, demanding legislation that, with the one hundredth anniversary of Lincoln's Emancipation Proclamation of 1862 looming, might make good on the promise that all men (and women) are equal in the eyes of the law.[2] While the civil rights movement spurred John F. Kennedy's affirmative action order in 1961 and the Civil Rights Act of 1964, activists played little role in deciding what compliance would look like. At first the Urban League and the NAACP created jobs banks and advised employers on how to recruit, but those contributions were short-lived. By the end of the 1960s, personnel administrators had taken the baton and were running the next leg of the relay on their own. As for that other social movement, the women's movement, it got rolling after personnel experts had already begun to define compliance. While activists went on to influence public policy, they no more designed corporate compliance than did civil rights activists.[3]

In the second act, politicians required federal contractors to practice equal opportunity in 1961, required employers to pay men and women the same wages for the same work in 1963, and required all employers to offer equal employment opportunity in 1964.[4] Books chronicling how policymakers negotiated these policies, and which legislators and regions led the charge, document just how these changes came about. Yet these studies also made clear that from the time policymakers outlawed discrimination, they did little to define compliance.

In the third act, federal administrators and courts shaped how these vague laws would be enforced.[5] Rather than encouraging a color-blind approach, for instance, federal administrators encouraged a race- and gender-conscious system of accounting for progress because they needed a metric by which to judge firms.[6] The federal reporting system focused employer attention on the issue of equal opportunity, but it did not define what employers would do. When bureaucrats or the courts took stands on compliance, most ratified what the Fortune 500 were doing. In 1971 the Supreme Court faulted Duke Power Company for excluding black applicants by testing them for skills not used on the job. That ruling ratified test validation practices that leading military contractors had embraced in the 1960s, based on decades-old advice from personnel psychologists. A generation later the Supreme Court's twin sexual harassment decisions of 1998, credited with encouraging companies to adopt harassment grievance procedures, in fact ratified procedures that 95 percent of employers already had in place. Over the years, then, personnel experts taught public officials what discrimination was through the programs they made popular.

Courts and bureaucrats played their part in defining compliance, but the popular corporate programs such as open job posting, job test validation, and maternity leave were worked out by personnel experts, not public officials. Judges rarely did more than give the nod to programs already popular among leading firms. Courts followed—they did not lead.[7] Congress rarely did more than allow innovations to stand, but in some cases it put popular practices into writing, as in 1978 when it required all employers to treat pregnancy like other disabilities. The Supreme Court's follow-the-leader approach is also evident in its rulings on affirmative action in education. In his 1978 opinion in the famous five-to-four *Bakke* decision, overturning quotas in university admissions but supporting integration as a goal, Justice Lewis Powell held up Harvard as an example, quoting its amicus brief: "The belief that diversity adds an essential ingredient to the educational process has long been a tenet of Harvard College admissions. . . . Harvard College now recruits not only Californians or Louisianans but also blacks and Chicanos."[8]

This book chronicles the fourth act in the drama, which began soon after John F. Kennedy signed Executive Order 10925 in 1961, requiring firms with federal contracts to take "affirmative action" to end discrimination. Personnel professionals crafted equal opportunity programs with instruments drawn from their professional arsenal, and those programs came to define fair employment and discrimination. It was personnel experts who decreed that managers should advertise jobs and that they should use performance evaluations to judge applicants for promotions.

Personnel took charge for three reasons. First, Congress, John F. Kennedy, and Lyndon Johnson had crafted bills and presidential edicts in high-minded, but vague, language. They outlawed discrimination without saying what it was. In the context of America's separation of powers and common-law tradition, this meant that civil rights law was ripe for what sociologist Lauren Edelman terms the "endogenous" definition of compliance.[9] Those being regulated helped to establish the terms of compliance. This happened in part because Congress had decided not to create a regulatory agency with independent authority to set compliance standards—an agency in the mold of the National Labor Relations Board.[10] The result was a system in which scattered judges across the country evaluated claims about compliance. Judges were in no position to invent compliance standards from scratch, so they took their cues from leading firms.

Second, personnel experts took charge because they saw an opportunity to push programs they had long favored, at a time when unions were in decline and thus when many of their traditional duties were on the wane. They used civil rights law to expand their duties, and numbers, within the firm. They now snuck virtually every element of the "modern personnel system" of the fifties in through the back door as an equal opportunity measure, arguing that programs to rationalize the allocation of people to jobs, and their movement up through the ranks, would increase efficiency while eliminating bias. By the end of the century the profession had grown tenfold, while the workforce had only doubled.

Third, the other principal contender for defining compliance was the legal profession, but lawyers were not so anxious to take over this task. Personnel experts succeeded by arguing that bureaucratic innovations could keep firms out of court, but lawyers balked at the idea of peddling remedies that the courts had not approved. That was not part of the profession's modus operandi. Thus personnel experts came to define compliance in part because they had something lawyers were not offering, plausible bureaucratic vaccines against litigation. Despite the absence of evidence that those vaccines stopped discrimination, judges gave companies that adopted those "best practices" credit for acting in good faith. They were suspicious of firms that weren't doing all of the latest things.[11] And so what personnel made popular gradually became lawful.

How Public Policy Spawned Legal Codes in Companies

Because Washington never codified fair employment regulations, companies inscribed their own regulations in their human resources manuals. Perhaps if fair employment advocates had won a powerful administrative agency, that agency might have set clear standards. Instead, two toothless federal agencies and dozens of state fair employment agencies oversaw firms, and hundreds of judges were responsible for interpreting the law. No single official could demand that an employer cease discriminating and sanction the employer who did not.[12] Thus no one could give employers a clear answer to the question, "How do we stay out of court?"

The Paradox of America's Weak State

The fragmentation of the U.S. state, with powers dispersed across federal, state, and local governments, and with legislative, judicial, and administrative branches at each level, is usually described as a weakness. The paradox of this particular kind of weakness is that it led to extensive corporate compliance efforts by firms worried that agencies and courts might change compliance standards. Executives tried to anticipate where the law would move next and installed entire departments devoted to tracking legal change.[13] Fragmentation made the law unpredictable in part by giving citizens so many venues for pursuing change. They could appeal to Congress to clarify and expand statutes, to federal judges to reinterpret statues, to state judges to assess liability under tort laws, to state legislatures to expand the definition of discrimination, to federal bureaucrats to issue new guidelines, and to city governments to outlaw newly recognized kinds of discrimination. The result is that the state was "porous," open to input.[14] This system allowed citizens to appeal to judges and bureaucrats to reinterpret even laws that were written with crystal clear language, with the express purpose of preventing judicial expansion.[15] Thus the Civil Rights Act, designed explicitly to protect against judicial expansion, was expanded by judges nonetheless.

Corporate equal opportunity experts speculated about how interpretation of the law might evolve, and how legislation might change. The speculations often followed new social scientific ideas, such as the idea of institutional discrimination or the idea of cognitive bias. Experts then set up their own regulatory systems within firms consisting of practices ranging from bureaucratic promotion procedures to halt institutional discrimination to mandatory diversity awareness programs to end cognitive bias. Discrimination came to be defined as the absence of such measures.

Seeing the rise of big corporations, the nineteenth-century French philosopher Henri de Saint-Simon feared that they might overwhelm weak states and threaten the rights of citizen-employees. Democratic nations that shared Saint-Simon's concern created legal protections for employees. Paradoxically, in the United States, some of those very protections, such as civil rights laws that seemed to their champions to be too vaguely worded and spottily enforced, led corporations to create their own private codes of legal conduct. America's weak state stimulated private-sector activism in the protection of citizens' rights.

While some firms created their own elaborate equal opportunity systems, the absence of a strong central authority with clear standards meant that others did nothing. Leading firms had diversity task forces, diversity performance evaluations, and sexual harassment counseling programs by the turn of the century, but no one made the laggards follow suit. The vagaries of the law produced tremendous managerial activism, but uneven use of new innovations.

Other countries look very different. In France's civil law system, for instance, the courts do not offer broad new interpretations of legislation, and bureaucrats do not issue guidelines that stray far from the original language of legislation. Government authority is centralized in Paris, not dispersed to the provinces and towns. It is not that French laws are more precise than U.S. laws, but that the French legal system doesn't permit expansive reinterpretation or significant regional variation. In consequence, in France firms did not play the game of trying to guess where antidiscrimination laws would move—they guessed correctly that such laws would not be reinterpreted—and firms did not build their own elaborate internal legal codes.

Corporate Codes and Legal Consciousness

By decentralizing authority over interpretation of the law, the American system allowed legal consciousness to evolve over time, as activists promoted new definitions of discrimination, social scientists identified new dimensions of bias, and personnel experts concocted new measures to expand opportunity.[16] Legal consciousness often corresponds not to black letter law but to social ideas about what should be lawful, and so it is not just that case law changed over time, but that notions of what should be lawful changed.[17] Those ideas changed in the 1950s as American personnel systems were organized around the notion of employee citizenship. Employees came to talk as if the inalienable rights of citizenship carried over to employment.[18] By the late 1950s, a chemical industry personnel executive reported, "Because of the type of country we live in, . . . a man carries this idea about his rights into his work." The head of personnel at a food-processing plant argued that even union members saw their rights as extending beyond the contract:

> Implied rights are implicit in the expectations of the mutual parties to a relationship—like the employment relationship. Usually, when employees talk about their rights, they are not referring to contract provisions. Employees use the term in a broader sense. For example, if an employee feels his supervisor has treated him ill, he speaks of his rights as an individual with human dignity.[19]

Employees thought that the law must protect rights they believed they should have.

The Civil Rights Act was revolutionary, for it seemed to extend certain rights citizens held vis-à-vis the state to relations between citizens. The relationship between employer and employee had been governed by implied or express contract. The principle of freedom of contract meant that the employer and employee could contract with whomever they chose, and terminate the contract at will. The Civil Rights Act changed that, and in so doing, contributed to rights consciousness in the realm of employment. People came to think not only that no-Negroes policies were illegal, but that anything that smacked of unfairness might be illegal. This resonated with the American myth that human rights are inalienable, created not by the state but by the state of nature.

The fact that Title VII case law was voluminous and ever changing encouraged the view that the law must contain many specific prohibitions. Americans came to view as unlawful what personnel manuals prohibited. Even those who wrote the manuals thought this way. I have conducted hundreds of interviews with human resources managers since the early 1980s. They typically report a litany of actions proscribed by law—asking a woman applicant if she is married, firing a minority for not showing up for work, hiring someone without advertising the job, patting a subordinate below the first lumbar vertebra. The things they mention are covered in company manuals and diversity management "best practices" lists, but rarely in legislation or case law. For authority those managers are as likely to cite a discrimination complaint from the six o'clock news or the situation comedy *The Drew Carey Show*, whose main character is an HR manager, as they are to cite a Supreme Court ruling. Indeed, because journalists often cover the most ludicrous discrimination charges, personnel managers, like the rest of us, can end up with a warped sense of what the courts forbid.

The Invention of Equal Opportunity

The history of equal opportunity challenges the conventional wisdom about how social movements, the professions, corporations, and government interact in the United States. According to that wisdom, each citizen has a set of interests that derive from her place in society. Social movements arise to assemble people whose interests are not well represented. Government reacts by altering the distribution of resources or the rights and responsibilities of groups. Corporations either go along with new laws or fight them. Professionals such as lawyers carry out new policies, translating social movement agendas into action.

Journalists and social scientists mostly admire this portrait of the polity, journalists adding to it by showing flaws and social scientists by showing more complexity than meets the naked eye. My contribution is to point out that the conventional wisdom is a caricature that depicts a set of roles and relations. It shapes reality as well as describing it, because people who believe it behave according to its dictates.[20] This particular caricature is mistaken in part because it is static. Because roles and group relations and social norms are social inventions, they are in constant motion. Neither social movements nor professions, neither corporations nor governments follow any particular script for long. All are in constant flux, changing memberships, forms, roles, and interests, and we can see those changes in action by tracing the history of corporate response to equal opportunity law.

Social Movements

According to the conventional wisdom, social movements arise when people whose interests are poorly represented band together to influence the political process. The civil rights movement arose in the 1950s to represent disenfranchised blacks, with the goal of pushing Congress to eliminate discrimination in all realms of life. After Congress passed the Civil Rights Act of 1964, activists picketed employers who wouldn't hire blacks, organized jobs banks, and filed charges against companies that discriminated. Otherwise the movement turned to new tasks, and gradually petered out.

Soon a new social movement emerged, within the personnel profession, to carry the civil rights project forward. But because we don't have a language for describing a national network of professionals as a social movement, we have been blind to its emergence. Many personnel experts fought change, but by the late 1970s there were equal opportunity experts in every major personnel department, most of them women. By the end of the century, seven out of 10 personnel experts were women.[21] They were rarely the same people who marched for civil rights in Selma and Washington, but they continued the work of that social movement just the same. Personnel was transformed from a bastion of white men with backgrounds in labor relations to a bastion of white women attracted by equal opportunity goals. Civil rights was neither the first nor the last social movement to morph into a professional project. From the 1930s, labor leaders and labor relations experts institutionalized the labor movement and its corporate opposition. From the 1970s, environmental engineers carried the green movement forward within the firm. Gynecologists and abortion clinics carried the women's reproductive rights movement forward.

The American model of the social movement as a force outside of the party system had arisen in the nineteenth century with the Second Great Awakening, and had only been institutionalized as part of the political process with the temperance, suffrage, and labor movements.[22] The civil rights movement helped to reestablish that model for a new round of movements in the 1970s championing the rights of women, Latinos, the disabled, and many others.[23] The grassroots women's movement, for instance, was launched by women's advocates in government, building on the model of the civil rights movement.[24] The conventional wisdom about social movements, then, dates to a time when most Americans worked in farming, outside of corporations. As corporations absorbed more of the working population, and hired professional managers, they created the potential for social movements to be institutionalized in this way.

Professions

According to the conventional wisdom, the role of the professions in regulation is to make sure corporations act in accordance with the law. Historically the liberal professions fought to win state licensure and monopolies of authority over specific arenas of expertise. Within the firm, lawyers wrote contracts and approved legal documents and accountants produced financial reports, both groups with the blessing of state licenses.

Because it depicts the law as clear in its requirements, the conventional wisdom misses the role of networks of professionals who span firms in actively constructing and making sense of the law. The personnel profession created a national network of specialists who invented the compliance strategies companies tried out. Because it was personnel experts who won control of the area, rather than lawyers or accountants, virtually all of the new compliance strategies were recycled from the personnel arsenal. New recruitment and training programs of the 1960s, formal hiring and promotion systems of the 1970s, diversity management programs of the 1980s, work life and harassment programs of the 1990s—all of these came from the profession's toolkit. If lawyers had won control, firms might have bureaucratized fewer personnel procedures and codified more employee rights. If accountants had won control, firms might have instituted systems to scrutinize wage inequities and hiring disparities. In other regulatory arenas, such as benefits regulation or health and safety, it was other professionals who took charge, and they did indeed rely on their own professional kit bags.

By spawning a professional specialty devoted to managing compliance, equal opportunity law ensured that compliance would succumb to management fads. Once they had instituted one round of innovations, the experts looked for new things to try, building programs around emergent ideas from academia and from activists. Formal promotion systems and diversity training and flextime spread through the network of corporate equal opportunity managers just as matrix management and quality management spread through corporate operations managers.

Another piece of conventional wisdom about the professions is that they compete for licensure from the state. In this case, personnel experts appealed to CEOs for unofficial licensure to control the domain, and they did so by proffering compliance solutions. This represents a new pattern, for professional groups are handling compliance in realms ranging from environmental protection to securities regulations to corporate governance. In these realms government policy establishes standards, but not the means for reaching those standards.[25] Professional groups then vie to win corporate approval of their strategies. In effect it is now the CEO, not the king, who grants professional licenses by choosing which group will handle compliance in each regulatory realm.

Corporations

According to the conventional wisdom, corporations respond to new regulations either by complying or by battling to have them changed. Corporations responded to the Civil Rights Act by eliminating bans on hiring blacks and married women, and by fighting against other requirements that emerged in case or administrative law. They fought guidelines requiring them to treat pregnancy like other disabilities and won in court, although Congress responded by passing a new law. They fought the definition of sexual harassment as sex discrimination and lost.

Because the conventional wisdom depicts new rules and regulations as codified in legislation, case law, and administrative law, it has blinded us to the fact that rules and regulations can be codified in internal corporate legal codes. Every major corporation developed lawlike rules governing hiring, promotion, discharge, discipline, maternity leave, sexual harassment, and a host of other issues. In embracing these innovations, corporations established compliance norms. Corporate practices were influential in part because federal officials, judges, and members of Congress had little relevant expertise. While each company developed its own legalistic code of behavior, that code resembled others because the components spread through a national network of professionals. Corporations increasingly became states unto themselves, but states that were similar to one another. What a manager could do, and could not do, in the realm of hiring and promotion and discipline and discharge was, for the most part, defined vaguely in legislation and case law but quite precisely in the intercorporate network. At first it was personnel managers at leading federal contractors, worried about losing contracts, who devised equal opportunity measures in the private-sector Plans for Progress group. Personnel and management associations and journals took over the job of promoting equal opportunity innovations in the 1970s, and a new specialty of diversity consultants arose to invent and promote new programs to corporations. That same pattern of policy homogenization can be seen in the world of nation-states, where consultants and academics devise new policy norms that make nation-states look much alike in any policy arena.[26]

Here our fascination with judicial decisions led to a misreading of the role of the courts. Seeing that many companies have sexual harassment policies and procedures that are in line with Supreme Court guidelines, for instance, many conclude that the Court's rulings were successful. In fact, human resources experts devised guidelines for corporations, and then the court vetted them. It was corporations that guided the judiciary, not the other way around. Congress and federal bureaucrats also took their cues from employers, approving some innovations and overturning others. For the most part, they went along with what leading employers were doing, though they rarely ruled that any one innovation, or any concoction, would fully protect employers. This was the case in part because, while the courts were the final arbiter, they did not have the authority to make law. Never knowing quite what might protect them, employers added one innovation after another in the belief that each might one day contribute to a "good-faith effort" defense.

Government

According to the conventional wisdom, Congress enacts new legislation in response to the changing political preferences of the electorate, conveyed through social movements and directly through elected representatives. Then the executive and judicial branches do their best to make sense of new edicts as citizens present their cases for how laws should be enforced. The three branches of government work together, and each checks the power and caprice of the others. The government determines what new laws mean and how they will be carried out.

This system of checks and balances is thought to make America's federal state unusually weak, because the legislature is hemmed in by constitutional constraints. In fact, the vicissitudes of case law led to elaborate corporate compliance efforts, and so this weak state's edicts had strong effects on firms. Fair employment laws led to more extensive corporate responses in the United States than elsewhere precisely because no federal authority could establish a simple litmus test for compliance. If the executive branch could have established simple compliance criteria, as bureaucrats did in other countries, firms would not have had to guess where the law was going. Personnel experts not only created regulatory regimes internal to the firm. In defining how firms could comply with the law, they also defined what was illegal. They defined pregnancy discrimination as illegal by embracing maternity leave in the 1970s, and hostile environment harassment as illegal by banning it in corporate sexual harassment policies in the 1980s. Courts and legislatures followed their lead.

The conventional wisdom also depicts public policy as shifting dramatically with particular historical watersheds, such as the Civil Rights Act. That view is belied by the history of the enforcement of the act. Personnel experts expanded on the original definition. So did women's movement activists, judges, and members of Congress. Together these small steps amounted to a revolution, but a gradual revolution of small steps and missteps that continues today.[27]

The equal opportunity policy nexus reveals blind spots in the conventional view of social movements, professions, corporations, and government. For instance, we see social movements as composed of activists who picket statehouses and corporate headquarters, not of personnel experts administering promotion rules. In the courts we see legal precedent leading everything else, not as responsive to what personnel experts convince firms to do. We see corporations as following the policy dictates of legislators and bureaucrats and judges, not as the locus of policy experimentation and evaluation. But, as we will see, human resources innovations were built on equal opportunity programs spawned by the state. We see the professions as competing for authority in the eyes of the state. But they are increasingly appealing to executives for authority, even over matters of legal compliance, and executives rather than state officials may ultimately choose which profession will reign.

Wave upon Wave of Corporate Programs

The role of the personnel profession in defining equal opportunity is the part of this story that has been least well documented. Personnel experts promoted one round of compliance measures after another. In the 1960s, they wrote nondiscrimination policies based on union nondiscrimination rules, and set up recruitment and training programs for women and minorities. In the 1970s, as the profession more than doubled in size and as the proportion of women rose from a third to nearly a half, they formalized hiring and promotion with performance evaluations, salary classification, and other measures to eliminate managers' opportunities to exercise bias.[28] In the Reagan years, when affirmative action was on the ropes, they changed course, arguing that the new hiring and promotion practices helped to rationalize "human resources management" and relabeling "equal opportunity" programs as "diversity management" programs. Then in the 1990s and 2000s, the increasingly feminized human resources profession focused on women's issues, pushing for the expansion of work and family programs and antiharassment programs. In each period the meaning of discrimination changed, and the roles of social movements, organizations, the professions, and the government evolved in ways that challenged the conventional wisdom.

Equal Opportunity versus Affirmative Action

While politicians and pundits often make a sharp distinction between equal opportunity and affirmative action, in practice the legal requirements for the two programs were only subtly different. All employers were required to practice equal opportunity, and federal contractors were required as well to take "affirmative action" to equalize opportunity. Contractors must write affirmative action programs and open their doors to Department of Labor inspectors. Yet the main legal risk to employers came from lawsuits filed under the Civil Rights Act, which covered everyone, and personnel experts recommended the same compliance strategies to all employers. Sometimes federal contractors installed innovations before noncontractors, but in the end, the two groups of firms installed the same measures for the most part.

The 1960s: Ending Jim Crow in Employment

In response to Kennedy's 1961 order requiring federal contractors to take "affirmative action" to equalize opportunity, personnel executives began to dismantle de jure discrimination. Experts at Lockheed's Georgia aircraft factory were first to propose changes, soon after Lockheed won a billion-dollar air force contract. In short order a network of firms with government contracts organized Plans for Progress as the private-sector arm of the President's Commission on Equal Employment Opportunity (PCEEO), which was headed by Vice President Lyndon Johnson. That group soon had 300 members that pledged to strike rules that excluded blacks, Latinos, and women from jobs ranging from meat cutter to chief executive.

Personnel experts modeled new job posting systems on union posting requirements, so that minorities would hear of openings. Then they built on traditional recruitment programs, which targeted Harvard and Yale and the Big 10, with recruitment programs for blacks and women, targeting Howard and Spellman, Wellesley and Mount Holyoke. They recruited production workers not only in white high schools, but in inner-city high schools that had never before seen recruiters. They built on conventional skill and management training programs, establishing programs designed for blacks and women. Through these changes, personnel experts defined discrimination first as the categorical refusal to consider minorities and women for jobs, and then as systems of recruitment and training that worked only for white men.

Federal agencies in charge of Title VII and affirmative action enforcement looked to what Plans for Progress employers were doing for guidance. The foot soldiers of equal opportunity were to be found not on the streets of Selma, but in the personnel office at Lockheed's Marietta, Georgia, plant. They weren't always willing conscripts, but now the personnel profession had added a specialty, and the old hands would have to change their focus from guarding against unions to protecting equality of opportunity.

The 1970s: Bureaucracy as the Antidote to Discrimination

Washington strengthened civil rights regulations in the early 1970s. The Supreme Court extended the definition of discrimination in 1971, in *Griggs v. Duke Power Company*, striking down employment practices that excluded blacks absent evidence of intent to discriminate. The Department of Labor expanded affirmative action reporting and enforcement. In 1972 Congress gave the EEOC power to bring lawsuits itself. The number of civil rights suits skyrocketed by the end of the decade, from several hundred a year to over five thousand.[29] With its new powers the EEOC negotiated $75 million in consent decree settlements in 1973 and 1974 with AT&T, the first in a string.[30]

The federal government clearly meant business, but no one knew what it expected of employers, not even government officials. Personnel experts like Barbara Boyle, who designed IBM's first equal opportunity program before opening a consultancy, now argued that the courts would question many common employment practices. They championed new equal opportunity programs built on the foundation of classic personnel administration, beginning with formal hiring and promotion practices to stop managers from discriminating.[31] They recommended test validation procedures pioneered by industrial psychologists and recently championed by Plans for Progress. They designed quasi-judicial grievance and disciplinary mechanisms—adapted from their union management toolkit—to intercept discrimination complaints before they reached the courts.[32]

In the process, Boyle and the growing cabal of equal opportunity experts defined formal, legalistic employment rules as the antidote to discrimination, equating fairness with the rule of law. Bias wasn't a problem of individual prejudice, but of management practices that had not been modernized. Eldridge Cleaver's attack on institutional racism gave force to their arguments. Individual bias might be difficult to counteract, but institutional racism could be fought with new institutions.

Personnel managers began to see equal opportunity law as the profession's best chance for expansion. Meanwhile the courts looked to leading firms to define compliance. The women's movement took off in this decade, modeling itself on the civil rights movement after women's advocates in the federal government called for grassroots support. That movement emerged not from the bottom up, but from the top down, organized by elites to build consciousness and support for women's issues.

The 1980s: How Reagan Promoted Diversity Management

Uncertainty about what the Civil Rights Act implied had led firms to appoint experts to track changes in the law and devise compliance strategies. These experts played the role that the courts are supposed to play, adjudicating debates over compliance. When Reagan suggested that affirmative action had done its job and could be dismantled, these experts came to the defense of their programs. They framed performance evaluations, skill training, and job-posting systems as part of an effort to rationalize the allocation of "human resources."[33] Those programs had been torn from the modern personnel administration manual of the 1950s, and rebranded as affirmative action measures, and so now they came full circle. In *The Economics of Discrimination*, economist Gary Becker had argued that discrimination raised wage costs by shutting some groups out of the labor market.[34] Experts now argued that it was inefficient to allow middle managers to favor workers of their own sex and race, and pointed out that new workers would be disproportionately female and minority.[35]

The efficiency argument worked for programs like job-posting systems, which had nothing connecting them to equal opportunity law. For other programs, experts like uber-consultant R. Roosevelt Thomas dropped the language of legal compliance for a language of "diversity management."[36] Diversity training, culture audits, and diversity performance evaluations were built on personnel's sensitivity training, attitude surveys, and performance evaluations. To the extent that diversity experts could frame these programs as key to corporate effectiveness, they could win a permanent role for them. Experts aligned the new programs with ideas from the social sciences. The cognitive revolution that had swept though academia suggested that mental categories shape the behavior of managers and workers alike, and influence hiring and promotion decisions. One remedy was diversity training to alter managerial cognition. For disadvantaged workers, stereotyping can impede ambition and lead to self-handicapping. The remedy was mentoring and networking programs that would impart the skills and insider knowledge necessary to succeed, and at the same time offer positive role models.

The 1990s and 2000s: Gender Discrimination at Center Stage

The human resources profession had gradually become feminized between 1970 and 1990, and leaders came to champion women's issues. In the 1970s, personnel experts pushed firms to install maternity leave programs to comply with civil rights law, until the Supreme Court ruled in 1976 that Title VII did not require maternity leave. By that point, leading firms had maternity leave programs on the books, and so personnel experts' advocacy for them helped to quell corporate opposition to the Pregnancy Discrimination Act of 1978. After that, personnel experts did not argue that other work life programs were required by the Civil Rights Act, but they did argue that flexible working arrangements and child care supports could be part of a "good-faith effort" defense against claims of gender discrimination. The link between Title VII and work-family programs remained tenuous, but the proponents of Title VII programs and work-family programs within firms were one and the same. Public officials had created tax incentives and federal demonstration projects that supported on-site child care, dependent care expense accounts, flextime, and part-time career options, and these helped personnel experts to build a case for work-family programs.

Women's advocates in personnel did, by contrast, tie new programs to fight sexual harassment at work directly to Title VII. The women's movement focused attention on the issue of harassment at work in the 1970s. It was personnel experts who proposed the remedy: sexual harassment grievance procedures, modeled on union grievance procedures, and harassment sensitivity training, modeled on diversity training and ultimately on the management sensitivity training seminars of the late 1960s.[37] In 1991, Anita Hill's charge that Supreme Court nominee Clarence Thomas had sexually harassed her at the Equal Employment Opportunity Commission focused national attention on the issue, and it was human resources experts who pushed again for firms to create systems for fighting harassment. The press coverage helped win congressional support for the Civil Rights Act of 1991, which gave women the same right to sue for punitive damages that African-Americans had.[38] By popularizing harassment training and grievance procedures, human resources experts helped to win judicial support for them in 1998, when the Supreme Court found that these practices could inoculate employers against liability in some hostile work environment cases. The court came to view practices that were widely popular as adequate compliance efforts.

A Note on Evidence

In the coming chapters I present graphs tracing the diffusion of dozens of different equal opportunity practices across firms. The data come from surveys I conducted in 1986 with colleagues John W. Meyer, W. Richard Scott, and John Sutton, in 1997 with Erin Kelly, and in 2002 with Alexandra Kalev. They cover 279, 389, and 829 employers respectively, and each sample covers a broad cross-section of industries.[39] Each covers small and middling firms as well as the corporate giants that most surveys focus on. To develop these longitudinal graphs my collaborators and I collected life histories of employment practices by asking managers whether, and when, they had used each practice The surveys offer a picture of the diffusion of innovations. I report evidence from many cross-sectional surveys as well, and these typically show that the biggest firms were the first to embrace innovations. In later chapters I also quote from in-depth interviews with human resources managers, mostly conducted in collaboration with Erin Kelly, Alexandra Kalev, and Shawna Vican between 1997 and 2008. To chart the evolution of the personnel profession's position I rely on histories of firms, reports written by personnel experts, oral histories, studies done by management groups, and in particular, articles in the management press by personnel experts promoting new equal opportunity innovations.

Conclusion

Before 1960, it wasn't merely difficult for a black man or a white woman to get a job as a manager in most firms, it was impossible. Most American employers wouldn't hire women, blacks, or Latinos for any job a white man would take. There were some seeming exceptions, as when the Rosie the Riveter campaign brought women onto the factory floor during World War II. But Rosie was out of luck the moment veterans returned from the war. Many firms put it in writing: women and blacks were not eligible for skilled or management jobs. Federal rules against discrimination by munitions contractors and state laws against discrimination in government service had done little to change this.

The Civil Rights Act of 1964 revolutionized America's long-standing treatment of employment as a matter of free contract. Originally, employers could hire whomever they pleased under whatever terms they could

get. They could barter passage to the New World for seven years of inden-
tured servitude. With the 1964 act, Congress extended the right of equal
protection from the citizen-state relationship to the employee-employer
relationship. Washington had already extended certain rights to employees, such as the right to bargain collectively, but the idea that you could
not hire whomever you pleased was new in the eyes of many.

The law did not require anything specific, it merely outlawed discrimination. In the face of uncertainty about just how judges would
interpret this ban, entrepreneurial personnel experts promoted one
wave after another of equal opportunity innovations. Most of the programs were based on old personnel standards, such as the grievance
procedure. This saga lays bare a peculiar dynamic between the state
and society in the United States. The constitutional constraints on federal power—the separation of powers, the common-law tradition, and
the sharing of authority with the states—opened the government to
invasion, allowing activists, social scientists, and more than any other
group, personnel experts to champion new ideas about what the law
should require employers to do. Activists called for civil rights law to
cover harassment. Women's rights advocates in federal posts called for
it to cover pregnancy discrimination. Social scientists argued that firms
should protect against institutional racism and cognitive bias. Personnel experts designed practices and programs to respond to all of these
ideas, and many notions of their own, even before federal officials ruled
on them.

The constitutions of most other countries did not admit such changes
in the meaning of the law. Thus, for instance, while the U.S. Supreme
Court found in 1971 that seemingly neutral employer practices could
be discriminatory if they had a "disparate impact" on disadvantaged
groups, it was 30 years before a similar prohibition found its way into
French law, and that only came through new legislation responding
to the European Union's Race Directive of 2000.[40] France's less porous
civil law system meant that employers did not worry that judges would
reinterpret the laws against race and gender discrimination, and one result was that employers did very little to comply with those laws. That
was true in nearly every country but the United States.

The great paradox of our federal system is that the constitutional
weakness of our state contributes to a powerful collective culture. The
1964 law created not a single, episodic, change in public policy but a
decades-long public debate about the definition of discrimination
among civil rights leaders, women's movement activists, social scientists, personnel experts, corporate executives, pundits, judges, federal
bureaucrats, and legislators. Even though the statutory definition of discrimination remains nearly as vague as it was in 1964, in debating what

the law meant, we have come to a broad consensus about the details. We now think that sexual harassment constitutes employment discrimination and that stereotypes can affect promotion decisions. Workers see institutional racism and cognitive bias around them, largely because the law stimulated this debate and led an army of equal opportunity experts to devise remedies to these forms of discrimination. Americans encountered new definitions of discrimination at work, in the form of promotion systems to counter institutional racism and training programs to fix cognitive bias.

Americans have long seen their social institutions and national culture as originating in the community rather than in the state. We see culture as arising from below, even when it is stimulated by public policy. The form that equal opportunity law took contributed mightily to the view that fair employment practices were private inventions. Equal opportunity experts claimed civil rights grievance panels and diversity training as their own innovations, not as mechanistic responses to the law. That reinforced a long rhetorical tradition of laissez-faire that suggested that government interventions were illegitimate, and so were the compliance strategies they elicited. In defining equal opportunity measures as private innovations, personnel experts left the door open to redefine them as good business—as efficient in their own right. Near the end of the first decade of the twenty-first century, Fortune 500 companies have extensive diversity management offices, which administer relabeled compliance programs, and slim affirmative action offices, which write mandatory affirmative action plans and fill out federal forms. The link between most compliance programs and the law has been deliberately severed. The result is that most everything American firms did to comply with equal opportunity law, they now define as stimulated by one new management paradigm or another. In a nation that has long defined government regulation as illegitimate, this was perhaps the surest way to guarantee the survival of compliance measures.

The history of the Sherman Antitrust Act of 1890, designed to prevent large companies from quashing their smaller competitors through restraint of trade, may portend the future of equal opportunity. Sherman was roundly villainized by corporations as unwanted, inefficient, government meddling in industry, or as the beginning of a new form of tyranny. But it stuck, and through a Herculean effort of mass cognitive dissonance, Americans came to view it as reinforcing market competition. For most of the twentieth century, it was heralded as one of the foundations of America's greatness for its role in reinforcing the natural laws of the market. Americans came to see it not as an intervention at all. If one key to maintaining Americans' belief in laissez-faire was to frame compliance practices as private inventions, the other key was to deny government policies as interventions, and to frame them as supports for natural market mechanisms. The Sherman Act was so redefined. Equal opportunity laws are not there yet, but when Reagan sought to tear down affirmative action, corporate America stood together to oppose the idea, arguing that it had improved corporate use of talent and made personnel systems more efficient. Equal opportunity laws may one day be viewed as outlawing price discrimination in the labor market just as antitrust outlaws it in the product market, preventing firms from paying more for white male labor than for black female labor.

One of the most surprising things about the compliance regimes that corporations popularized is that they remain largely untested. They spread among firms, and were vetted by courts, without evidence of their efficacy in equalizing opportunity. We still know little about whether the recruitment programs of the 1960s, the performance evaluations of the 1970s, the harassment grievance procedures of the 1980s, the diversity training of the 1990s, or the diversity councils of the 2000s actually helped to integrate workplaces. What we do know is discouraging. We know that employers subject to affirmative action edicts saw some increases in racial and gender diversity beyond the increases their peers saw during the 1970s, and that, in the 1980s, contractors stopped outpacing others.[41] Yet even for the 1970s, we don't know which of the innovations helped federal contractors to hire and promote more blacks. Thus employers and regulators are still choosing strategies based on spin, rather than evidence. My colleagues and I are working on the question of which of these measures have been effective in equalizing opportunity, but the answer will have to wait for another book.[42]

Another issue I do not take up in any detail is equal opportunity for the disabled. As corporate response to disability protections has not been to remaster favorites from the personnel playlist, a discussion of disability would not fit within the confines of this book.

WASHINGTON OUTLAWS
DISCRIMINATION WITH A
BROAD BRUSH

KING DAVID HOLMES GREW UP in Connecticut and worked in a brass mill before he went off to college in the 1940s. When he returned with his college degree in hand at the end of the decade, he went back to the mill: "I came back, went in the employment office, said 'I want a job.' I filled out my form—'College graduate.'" Holmes wanted a job in sales, a job that college men were eligible for. He asked: "Well how about [a job] selling some of this brass?" The personnel officer made no bones about it, they weren't hiring blacks in sales: 'Oh, that's reserved' he said, 'I see your uncle works here.'" They put Holmes in the old north mill, making sheet metal, in a job that didn't require reading and writing.[1]

In Chicago, there had been an influx of black migrants from the South during the Great War, and many metal products and meatpacking plants had hired blacks as laborers or production line workers. But there was no moving out of those jobs. Things hadn't changed much by the early 1950s. A black machine operator who worked for Swift meatpacking reported, "Advancement is not for colored people. I've seen colored fellows more qualified than the foreman. I've thought of being a foreman. Don't take long to catch on." Swift wasn't promoting blacks, qualified or not. "I've had ninth grade. It don't call for much education for being a foreman. They got schools anyway. . . . [But] I don't carry a chip on my shoulder." Swift didn't have a rule against promoting blacks to foremen, but it never seemed to happen. Another machine operator reported, "I had four years at Englewood High School. I took an exam for a checker's job. The foreman told me I failed. Another fellow got the job, a foreigner who could hardly speak English. He didn't take the exam. I didn't say anything to the foreman. I just took it. . . . I don't let it bother me. Just keep on working at $1.24 an hour."[2]

Blacks who had dropped out of school often lost out to whites, but then so did blacks who had not dropped out. At Swift, the best-educated production workers were black women, for Swift put white women with some schooling in comfortable office jobs but would only hire black women on the meatpacking line.[3]

Swift was typical of large employers who set aside a few jobs for blacks and a few for women, but who didn't countenance blacks and whites, or men and women, working side by side. Economists have tried to gauge the extent of discrimination before the civil rights era by looking at whether firms hired more women and minorities after discrimination was outlawed, and at whether the effects were magnified in federal contractors subject to affirmative action regulations.[4] Researchers find that equal opportunity law had modest effects, but that may be because the law did not quash discrimination overnight rather than because there was little discrimination to quash.

Some military contractors began to change during World War II when they were required to offer equal opportunity. Some firms in the 23 states that had their own fair employment laws by the early 1960s had begun to change as well. But change was slow before 1964, and it was slow after.[5] Thus even after General Motors pledged in 1961 to comply with Kennedy's demand that federal contractors end discrimination, NAACP labor secretary Herbert Hill found that at GM's Fisher Body plant in Atlanta, company guards "prevent Negroes from even entering the plant grounds to apply for employment in production jobs that have been advertised." Blacks could still only apply for a handful of menial jobs, and in bad times were laid off from those bad jobs ahead of whites with less seniority.[6]

Before sketching federal antidiscrimination laws of the early 1960s, I discuss the systems of discrimination that those laws attacked. Employment traditions in quarries, clothing factories, steel mills, auto plants, and government agencies separated men and women, blacks and whites, through different mechanisms.

Systems of Segregation before Civil Rights

The industrial revolution drew workers from farms to factories from the 1820s to the end of the twentieth century. Farmers made up 97 percent of the working population in 1800, 63 percent in 1900, and only 1 percent in 2000.[7] New industries sorted people systematically by gender, race, and ethnicity. In 1840, Massachusetts textile mills hired only young women from farm families to work on the mill floor. In 1890, Philadelphia railroads hired only men, and segregated them by race and nativity, with nine-tenths of blacks working as laborers, and native-born whites evenly divided between white-collar jobs and skilled blue-collar jobs like engineer and brakeman.[8]

Many employers matched people with jobs based on ability, but only after dividing them by race and sex. Women who could type would be typists, those who couldn't would answer the phone. But women would never go down into the mine, or up into the corner office. Young black men would shovel gravel; old ones would clean bathrooms. But blacks would never get skilled jobs or join management training programs. Federal agencies assigned jobs on the basis of civil service examinations, but they reserved some categories of jobs for women and others for men.[9] By the mid-1950s, four out of every 10 factories had a merit rating system, as did half of offices.[10] Yet because firms created distinct career lines for men and women, merit systems could only help the best-qualified white men to move up. They did not help to integrate the workplace.[11]

Defenders of these systems pointed to the natural proclivities and talents of men and women, blacks and whites. In the insurance industry, by 1970, women made up 83 percent of clerks, but scarcely 3 percent of agents. Executives explained this pattern in terms of nature: "Most girls don't have what it takes. They don't have the killer instinct." Even in the 1980s, firms that did allow women to sell insurance kept them on the phone and out of the field.[12] Change was slow, as it was in Europe and Asia.[13]

Before the Civil Rights Act of 1964 there were a handful of common systems for hiring and managing workers. All of these systems started at the front door, sorting new hires based on sex and race into jobs that differed in wages and working conditions and in chances of promotion. Where you ended your career with the railroad depended on whether you started as a ticket agent or a laborer.

The "Drive System" and Segregation

After World War II many firms continued to use the rudimentary hiring and firing routines that labor economist Sumner Slichter had in 1919 dubbed the "drive system."[14] Foremen did the hiring and firing themselves in dressmaking workshops, in stone quarries, and on farms, and used the threat of discharge to motivate workers. They hired by sex and race, choosing women to run sewing machines, men to work in quarries, and blacks and Mexican immigrants to pick fruit. Foremen often chose workers from their own neighborhood and ethnic group, and so in some plants, nearly all jobs were held by Italian or Irish or Polish immigrants. The personnel office—where there was one—played little role in hiring and promotion decisions, leaving foremen free to hire relatives and friends-of-friends for the best jobs.[15] One result was that people worked alongside others like themselves, and upper management often knew little about what went on on the shop floor.

Scientific Management and Segregation

In 1912, the original management guru, Frederick Taylor, argued before Congress that the rational employer would test each new worker, and observe him at work, to match the man to the job. The idea was to find, for each employee, "the most profitable class of work for which his natural abilities fit him."[16] The military built on that model during World War I, and by 1920, the basic ideas from Taylor's system of scientific management had been taken up by automakers and other mass-manufacturing magnates.[17] By the 1950s, blue- and white-collar employers tested men to sort them into suitable jobs: "the worker came to be viewed as an embodiment of aptitudes and feelings, which had to be assessed so that his job assignment would be advantageous to him and profitable to the enterprise."[18]

If the first cornerstone of scientific management was that science could be used to match the man to the job, the second cornerstone was that men were born to be either managers or workers.[19] Those born to be managers should engineer production, dictating how manual work was to be done by others, whose natural gifts lay in brute strength or the capacity to repeat the same monotonous task day in and day out. Some entire races were made for manual work, and so many factories tested native-born whites for different white-collar jobs, white ethnic immigrants for different blue-collar jobs, and blacks for different laborer jobs. Sorting by ability happened, but only within each group. The principle of merit stopped at the color line.

Another dividing line was sex. The gypsum mine that sociologist Alvin Gouldner studied in the 1950s, as well as the General Motors plant that sociologist Ruth Milkman studied three decades later, placed only men in their skilled assembly line jobs, but they placed them based on aptitude.[20] Women had won unskilled production jobs at GM, but most remained in low-wage, white-collar jobs.

Union Plants and Segregation

American workers joined unions in droves after 1935, when the Wagner Act made collective bargaining a right. Union membership rose from 14 percent to 36 percent between 1935 and the end of World War II in 1945, and had declined by only four percentage points by 1960.[21] Following the Wagner Act, mass-manufacturing firms developed a legalistic industrial-relations system in which unions negotiated rules about hiring, promotion, and discharge. What labor historian David Brody calls "workplace contractualism" narrowed the latitude of workers and managers alike. At the gypsum mine that Gouldner studied, rules negotiated by the union governed promotion, to guarantee that managers would not discriminate against union leaders.[22] Seniority rules guaranteed that experience would guide promotions and layoffs.[23] Open bidding rules guaranteed that union activists could vie for vacancies. Negotiated job descriptions prevented low-wage workers from doing skilled work. Once you were on the job, rules protected you against managerial favoritism and antiunion campaigns.

The hiring process in union sectors, by contrast, was not rule-governed. That was just as true for American Federation of Labor craft workers, in industries such as printing and glassmaking, as it was for assembly line workers who joined industrial unions.[24] Printer's apprentices and auto assembly line operatives were recruited by existing workers, through kinship and community networks. Entire departments, and sometimes entire factories, were ruled by Italians or Poles or WASPs. As a gypsum mine trucker observed, "They have lots of fathers and sons or brothers here." The head of personnel used existing workers to find new recruits: "I always tried to hire local help on the recommendation of the other men in the plant, who grew up with him." He favored farm-bred white boys—"there is a willingness to work in the farm boy you will never find in a city boy"—and so blacks and immigrants stood little chance.[25] Where blacks were union members, they belonged to segregated unions with access only to dirty, dead-end jobs. Segregated unions and seniority systems meant that in downturns, blacks would be laid off first.

Because entrenched, segregated unions protected their members, they were slow to promote equal opportunity. By the late 1960s there were no women and few blacks on the production line at General Motors' Linden, New Jersey, plant. Over the next 20 years, GM hired more blacks and women, but blacks got dirty jobs and women got unskilled jobs, like bumper polishing. By 1985, minorities held nearly four in 10 production jobs, but only one in 10 skilled jobs. Women held 15 percent of jobs, but only two of the 375 skilled jobs. Two-thirds of women were concentrated in five of the 89 production jobs. As one woman explained to sociologist Ruth Milkman, GM sorted people when they first walked in the door: "I hate to say this, but they have 'women's jobs' and they have 'men's jobs.'"[26]

By the late 1970s, sociologist David Halle found that 90 percent of blue-collar workers in New Jersey chemical plant were white ethnics; only 2 percent were black. Not a single woman was to be found among its 121 blue-collar production jobs. By the mid-1980s, women held 15 percent of production jobs but only 1 percent of the desirable skilled jobs.[27]

The Civil Service and Segregation

Since 1940, at least one in eight Americans has worked for the government.[28] Civil service systems bureaucratized hiring and promotion in federal, state, and city jobs as part of the effort to quash patronage and professionalize government work.[29] These systems came closest of all to the idealized bureaucracy that the early German sociologist Max Weber described, organized around credentials, experience, and tests to sort applicants into jobs. Each job was given a grade corresponding to prerequisites in education and experience. Formal job ladders determined the course of promotion.

The civil service epitomized meritocracy in form, but in practice, sex and race determined one's prospects. The structure of job ladders proved to be the key to this effect. Entry-level jobs were segregated, and so were the jobs they fed into. By the 1950s the federal civil service operated a dual white-collar career system, both in the professional services and in the administrative services. In the professional services, such as law and medicine, there were two career ladders, one for those with professional training that led to the top and one for clerical workers that had only a few rungs.[30] The logic was that only professionals could manage professionals. But the same dualism was found in administrative services, where many workers held nonprofessional college degrees. Management jobs were on (long) job ladders dominated by white men. Clerical jobs were on (short) ladders dominated by women and minorities. By sorting women and minority applicants into these clerical tracks, personnel departments kept them out of the running for managerial jobs.

The armed services were another matter. They used highly bureaucratized career systems, but unlike the civil service, they practiced Jim Crow until 1951, when they implemented a three-year-old order from Harry Truman to desegregate. Even then they continued to exclude women from combat jobs, which kept women out of the running for top uniformed positions.

Personnel management had progressed since the mid-nineteenth century, to be sure. The drive system had been replaced by scientific management in some sectors, by formal career systems inscribed in union contracts in others, and by formal civil service rules in government. But, as of 1960, none of these systems extended the principle of meritocracy beyond the ranks of white men. All of them sorted women and minorities into different career tracks at the point of entry, and those career tracks determined their futures. Personnel managers often viewed the sorting as a consequence of self-selection, or of natural proclivities, but where there were formal rules governing hiring and promotion, those rules often excluded women and blacks.

Formal Rules Excluding Women and African-Americans

At the dawn of the twentieth century, few firms outside of railroading and banking had formal personnel systems. But as those systems spread to other industries, so did formal rules excluding women and blacks from certain jobs. Many firms wrote rules excluding married women and women with children from all jobs, and all women from management jobs. Many excluded blacks from all but a handful of poorly paid jobs, such as janitor, laborer, and washroom attendant.

The Exclusion of Women

Before World War II, it was common for companies to refuse to consider applications from married women and to fire women who married while on the job. In a 1935 survey of medium and large companies, 52 percent said that they did not hire married women, and 46 percent said that they required women who married to resign (see figure 2.1). The need for labor during World War II led many firms to drop restrictions on hiring married women, but many reinstated restrictions after the war.

Company policies requiring pregnant women to resign also abounded before the war, and after the war they enjoyed renewed popularity. In 1954, 44 percent of the medium and large firms surveyed by the National Industrial Conference Board put it in writing: pregnant workers must resign. By 1964, fully half of employers had such policies. State fair employment laws, which outlawed marriage bans for women, may have actually popularized pregnancy bans as an alternative. Even the Civil Rights Act did not quash pregnancy bans right away. Only after

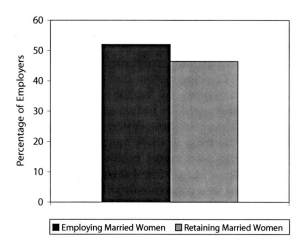

Figure 2.1. Employers with Policies Against Employing or Retaining Married Women (1935)

Source: Peirce School 1935.

the courts refused to define pregnancy bans as discriminatory did Congress pass the Pregnancy Discrimination Act of 1978.

Age restrictions, coupled with pregnancy restrictions, often meant that childbearing marked the end of a woman's career. Figure 2.2 shows that a quarter of firms surveyed by the Conference Board had formal rules against hiring older workers in 1937, and four in 10 had such rules by 1954, when the typical maximum age was 50 for men and 40 for women. Many women who were forced to resign when they became pregnant found that they were too old to return to work when their children were grown.[31]

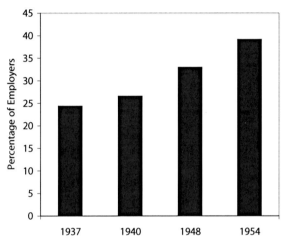

Figure 2.2. Employers with a Maximum Hiring Age (1937–54)

Source: Brower 1937; Earl 1940; National Industrial Conference Board 1964; Seybold 1948, 1954.

Even unmarried, childless women, however, were excluded from the best jobs in most firms. In a surprising number of firms, these exclusions were put in writing. In a 1967 survey the Bureau of National Affairs asked leading employers the equivalent of "When did you stop beating your wife?" They asked: have you *opened* any jobs that had been closed to women? Forty-three percent had opened jobs. The jobs they mentioned opening were not those at the top of the pyramid, but jobs such as personnel clerk, accounting clerk, payroll clerk, machine operator, and sander.[32] As of 1967, three years after passage of the Civil Rights Act, only 18 percent of companies reported that women were excluded from *no* jobs. Another 18 percent excluded women from jobs to comply with working conditions laws. The remaining 64 percent still excluded

women from jobs that they deemed them unfit for, in sales or management, or in physically demanding fields that working-conditions laws
did not exclude women from.[33]

The Exclusion of African-Americans

Employment agencies did much of the work of excluding blacks. Agencies often made the first cut based on race and religion. In New York,
which had its own fair employment law on top of the Civil Rights Act,
one insider told the *New York Times* in 1967 that agencies coded the
race and religion of applicants: "a One is a Puerto Rican, a Two is a
Negro, and Three, Four and Five are reserved respectively, for Jew,
Catholic, and WASP. Of course, when the investigator from the State
Commission for Human Rights drops by and asks which applications
are from Negroes the proper answer is: 'I don't know.'"[34]

Companies themselves often had unwritten rules excluding blacks.
Personnel surveys did not regularly ask about policies against hiring
blacks, perhaps because all military contractors and private-sector employers in certain states were forbidden to practice racial discrimination. Thus the Bureau of National Affairs did not report in 1967 on the
number of companies that had excluded blacks before the Civil Rights
Act, but it did discuss individual companies. One company reported
that it had "opened quality jobs to Negroes." Another reported that it
had previously restricted blacks to three jobs, but had opened another
38 job categories.[35] Lockheed's Marietta, Georgia, plant had excluded
blacks from skilled jobs, relegating most to jobs as janitors and washroom attendants, but opened dozens of jobs after Kennedy's 1961 affirmative action order.[36] In Atlanta, GM had few blacks who were not
janitors before 1962, when it opened up all jobs under the threat of losing government contracts.[37]

Two decades after Franklin Roosevelt banned discrimination by federal contractors, and a year after Kennedy's renewed commitment,
many contractors still relegated blacks to the worst jobs. In July 1962,
Attorney General Robert F. Kennedy announced an agreement with
four big oil refineries in Lake Charles, Louisiana. "These plants, with
the approval of the previous Administration's committee on equal employment [headed by Vice President Richard Nixon], had completely
segregated facilities—even parking lots—and *in job opportunities had excluded Negroes entirely from fifteen out of seventeen categories.*"[38]

While 99 percent of big companies had some women workers, and 93
percent had some blacks, according to the Bureau of National Affairs'
1967 study, many companies had closed promotions to those groups.
Between 1965 and 1967, 16 percent of companies abolished policies
against promoting women, and 19 percent abolished policies against

promoting blacks.[39] Not all firms had excluded blacks, of course. The *New York Times* reported in 1965 that J. C. Penney, Xerox, IBM, Celenese, and J. Walker Thompson "are among the several large corporations with a history of hiring Negro college graduates for any position for which they are qualified."[40] Even in these companies, blacks were seldom seen in management.The consequences of exclusion were evident across the nation. The black unemployment rate was double the white unemployment rate. Black college graduates earned less than white high school dropouts. *Fortune* editor Richardson Wood estimated the cost of racial discrimination in Kansas City in 1950 at $37.5 million annually in foregone income "that could be earned by Negro workers if they were permitted to work at all jobs for which they can qualify."[41] And blacks rarely qualified for the best jobs, for a pattern of discrimination had led blacks to despair of succeeding, and to high school dropout rates that exceeded 50 percent in many places.

When Congress faced the issue of employment discrimination, it faced a long history of exclusionary practices. In some sectors exclusion was largely a prerogative of the foreman. In others it was inscribed in long-standing personnel policies. Most employers had arrived at one scheme or another for sorting women and minorities into the less desirable jobs and keeping them there. The challenge was to end all of these forms of exclusion.

Outlawing Discrimination in Broad Strokes

The civil rights movement put the issue of racial inequality on the public agenda in the 1950s, and John F. Kennedy came into office in 1961 with a commitment to moving racial equality forward. In the Civil Rights Act of 1964 Congress created a broad mandate short on specifics and left it to the courts to define compliance. Congress thus created an opening for personnel experts to take the ball and run with it. American state fragmentation meant that three *branches* of government would listen to supplicants with new definitions of discrimination, and three *levels* of government would hear complaints.

We now see the Civil Rights Act as a simple elaboration of the right to equal protection, guaranteed by the Fourteenth Amendment of 1868, to the realm of employment. In keeping with the amendment's guarantee of equal protection under the law, the Civil Rights Act mandated equal treatment in public education and accommodations. But Title VII of the act went further, guaranteeing equal treatment in private employment. Previously, the federal government had treated employment as contractual. Under common law, contracts between private parties were private matters. The government had outlawed contracts that required servitude, but managers still viewed the employment contract as akin to the marriage contract. They could contract with whomever they pleased, rebuffing blacks at the door, and break it when they pleased, firing pregnant women.

Before the 1960s, the legal treatment of employment as a free contract prevailed despite regulatory encroachment. Congress and the states had regulated wages, hours, and working conditions to prevent abuse and had guaranteed the right of employees to bargain collectively. When Roosevelt, Truman, and Eisenhower had decreed that companies with federal contracts must practice equal opportunity, they in effect conceded that other private employers could hire whomever they pleased.

Kennedy's Broad Affirmative Action Edict

In 1941 Roosevelt's Executive Order 8022 required World War II defense contractors to sign nondiscrimination clauses and established the Fair Employment Practices Committee to investigate complaints of racial discrimination. Further orders expanded the scope to all contracts emanating from the Department of War, the Department of the Navy, and the Maritime Commission. In 1948, Harry Truman signed Executive Order 9981, ending racial segregation in the armed forces themselves. The prohibition against discrimination in defense contracting survived the war, and in 1951 Truman extended it to eight other federal agencies involved in defense, in the belief that racial minorities were due "fair and equitable treatment in all aspects of employment on work paid for from public funds."[42] Truman set up the Committee on Government Contract Compliance, succeeded in 1953 by Dwight Eisenhower's President's Committee on Government Contracts.[43]

In 1961, John F. Kennedy extended the ban on discrimination by military contractors to all federal contractors. Executive Order 10925 did not require contractors to hire blacks and Latinos before better-qualified whites, but it did require them to take "affirmative action to ensure that applicants are employed, and that employees are treated during employment, without regard to their race, creed, color, or national origin."[44] The term *affirmative action* had first appeared in the Wagner Act of 1935, which directed judges to take "affirmative action" to compensate union organizers who had faced discrimination, action such as reinstatement with back pay.[45] In Kennedy's order, the idea was that employers would make things right for blacks who had faced discrimination.[46] The order required that bidders for contracts to submit a "Compliance Report," but did not specify compliance standards.

The ban did not cover sex discrimination, but after passage of the Civil Rights Act in 1964, Lyndon Johnson amended 10925 in 1967 to cover sex discrimination as well.

Kennedy's affirmative action order was specific about coverage—which employers were subject and which groups were protected—but it was mute on how compliance would be judged. An interagency committee, the President's Committee on Equal Employment Opportunity (PCEEO), was to oversee the order. Its illustrious members lacked statutory authority to define and promulgate compliance practices, and lacked authority to enforce compliance, beyond the capacity to recommend termination of the employer as a federal contractor. The lack of specificity about compliance, and lack of clear authority to define the terms of compliance, proved all-important, for these things opened the way for personnel experts to daydream about programs they might sell to their bosses as equal opportunity measures.

Plans for Progress: *The Private Sector Sets Standards*   The PCEEO was to advise the 27 federal agencies that contracted with private firms, for everything from jet planes to paper towels. Kennedy put Vice President Lyndon Johnson in charge and appointed labor secretary Arthur Goldberg, as well as the secretaries of Commerce; Defense; and Health, Education, and Welfare, and heads of the Civil Service Commission, the General Services Administration, the Atomic Energy Commission, NASA, and secretaries of the navy, army, and air force. Private-sector members came from Who's Who and from the civil rights movement.[47] The committee's support staff of 40 was spread out between Washington, Chicago, and Los Angeles. Five subcommittees covered apprenticeship, vocational education, promotion and upgrading, franchised industries, and religious cooperation, but the subcommittee that was most influential was spearheaded by Atlanta lawyer Robert Troutman. Plans for Progress organized voluntary compliance among federal contractors. Within a year, 85 leading companies had signed on, many in well-publicized Oval Office ceremonies.

The all-volunteer Plans for Progress became the breeding ground for affirmative action practices. Its members first built on the practices Lockheed Marietta's personnel experts designed in 1961, when the company won a billion-dollar defense contract just three days before Kennedy's affirmative action order to federal contractors. Lockheed acted quickly to signal its commitment to fair employment, and Plans for Progress codified Lockheed's steps for other contractors to follow. For Troutman, the idea was to set an example: "Compulsion is not the thing. I'm a lawyer. I can show you how to get around the Executive Order. It's got to be voluntary."[48] The Plans for Progress experience proved that companies would mimic industry leaders. Regulators and judges later built on the experience, making examples of brand-name companies.[49]

Plans for Progress trumpeted participants' innovations far and wide, while other subcommittees twisted executives' arms behind the scenes, hoping to change their ways through persuasion rather than by making examples of them. The committee talked of canceling contracts to punish the recalcitrant, but Johnson agreed with Troutman that setting a good example was the way to win converts. Despite tough talk, a year into its life the committee had not canceled a single contract.

The Equal Pay Act of 1963: Employers Define "the Same Work"

Congress took another step toward fair employment with the Equal Pay Act of 1963, protecting women against wage discrimination. During World War II the War Labor Board had ordered employers to offer women and men equal pay for "comparable quality and quantity of work," and, by the mid-1950s, 17 percent of union contracts had equal pay clauses. By 1963, 17 states had passed equal pay laws. Yet in the early 1960s, companies were still advertising jobs with one hourly wage for men and another for women. The Women's Bureau of the Department of Labor spearheaded the fight for federal legislation. The Equal Pay Act led many companies to change their ways, but the act's effects were muted by the courts. When employers created different job titles for men and women doing similar work, judges mostly let the practice stand. As sociologists Robert Nelson and William Bridges document in their book *Legalizing Gender Inequality*, attorneys defending these employers successfully argued that market forces, not bias, had produced wage differences.[50]

While the Equal Pay Act did not live up to its promise, it did open the way for the Civil Rights Act, for it helped to establish the principle that the federal government had a right to regulate employment, and that the contractual view of employment had its limits. Washington had assumed the right to outlaw wage discrimination and next would outlaw employment discrimination itself.

The Civil Rights Act: Outlawing Discrimination without Defining It

The idea that the federal government should promote equal opportunity in employment was not a new one when Congress debated the Civil Rights Act of 1964. It had been around for nearly a century, since the Freedman's Bureau had helped former slaves find schools, housing, and jobs during Reconstruction. During the 1930s, Franklin Roosevelt's National Industrial Recovery Act outlawed discrimination based on race, religion, and national origin in public works programs, and in wartime Roosevelt prohibited discrimination by military contractors.

The idea that Washington could forbid discrimination in private employment seemed at odds with the principle of freedom of contract, and yet that principle had been abridged when the Wagner Act of 1935 gave union members the right to representation and forbade discrimination against unionists. It stood to reason that Congress might outlaw other forms of discrimination. So the two pillars underlying Title VII of the Civil Rights Act had been established—the idea that the federal government should regulate employment discrimination and the idea that public purposes sometimes trumped freedom of contract.

Title VII of the Civil Rights Act outlawed discrimination on the basis of race, color, religion, sex, or national origin for employers with at least 25 workers. The new Equal Employment Opportunity Commission was to administer the law. While the commission and employers agreed that Title VII made Jim Crow illegal, no one had a good idea of what the law implied beyond that or of whether it implied anything at all.

The Democrats who had first proposed a federal fair employment law envisioned, if not a law that was clearer in terms of the requirements for compliance, at least a federal agency with the authority to set clear compliance standards. They did not get that, and some in Congress were concerned that Washington had only tenuous authority to regulate employment. Thus the act specified that the Constitution's interstate commerce clause gave it authority: "The term 'employer' means a person engaged in an industry affecting commerce."[51]

Congressional opponents questioned both the authority to regulate employment and the wisdom of trying to, and in the end the act outlawed only the most egregious, deliberate forms of discrimination. Title VII offered little guidance as to which of the various employment traditions discussed in the previous section would be illegal. It reads:

> It shall be an unlawful employment practice for an employer—
>
> 1. to fail or refuse to hire or to discharge any individual, or otherwise to discriminate against any individual with respect to his compensation, terms, conditions, or privileges of employment, because of such individual's race, color, religion, sex, or national origin; or
> 2. to limit, segregate, or classify his employees in any way which would deprive or tend to deprive any individual of employment opportunities or otherwise adversely affect his status as an employee, because of such individual's race, color, religion, sex, or national origin.

The act also explicitly outlawed discrimination by employment agencies and labor unions, which proved important because unions adopted nondiscrimination policies that became models for corporations.

Employers who believed that women and minorities chose to be in the jobs they were clustered in thought that little would change, for the law did not require specific changes in employment policies.

The core language was quite abstract, and the act got specific only when it came to what it did *not* cover. Section 706g, which covers judicial enforcement, reads: "If the court finds that the respondent has *intentionally engaged* in . . . an unlawful employment practice . . . the court may enjoin the respondent" from engaging in the practice and may require remedial measures.[52] This language seemed to let employers off the hook for unwitting discrimination. Moreover, Senator Everett Dirksen had worked out a compromise to ensure that the law would not be used to force employers to give preferential treatment to women or minorities.[53] The final draft read:

> Nothing contained in [Title VII] shall be interpreted to require any employer . . . to grant preferential treatment to any individual or to any group . . . on account of an imbalance which may exist with respect to the total number or percentage of persons of any race, color, religion, sex, or national origin employed by any employer.[54]

In the congressional debates as well, the bill's sponsors made clear that the bill referred to *deliberate* discrimination.[55] Because the courts take congressional intent seriously, sponsors' testimony for the *Congressional Record* assured members of Congress who were on the fence that the bill covered only deliberate discrimination.

The language that Dirksen included to prevent courts and bureaucrats from getting carried away seemed to rule out quotas, but did not specify what employers should do or how the courts should interpret the act. In the end, the courts ignored even the language that seemed to rule out quotas. While the Supreme Court discouraged job quotas not ordered by judges, it imposed quotas on recalcitrant police and fire departments, and permitted training quotas not ordered by judges.[56] So even when it came to the one compliance approach the law seemed to forbid, the courts did not take a consistent line.

The act did nothing to define positive compliance measures. It might have required employers to advertise all jobs, or to eliminate race and gender exclusion. Or it might have required employers to keep records of applicants and their qualifications. Or it might have imposed quotas for hiring blacks and Latinos in proportion to their representation in the local labor market. All of these approaches would emerge over time, but because the act did not settle on one or another, employers were left to their own devices.

Sex as a Bona Fide Occupational Qualification   The act was also unclear as to whether sex discrimination was verboten. Sponsors had wa-
vered on whether to outlaw sex discrimination, and in the end, the bill
covered sex but included an escape clause. Kennedy's affirmative action order from early 1961 had not covered sex discrimination. Adam
Clayton Powell Jr.'s original November 1961 draft of the Civil Rights
Act covered sex, but sex was dropped in negotiations, only to be reintroduced by a southerner who was no friend of the bill.[57] For some, sex
was reintroduced as a poison pill. For others, the inclusion of sex was
a victory for women's rights.[58] Either way, sex stuck, but with an important caveat. The act specifically permitted sex discrimination where
sex is a "bona fide occupational qualification," which the Equal Employment Opportunity Commission would later interpret to cover wet
nurses and sperm donors. For years, however, employers interpreted
this clause to have quite broad implications, allowing them to exclude
women from management jobs, for instance, with the argument that
women might leave to have children (or be forced to leave, because
most employers retained pregnancy bans).

A Weak Equal Employment Opportunity Commission   Had an early
version of the act passed, the terms of compliance might not have been
up for grabs. The early proponents of a federal fair employment law
favored an administrative agency parallel to the National Labor Relations Board (NLRB), with the authority to sanction firms and to establish
compliance criteria.[59] In the end, those who had sought to weaken the
bill by preventing an authority like the NLRB got their way, but this left
enforcement to the courts. Judges eventually went much further than
even the bill's most ardent proponents might have hoped for.

Title VII gave the new Equal Employment Opportunity Commission
(EEOC), an independent agency of five presidential appointees, no powers of enforcement. The commission was to investigate complaints and
seek voluntary conciliation where it found discrimination. Individuals
had the right to bring suit, but the EEOC had no authority to bring suit
or to otherwise enforce its own rulings against employers. The attorney
general could bring suit in cases where a "pattern or practice" of resistance to Title VII was identified, but rarely exercised this power, for the
Justice Department's "priorities and budgetary requirements did not
fully coincide with the EEOC's interests," as Antonia Chayes wrote in
the *Harvard Business Review* in 1974.[60] To win support for the bill, Everett
Dirksen had removed clauses that would have allowed nonprofits such
as the ACLU and the NAACP to sue on behalf of plaintiffs, and the attorney general to sue in individual discrimination cases. Critics of the
bill thought that these limitations would prevent frivolous suits. Under

the act, the EEOC could draw up guidelines for nondiscrimination, but these guidelines had no legal standing.[61] Because the EEOC's powers were so carefully hedged, it was clear that its rulings would be effective only insofar as employers chose to comply, or the courts chose to compel them to comply. In 1971 Congress did give the EEOC the power to bring suits, but federal judges were still left to interpret and enforce the act.

The Addition of Age and Disability By beginning with a laundry list of protected categories—race, color, religion, sex, and national origin—instead of targeting one group, such as descendants of slaves, sponsors left civil rights law open to the inclusion of new categories.[62] Congress protected those aged 40 to 65 in 1967 by adding them to the list, and then for the public sector protected the physically and mentally impaired through the Rehabilitation Act of 1973.[63] As Arthur Gutman argues of that act, "Congress prayed that model programs for federal entities would trigger widespread voluntary efforts in the private and state/local sectors—a prayer that went unanswered."[64] It required executive agencies to practice nondiscrimination, "affirmative action," and "reasonable accommodation," for people with physical or mental impairments, current, past, or only imagined. These acts were later reinforced by 1986 age discrimination amendments protecting most workers over age 70, and by the 1990 Americans with Disabilities Act extending protections to disabled workers in private enterprise.

Johnson's Reinforces Kennedy's Vague Affirmative Action Order

In 1965 Lyndon Johnson updated Kennedy's original affirmative action order for federal contractors. Like Kennedy's order, Johnson's Executive Order 11246 of September 24, 1965, prohibited discrimination among contractors, requiring them to "take affirmative action to ensure that applicants are employed, and that employees are treated during employment, without regard to" race, color, or national origin. In 1967 Johnson added sex to the list, and in 1968 he added religion. Johnson's 1965 order extended coverage to *all* work done by contractors and subcontractors, not just contracted work. Like Kennedy's order, it required federal contractors to submit regular reports detailing workforce composition. Like Kennedy's order, it encouraged employers to take positive steps to end discrimination. Johnson replaced Kennedy's President's Committee on Equal Employment Opportunity in the Executive Office with the Office of Federal Contract Compliance (OFCC) in the Department of Labor.[65] Federal guidelines from 1968 stipulated that employers with contracts of over $10,000 must practice affirmative action, and those with contracts of over $50,000 must maintain written affirmative action plans for each establishment. The OFCC was to "issue regulations to implement the order, investigate complaints, conduct compliance reviews, hold hearings and impose sanctions, and to supervise and coordinate the compliance activities of the contracting agencies."[66]

The contract compliance office could terminate contracts and debar firms from future contracts, but it rarely used that power. Not a single major federal supplier was terminated or debarred in the 1960s.[67] Neither employers nor the OFCC knew what the order required firms to do, beyond eliminating the most blatant forms of discrimination.[68] The compliance office could conduct on-site "compliance reviews," but it did not have independent standards of compliance because Johnson's order did not spell out any.[69]

By 1968 it was clear that Washington would not set out compliance criteria either for federal contractors subject to affirmative action edicts, or for firms subject only to equal opportunity law. It was clear that federal agencies would reinforce what leading firms chose to do. After Plans for Progress companies put in special recruitment and training programs for blacks on their own initiative, the Department of Labor issued affirmative action guidelines in 1968 encouraging recruitment and training. The National Association of Manufacturers and Plans for Progress set up meetings between employers and federal officials to try to educate business leaders about what was required of them, but, as a business association noted, "In spite of these meetings, the concept of 'affirmative action' remained fuzzy."[70] It would be defined in the future by the actions of firms more than by anything else. The PCEEO and its successor, the Office of Federal Contract Compliance, looked at whether firms were making the same "good faith" efforts their peers were making rather than inventing their own norms.[71] The EEOC took its cues about what the Civil Rights Act required from the same firms, and so when the agency cited the Allen-Bradley Company for lack of progress in 1968, it pointed to the absence of a recruitment program for blacks like the programs found at Plans for Progress firms.[72]

Conclusion

Employers had excluded women and minorities in a myriad of different ways in the late 1950s. When King David Holmes went back to Brass Valley in Connecticut after college in the 1940s, the personnel officer told him that sales jobs were "reserved" for whites. Segregated unions recruited brothers and cousins of members, excluding anyone not in the kinship network. Civil service officers steered women into jobs without promotion prospects. Armaments manufacturers kept blacks out of skilled manufacturing jobs, offering them jobs as janitors and laborers. Insurance companies recruited at colleges that practiced discrimination, and used employment agencies that only sent them white candidates. Exclusion took so many forms that it was probably beyond the capacity of Congress to outlaw it in all of its specific incarnations.

Because the mechanisms of discrimination were so varied, perhaps federal officials would inevitably have had to work out what the law meant in different sectors. Congress might have done two things to make the terms of compliance clearer, however. First, it might have set out terms in the original legislation. It might, for instance, have required employers to advertise all jobs and keep the records of all applicants. Second, it might have set up an executive branch agency on the model of the National Labor Relations Board, with authority to set standards and enforce them. In the case of the NLRB, its rulings on collective bargaining certainly evolved, but at any one point in time the terms of compliance were clear enough. By outlawing discrimination without setting up a system for defining it, John F. Kennedy, Lyndon Johnson, and Congress put employers in a bind. While affirmative action and equal opportunity law ruled out the most egregious forms of discrimination—"No Negroes" signs and bans on employing married women—employees and activists were free to argue that it required much more than this. Hundreds of judges across the country would be the eventual arbiters of compliance, yet those judges would not speak with a single voice.

Personnel experts would respond by playing a defensive game. They would try to protect against every imaginable eventuality, predicting where the courts would move in the future based on general principles from the past. Thus because Washington had settled on grievance panels to resolve union disputes, personnel experts would recommend them to resolve civil rights disputes. Because firms governed labor relations with their own bureaucratic personnel systems, managers would set up bureaucratic personnel systems to govern equal opportunity. It was up to the courts and the Department of Labor to figure out what was lawful and what was not. With little knowledge of personnel systems, judges and federal officials would take their lead from leading employers.

■   ■   ■   ■

THREE

THE END OF JIM CROW
The Personnel Arsenal Put to New Purposes

AS A JUNIOR MAJORING IN PSYCHOLOGY at Howard University in 1963, Leon Butler thought he had little chance of a career in industry. The alma mater of Thurgood Marshall, Howard had been established for blacks two years after the end of the Civil War. As Butler explained to the *New York Times* in 1965, since his junior year there had been "a fantastic rise in the number of corporation recruiters coming to campus." Those recruiters had been going to area schools like George Washington and Georgetown for years. Now for the first time they were visiting historically black colleges. Butler interviewed with Western Electric representatives when they came to campus in his senior year, and five interviews later found himself with a job using his psychology degree in the company's management training program.

A black man helping to train Western Electric managers would have been unimaginable the year Butler entered Howard. In July 1961, the company employed 14,708 supervisors and managers. One was black. Three years later, the number had risen to 41. In the meantime, Western Electric and other members of Plans for Progress, the private-sector wing of Kennedy's Presidents Committee on Equal Employment Opportunity, had acted on the White House's call to open the doors to blacks.[1]

Kennedy's Executive Order 10925, issued in March 1961, required federal contractors to take "affirmative action" to equalize employment opportunity, but it mentioned nothing specific. It was personnel managers who made the order concrete. Civil rights groups charged companies with discrimination, organized demonstrations, and set up jobs banks for black workers, but they did not draw blueprints for corporate equal opportunity programs. Federal bureaucrats collected detailed data on minority and female employment from private firms and investigated charges of discrimination, but they did not redesign the personnel system. Congress strengthened agency oversight and periodically added new regulatory teeth, but did not specify how employers should change. The courts overturned some compliance strategies as discriminatory and vetted others, but it wasn't judges who designed corporate programs.

It was personnel experts who built the first equal opportunity programs, on three distinct pillars of classical personnel administration. First, they modeled corporate policies forbidding racial discrimination on contract clauses prohibiting discrimination against union activists that first appeared in the 1930s. Second, they fashioned recruitment programs for blacks on those they had used for whites, focusing now on black high schools and colleges, black newspapers and magazines. Third, they based new management and skill training programs for blacks, Latinos, and women on programs that had been open only to white men. These innovations would become the hallmarks of equal opportunity programs in the 1960s.

In choosing these interventions, personnel experts redefined the public's understanding of workplace discrimination. Federal officials soon argued that employers without nondiscrimination policies weren't serious about stamping out discrimination. They soon argued that employers who didn't recruit at black high schools and women's colleges didn't want women or blacks. They soon argued that employers who didn't enroll blacks and women in training didn't want to integrate. These ideas came from personnel managers.

It was personnel managers meeting first under the auspices of Plans for Progress, and then in professional associations and business groups, who decided what equal opportunity meant in the 1960s. Some activists and politicians kept pressure on firms, but the nexus of action shifted to the firm once Kennedy's affirmative action edict and the Civil Rights Act were in place. The shop floor was where change took place. Firms might have chosen any number of other strategies. They might have simply eliminated explicit barriers to blacks and women—"No Negroes" signs and marriage bans. That is what most European employers did when faced with similar laws. They might have created hiring quotas. They might have created whistleblower programs to identify and remove managers who discriminated. Instead, they adopted three tools drawn from the personnel arsenal.

This chapter shows how important personnel professionals and employers were in defining discrimination and equal opportunity. The broader lesson is that, in the American context, professionals and organizations play an underappreciated role in designing regulatory compliance. Congress's Civil Rights Act and both Kennedy's and Johnson's affirmative action orders left it to employers to figure out how to comply, and to the courts to judge whether their innovations were lawful.

Personnel Defines Equal Opportunity

John F. Kennedy's executive order outlawing discrimination in government agencies and federal contractors led to a sea change in the personnel profession. The profession had been focused on labor relations since the 1930s, when the Wagner Act gave unions new powers to organize. Personnel managers in many nonunion firms spent their time fending off organizers, while those in union firms specialized in negotiations and contract management.

Many personnel experts who had spent their careers dealing with labor regulations were none too pleased when Washington added another layer of regulation. Nearly a decade after the Civil Rights Act, a *Harvard Business Review* article reported on executives' attitudes toward equal opportunity at 20 of America's largest firms. One described them as "foolhardy investments in still another government thorn in management's side." Another complained, "Two years ago, our annual report featured blacks; last year, pollution equipment; this year, women; next year, your guess is as good as mine." Another summed up his views of women in management: "As the person responsible for developing this organization's human resources, I often find it hard to justify investing in females in managerial positions. No matter if it is the result of biological or social factors; women present the added risk of possibly terminating for purely personal reasons."[2]

Yet a growing number of personnel executives saw that equal opportunity law would enable them to expand their role in the firm. The national network of personnel experts that came together in 1961 in Plans for Progress, the private-sector arm of the President's Committee for Equal Employment Opportunity, championed equal opportunity programs. The 300 firms that signed on as Plans for Progress members served as proving grounds for new strategies for fighting segregation. The network helped to convey new ideas to companies across the country, as smaller firms mimicked regional and industry leaders.

In defining new solutions to the problem of discrimination, the personnel profession defined the nature of the problem. If the solution was new recruitment programs, the problem was the old recruitment program. If the solution was new training systems, the problem was the old training model. As federal agencies endorsed these new strategies, they vetted the definition of discrimination that the personnel profession was promoting. This pattern would continue as personnel experts promoted one round of compliance strategies after another.

Labor Law and the Rise of Personnel Administration

Lawyers might have taken charge of equal opportunity compliance, but personnel experts had begun to handle regulatory compliance after passage of the Wagner Act of 1935, when union membership skyrocketed. Whereas a tenth of the industrial workforce was unionized in 1935, eight-tenths were unionized by 1946 (see figure 3.1). The personnel profession grew to manage unions, building bureaucratic systems

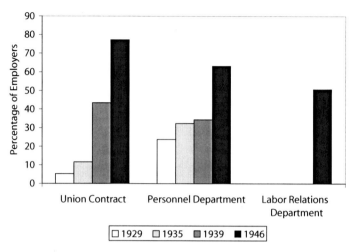

Figure 3.1. Growth of Unionization and Personnel Departments (1929–46)
Source: National Industrial Conference Board 1929, 1936, 1940, 1947.

to handle labor regulations and union contracts. Meanwhile, the record unemployment of the 1930s gave way to record employment during the war. To manage the tight labor market, Washington exercised new controls over job changes and demanded that firms justify their calls for more workers. Employers responded to this triple threat of increased unionization, a tight labor market, and new federal labor controls by hiring personnel directors.[3]

Firms also put in labor relations departments for the first time. By 1946, half of the firms surveyed by the National Industrial Conference Board reported labor relations departments, and 66 percent reported personnel departments, up from 34 percent in 1939, just before the war. In 1939 the Conference Board had not even asked about that brand-new offshoot of the personnel department, the labor relations department.

The personnel profession had grown in the 1920s by developing formal systems for recruiting, testing, and assessing workers. The Wagner Act encouraged personnel experts to further elaborate bureaucratic systems by focusing on workers' rights to hold fair elections, and the rights union contracts guaranteed. In the 1960s personnel experts forged equal opportunity programs from their bureaucratic labor relations toolkit. They wrote policies forbidding discrimination against women and minorities that paralleled their policies forbidding discrimination against activists. They expanded recruitment from white to black high schools and colleges. They expanded training to include minorities and women. Nothing in the law suggested that firms should take these particular measures.

Plans for Progress: The Private Personnel Office as Laboratory

It was the personnel profession that took on the job of complying with equal opportunity regulations in most companies. Regional and national professional associations played a role in promoting compliance strategies, but at first it was a self-organized group of company personnel officers that responded to Kennedy's call for "affirmative action" by sketching a blueprint for nondiscrimination. That blueprint would later be embraced by federal regulators at the EEOC and at the OFCC, the agency charged with overseeing federal contractors.

Personnel directors at big defense contractors were the first to change their ways after Kennedy ordered them to take affirmative action to eliminate discrimination. They worked together through Plans for Progress, the private-sector adjunct to the President's Committee on Equal Employment Opportunity. That group was set up by Atlanta lawyer and businessman Robert Troutman, a classmate of Joseph Kennedy at Harvard who devoted a year of his time, funded the operation out of his own pocket, and set up shop next to his own Atlanta law office. Lockheed was the catalyst, for on March 3, just three days before Kennedy ordered federal contractors to take affirmative action to end discrimination, it had signed a billion-dollar air force contract for C-141 cargo planes to be built at its Marietta, Georgia, plant.[4] In 1961 Lockheed's Marietta plant still practiced Jim Crow despite presidential orders forbidding discrimination in military contractors dating to World War II.

Lockheed-Georgia was the biggest industrial firm in the South, with 10,500 workers. Its Marietta plant had segregated facilities, and near-complete job segregation. Blacks were almost exclusively hired as janitors or washroom attendants. The rest, members of a "Negro" union, were in semiskilled jobs. The white union locals excluded blacks from apprenticeships for skilled jobs, and from the union itself. On April 7, barely a month after Kennedy's Executive Order 10925 established the President's Committee for Equal Employment Opportunity (PCEEO) under Vice President Lyndon Johnson, the committee received a complaint from the NAACP's Herbert Hill that Lockheed's contract made a "shameful mockery" of Kennedy's new order forbidding discrimination among federal contractors.[5]

The air force investigated the charge that Lockheed kept blacks out of skilled jobs and apprenticeships, operated segregated cafeterias, restrooms, and water fountains; and had signed a contract with a segregated white union. Committee staff director John G. Feild found the charges to be "substantially correct," and Lockheed quickly drafted what Feild called a "plan for progress," signed in the Oval Office on May 25 by Vice President Johnson, the secretary of labor, and Lockheed's president. Johnson said that this might become the model for defense contractors, and so it did.[6] Lockheed's personnel managers sketched a six-page plan promising a strict policy of nondiscrimination, a new recruitment program, training programs for blacks, and an upgrading program for underemployed black workers.

Hugh Gordon had come to Marietta in 1951, with an undergraduate engineering degree from Virginia Tech and a masters in science from Georgia Tech, looking for a people-oriented job. He landed a job in personnel. Lockheed was making planes for the Korean War. A California company, Lockheed tried to integrate the production lines by setting up an all-black line in the early 1950s for semiskilled workers and merging it with a white assembly line. The blacks they hired were mostly college graduates, who rankled at being supervised by whites with less education. They caught the attention of the NAACP's Herbert Hill, who helped to organize a protest. Little came of the protest, but it put Lockheed on Hill's radar. Even less came of the experiment.

Gordon stuck with the company and became the Marietta director of personnel in 1959. When Lockheed sought to comply with Kennedy's 1961 affirmative action order, Gordon's department sketched the plan for progress.[7] Under the recruitment component, Lockheed promised to "aggressively seek out more qualified minority group candidates in order to increase the number of employees in many job categories," and it accomplished this by visiting predominantly black high schools and colleges. Under the training component, Lockheed pledged to "make certain that qualified minority group employees are included in supervisory and pre-supervisory training classes and in other classes offered to employees on company time" and to end the union exclusion of blacks from apprenticeships. Under upgrading, it promised an inventory of current workers and an effort to place underemployed blacks in better jobs.[8]

Robert Troutman had brokered the deal to have this plan approved in Washington, and, on the day before it was signed, he proposed to the PCEEO that he chair a special subcommittee called Plans for Progress that would recruit other companies to follow Lockheed's lead. On July 12, eight other major defense contractors signed on—Western Electric, Boeing, Douglas Aircraft, General Electric, Martin Marietta, North American Aviation, the Radio Corporation of America, and United Aircraft—bringing to three-quarters of a million the number of workers under Plans for Progress pledges.[9] The newcomers wrote plans modeled on Lockheed's, promising strict nondiscrimination policies for hiring and firing and new recruitment efforts for blacks, including visits to historically black colleges. Some vowed that no numerical targets would be used, but promised to monitor progress in both training programs and jobs. Troutman set to work recruiting other big defense contractors who depended on federal contracts for their livelihood. He had signed 52 firms by the fall of 1961, and 105 within a year.[10]

Lockheed's Hugh Gordon described the role of Plans for Progress in a 2000 interview: "We entered into a plan to go out and recruit and train . . . and just step up our affirmative action to integrate the plant and give blacks opportunities to be hired." The result was not only a local change, but

> a national business government partnership with headquarters in Washington run by business volunteers in conjunction with the government. But it was a business organization and it went around the country and signed up other companies to similar pacts.[11]

First it was Troutman who did this, and then personnel executives from participating companies.

For Gordon, personnel executives at leading contractors were carrying out Kennedy's pledge to eradicate discrimination. Plans for Progress "was one of the major factors in changing . . . opportunities for blacks. Nothing has ever been written about that. . . . That story has never been told. Those companies . . . had in excess of eight million employees. No single event in history . . . produced more immediate results than that [group]" when it came to ending discrimination.[12] And so it was that the new norms developed by personnel executives at Lockheed were embraced by leading employers across the country.

Within Plans for Progress, committees of personnel executives from member firms handled the different components of the plans, such as training and recruitment. Hugh Gordon served on the 10-member Community Relations Committee in Washington, which focused on establishing recruiting relationships with minority schools and communities. In eight southern states the committee set up local merit employment councils devoted to recruiting and to getting the word out about the skill requirements of industry. They also set up institutes to train high school guidance counselors in how to steer minority students into jobs in participants' firms.[13] Merit employers associations in major cities across the country brought together personnel executives with educators to step up recruitment.

While Plans for Progress made news, other subcommittees of the PCEEO worked behind the scenes to persuade companies to change their ways. Jerry Holleman, executive vice chairman, told the Industrial Relations Research Association in July 1961 that his idea was to get others to join the bandwagon by quietly investigating complaints and pointing out problems to companies, not through public shaming.

> I do not brandish this enforcement power as a threat. It is a weapon I would just as soon the committee would never have to use. . . . We are not a publicity-seeking outfit. We do not intend to grab headlines by releasing information about complaints received. . . . We are not engaged in witch hunts. . . . If there is fault, we intend to find it, but we will seek to get the fault corrected peacefully and quietly, without fanfare.[14]

And so the investigations of Johnson's committee were kept quiet, and it was the programs of the Plans for Progress employers that took up column space in the *Wall Street Journal*, the *New York Times*, and the *Washington Post*.

Seeing how rare sanctions were, and how many firms continued to discriminate, civil rights advocates complained that, in its first year, the PCEEO relied too much on voluntary efforts by Plans for Progress firms and not enough on conventional enforcement. Troutman, they said, went too easy on participants. As Herbert Hill of the NAACP argued on the first anniversary of Plans for Progress, change had been largely "symbolic," and firms regarded participation as "a way of securing immunity from real compliance with the antidiscrimination provisions of their Government contracts." "Plans for Progress" was "simply a euphemism for what a previous administration called 'voluntary compliance.'"[15] Or as Whitney Young Jr., new head of the National Urban League, said in 1962 about Plans for Progress, "We've tried the voluntary approach for years, and nothing's happened."[16] The Washington oversight board of Plans for Progress largely left companies to their own devices.

On the Fourth of July, 1962, the NAACP's Herbert Hill announced that he would file charges against 40 of the first 85 Plans for Progress signatories, a slap in the face to Troutman. The PCEEO publicly reasserted its commitment to active enforcement, leading Troutman to resign that August.[17] Plans for Progress moved from Atlanta to Washington, and continued operations as a business association under the loose control of the PCEEO. It continued to gain members, even though its star performer had exited the stage. By mid-1965 it had signed over 300 firms.[18] Now Plans for Progress operated as a network of personnel executives at leading firms, organized into committees, under a Washington headquarters with a small staff.

Lockheed's original innovations continued to provide the main template for companies in the 1960s, and thus to define what it meant to practice fair employment. The Plans for Progress pledges that most firms wrote "follow the basic pattern established by Lockheed," concluded Columbia Law's Michael Sovern in his review of the plans.[19] The PCEEO didn't have a blueprint of its own, and in its view, its job was to make sure that firms stopped discriminating, not to dictate how firms should go about it. The committee worked toward that goal by collecting statistics and adjudicating discrimination charges. When it found fault, it did not redesign the personnel system, but required the employer to hire the rejected applicant or promote the worker who had been passed over. Innovative employment practices were developed by Lockheed, not by the committee, and later by others in the Plans for Progress network.

To implement their new programs, the firms shared information through the PCEEO, which monitored them, and through conferences and meetings organized by the committee and professional associations. In early 1964, for instance, the committee sponsored a meeting of representatives from 70 historically black colleges and over 300 firms to discuss training and recruitment of black college graduates.[20] At a meeting of business firms in November, sponsored by the Wharton School, personnel executives E. G. Mattison of Lockheed, Harry Baker of International Harvester, Harold McFarland of General Motors, R. G. Lawrence of Western Electric, Virgil Day of General Electric, and Gerry Morse of Honeywell described their companies' plans for others to emulate.[21]

The personnel executives who devised these programs reported that they worked. By 1963, early Plans for Progress employers were hiring nearly 10 times the number of blacks they had hired just three years earlier. Whitney Young of the Urban League had criticized Troutman's Plans for Progress in 1962 as too voluntary, but late in 1963 he announced that 115 companies in Plans for Progress had hired nearly 15,000 new blacks in the third quarter of that year—25 percent of new workers in these companies were black. Before Plans for Progress, blacks had never made up more than 3 percent of new workers in any quarter.[22]

Why Firms Joined the Bandwagon

Why did Kennedy's affirmative action order grab the attention of employers who had ignored similar orders from Roosevelt, Truman, and Eisenhower? First, Kennedy put together an oversight committee of people devoted to the cause, spearheaded by Lyndon Johnson, and including four cabinet secretaries, secretaries of the army, navy, and air force, heads of major federal agencies, and private-sector luminaries.

Second, he promised to enforce the edict by cutting off contractors. In 1962, committee executive director John G. Feild warned: "the government will not hesitate to cancel contracts if either labor or management fails to comply with fair employment practice laws. . . . We will attempt to bring equality control as well as quality control into industries handling government work."[23] In 1966, the *Wall Street Journal* carried a front-page story titled "Job Bias Showdown" reporting that more than a dozen major federal contractors were on the verge of losing their contracts.[24] Third, civil rights groups now pledged to hold contractors' feet to the fire. NAACP labor secretary Herbert Hill actively investigated complaints, and went to the committee for answers. The Urban League also pressured the committee to achieve results.

Hill told a House committee in December 1968 that, in spending $54 billion buying goods and services from private companies, many of which practiced discrimination, "the Government is directly subsidizing racial discrimination." As yet, Washington had not made good on its threat to cancel contracts: "only one instance of genuine enforcement, one contract canceled, would have been real evidence of intent to use the enforcement powers provided."[25] PCEEO members believed that the threat of contract termination had done the job. In 1962, the committee found discrimination at five Comet Rice plants in the South, and at Danly Machine Specialties in Cicero, Illinois. When management refused to make changes, the committee announced the plants would be barred from future contracts. Management came around.[26]

Companies signed on with Plans for Progress (PfP) in part because they believed that signing would inoculate them against all penalties. A PfP pledge in fact did not prevent lawsuits or debarment, and a number of firms were later debarred, but Plans for Progress did not disabuse companies of the idea. One advantage PfP firms did have was that they could submit their own progress reports to Plans for Progress, rather than the standard forms required of other contractors beginning in April 1962.[27]

The race riots of the summer of 1965 gave employers another reason to join. As the *Wall Street Journal* reported on August 19, a campaign to end job discrimination,

> may prove to be a crucial factor in the troubled racial situation in the nation's urban areas. Many sociologists say that the rioting here and in Los Angeles last week was mainly caused by the overwhelming sense of frustration of Negro youths who feel there are no opportunities for them in a dominant white society. Such riots "could potentially happen in almost every one of the central cities in the 215 metropolitan areas in which half of the Negro popula-

tion of this nation is now concentrated," says Philip M. Hauser, a University of Chicago sociologist.[28]

Or in the words of President Lyndon Johnson, "Aimless violence finds fertile ground among men imprisoned by the shadowed walls of hatred, coming of age in the poverty of slums, facing their future without education or skills and with little hope of rewarding work."[29] In 1967, *Nation's Business* would write, "Quietly, across the face of America, business and industry are taking the initiative to shatter barriers of discrimination. . . . This effort is having notable success even in cities rocked by racial violence where the militants lay the blame for civil disobedience largely on the supposed scarcity of job opportunities for Negroes."[30]

Personnel Committees Spread the Word in Every Town

Personnel directors in big national firms shared information on how to comply with the law through Plans for Progress and the conferences and meetings organized for members. Meanwhile at the local level, personnel experts in smaller firms popularized the recruitment and training programs that Plans for Progress firms like Lockheed and GE had developed. They banded together in regional associations, like the merit employers councils that Hugh Gordon and his Washington-based committee organized across the country, to spread the word.

In Boston, Polaroid organized a nonprofit Jobs Clearing House in September 1963 to match blacks with job openings, signing up 700 area employers. The no-fee agency used volunteer personnel experts to interview prospects and match them to jobs, and created a center to promote new recruitment strategies among member companies, such as sending current black employees to recruit at urban high schools.

At the new Chicago Merit Employment Committee, set up in 1965 by leading Chicago businesses to improve recruitment of minorities, personnel managers and executives met over lunch to hear presentations about how to end bias. They saw slide shows documenting the growing market power of the black community, and heard "strong testimonials from executives who have hired large numbers of Negroes." Like the merit employment committees across the South, they helped build conduits from black schools and colleges to area employers.[31]

After the Watts riots of 1965, 200 major firms worked with the American Society for Training and Development to create training and placement programs for the unskilled, from special ASTD offices in downtown L.A. and in Watts. The society was run by Dr. Carl Kludt, on leave as manager of personnel development at Hughes Aircraft, where he had run a pilot training program for the long-term unemployed.

Two years later, Chicago's Fair Employment Practices Committee (FEPCo.) employment agency launched the Eager Beaver campaign to convince 1,000 employers to hire 1,000 black men and women for white-collar jobs and prepare them with training programs. FEPCo. president William Dasho argued that, because of past discrimination, many blacks lacked the work experience to pass standard "employability tests": "They can't get the experience until they are hired. It has become a vicious circle." FEPCo. championed corporate training programs that would help blacks to get ahead.[32]

In Indianapolis, by 1967 the Center for Independent Action (CIA) had brought together 26 of the city's biggest businesses to improve the lot of the disadvantaged. CIA asked 500 Indianapolis businesses to pledge to do more than the law required, adopting aggressive recruitment tactics to integrate their workforces. At CIA's first job fair more than 100 employers listed 2,000 openings, resulting in 560 hires.

Meanwhile in Sacramento, Dr. Philip Brunstetter, manager of personnel development for Aerojet-General, hosted a weekly television show with job-seekers, employers, and government officials aimed not only at matching people and jobs, but at helping employers develop new recruitment programs. As C. S. Woodruff, general manager of Pacific Telephone and a sponsor of the program, argued, "Business has realized there is no forum to talk about minority employment problems. We need to communicate in the business community and share our experiences on employing members of minority groups."[33]

Local merit employment associations, spearheaded by Plans for Progress, were joined by local chapters of the American Society for Personnel Administration (ASPA) in promoting recruitment and training programs.[34] Monthly meetings covered topics such as how to recruit black workers, and how to help Latinos arrange transportation to work.[35] The journals and annual meetings of the ASPA and other personnel groups increasingly focused on how to integrate the workforce and comply with equal opportunity laws.

Nondiscrimination Policies Copied from Union Contracts

The first step most personnel managers took was to craft their own nondiscrimination pledges. Kennedy required federal contractors to post a notice stating: "The contractor will not discriminate against any employee or applicant for employment because of race, creed, color, or national origin."[36] On the face of it, a separate company pledge was redundant, but companies adopted their own policies following Lockheed's example. The pledges were modeled on clauses in union contracts forbidding discrimination against activists. An old labor relations instrument, the nondiscrimination clause to protect union leaders won new life as an anti-bias instrument.

Union Nondiscrimination Clauses and the Color Line

State laws had done little to stop unions from excluding blacks, and by the early 1960s, many unions rejected blacks or operated segregated locals. Massachusetts surveyed unions in 1962 to gauge compliance with its prohibition against race discrimination. Only a third of unions completed the survey, and only 1.5 percent of their members were black, as compared with 9 percent of the state's population.[37] Segregation of locals meant that, as of 1960, black unionists were ineligible to train and bid for skilled work in aircraft, oil, and many other industries. Segregation also meant separate seniority lists affording late-coming whites job protection over blacks of long standing.

In June 1961 the segregated unions at Lockheed's Marietta plant pledged to merge. By the middle of 1962, unions at other Plans for Progress signatories—like U.S. Steel's coal and iron plant at Birmingham, employing 6,000 blacks and 14,000 whites—had made similar pledges. That year the AFL promised to stamp out segregated unions across the country, to allow blacks to hold elective office, and to put an end to dual seniority lists.[38] Personnel managers and union leaders now built racial nondiscrimination policies into contracts. These contracts were modeled on clauses forbidding discrimination against union organizers. As early as 1967, a survey found that 52 percent of companies had signed a union contract forbidding race discrimination.[39]

Civil Rights Nondiscrimination Policies

Personnel experts recommended that firms follow Lockheed's model and adopt nondiscrimination pledges for all workers, pointing out that government prohibitions alone hadn't ended discrimination in fair-employment states like Illinois and Massachusetts. A Chicago study from October 1962 found that companies routinely ruled out blacks, Catholics, and Jews in their job orders to employment agencies. At one agency, 14 percent of 1,070 sampled job orders ruled out "negroes" or Jews, or stipulated Protestant, gentile, or "Nordic only." At another agency, at least 20 percent of job orders ruled out certain groups. Half a dozen of the offending employers had signed Plans for Progress agreements, pledging in writing to "make explicit their nondiscriminatory hiring policy in employment advertising."[40]

Plans for Progress companies had published explicit pledges, and reiterated these pledges in job advertisements. Bethlehem Steel ended its ad in the MIT campus paper in 1967 with the tag line, "An Equal Opportunity Employer in the Plans for Progress Program."[41]

The policies caught on quickly. By November 1963, the *New York Times* would trumpet: "Many national concerns with headquarters in New York City have announced new nondiscrimination policies."[42] By mid-1965, most of the 300 Plans for Progress companies had written nondiscrimination policies. By 1967, 71 percent of medium and large employers surveyed by the Bureau of National Affairs had nondiscrimination policies.[43] The policies spread to smaller employers after 1970. In my broad-based employer survey, one in five had a written policy protecting minorities by 1970, but nearly half had a policy by 1980 (see figure 3.2).[44] Policies covering women lagged behind those covering minorities, for Kennedy's 1961 affirmative action order did not cover sex discrimination.

Washington's response was a preview of what was to come. Once corporate nondiscrimination policies were widespread, administration officials endorsed them. When the Allen-Bradley Company of Milwaukee was challenged by the Department of Labor in 1968, Secretary of Labor George P. Shultz said that the company must do as other companies had done and announce a policy change:

> Affirmative action means . . . the Company taking those steps with respect to its own recruitment and hiring practices which will make clear to those seeking work in Milwaukee that race, creed, color, and national origin make no difference when some-

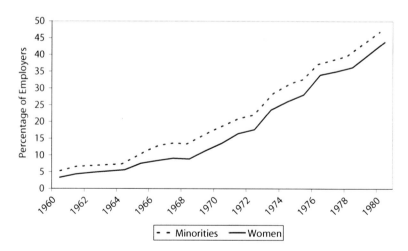

Figure 3.2. Employers with Antidiscrimination Policies for Minorities and Women (1960–80)

Source: Author's survey of 279 employers in 1986 (Dobbin et al. 1993).

body applies for work at Allen-Bradley. *These steps include both public representation to this effect*, and action which will give such representation its validity.[45]

Schultz suggested that the company should follow the crowd, and that a local nondiscrimination policy was key to attracting new minority talent. Personnel experts defined what compliance meant, and now Schultz endorsed that definition.

The Mixed Blessing of Seniority Rules   Unions had done two things to prevent discrimination against their members and leaders: written nondiscrimination clauses and set up seniority systems. The clauses served as a blueprint for policies forbidding racial bias, but seniority policies that continued in force had perverse effects on integration.

As early as 1900, craft unions negotiated for seniority rules to stop firms from firing activists or giving them the worst jobs.[46] After 1935 seniority rules spread to unskilled mass-manufacturing sectors. Non-union industries seeking to forestall unionism followed, and by 1946, 80 percent of the middling to large firms surveyed by the National Industrial Conference Board had seniority policies (see figure 3.3).[47]

Seniority rules would protect women and minorities from unjust dismissal eventually, but in the short term "last hired, first fired" worked against them. In her study of a New Jersey automobile factory, *Farewell*

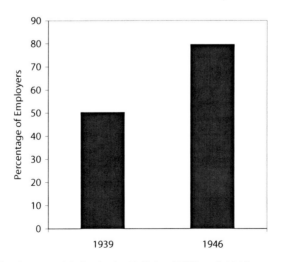

Figure 3.3. Employers with Seniority Policies (1939 and 1946)
Source: National Industrial Conference Board 1940, 1947.

to the Factory, Ruth Milkman finds that even in the 1980s, seniority-based layoffs cleared virtually all women out of the ranks with each economic downturn.[48]

Segregated Job Advertisements and Mothers' Exclusions Companies wrote nondiscrimination policies in their personnel manuals and in their job advertisements. Yet many companies continued to exclude women by advertising jobs for men and women separately, by excluding mothers from certain jobs, and by banning pregnancy. In the late 1960s, Lockheed and General Electric were publishing ads in the *Times* with the tag line "an equal opportunity employer" under the heading "Help Wanted, Male." While the EEOC had issued guidelines in 1966 forbidding employers to ban married women or women with small children, it let segregated job ads stand.[49] The agency's Sonia Pressman Fuentes later recalled the situation:

> Now, if you just looked at that issue as a lawyer, it was obvious that the law required one set of ads. But the country was at first unwilling, advertisers were unwilling, to do that. So, at first the EEOC came up with this cockamamie solution. They required a box on the classified advertising page that said something like, "While we're listing ads under 'Help Wanted, Male' and 'Help Wanted, Female,' we don't really mean it, and anybody can apply." Ridiculous![50]

The newly formed National Organization of Women fought the EEOC, sending picketers to five of its offices and suing the agency for failure to prevent sex discrimination in hiring.[51]

By 1969 the EEOC had changed its position, requiring nondiscrimination in advertising except where a "bona fide occupational qualification" (BFOQ) limited the job to one sex.[52] The agency also defined the term, so as to end the common practice of excluding women from such jobs as firefighter, police officer, and construction worker. According to the guidelines that Pressman drafted, "the only jobs for which sex could be a BFOQ were sperm donor and wet nurse."[53]

Many companies had banned married women, pregnant women, or women with young children from some or all jobs. Most dropped marriage bans, but kept pregnancy and mothers' bans until the EEOC ruled against them in the early 1970s. The Supreme Court did not take a hard line against pregnancy bans, but it did side with women's advocates in the EEOC on mothers' bans. In a 1971 case against aircraft maker Martin Marietta, which excluded women with young children, the Court ruled that the company could not permit "one hiring policy for women and another for men—each having pre-school-age children."[54] Thurgood Marshall objected to a loophole in the majority opinion, allowing the company to exclude women with young children if they could show that those women underperform: "The Court has fallen into the trap of assuming that the Act permits ancient canards about the proper role of women to be a basis for discrimination."[55] Despite some backpedaling, personnel managers now applied their nondiscrimination pledges more broadly, opening most jobs to women.

New Recruitment Programs Modeled on the Old

The company recruitment program was the second pillar of the equal opportunity program of the 1960s. In most industries the leading firms—Lockheed, Proctor and Gamble, Chase Manhattan Bank—had well-established recruitment programs for executives and production workers. They visited Ohio State, Columbia, and Yale to find management trainees, and local vocational and high schools to find production workers and bank tellers. As early as 1935, a survey of 254 medium and large employers found that 51 percent recruited directly at high schools and colleges.[56] The Conference Board's 1965 survey of almost 300 leading service sector firms found that 72 percent actively recruited at high schools, 57 percent visited colleges, and 47 percent visited business or trade schools.[57] Plans for Progress firms built on this model to create special recruitment programs to target blacks. They sent recruiters to historically black colleges and inner-city high schools. Later they developed special recruitment programs for women.

There was some resistance to these targeted programs. One executive told the Bureau of National Affairs that he couldn't in good conscience recruit in new areas: "I have given instructions as of 1965 . . . that if any good Negro applicants appear and if we have any openings, hire them. We have had none during this period . . . to go outside our area and recruit them would discriminate against local applicants."[58] But executives at leading firms overwhelmingly supported the idea. A national survey of Fortune 750 companies in 1969 found that 100 percent of top executives thought companies should make special efforts to hire and train blacks for skilled jobs. Just over half of line managers agreed.[59]

Special Recruitment for African-Americans and Women

Many federal contractors saw that they did not have enough blacks in the ranks. Blacks made up 21 percent of the population in the South, but only 4 percent of Lockheed-Georgia's 1961 workforce of 10,500.[60] Lockheed's personnel managers proposed to recruit from the Georgia State Employment Service, which in turn promised in writing not to discriminate in referrals.[61] Within two months of Kennedy's executive order, the heads of training at Lockheed had made recruitment visits to all six of Atlanta's segregated black high schools. Lockheed personnel managers began recruiting engineers and professionals through black colleges, professional associations, and civic organizations.[62]

According to Hugh Gordon, whose personnel department at Lockheed stationed a black personnel representative to Atlanta to recruit in the black community, companies that had discriminated in the past needed to get the word out that they were accepting applications from blacks. Visits and personal contacts could help, just as they had helped firms recruit for hard-to-staff occupations. In Gordon's words, "You had the situation in the South all over that blacks who had been denied jobs just didn't have the confidence . . . to apply for jobs in companies where they thought they were not wanted. So it's understandable we had to make an effort to get the applicants."[63] Lockheed brought "Negro college students by the busload" from Tuskegee Institute in Alabama to spend a day in the plant, and brought "a group of Negro high school counselors" to the plant for an "all-day educational program, showing in detail the industrial application of high school math and other subjects to the apprenticeship program."[64]

Part of Lockheed's Plan for Progress was to recruit through new Merit Employment Councils. Lockheed had set up such councils in California in the 1960s to get the word out about the kinds of skills it needed. Gordon sat on a national Plans for Progress committee that established these councils across the country to help employers recruit from minority communities.[65] Then in 1965 Gordon and his counterpart at Coca-Cola set up a national Merit Employment Association with local chapters doing the work of targeting minority high schools. Whitney Young, director of the Urban League, got on board and encouraged businesses to fund merit councils locally.

Targeted recruitment was a centerpiece at all nine Plans for Progress pioneer companies. International Harvester added 11 historically black colleges to its roster of recruitment sites.[66] Western Electric added four black colleges by 1962, and 12 by 1964.[67] All pledged to recruit through black colleges, civic groups, and newspapers.[68] All promised to work with state employment agencies. Public employment agencies had practiced their own version of Jim Crow. The Georgia State Employment Service had a black service and a white service. If an employer wanted a black worker, he listed a job with the black service. Before 1961, Lockheed had listed all janitorial jobs with the black service, and had nothing but black janitors. State agencies pledged to stop segregating workers, but Plans for Progress leaders argued that firms would have to establish their own recruitment programs if they wanted to see real change, because state agencies did not get out and beat the bushes for workers.[69]

Federal personnel managers set up their own targeted recruitment programs. The Bureau of Veterans Affairs (VA) sent its new recruitment task force to black colleges, under VA director John Gleason's order: "If Negroes are qualified, hire . . . them now." After Kennedy's 1961 executive order for federal agencies and contractors, the VA added 11,000 black employees over 18 months, for a total of 35,000 blacks on the payroll, or 23 percent of the workforce—the largest proportion of blacks of any federal agency. Before long black doctors were scattered across the country in VA management. A 1963 study found that 8 percent of jobs in the middle pay grades were held by blacks.[70]

By 1963, the *New York Times* would report that, among national firms headquartered in New York, "Personnel officers are taking a new look at their recruiting methods and seeking advice from Negro leaders on how to find and attract the best-qualified Negroes."[71] In that year, Kodak's industrial relations director Monroe C. Dill began targeting blacks for recruitment at the Rochester headquarters. Despite a growing population of black migrants from the South, Kodak had hired few blacks because, according to Dill, migrants were poorly educated, with skills suited to farming: "We don't grow many peanuts in Eastman Kodak. Most of the young Negroes in Rochester haven't even had the advantage of the kind of education one gets in the Rochester school system." The old recruitment system didn't turn up many black prospects: "Sure, we'd pick up a Negro here and there in the state universities and the private schools, but we never took a look at a Negro school. We were discriminating by omission. Now we're exposing ourselves to what the Negro market is so that we can make fair decisions."[72]

By 1965, Western Electric personnel director R. G. Lawrence not only sent recruiters on visits to historically black colleges such as Howard (where he found Leon Butler, who was introduced at the start of this chapter), he "guaranteed that ads in campus publications show Negro engineers and management personnel at their jobs."[73] Meanwhile Pacific Telephone sent black and Spanish-speaking recruiters not only to high schools and colleges, but to stores, barbershops, beauty parlors, and pool halls, and Metropolitan Life set up a program in New York using the Urban League, social service agencies, and Harlem nonprofits to find new recruits. By 1967, Mobil Oil's personnel department asked the few blacks who worked in white-collar jobs to help them recruit at black high schools. Gilroye Griffin Jr., a black lawyer recently hired at Mobil's White Plains office, went on high school recruiting visits to Bedford-Stuyvesant in Brooklyn, bringing the company's message: "Hang on. Finish school. There are jobs available."[74]

Part of the recruitment formula was to rethink job requirements. Met Life now paid less attention to employment exam scores and more to "native intelligence."[75] In 1967 Bruce Cole, whose Chicago's Jobs Now Project found jobs for minority youth, asked companies to drop experience requirements that excluded black novices who had suffered discrimination in the past: "We ask them to waive all the normal standards that have been set up to sort out whom you hire and whom you don't hire, to forget the high school diploma." Cole also asked employers to overlook police records: "It is pure luck if you don't get arrested if you grow up in the slums of Chicago or in the slums of any other city." In Massachusetts, Polaroid had come to the same conclusion about police records.[76]

An Invasion at Historically Black Colleges   By 1965 America's historically black colleges faced an onslaught of recruiters. Howard, Morehouse, Fisk, North Carolina College, Hampton Institute—all of the elite black colleges were deluged. President Stephen Wright of Fisk College in Nashville reported that, for the graduating class of 1963, 11 company recruiters and 16 government recruiters had come to campus. For the class of 1964, Fisk saw 58 company recruiters and 25 government recruiters. In Atlanta, Morehouse had to assign two full-time employees to handle 1963–64 recruiting visits—50 from industry and 36 from school districts. Howard had an unprecedented 400 recruitment visits in 1964 and again in 1965, for a graduating class of 450. Ohio's Central State College had 300 recruitment visits in 1965 for a graduating class of 315. A black college president told the *Washington Post* in 1965, "I had a Ph.D. for 10 years before I could command the salary that many of these kids are starting out with."[77] The *Post* wrote in 1964 that Plans for Progress firms were among the first to send recruiters to black colleges: "The firms that are seeking Negro graduates include many in the Plans for Progress program . . . those that have signed pledges to hire and promote without discrimination," such as Western Electric, Allied Chemical, Alcoa Aluminum, and American Telephone & Telegraph.[78]

William Nix, placement director at Morehouse, reported in 1964 that early candidates had changed the attitudes of recruitment directors at big companies: "the few Negroes who cracked the color line a few years ago were good ambassadors for the race." When two representatives from a firm in the North visited campus to look things over in 1961, they expressed surprise: "I took them to see Atlanta's Negro community. They were very impressed after visiting one of the homes. They said, 'We don't have Negroes of this kind in our home town.' And I said, 'yes you do.' And they discovered that they did." Morehouse couldn't attract recruiters before 1961, and now it had as many as it could handle.[79]

Personnel managers later set up special programs to recruit women. Edward D. Goldstein, president of Glass Containers Corporation, outlined the new approach in the early 1970s: "We're not going to wait for women to knock on our doors. I'm serious about solving the problem. We're going out and searching for qualified women who have the talent and potential to advance in our company." Waiving experience requirements was key for women as well as for blacks, according to Goldstein: "I know their qualifications won't always be the same as the men's; in sales, for example, just add 'ten years of experience' as an important criterion and you've eliminated most women."[80]

Targeted Recruitment Catches On   The Bureau of National Affairs 1967 survey found that targeted recruitment of minorities was common among members of its Personnel Policies Forum, a group of leading firms interested in personnel issues, more than a quarter of whom had signed Plans for Progress pledges. Thirty-one percent of firms created new recruitment systems for blacks in the two years after the Civil Rights Act came into force, and many contractors had set up special recruitment even before that.[81] More than half of the firms were now advertising through organizations like the NAACP and the Urban League. Forty percent reported that they advertised in newspapers and magazines with "high Negro circulation." And a third sent recruiters to "predominantly Negro high schools and colleges." Fewer companies made similar efforts for women—only 18 percent recruited at women's colleges.[82]

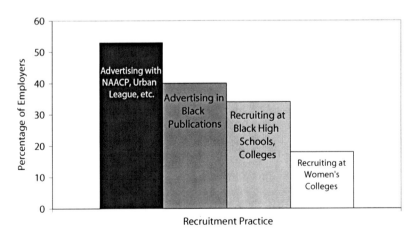

Figure 3.4. Employers with Recruitment Programs Targeting Blacks and Women (1967)

Source: Bureau of National Affairs 1967.

Big federal contractors pledged active recruitment campaigns, but these only took hold in work sites that already had recruitment programs in place. In Atlanta, big Plans for Progress work sites with recruitment directors made good on their pledges, according to a 1963 *New York Times* article, "Negro-Job Pledge Is Found Flouted." Not so for the smaller sites. Only the four largest Atlanta Plans for Progress sites were actively recruiting; 20 smaller sites were doing nothing. But the big workplaces accounted for 18,325 of the 23,084 employees at Atlanta Plans for Progress sites.[83]

Not everyone went along willingly. One industrial relations vice president argued in 1967 that targeted recruitment was tantamount to reverse discrimination: "Our company is . . . in a labor market where there are very few Negroes. . . . We are in strict compliance with all applicable laws." For firms like his that had filled all jobs by word of mouth, advertising so as to attract blacks seemed unfair to the white population: "Our attitude is that we will not practice reverse discrimination, i.e., advertising for Negro employees when we would not advertise for whites, or hiring Negro employees who live at distances from our plants where we would not hire whites."[84]

Still, the new recruitment techniques took hold and remained popular. Well over half of firms in the Bureau study reported special recruitment programs for minorities and women by 1975 (see figure 3.5). Ten years

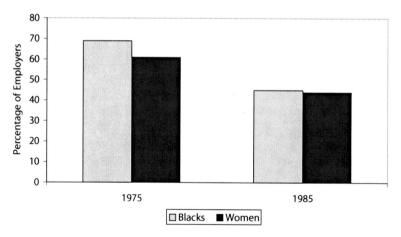

Figure 3.5. Employers with Recruitment Programs Targeting Blacks and Women (1975 and 1985)

Note: For women in 1975, the BNA asked about special recruiting programs "for women in traditionally male jobs."

Source: Bureau of National Affairs 1976, 1986b.

later, nearly half of firms still reported special recruitment. The percentage *reporting* special recruitment programs declined a bit, though that may have been because what was "special" in 1975—going to women's colleges as well as men's colleges—had become routine by 1985.

While many companies now used targeted recruitment, many still relied as well on word of mouth. In a 1965 survey, firms reported personal recommendations as their most effective recruitment tool, yet that method tended to reproduce the status quo.[85] At the New Jersey chemical plant sociologist David Halle studied in the late 1970s, 37 percent of the 121 blue-collar workers had a relative in the plant. Others had found their jobs through fathers and uncles now retired: "To be hired at Imperium, and at many of the plants in the area, the most important condition is to know somebody already there. Workers take it for granted that this is how good jobs—in refining or chemical plants or construction or the docks—are obtained."[86] And so, 15 years after passage of the Civil Rights Act, there were no women and only two Hispanics and two blacks on the job. Two-thirds of workers had been born within two miles of the plant.[87]

Training Retooled for Equal Opportunity

One of the first steps personnel took at Lockheed Marietta, just weeks after Kennedy signed Executive Order 10925 in 1961, was to implement a plan to open the on-site skill-training program to blacks. The other Plans for Progress employers pledged to open up training for both skilled jobs and management jobs, and, before long, training current workers for better jobs became a key component of equal opportunity programs nationally.[88] By 1964, GM's personnel director boasted that "nonwhites" participated in apprentice training programs for skilled jobs; enrolled in the company-sponsored engineering school in Flint, the General Motors Institute; and participated in cooperative training programs for high school and college students. GM set up a cooperative training program with Alabama's historically black Tuskegee Institute.[89] Western Electric's personnel chief, R. G. Lawrence, reported that the company had a special program to recruit nonwhites for skill training, and sponsored special secretarial training programs in New York and Chicago for nonwhites.[90]

Classical Skill and Management Training

Skill and management training programs were nothing new. Before World War II personnel departments had developed training programs for skilled production workers, clerks, foremen, managers, and executives. The National Office Management Association found that

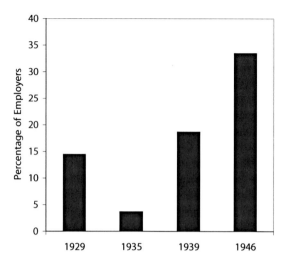

Figure 3.6. Employers with Training Programs for Supervisors (1929–46)
Source: National Industrial Conference Board 1929, 1936, 1940, 1947.

31 percent of employers had classroom training for office employees in 1935.[91] The National Industrial Conference Board surveys show that training programs for supervisors languished during the Depression but rebounded in the late 1930s (see figure 3.6). By the end of World War II, about a third of companies had training for supervisors.

By 1946, some 40 percent of firms had apprentice training programs, nearly 30 percent had training for production workers, and more than 10 percent had training programs for office workers and for college graduates, the latter typically designed for prospective managers (see figure 3.7).

Skill and Management Training for African-Americans and Women

Now Plans for Progress personnel managers opened up existing training programs to blacks, Latinos, and women. Personnel at the Western Electric plant in Newark had set up an apprentice program in 1937 to train machine-shop operators, but by 1960 the plant had few black apprentices even though Newark had a growing black community. Under its plan for progress, personnel managers began actively recruiting black trainees in the early 1960s and, by 1967, 80 percent of trainees were black.[92]

Many personnel experts argued that firms would have to train minorities themselves, for unions and vocational schools continued to discriminate, even though unions had pledged to integrate and now had nondiscrimination clauses in their contracts. Herbert Hill, spokesman

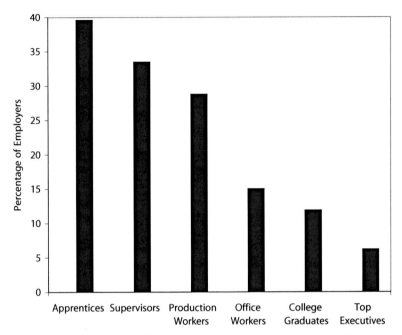

Figure 3.7. Employers with Training Programs for Various Groups (1946)
Source: National Industrial Conference Board, 1947.

for the NAACP, complained in 1962 that Johnson's PCEEO had been "powerless to effect changes" in the lot of blacks in textiles, public utilities, railroads, and construction, "where labor unions restrict access to employment and admission into apprenticeship training programs."[93] White unions still excluded blacks from apprenticeships.

Now personnel experts retrofitted the training schemes they had installed to deal with wartime labor shortages. At defense contractor Hughes Aircraft, personnel development manager Dr. Carl Kludt ran a pilot project to train the hard-core unemployed for clerical, drafting, and electronics jobs. Kludt placed 120 graduates of the training program. Meanwhile personnel managers at California's Pacific Telephone and New York's Metropolitan Life offered training not only in work tasks, but in basic math and English skills and in how to hold down a job.[94]

Equitable Insurance of New York had excluded blacks altogether before World War II and had hired only a handful before joining Plans for Progress. By 1965 Equitable had a new training program for blacks, in which it hired high school dropouts who scored well on IQ tests and enrolled them in night school to finish their degrees.[95] Between 1962 and 1965 New York Telephone recruited 2,500 black workers to its on-the-job training programs.[96] In Chicago, the FEPCo. employment agency challenged executives to set up on-the-job training programs for the black employees it placed.[97]

While blacks trailed whites in high school and college graduation rates, many employers had plenty of well-educated blacks on their payrolls in unskilled jobs. Personnel experts reasoned that they could readily move into white-collar jobs after some training. Theodore Purcell's 1960 study of Swift meatpacking plants in Chicago, Kansas City, and East St. Louis found that black women were the single best-educated group on the production line, but were relegated to unskilled jobs.[98] Black women and men had been given the worst jobs, regardless of their qualifications, and so many were ripe for promotion after a training stint.

Early training programs targeted blacks and Latinos, who were covered by Kennedy's 1961 affirmative action order. Many were expanded to include women after the Civil Rights Act protected women. Some firms put in special programs, but many put in general training programs and put extra effort into recruiting minorities and women, or set up quotas. As Barbara Boyle, an IBM executive turned equal opportunity consultant, concluded, "In addition to specialized [career development] seminars, many companies have specified that even regular management training and development programs include some qualified minority and women applicants."[99] Many had work to do to open up all training opportunities. Management trainee positions had long been informally reserved for men, as Boyle discovered in talking to managers:

> At a recent equal opportunity conference, a woman asked a top executive if he had ever considered naming a woman as his administrative assistant. "You don't understand the nature of that position," he replied. "The idea is to bring a man in for a year or two, to give him the experience of working with a top executive. . . . In short, to give him exposure to the entire company. . . . To develop him for increasing responsibility. . . ." He went on for several minutes, employing the words "man," he," and "him" at least 17 times. Then he stopped and blushed faintly at what he was saying. "I guess maybe some of us here ought to rethink that program," he said.[100]

For Boyle, women faced an obstacle because managers often thought, "after all, she'll leave after a couple of years to get married." Boyle argued that managers don't look closely enough at the turnover data: "It is generally true that women's attrition rate is higher than men's. But as

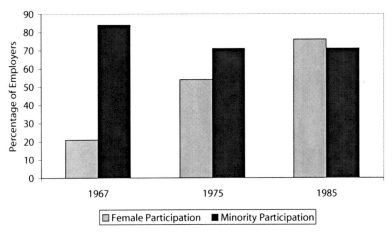

Figure 3.8. Firms with Women and Minorities in Apprenticeships (1967–86)

Note: Percentage of employers with apprenticeship programs who enrolled at least one member of each group in programs.

Source: Bureau of National Affairs 1986b, 14.

in the other areas of discrimination, going beyond the surface statistics reveals interesting facts. Within a given job level there is often no significant difference between the percentages of men and women leaving a company; attrition is higher in low-level jobs, and that is where most women are."[101]

More and more firms set up supervisory and management training programs to prepare current female and minority workers for advancement, according to the BNA surveys. Forty-seven percent of employers offered supervisory training in 1967, and that rose to 72 percent in 1975 and 78 percent in 1985. Thirty-one percent of firms offered management training in 1967, and that rose to 60 percent in 1975 and 69 percent in 1985. Setting up the programs was often not enough, and thus in 1967, 21 percent of firms reported that they used special recruitment strategies to attract minorities to training. Twelve percent used special recruitment strategies to attract women. These companies were likely ahead of the crowd, because a quarter were in Plans for Progress as of 1967, and three-quarters were federal contractors as of 1975.[102] Most of these companies reported that, before Kennedy's affirmative action order in 1961, they had not enrolled any women or minorities in supervisory or management training.

My own survey, which covers more small firms than the BNA studies cover, shows that management training became increasingly popular

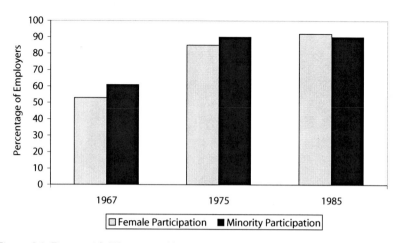

Figure 3.9. Firms with Women and Minorities in Supervisory Training (1967–86)

Source: Bureau of National Affairs 1986b, p. 14. Employers offering supervisory training: 47 percent in 1967, 72 percent in 1975, and 78 percent in 1985.

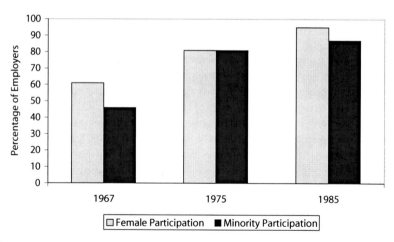

Figure 3.10. Firms with Women and Minorities in Management Training (1967–85)

Note: Employers offering supervisory training: 47 percent in 1967, 72 percent in 1975, and 78 percent in 1985.

Source: Bureau of National Affairs 1986b, 14.

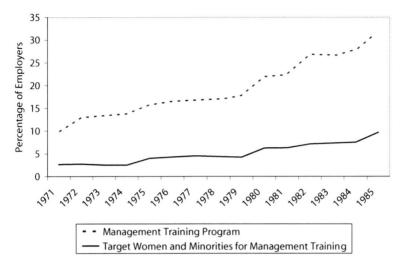

Figure 3.11. Comparative Growth in Management Training Programs and in Firms Targeting Women and Minorities for Management Training (1971–85)

Source: 2002 survey of 829 firms (Kalev, Dobbin, and Kelly 2006).

during the 1970s, and that programs targeting women and minorities for management training also grew. Training programs would continue to grow, so that, by 2002, nearly 70 percent of firms offered management training and nearly one in five targeted women or minorities.

While civil rights law made management and skill-training programs widely popular, many of the programs carried no equal opportunity label, and before long their origins were forgotten. A reverse discrimination lawsuit Brian Weber brought against Kaiser Aluminum, challenging Kaiser's 1974 quota of one black for every white in a new skill-training program, discouraged quotas and equal opportunity language. The Supreme Court upheld Kaiser's quota in 1979, but only after years of litigation. Many personnel managers soft-pedaled the equal opportunity function of training. Indeed, Bureau of National Affairs data show that firms with training programs targeting women declined from 14 to 12 percent between 1975 and 1985, and those with programs targeting blacks declined from 16 to 8 percent.[103]

Washington Endorses Personnel's Solutions:
Recruitment and Training

When Lyndon Johnson established a new affirmative action advisory office in the Department of Labor in 1965, with Executive Order

11246, he left it to federal agencies to conduct compliance reviews and investigate charges of discrimination. Until 1978, the individual agencies conducted compliance reviews, but the Office of Federal Contract Compliance issued regulations, typically based on the "best practices" of leading firms.[104]

In its 1968 guidelines for employers the OFCC endorsed two Plans for Progress mainstays, special recruitment and training. As the Conference Board's Ruth Shaeffer wrote, the agency opposed quotas, but made clear that they expected companies to follow the Plans for Progress example: "The OFCC . . . assured companies that they need never lower their job performance standards in order to comply. However, the OFCC added that appropriate affirmative action might include special recruiting and/or training programs."[105] These guidelines were all federal contractors had to go on.

Plans for Progress convened a series of seminars jointly with the National Association of Manufacturers to help employers understand the guidelines. One message was that the OFCC would scrutinize the workforce reports that contractors had been required to submit since 1962, and would expect progress. Yet as Ruth Shaeffer of the Conference Board reported, "In spite of these meetings, the concept of affirmative action remained fuzzy."[106]

When it did offer recommendations, the OFCC and Department of Labor pointed to the recruitment and training programs that Plans for Progress firms had put in. When the OFCC cited the Allen-Bradley Company for a pattern of rebuffing black applicants in 1968, the company took up the Plans for Progress checklist. Secretary of Labor George P. Schultz personally commended the company for its proposed recruitment program, including advertising directly with the National Urban League and recruiting through minority community groups and in minority-dominated high schools.[107]

The courts as well found in favor of plaintiffs who argued that their employers were not doing what Plans for Progress prescribed. In 1973 a judge found merit in a charge that AT&T failed to recruit women to its training program, as many Plans for Progress firms had been doing. Judge Constance Motley found that, at AT&T, "The wide statistical disparities . . . in the company's employment of women in various job categories and in training programs places a burden on the defendant to show that the disparities are not the product of discrimination against women on the basis of their sex."[108] That same year, the National Organization for Women (NOW) and the Urban League filed a charge against General Mills for excluding women and minorities from a management training program that enrolled 65 trainees, 64 of them white males. "Not only was the publicity damaging, but both groups threatened to launch a nationwide boycott against the company's Betty Crocker products, Wheaties, Cheerios, and Gold Medal flour."[109]

The OFCC issued a new order in late 1971 prescribing special recruitment and training programs in even clearer terms. In nearly 400 words on the topic, the OFCC offered "Suggested techniques to increase recruitment and improve the flow of minority and female applicants." The order advised firms to recruit through civil rights and women's organizations, and detailed plans for recruiting at historically black colleges, women's colleges, and high schools with large numbers of minorities. Recommendations for special training programs included participation in the merit employment associations spearheaded by the Plans for Progress committee that Lockheed's Marietta personnel director Hugh Gordon had served on, as well as special on-site job-training programs, remedial training programs for current employees, co-op programs to help train minorities and women still in school, and summer job programs to attract and train women and minorities.

The OFCC had taken bullet points from the Plans for Progress outline to build its own list of recommended actions.[110] The personnel profession designed the new compliance systems, and only once they had become nearly ubiquitous among federal contractors did federal agencies and the courts come to back them. Bureaucrats and judges played important parts in vetting personnel's preferred solutions, to be sure, but they did not invent the solutions.

Conclusion

The movement led by Martin Luther King Jr., the NAACP, and the Urban League spurred Kennedy to require federal contractors to take affirmative action in 1961 and Congress to outlaw employment discrimination in all workplaces in 1964. Activists were ultimately responsible for what progress employers did make during the 1960s. They championed new laws, and then kept pressure on federal agencies and on employers. The Urban League and NAACP set up skills banks, filed charges against companies, and picketed stores and factories that turned away black applicants.[111]

With passage of the Civil Rights Act, however, the civil rights movement passed the baton to personnel directors. The NAACP and Urban League didn't design corporate compliance systems, personnel experts did. Congress might have fixed compliance standards, or it might have set up a federal agency with the power to write and enforce them, but it did neither of those things. Congress left the law vague and left enforcement capacity weak.

Personnel experts became the architects of new corporate compliance strategies, then, largely because Congress had declined to create an agency to monitor equal opportunity compliance on the model of the National Labor Relations Board.[112] Kennedy and Johnson left affirmative action enforcement first to a committee, and then to a department under the secretary of labor that depended on persuasion rather than sanctioning, and that chose to promote whatever leading employers were doing.

In the 1960s and early 1970s, personnel managers introduced three principal changes: corporate nondiscrimination policies, special recruitment programs for blacks, Latinos, and women, and training programs to bring these groups into skilled jobs and the management ranks. Personnel experts saw new federal regulations as an opportunity to expand their purview, and retrofitted existing implements from their professional arsenal to open opportunity.[113]

In 1960 the typical union employer had a policy guaranteeing that it would not discriminate against union activists. Unionists could file complaints if they were passed over for promotion, or laid off before a more recent hire. But these rules applied to workers within segregated unions. Now unions and personnel departments wrote nondiscrimination policies covering race and then sex. Nothing in the law suggested that firms needed their own nondiscrimination policies. Washington had written a nondiscrimination policy for federal contractors to post, and thus a separate policy for the firm was redundant, but personnel experts had a union nondiscrimination policy in their arsenal and figured that they might as well rewrite it for this new purpose.

In 1960 big employers had formal recruitment programs in place. They advertised in regional newspapers. They went to high schools and colleges to find workers with vocational training or management potential. But those programs targeted white men for the most part. Now personnel departments reasoned that they could use the same mechanisms to include rather than to exclude, and designed new programs for blacks and women.

In 1960, big firms offered skill training to unskilled workers and management training to college recruits. The typical company, however, excluded women and blacks from these programs, either by rule or by tradition. Now personnel executives created new skill and management training programs, and actively recruited women and minorities. Many personnel executives used this opportunity to create a training program for the first time. Training became more popular, and surveys showed that many firms enrolled some women and minorities.

Private-sector personnel executives affiliated with Plans for Progress pioneered these strategies. Plans for Progress was spearheaded by a group of big federal contractors with a lot to lose if they fell out of favor in Washington. All three of the changes that became the mainstays of equal opportunity in the 1960s were outlined in Lockheed-Georgia's 1961 "plan for progress," the first in a series of several hundred. The next group of eight Plans for Progress firms copied Lockheed's program, and then the components spread through local merit employment councils and equal opportunity groups, through meetings organized by Plans for Progress, and through local and national meetings of personnel officers.

The antidiscrimination policies, recruitment programs, and training programs pioneered by Plans for Progress firms were soon embraced by federal agencies. The Equal Employment Opportunity Commission endorsed them as the best practices of leading firms. The Department of Labor's OFCC, charged with overseeing federal contractors, issued guidelines modeled on the Plans for Progress program.[114]

Civil rights leaders, and officials on the PCEEO, had called for active federal enforcement of presidential affirmative action orders as early as 1961. The rub was that the law didn't specify what employers should be doing. What was there to enforce? Without clear federal rules, it was hard for employers to know what to do, and it was hard for the PCEEO to carry through on its pledge to cancel contracts of employers who did not make progress. How could you judge an employer without clear compliance guidelines? While there was good evidence that some Plans employers weren't keeping their nondiscrimination pledges, most big federal contractors did at least have nondiscrimination policies, recruitment systems, and training programs on the books.

These events precipitated a revolution in personnel administration. The focus on labor relations began to give way to a focus on nondiscrimination. By 1966, Boston Edison, the electric utility, had hired as personnel director an MIT graduate who wrote a thesis on an employment agency designed to place blacks.[115] It would have been hard to imagine a unionized company making such a move five years earlier. Hugh Gordon, who had been personnel director at the unionized Georgia Lockheed plant since 1959, became associated with one activity in the minds of Lockheed management: "When I would walk into a manager's office at Lockheed, it was the standard joke, 'Here comes the EEOC.'"[116] Among big federal contractors, compliance became a major undertaking. As Virgil Day, personnel VP at General Electric, wrote in 1965, "Implementation in a widespread, diversified, decentralized company of 250,000 people of an equal opportunity policy is infinitely more complex than taking a discriminatory sign off a door."[117]

By the end of the 1960s, a revolution had taken place at companies such as Lockheed. It was only a revolution because those companies had so systematically excluded blacks, Latinos, and women from skilled, professional, and managerial jobs, but it was a revolution to the extent that these groups had made some inroads. Even at pioneer companies, however, segregation persisted in many units. International Harvester had announced a nondiscrimination policy in 1948 and had revived it in 1961, yet by 1965 Harvester's personnel director Harry Baker reported that, at some plants, blacks were still steered into a small number of bad jobs: "There are a few operations where . . . Negroes are employed in substantial numbers, yet somewhat inexplicably, they are not employed in certain work areas or departments."[118]

Many personnel executives were surprised to be part of this revolution. National firms headquartered in the North expected that the Civil Rights Act would only affect firms in the Jim Crow South. One later told the Conference Board: "We were the good guys. We never dreamed they meant us. The major thrust of the law seemed to be aimed at 'the other fellow'—at smaller, or less enlightened, or regional employers and at certain obviously discriminatory unions—but only occasionally or very indirectly at important national employers like us."[119] Many personnel experts thought that, so long as they did not post signs reading "No Negroes Need Apply," they could not be charged with discriminating.[120] But federal contractors soon saw that it would take more than this to comply with affirmative action orders, however weak enforcement was. And personnel executives saw that Washington had left it to them to figure out how to comply.

WASHINGTON MEANS BUSINESS
Personnel Experts Fashion a System of Compliance

THROUGH THE 1960s MANY EMPLOYERS believed that equal opportunity law would forbid only the most blatant forms of discrimination, and that sanctions would be rare. In the early 1970s, Washington ramped up enforcement, and the Supreme Court interpreted Title VII as covering practices that appeared to be racially neutral. No one knew quite what discrimination was in the eyes of the law. Executives also worried more about social unrest after the urban riots of the late 1960s. According to General Electric's 1970 equal opportunity missive, there could be found in the "growing militancy and impatience of the minority community, a demand for action, not promises—now. Any company that is perceived as uncommitted, inactive or only half-hearted in its efforts, may well become the target of product and labor boycotts, or even of more violent action."[1]

Experts now dusted off weapons from the personnel arsenal to fend off discrimination complaints. They relied on equal opportunity officers who could track changes in the law and implement new innovations; equal opportunity performance evaluations to make managers responsible for equal treatment; and grievance procedures to intercept complaints. Together, these things made up a new compliance system. Meanwhile personnel experts were building bureaucratic hiring and promotion systems to quash bias, as I describe in the next chapter.

First, personnel managers argued that companies needed experts who could track changes in the law and implement corporate innovations. This was a direct reaction to expanded enforcement of an ambiguous law administered by federal judges and bureaucrats of all stripes. No one knew what the law meant, but they did know from experience that judges and bureaucrats could reinterpret the law at every opportunity. In 1969, Frank J. Toner set up General Electric's new Equal Opportunity/ Minority Relations Office, where he created executive committees and task forces focused on helping minorities to advance and tracking changes in compliance norms. Personnel experts had followed the same strategy before. When the Wagner Act of 1935 had created regulatory uncertainty over union rights, personnel specialists prescribed the labor relations department. When the War Labor Board of the 1940s created uncertainty over federal labor allotments in wartime, personnel experts recommended employment offices. Now with growing uncertainty about what equal opportunity meant in practice, they created equal opportunity offices to take charge of compliance.

This decision was pivotal, for, in hiring experts, companies created an internal constituency to champion the cause of equal opportunity. Whereas labor relations experts often fought unions, equal opportunity experts became cheerleaders for integration. A new social movement arose: a network of equal opportunity managers who would promote future rounds of compliance mechanisms, further expanding the meaning of discrimination.

Second, experts argued that new federal affirmative action goals and timetables could serve as the platform for managing equal opportunity through performance controls. In recent years, conglomerates such as GE had replaced the command-and-control management system with financial accounting control over independent business unit managers. Alfred P. Sloan had championed General Motors as a model.[2] CEOs did not dictate strategy to unit managers; rather they tracked data on unit growth and profits, and rewarded business unit managers through performance evaluations affecting bonuses and promotions. Personnel had first developed formal rating systems for the rank and file in the 1930s, and, by the 1960s, conglomerates had built on those systems to develop elaborate performance evaluations for executives. In the 1970s, personnel experts recommended systems for tracking equal opportunity goals, and an "equal opportunity performance evaluation" to assess managers on goals they had set in affirmative action plans. GE's Frank Toner emphasized that such performance ratings could make individual managers take responsibility for equal opportunity.[3] These performance ratings spread to all kinds of firms only in the 1990s, but leading firms had them in place by the end of the 1970s.

Third, personnel experts proposed equal opportunity grievance procedures modeled on the union procedure, which dated to the 1930s. Now that there were thousands of discrimination complaints being lodged every year, consultants argued that equal opportunity grievance procedures could intercept complaints headed for the courts and keep the firm out of the news.

Personnel experts had devised a new system for managing equal opportunity compliance, with an office to track legal changes, performance evaluations to make managers accountable for change, and a grievance mechanism to handle complaints. These things, they argued, could prove an employer's "good faith" in court. Personnel experts had a long history of inventing regulatory compliance strategies and lobbying for judicial approval. Judges struck down the company unions they recommended in the 1920s as an alternative to real unions, but accepted the binding arbitration schemes they crafted as an alternative to National Labor Relations Board hearings.[4] The courts allowed new fringe benefits packages personnel experts recommended during World War II to circumvent the wage freeze.[5]

Personnel gained control of equal opportunity compliance with innovations they claimed the courts would look favorably upon. As there were no federal compliance standards, perhaps the courts would recognize a department devoted to creating equal opportunity. As it was difficult to control individual managers, perhaps the courts would accept the equal opportunity performance evaluation. As Washington required union complaints to be addressed through union grievance procedures, perhaps it would do the same for discrimination complaints and equal opportunity grievance procedures. Lawyers, by contrast, were unwilling to recommend compliance strategies not yet vetted by judges. Professional norms directed them to advise clients about black letter law, and not to speculate wildly about what the courts might or might not approve. For a personnel expert to extol the legal benefits of these measures was perhaps wishful thinking, but for a lawyer to do so amounted to malpractice. And so it was personnel experts who invented new compliance strategies.

Personnel experts spread these new ideas in articles in professional publications, like *Personnel* and the *Personnel Journal*, and in general management publications, like *Business Week* and the *Harvard Business Review*. Consultants brought innovations from Plans for Progress participants like IBM and General Electric to companies that were new to the game. Business groups like the Bureau of National Affairs, the Conference Board, and the National Association of Manufacturers published how-to articles and reviews of what leading employers were doing, and set up training sessions for personnel managers seeking compliance strategies. New norms were promulgated, then, not by public policy, but by the intercorporate network of management experts.

Word from DC: Washington Means Business

Progress on workplace integration was slow in the 1960. In the early 1970s Washington expanded enforcement and opened the door to a much broader definition of discrimination. This happened piecemeal, not as part of a master plan, in keeping with the American government's fragmented system of authority. One change came from the administrative branch. In 1970 and 1971 the Department of Labor required new workforce reports and new affirmative action plans from federal contractors, and stepped up compliance reviews. One change came from the judiciary. In 1971 the Supreme Court defined discrimination to include employer practices that were not explicitly discriminatory, but which had a "disparate impact" on women or minorities.[6] One change came from the legislature. In 1972 Congress expanded the coverage of Title VII and gave the Equal Employment Opportunity Commission the authority to sue employers, alongside private parties and Justice. A fragmented state had produced a fragmented set of regulatory changes, the upshot of which was that enforcement would be strengthened, while the meaning of discrimination would be even muddier than before. In the context of recent racial strife in big cities, these changes emboldened personnel experts to introduce new compliance measures.

New Affirmative Action Requirements

Roosevelt, Truman, Eisenhower, Kennedy, and Johnson had ordered military contractors, and then all federal contractors, to end discrimination but had done little to enforce those orders through the 1960s.[7] That changed in the early 1970s, when Washington ramped up enforcement. In 1970, the Department of Labor required all firms with federal contracts worth $50,000 or more to establish goals and timetables for hiring minorities in written affirmative action programs. Then in December 1971 the department established more stringent requirements for goals and timetables and required a mechanism for evaluating program effectiveness. Employers now had to set goals for each job category in each establishment.[8] Contractors would now be judged on the bottom line, integration.[9]

The goals and timetables approach had been borrowed from the Nixon administration's "Philadelphia Plan" for construction firms, yet the idea that firms should write down the components of their own compliance programs in the form of pledges was borrowed directly from the private-sector Plans for Progress group. As the Department of Labor wrote in 2000, the "current blueprint for affirmative action" has its "origins in Plans for Progress (PfP), conceived and successfully implemented in 1961 by a group of 300 leading corporations committed to achieving equal employment opportunity through voluntary affirmative action." The establishment-level plans for action that the PfP firms adopted became the model for the affirmative action plans that the department required. "Each company adopted a 'plan for progress' for the corporation as a whole and for each of its individual establishments. These plans for progress, as a management tool for achieving equal employment opportunity, were the precursors to the current written affirmative action programs."[10]

Like the Plans for Progress pledges, written corporate affirmative action programs put responsibility for devising solutions in the hands of personnel managers. Regulators did not require firms to change X, Y, and Z. Companies designed their own programs. New guidelines did suggest what some of the components should look like. They reiterated the call for active recruitment and training programs, for instance. The elements in the guidelines were also torn from the Plans for Progress manual, according to the department's own history: "On February 7, 1970, the Office of Federal Contract Compliance incorporated PfP's Guidelines on Affirmative Action as the centerpiece of its affirmative action program of regulations applicable to larger Federal [contractors]."

Every corporate affirmative action plan would include a "workforce analysis" detailing whites and blacks, Hispanics and Asians, in every job in every department. An "underutilization" analysis was to compare the firm's labor composition with the area labor pool and identify employees who could be upgraded through training and reassignment.[11] Management experts championed the new workforce goals and timetables as a way to focus attention on the issue. As a veteran manufacturing manager argued, managers are trained to work toward a goal: "You have to understand the sort of climate you're working in. We have all sorts of priorities and unless you give us numbers and dates, nothing will ever get accomplished. It's just easier to fill a job with a male applicant than to go out of your way to look for a woman."[12]

The 1971 order prohibited "rigid and inflexible quotas" and stipulated that the goals must be "targets reasonably attainable by every good faith effort."[13] Quotas would have made compliance straightforward. Instead, the guidelines required contractors to write their own plans, and provided only very broad guidance about what should be in them. Meanwhile the Department of Labor started conducting more compliance reviews, which sent employers the message that they had better create programs. Field officers would visit firms to conduct compliance reviews and look for discriminatory recruitment, hiring, promotion, and firing practices. By 1976, a Bureau of National Affairs survey of large employers found that over 60 percent had had a compliance review. While the Department of Labor rarely terminated contracts, contractors now felt someone looking over their shoulders.[14]

A New Source of Lawsuits: The EEOC

Democrats had been dissatisfied with Title VII from the start and in March 1972, Congress passed the Equal Employment Opportunity Act, extending coverage to state and local agencies and public schools, colleges, and universities, and allowing the EEOC to sue employers on

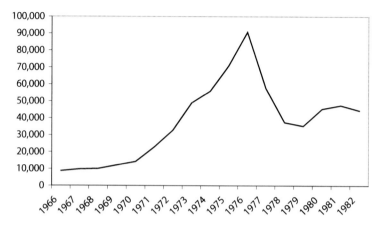

Figure 4.1. Complaints to the EEOC (1966–82)
Source: Burstein and Monahan 1986.

behalf of people who had faced discrimination.[15] Previously, individuals could sue employers, and the Justice Department could sue where it saw a "pattern and practice" of discrimination. Yet the EEOC, which was receiving 10,000 complaints a year by the late 1960s, could not sue when its conciliation efforts failed. Many individual complainants lacked the resources to sue, and many had suffered damages too small—a few months of back pay, or lost wages after a failed bid for promotion—to entice an attorney.[16]

To get results, an emboldened EEOC concentrated its investigatory and prosecutorial efforts on high-visibility employers. By 1974 it had filed 180 suits, and the business press noted that losing a case to the EEOC could be costly and embarrassing.[17] Complaints to the EEOC skyrocketed, from 10,000 per year in the last half of the 1960s to a peak of 90,000 in 1976.

A New Definition of Discrimination

In 1971 the Supreme Court redefined discrimination, ruling that an employment practice that appeared to be racially neutral could be discriminatory if it had a "disparate impact" on racial minorities. In *Griggs v. Duke Power Company* and again in *Albemarle Paper Co. v. Moody*[18] the Court found that employers were liable for the discriminatory effects of their employment tests, regardless of the intent. Now unintentional discrimination was against the law, except where the courts could be convinced that there was a "business necessity" for practices that had a disparate impact on women. The Court had rendered suspect virtually any employment practice that disadvantaged women or minorities.

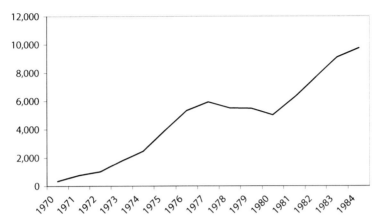

Figure 4.2. Federal Title VII Cases Commenced in District Courts (1970–84)
Source: Burstein and Monahan 1986.

Federal cases skyrocketed. In 1970 plaintiffs commenced 344 federal district court cases under Title VII; by 1976 they were commencing at least 5,000 a year.[19] As an article in the *Personnel Journal* concluded, by shifting the burden of proof to the employer, the Court "made it easy for the EEOC and private plaintiffs to win class action Title VII suits. As a direct result, many employers found themselves losing Title VII cases and being saddled with huge back pay awards in cases based strictly on statistics."[20] Plaintiffs could now make their cases with statistics showing a disparate impact on a protected group, without proving intentional discrimination.

While most of the new cases were not disparate impact cases—in 1972 and 1973 only 9 percent of cases were disparate impact cases, and by the late 1980s less than 5 percent were—those cases had a profound effect because most were class actions, prosecuted by the EEOC, targeting major firms, seeking large dollar settlements, and aiming at traditional personnel practices.[21]

Executives Take Notice

This one-two-three punch—mandatory affirmative action plans, an EEOC filing suits on its own, and a new definition of discrimination—caught executives unaware. The fear, as Carey Thorp wrote in *Personnel Journal* in 1973, was that those who "ignore the whole mess" of regulations "run the risk of spending a great deal of time in the legal maze of investigations, conciliation conferences, public hearings, and court trials."[22] Antonia Chayes wrote in the *Harvard Business Review* in 1974, "More vigorous enforcement . . . has now compelled the kind of attention long given to antitrust laws. . . . Now the penalties imposed under employment discrimination laws are seen as posing a severe financial threat."[23]

Pressure for change came not only from the government and movement leaders, but from within industry. Levi Jackson, who had been the first black captain of the Yale football team, was a vocal advocate from his pulpit in the personnel office at Ford, convincing the company to hire thousands of blacks in the years after the 1967 riots.[24] Industries that catered to women were susceptible to the argument that they would alienate customers if they weren't careful. As the business manager of a leading women's magazine said in 1973: "Let's face it—we sell primarily to women and many of them are becoming increasingly aware of discriminatory behavior. Unless we do something to improve the situation of women here on the magazine from a long-range standpoint, our future is in jeopardy."[25]

Personnel Plays Old Standards

The regulatory changes of the early 1970s made antidiscrimination law more powerful, but executives had trouble figuring out how to avoid liability. That was partly because, after the Supreme Court's 1971 *Griggs* decision, allowing suits for discrimination without evidence of intent, the law was a moving target. As one popular personnel management text from 1977 warned, "judges interpret [civil rights] law differently, and decisions are often reversed in higher courts."[26] So changeable was the law that the private Bureau of National Affairs published the *Equal Employment Opportunity Manual* as a serial.[27]

For federal contractors, affirmative-action goals, timetables, and plans established a new yardstick for measuring progress, but executives would have preferred a clear litmus test for discrimination. Many wanted the government to vet concrete hiring and promotion practices. As an insurance company vice president said in 1973 of federal compliance reviews, "We pull out all of our records for a review, which in itself takes precious time, and then the only comment we get is, 'You haven't met your objectives yet.' We knew that before the . . . investigator walked in. Why can't the government offer us constructive practical suggestions?"[28] Contractors almost never met goals, according to a study by Berkeley economist Jonathan Leonard,[29] and yet Washington had not spelled out what they should do about it.

The courts and administration had ruled some strategies out. *Griggs* made unvalidated job tests verboten.[30] Title VII, the Department of Labor's orders, and early reverse discrimination suits, made clear that quotas were illegal unless approved by a judge.[31] But the courts and administration did not do much to rule other strategies in. Compliance ambiguity created an opening for people who knew something about personnel to style themselves as equal opportunity experts. Before long, nearly every leading company had an equal opportunity consultant on retainer and a new office devoted to equal opportunity.

Equal Opportunity Specialists and Departments

In the past, personnel had responded to complex new regulations by setting up specialty departments.[32] After passage of the Wagner Act in 1935, personnel experts recommended labor relations departments.[33] When the War Labor Board regulated the movement of workers, personnel suggested employment departments. After wartime wage controls, personnel advocated benefits departments to craft fringe benefit packages in lieu of wage increases. Following state safety regulations, personnel touted safety departments. Thus by 1946, a survey of large American companies found that 63 percent had employment departments, 51 percent had labor relations departments, 52 percent had safety departments, and 29 percent had benefits departments.[34]

Organizational sociologists were coming to recognize the pattern. Harvard Business School professors Paul Lawrence and Jay Lorsch had argued that firms grow internally in response to external demands such as regulations.[35] Sociologist James Thompson from the Cornell business school argued that organizations create departments that mirror the players they face in the environment, such that the internal structure comes to mirror the regulatory environment.[36] Stanford Business School professor Jeffrey Pfeffer described department creation as a form of "protest absorption," in which the demands of internal groups like unionists and external groups like federal regulators can be contained. These add-on departments may be only loosely connected to daily operations, so that "various groups may be satisfied simultaneously. . . . [W]orkers wanting more control can appeal to the personnel or industrial relations department, while minorities can articulate their interests through affirmative action offices"—all without much disruption to day-to-day functioning.[37]

Stanford organizational sociologists John Meyer and W. Richard Scott argue that this pattern is uniquely American: our fragmented system of employment regulation, with different agencies and levels of government regulating different workplace matters, produced departmental fragmentation within the firm. Each American organization thus has distinct offices and "officers that symbolize safety, the environment, affirmative action," each to handle interactions with a different component of the bureaucracy.[38] In Sweden or Germany, by contrast, where government regulation of employment is more unified, corporate response is not to proliferate compliance activities but to concentrate them in one department.

A new round of federal regulations in the 1960s and 1970s gave the personnel profession an opportunity for stunning growth, according to labor economists Thomas Kochan and Peter Cappelli.[39] Equal opportunity and affirmative action regulations were key, but new environmental, wages and hours, safety, and benefits regulations contributed. As the *Harvard Business Review* reported in 1977, "In 1940, the U.S. Department of Labor was responsible for enforcing 16 statutes and executive orders. By 1960, the number had grown to 40. Today it is more than 130."[40] Personnel managers were having a field day creating new positions and programs to manage legal compliance.

Regulations that were crystal clear didn't seem to elicit new departments. When it came to wages and hours regulation, or federal overtime regulations, companies didn't create departments, but the Wagner Act's complex requirements were another matter. In the 1960s, when employers believed civil rights and affirmative action law to be fairly straightforward, only a handful of military contractors created compliance departments. Under the new legal uncertainty of the early 1970s, equal opportunity experts in a wide range of firms got their own departments.[41]

General Electric had long been ahead of the curve. President Gerard Swope, who had worked his way up from a dollar-a-day helper in 1893 and would later be recognized by Forbes as one of the 20 most influential businessmen of all time, introduced a widely imitated corporate welfare program in the 1920s and committed the company to fair employment in 1935: "There shall be no discrimination by foremen, superintendents, or any executives of the Company against any employee because of race, or creed."[42] In 1961, General Electric was one of the first nine employers to join Plans for Progress. As a major military contractor with urban plants that felt the racial unrest of the 1960s, GE had more than one reason to promote equal opportunity. In 1968, CEO Fred Borch made a film advertising the company's commitment to equality, and on the advice of personnel experts set up a new Equal Opportunity/Minority Relations unit, arguing:

> We can no longer delay action. We cannot—as a society—bear the cost of chaos in the lives of millions of our citizens. . . . General Electric . . . must face up to a new corporate responsibility. . . . The successful manager of tomorrow will be the individual who can effectively manage the new work force in our changing environment.[43]

Frank J. Toner was in charge of the new office, which was to pursue GE's "new, intensified effort to hire and train and, more importantly, to provide upward mobility for the minority citizens of the United States."[44] Toner set up an executive policy advisory panel, a panel of middle managers, and a panel of minority professionals to review proposals "from the point of view of minority interests."[45] Those panels put together 27 different task forces charged with evaluating what other companies were doing, reaching out to community leaders, writing guidelines for dealing with federal affirmative action compliance reviews, tracking current equal opportunity law, setting up management training in "social awareness," and evaluating affirmative action programs.[46]

Soon after Washington ramped up enforcement in the early 1970s, the Office of Federal Contract Compliance Programs (previously the OFCC) recommended that firms appoint affirmative action officers to handle compliance. Personnel journals advised employers to follow General Electric's lead of creating a new office and enumerated arguments that could be used to sway chief executives. First, there was the job of managing compliance. As two consultants wrote in *Personnel* in 1974, new departments could guide Department of Labor officials through compliance reviews.[47] In 1975 an Arthur Young consultant and a New York University management professor wrote, in *Personnel,* that specialists could fill out the workforce reports the EEOC demanded and develop affirmative action plans.[48]

Second, new departments could create antidiscrimination programs to preclude litigation and contract cancellation. Barbara Boyle wrote in the *Harvard Business Review* that costly litigation made an autonomous antidiscrimination office "at the highest practicable level in the organization (i.e., outside the personnel office)" well worth the price: "The establishment of an affirmative action program is not costly—its absence is."[49]

Third, an equal opportunity office could "strengthen the position of personnel managers in their dealings with operating managers." The idea was to give personnel oversight over hiring, promotion, and discipline, so as to prevent managers from falling into old patterns of using race and gender as bases for personnel decisions. In "A Total Approach to EEO Compliance" Giblin and Ornati pointed out that leading firms had already created affirmative action offices: "The affirmative action office, which usually resides in the personnel organization, often influences recruitment and hiring practices." The affirmative action office would need close ties to other personnel departments, "wage and salary administration, benefits administration, manpower planning, and training and development" to ensure compliance across the board.[50]

Fourth, such departments could provide job insurance to CEOs. In her 1974 *Harvard Business Review* article, Antonia Chayes noted that recent changes had brought "serious top management attention to anti-discrimination legislation," and she advised executives to set up EEO and AA programs that could prevent liability.[51] Executives worried about ouster, and in some firms compensation was being linked to affirmative action success. A department could make sure the firm was doing what could be done.[52]

Perhaps the best reason to create a dedicated affirmative action office, consultants advised, was that Congress and the courts were constantly changing the rules. In a *Personnel* article, "Conducting an Internal Compliance Review of Affirmative Action," business school professor Kenneth Marino advocated what he termed "The Good-Faith-Effort Strategy."[53] The key, others argued, was to create an office that would signal to Washington that the company was doing its best to figure out how to comply.[54] Offices served a public relations function, contributing to "the appearance of social responsibility."[55] As Robert Ackerman concluded in his 1975 study of corporate social responsibility in nine leading firms, "A new department tended to provide greater leverage for the chief executive and more visibility and emphasis for the issue" than a new staff position alone.[56]

At the time, in the early 1970s, American firms were setting up other new compliance departments as well, in response to the ever-changing regulations brought about by the new Occupational Safety and Health Act (OSHA) and the 300 pages of regulations that accompanied the pension reform act of 1974 (ERISA).[57] A 1977 article in the *Harvard Business Review* advised: "The various requirements of state and federal regulations . . . make increasing demands on both profit and nonprofit organizations. . . . Compliance with the laws relating to OSHA, EEOC, and ERISA demands expertise."[58] Specialists in each regulatory realm were needed for "surveying what is happening in the outside world," in both the law and employer response.[59] Frank Toner's General Electric department set up one committee devoted solely to tracking what other companies were doing.

Following the lead of General Electric and a few other big military contractors, many companies put in new departments staffed by experts who acted as "quasi-lawyers."[60] A study from the late 1980s of 141 Tennessee manufacturers with at least 100 workers found that over half had affirmative action offices.[61] In our 1986 survey of employers with at least 50 workers, we found that in 1972 only 4 percent had equal opportunity offices, yet by 1986, 20 percent had them.[62] More than a quarter had affirmative action officers (see figure 4.3). In Lauren Edelman's national survey, only 4 percent of employers had affirmative action offices in 1970, but 18 percent had them in 1990 (see figure 4.3).[63]

Firms too small to support autonomous equal opportunity offices often set up personnel departments for the first time in response to the

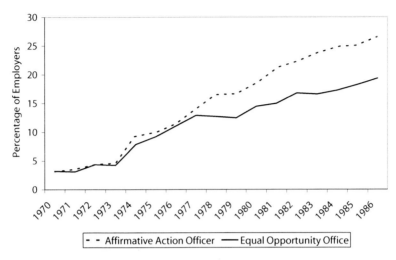

Figure 4.3. The Growth of Equal Opportunity and Affirmative Action Offices (1970–86)

Note: Some organizations were not in operation at the beginning of the period. The denominator varies over time.

Source: Survey of 279 employers in 1986 (Dobbin et al. 1993).

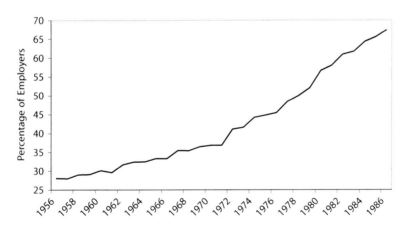

Figure 4.4. Growth of Personnel Offices (1956–86)

Source: Survey of 279 employers in 1986 (Dobbin et al. 1993).

new enforcement activities. In my 1986 sample of medium and large employers, the rate of personnel office creation increased in the early 1970s. Between 1956 and 1970, the prevalence of personnel offices grew from 28 to 37 percent. At that rate, by 1986, 44 percent of employers would have had personnel offices. By 1986, 67 percent had them.

Most large firms had equal opportunity offices by the early 1980s, responsible for tracking compliance trends and putting new practices into place. What could employers do to make individual managers participate?

Equal Opportunity Performance Evaluations: Making Managers Accountable

Industrial psychology professor Theodore Purcell's article "How G.E. Measures Managers on Fair Employment," published in *Harvard Business Review* in 1974, helped to popularize a new strategy of making individual managers accountable for change. Purcell had worked for Commonwealth Edison before entering the Jesuit order and studying psychology. In 1965 he conducted a two-year Ford Foundation study of race and employment in the electrical industry. GE was a model, Purcell argued, thanks to a system Frank Toner's team pioneered in 1969 for rating each of its 26,000 managers on equal opportunity performance.[64]

The measurement system began with GE's six-page equal opportunity form filled out by each department and group chief, detailing workforce composition, five-year goals, and programs to increase minority representation.[65] Managers were then evaluated annually on program implementation and progress toward goals. The key, Purcell wrote, is a "measurement system with rewards and penalties designed to produce behavioral changes in managers."[66] Bonuses and promotions are what managers respond to: "Since, generally, managers' motivation and performance is spurred by measurement and evaluation, it was felt that the only way of achieving the desired [equal opportunity] progress would be to make this activity a required part of the regular business review process."[67] When the Department of Labor required goals and timetables of federal contractors in 1971, GE synchronized its 1969 reporting system with the federal requirements.

Some firms created separate equal opportunity performance evaluations, and some folded an equal opportunity component into the regular performance evaluation system. Either way, managers in firms that installed these systems got annual feedback.

The equal opportunity performance evaluation took its form from the merit rating and performance evaluation systems that unions had lobbied for from the 1930s to ensure that promotion decisions would be based on merit rather than allegiance to management.[68] These new evaluations were for managers, however, and the more proximate blueprint was the financial performance metric used to assess how different business units, and their managers, were performing.

General Electric was a leader in the new breed of diversified conglomerates using financial accounting systems that made the manager of each division responsible for its bottom line. Conglomeration and divisionalization fueled the trend. Whereas in 1949, 63 percent of Fortune 500 firms were organized under a single president, by 1969 only 11 percent were so organized. Most firms now had multiple units operating in different industries. The traditional command-and-control systems that executives had used to manage the pyramidal, one-industry firm was now replaced by an accounting system pioneered by Alfred Sloan at General Motors.[69] Executives made decisions about where to apportion capital and about whom to reward with bonuses and promotions based on performance reports from each business unit. Executives in headquarters did not set operational policy, but used those reports to develop an overarching strategy.[70]

As Robert Ackerman wrote in *Harvard Business Review* in 1973, divisionalization made a command-and-control approach to affirmative action impracticable.[71] Instead, for affirmative action, as for other functions, top executives now managed through incentives and objectives. As a division manager at a big electronics firm put it: "Look, let's start with the idea that I don't need pollution control equipment or minorities to run my business. If the company wants me to do these things, they'll have to make it worth my while."[72] Running annual evaluations of managers was one way to make top management team goals clear to managers in a big, divisionalized company spread out across different industries.

Accountability was the codeword for the equal opportunity performance evaluations. As Barbara Boyle, IBM executive-turned-consultant, wrote in the *Harvard Business Review* in 1973, "Middle echelons have to know that top management is serious about the issue and that part of their performance appraisal includes results in the area of women's equality."[73] To make this work, the CEO also had to herald his commitment to equal opportunity. The CEO of Mobil Oil, Rawleigh Warner Jr., made a film championing the cause of equal opportunity that was shown to all managers. When a Mobil division manager was asked whether he would set up a program for promoting women, he replied: "What do you expect me to say? After hearing Mr. Warner up there telling me that it's a high-priority item, do you think I'd say no? Of course we're going to do it."[74]

C. F. Fretz and Joanne Hayman from the management consultancy Towers Perrin reported in *Harvard Business Review* in 1973 that, in the 20 leading firms they studied, equal opportunity was a component of the formal annual performance evaluation, if not a separate evaluation as at GE. These worked only when coupled with support from the top: "Without a determined commitment by top management, it is unlikely that poor performance in the equal opportunity area will detract from a manager's evaluation."[75]

Another 1973 *Harvard Business Review* piece quoted a consumer goods division manager who argued for holding line managers' feet to the fire: "The only way of implementing" equal opportunity policy is to "agree on minority hiring and advancement targets" with each manager and "hold them accountable for the results."[76] One company president wrote to his workers: "The most significant change this year—the one that is basic to all others—is to place responsibility for achieving equal opportunity objectives where it rightfully belongs, with operating management, with each of us." The key was to make managers understand that "achieving these objectives is as important as meeting any other traditional business responsibility." Equal opportunity success had to be a necessary condition for a positive overall evaluation: "No manager should expect a satisfactory appraisal if he meets other objectives, but fails here."[77] In a 1985 study of nine companies with exemplary equal opportunity records, every firm reported that it made promotions contingent on equal opportunity success: "Universally, performance reviews include assessment of a manager's affirmative action efforts. . . . All participating companies cited instances in which managers who consistently did not perform well in making such assignments were demoted or dismissed."[78]

The Bureau of National Affairs found in its 1975 study of big companies that four in 10 manufacturing firms, three in 10 service sector firms, and two in 10 nonprofits had equal opportunity performance evalu-

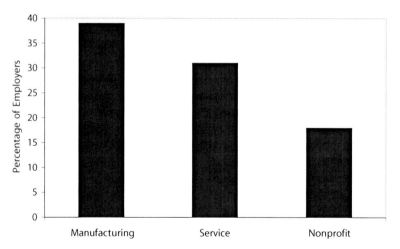

Figure 4.5. Equal Opportunity Performance Evaluations (1975)

Note: Survey of 160 employers with a median of 1,000 workers.

Source: Bureau of National Affairs 1976.

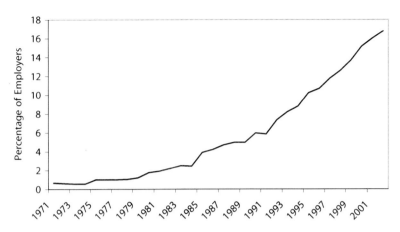

Figure 4.6. Diversity Performance Evaluations for Managers (1971–2002)
Source: Survey of 829 firms in 2002 (Kalev, Dobbin, and Kelly 2006).

ations in place.[79] Performance evaluations were quite popular among big firms (the median size of the largest establishment in each of these organizations was 1,000 workers), and more so in the contractor-heavy manufacturing sector. Outside of leading firms and contractors, however, equal opportunity performance evaluations were not so popular. When we asked about "diversity performance evaluations" in our national survey in 2002, we found that only 4 percent had them as of 1985. By 2002, nearly one in five firms had them.

Another much-touted approach to linking diversity performance to incentives was the diversity bonus, in which part of each year's bonus or salary increment is explicitly tied to diversity performance. The diversity-based bonus appeared later, and in our 2002 sample had spread to only 6 percent of organizations. But some leading firms in finance were promoting them. Merrill Lynch based up to 10 percent of the bonuses of its 10 executive vice presidents on division diversity performance as of the early 1990s.[80]

With equal opportunity offices tracking changes in the law, and equal opportunity performance evaluations keeping managers' attention focused on the issue, experts argued that companies needed one further component to manage enforcement, a system for airing complaints.

Equal Opportunity Grievance Procedures Modeled on Union Procedures

Some companies had resisted the binding arbitration and the grievance procedures that unions sought after passage of the Wagner Act in

1935 to protect unionists from unfair treatment at the hands of management. But managers came to see union grievance procedures as a way to intercept complaints en route to the new National Labor Relations Board.[81] The *Harvard Business Review* and other leading management journals provided templates and touted the benefits of resolving complaints locally.[82]

While the Wagner Act got the ball rolling, by the mid-1950s, not only had 99 percent of unionized firms installed grievance procedures, but 80 percent of big nonunion firms had put them in to help resolve conflicts or to keep unions at bay.[83] As a proponent of the nonunion procedure reported in 1980: "We did not develop this procedure because we are nice, but because we want the non-union employees to stay that way."[84]

Grievance procedures, formal disciplinary systems, and personnel department review of hiring and promotion decisions were part of a broader due-process revolution in the American workplace in the 1950s and 1960s. Among firms with skilled, high-wage, workers, procedures that guaranteed due process were viewed as a way to create an atmosphere of employee "citizenship."[85] In specifying employee rights and adjudicating complaints, personnel experts came to view themselves as employees' defenders against capricious line managers.[86] Howard Vollmer and Patrick McGillivray interviewed a shipyard personnel director at the end of the 1950s who reported: "I have as many arguments with the back office as I do with union leaders. Yesterday I had a fight with one of our managers to get him to give an employee adequate notice before discharging him." The personnel manager at an oil company sounded the same note: "I'm employed by the company, but my responsibility is to the employee as well as to the company. Sometimes I have to fight for an employee with management. I have to ward off the impulsive actions of division heads. Believe me, one has to have the courage of his convictions to do this." In the words of a steel company personnel executive: "There are times when we believe line management at the plant level is wrong. Then they say, 'God damn you, you're selling us down the river.' Then we must sell them on the right way to handle discipline. We may even have to go to the company president if we have a firm disagreement with the plant managers."[87] Grievance procedures had transformed many personnel managers into intermediaries, at least in their own minds. In matters of civil rights, they would revive that role.

The first procedure covering racial discrimination was spelled out in General Motors' 1961 United Automobile Workers contract covering 337,000 production workers in 130 U.S. plants, signed within months of Kennedy's affirmative action order. The new GM contract read:

It is the policy of General Motors and the UAW-AFL-CIO that the provisions of this Agreement shall be applied to all employees covered by this Agreement without regard to race, color, creed, or national origin. Any claims of violation of this policy may be taken up as a grievance.[88]

Civil rights provisions covering race spread like wildfire through union contracts.[89] By the early 1970s, Charlotte Hallam reported in the *Labor Law Journal*, union contracts increasingly forbade sex discrimination and spelled out compliant procedures.[90]

Personnel experts recommended freestanding equal opportunity grievance procedures for nonunion workers. One of the first was created at the Department of Justice in 1969.[91] That procedure famously failed to remedy a complaint of sexual harassment by Diane Williams, fired after having rebuffed the advances of her supervisor, Harvey Brinson. Neither the department's equal employment opportunity officer nor the complaint adjudication officer took Williams's side and so she went to court, where she eventually won a suit that helped to define harassment as sex discrimination.[92]

After the EEOC gained the power to file suit in 1972, personnel experts advised that a freestanding civil rights grievance procedure could intercept employees en route to complain to the EEOC and at the same time signal the employer's good faith in trying to quash discrimination.[93] They also counseled firms to install formal disciplinary procedures—warning systems and hearings—to protect against charges of discrimination in demotions, the docking of pay, and layoffs.[94] As Conference Board personnel expert Ronald Berenbeim wrote, "In areas such as discrimination and safety, where the employee's right to complain has some legal protection, the existence of a meaningful grievance mechanism may provide management with a valuable defense against a potential employee claim."[95] The idea was that judges would expect employees to make use of internal grievance procedures before appealing to the courts. The grievance procedure could be part of a defense based on a good-faith effort.

Universities joined the bandwagon. In 1973, MIT hired two "special assistants to the president"—"one black male, the other white female"—in response to Title IX of the Federal Education Amendments of 1972, extending equal opportunity law to universities.[96] The special assistants were to adjudicate complaints from nonunion employees and students. The preamble to MIT's procedure made it clear that they were there to hear complaints of discrimination: "Any M.I.T. student and any person employed at M.I.T. who believes that he or she has been treated unjustly for any reason, or that the Institute's stated policy of nondiscrimination has been violated, should have access to a clear means of seeking redress."[97]

By the beginning of the 1980s, personnel journals were unanimous in counseling firms to install nonunion grievance procedures to keep complaints in-house. Based on a poll of corporate equal opportunity specialists, business professor and consultant Kenneth Marino advised employers to "establish a formal EEO complaint procedure within the facility."[98] Gloria Gery, a manager at Aetna's Corporate Data Processing Consulting, advised personnel managers to set up a "grievance system . . . to ensure that all employees have an opportunity to resolve complaints . . . without having to appeal to external organizations such as the EEOC."[99] *Personnel* published an article arguing that, to protect themselves from discrimination claims, "enlightened personnel management typically embraces a formal grievance procedure as a means to ensure fair and consistent treatment of all employees."[100] Berenbeim's *Non-union Complaint Procedures*, distributed to personnel executives at Conference Board companies, offered blueprints for grievance procedures and pointed out that leading companies already had them in place.[101]

A change in the nature of discrimination suits speeded the diffusion of grievance mechanisms. Firing suits proved easier to pursue than hiring suits, and so Title VII became "a sort of implicit tort of wrongful discharge . . . for virtually all workers except white males under the age of 40," according to law professors John Donohue and Peter Siegelman.[102] This was exactly what the grievance procedure was designed for: current employees who felt they'd been unfairly treated.

While many of the new grievance procedures did not have the words *equal opportunity* in their titles, their purpose was clear. Xerox published tips for using its "formal open-door policy," beginning: "*Be sure your complaint is serious and not trivial* . . . affirmative-action matters are . . . serious: parking-space allotments, lost vacation days, office furnishings are not."[103] TWA's 1980 grievance procedure begins: "This grievance procedure is established to assure that the policies of the Company are applied to its employees in fair, reasonable, and nondiscriminatory fashion."[104]

MIT ombudsperson Mary Rowe wrote in 1984 that grievance mechanisms were catching on: "Many corporations, universities, and other institutions have, in the past decade, developed explicit, nonunion complaint systems. The nonunion complaint system at MIT is in many ways similar to those of several hundred universities and corporations."[105]

The Conference Board found that, by 1979, 88 percent of nonunion firms with over 5,000 workers had grievance procedures. Sixty-seven percent of big union firms had grievance procedures for their nonunion workers.[106]

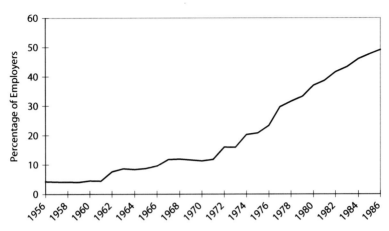

Figure 4.7. Rise in Nonunion Grievance Procedures (1956–86)
Source: Survey of 279 employers in 1986 (Dobbin et al. 1993).

Some nonunion grievance procedures predated the civil rights era, and so it could be that some of the new grievance procedures were adopted for reasons other than civil rights enforcement. But all evidence points to civil rights law being the main driving force. When Lauren Edelman surveyed employers nationally in 1989, she found that 31 percent had installed a grievance procedure specifically to handle discrimination complaints.[107] My colleagues and I surveyed employers in California, New Jersey, and Virginia with at least 50 workers in 1986. The timing of adoption in that survey suggested that the renewed civil rights enforcement of the early 1970s was the catalyst. Only 4 percent of employers added a nonunion grievance procedure between 1964 and 1972, for a total of 16 percent by 1972. Another 35 percent added a procedure between 1973 and 1986.[108] Civil rights laws had made grievance procedures popular even among medium-sized and small firms by late in the 1980s.

Formal disciplinary hearings often went hand in hand with the grievance procedure. Experts argued that they could prevent managers from behaving prejudicially in demotions, firings, and the docking of pay. Perhaps most important from the standpoint of legal risk, they could stop managers from discharging minorities and women without cause. My 1986 survey showed a dramatic increase in firms with formal disciplinary hearings after 1975, in a period when unionization was flat. Disciplinary hearings gradually grew in popularity between 1955 and 1975 to about 35 percent of firms, and then over the next decade spread rapidly (figure 4.8).

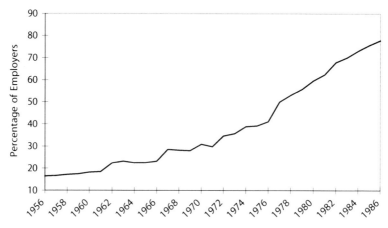

Figure 4.8. Increased Disciplinary Hearings (1956–86)
Source: Survey of 279 employers in 1986 (Dobbin et al. 1993).

Do Grievance Procedures Work?   If they work as advertised, grievance procedures should both head off complaints, reducing the number that reach the government, and protect employers in court, by demonstrating a good-faith effort to eradicate discrimination. Yet what evidence there is suggests that grievance procedures weren't of much use on either front in the 1970s and 1980s, when they were spreading. Consultants popularized procedures not by holding up evidence that they worked, but by telling a strong story.

First, grievance procedures were not reducing complaints to the government. Of the 70 human resources managers Ronald Berenbeim interviewed for his 1980 Conference Board report, two-thirds heard complaints of discrimination, but a majority said that the grievance system did not reduce complaints to the government.[109] An executive who had handled massive layoffs reported that people with gripes went straight to the feds: "I was shocked at how few people used our system" to resolve complaints; "the system was not effective in convincing people that they would get relief from us."[110] Sociologists Edelman, Uggen, and Erlanger analyzed data from their 1989 survey of more than 200 employers, finding that a civil rights grievance procedure did not reduce complaints to the government.[111]

If they did not reduce the number of charges filed with the government, did they at least inoculate employers against legal liability? Evidently not. One reason is that the courts had used, and continue to use, a strict liability standard in discrimination cases. They hold employers responsible for discrimination even when they have taken some precautions. In

1986 the Supreme Court indicated in *Meritor v. Vinson* that it might favor a special grievance procedure to deal with harassment, but gave no sign that a grievance procedure would protect employers in regular discrimination cases. When Edelman and colleagues searched tens of thousands of published rulings in federal discrimination cases, they found only 13 that mentioned grievance procedures up to 1986, and in only four of those did judges reduce liability, even in some small part, for the presence of a grievance procedure.[112] No one following the courts could have taken the lesson that grievance procedures protected employers by 1986, and by then, nine out of 10 big nonunion employers had them, and half of the employers in my broad national sample had them.[113]

After 1986, judicial mention of grievance procedures and deference to them, in harassment cases, in any event, rose.[114] But, as I will argue in chapter 8, judicial deference rose because judges saw their popularity. Popularity did not rise, it seems clear, because judges deferred to them.

Binding Arbitration for Civil Rights Complaints   Personnel experts hoped from the start that the courts would require workers with civil rights gripes to use in-house grievance panels and abide by their decisions.[115] Union contracts stipulated local grievance panels leading to binding arbitration, yet judges did not require nonunion workers to use civil rights grievance panels, or to abide by their rulings if they did use them. Workers could go directly to court, and they could appeal in-house rulings in federal courts.[116]

Late in the 1980s, personnel experts and lawyers proposed to have individual employees sign contracts committing them to use binding arbitration for all employment-related complaints. The securities industry was the first to embrace the idea. By 1994, the *Wall Street Journal* reported, "A majority of industry employees—more than 80 percent, according to some estimates—are required to submit all employment claims, including discrimination charges, to industry-run arbitration."[117] Other industries followed suit, though not always with the desired results. When the internet service provider Juno faced harassment complaints in the 1990s, binding arbitration didn't prevent salacious headlines or hefty settlements.[118]

On July 10, 1997, the EEOC issued a notice opposing binding arbitration for Title VII cases, yet most circuit courts upheld binding arbitration pledges. In March 2001, the Supreme Court overruled the last judicial holdout, California's Ninth Circuit Court, finding that Circuit City's binding private arbitration could substitute for judicial arbitration of civil rights cases. That case gave new ammunition to arbitration advocates.[119] The Court had accepted a remedy that leading firms, in the leading industry of finance, had made popular.

Conclusion

In the 1960s personnel experts who were unsure of what the Civil Rights Act required thought that when the dust settled, all would be clear. They removed rules barring African-Americans and women from certain jobs and married women from all jobs. They adapted conventional recruitment and training programs to the problem of finding and upgrading minorities and women. The management press suggested that leading firms had solved the problem. Then at the beginning of the 1970s, a significant change from each branch of government made clear that the dust would not settle. The administrative branch required federal contractors to submit elaborate new affirmative action plans and stepped up administrative reviews. Congress gave the EEOC the power to sue employers. The Supreme Court redefined discrimination to include practices that were on their face neutral but which had a "disparate impact" on minorities or women. Now it was apparent that the meaning of nondiscrimination would not be fixed, and that compliance strategies would need to be responsive to changes in legal interpretation.

Personnel experts responded with three distinct recommendations. One innovation was an approach personnel had used to handle previous regulatory uncertainty, a new compliance department. In response to the Wagner Act, personnel had recommended labor relations departments. In response to wartime labor restrictions, personnel had pushed employment departments. Departmentalization was becoming personnel's modus operandi for troublesome regulations. In the 1970s, personnel followed this path not only for equal opportunity regulations, but for new benefits and health and safety regulations.[120] The approach was soon theorized by the leading organizational paradigms, from contingency theory to resource dependency theory to institutional theory.[121] All described a stylized solution, in which firms establish distinct compliance offices in each key regulatory realm. Personnel executives saw their own interest in "feathering the nest" by expanding departments under their control. In corporate bureaucracies, after all, the best way to elevate yourself short of a promotion is to add to the pyramid on which you sit.[122]

A second innovation was to transfer accountability to individual managers. The annual performance evaluation was a mainstay of the personnel arsenal that had gotten a boost in the 1950s and 1960s from the rise of the diversified conglomerate, and the model of managing subunits not through command and control but through financial accounting and feedback. Benchmarks, numerical controls, and statistical performance measures were increasingly used to monitor managers. Personnel experts in diversified conglomerates such as GE were the first to propose diversity performance evaluations as a way to bring that management approach to the new task of quashing bias and integrating the workplace. The approach was to offer feedback on performance, rather than control behavior per se. Bonuses and future promotions were to hinge on performance measures. Four in 10 of America's big manufacturing firms had the new performance evaluations in place by 1975, but it was another decade before they took hold in smaller enterprises.

The grievance procedure provided the third leg of the new compliance system. In civil rights as in union rights, not every potential complaint could be precluded by bureaucratic rules forbidding discrimination against unionists, or against minority groups. A grievance procedure might keep complaints in-house. That had worked well in the field of labor relations. Judicial decisions expanding the meaning of discrimination coupled with new legislation allowing the EEOC to pursue suits itself led personnel experts to seek a way to intercept complaints, which were skyrocketing during the 1970s. While personnel managers were transferring responsibility for equal opportunity to managers with one hand, they were intercepting complaints en route to Washington with the other by installing civil rights grievance mechanisms.

All three of these innovations would survive, but the most consequential would be the equal opportunity office. By institutionalizing equal opportunity as a specialty within personnel, the profession created a place for an internal constituency to champion new rounds of equal opportunity and diversity measures. In the 1970s the job of personnel management was changing. Rare was the firm that fought a union organizing attempt, or even suffered a debilitating strike from an existing union. Now much of personnel's work involved compliance with equal opportunity law and with new benefits or safety regulations. And as we will see in chapter 7, the personnel profession was rapidly becoming feminized. By putting equal opportunity specialists into place within the firm, then, the personnel profession created both a nexus of advocacy and a beachhead where future equal opportunity innovations would be brought ashore.

The affirmative action programs that the Department of Labor required each federal contractor to write in 1971 shows the importance of private-sector leadership in defining compliance. The personnel profession's most visible response to Kennedy's 1961 affirmative action order was the corporate "plan for progress." Personnel experts at each company drafted a unique pledge, borrowing language from Lockheed's blueprint but in a configuration of their own making. When the Department of Labor issued guidelines requiring written affirmative action programs in 1970, they modeled them directly on the Plans for Progress pledges. This was the one thing regulators required for affirmative action compliance, and it was forged and popularized by private-sector personnel managers before being embraced by regulators. In turn, the required affirmative action programs shaped the future of corporate compliance. In requiring an annual written plan from each contractor, rather than dictating practices to be adopted by all, the Department of Labor gave personnel directors ongoing responsibility for defining compliance for their own firms. This meant that personnel experts would continue to scan the environment for innovations to include in next year's plan, and that equal opportunity compliance would continue to evolve. Firms without federal contracts were not required to write annual plans, but many wrote them anyway.[123] Firms with these plans were often the first to embrace new compliance innovations, from grievance procedures to harassment training.[124]

FIGHTING BIAS WITH
BUREAUCRACY

PERSONNEL EXPERTS AT LEADING military contractors designed
the equal opportunity programs of the 1960s. At Lockheed's Marietta,
Georgia, plant, they put in nondiscrimination policies to open jobs to
women and blacks, set up recruitment programs targeting black high
schools, and organized new skill-training programs. Those programs
spread widely across industries. By the early 1970s, in-house equal opportunity experts at a handful of firms, like General Electric and IBM,
were developing a new set of programs. They put in equal opportunity
departments, special performance evaluations, and civil rights grievance procedures, as described in chapter 4, and they were soon promoting a whole package of bureaucratic hiring and promotion practices.

Barbara Boyle spent 14 years at IBM developing the company's affirmative action policies and becoming the first manager for women's
programs in 1970. She took IBM's model on the road in the early 1970s,
setting up Boyle/Kirkman Associates to advise other firms. In her 1973
Harvard Business Review article, "Equal Opportunity for Women Is
Smart Business," she advocated a formal internal labor market system
that would base hiring and promotion decisions on rules and written
records, leaving little room for managerial bias.[1] Ultimate control over
placement and discipline would move to the personnel department.
What Boyle proposed was taken line by line from the personnel manual
of the 1950s. She described core personnel tools as mechanisms for erad-
icating bias. The equal opportunity prototypes Boyle proposed spread
rapidly in the context of the more vigorous enforcement of the 1970s.

Boyle and her fellow personnel experts found that they could put
their pet projects into place under the cover of equal opportunity law,
practicing what sociologist James March and colleagues describe as
the "garbage can" approach to innovation.[2] Faced with the problem
of stepped-up enforcement, they looked to the stockpile of personnel
programs and selected those that might be used to fight discrimination. In political scientist John Kingdon's terms, there was a "window
of opportunity" in which a problem, a plausible policy solution, and

advocates for that solution coalesced.[3] The problem was compliance with newly strengthened equal opportunity laws; the solution was bureaucratic hiring and promotion programs; the advocates were personnel managers hoping to expand their turf.

Equal opportunity experts argued that formal job descriptions and job requirements, open bidding systems for jobs, and salary classification systems that tied wages to skills and duties could stop discrimination. Those measures had been part of the labor relations portfolio created in the 1930s to prevent line managers from discriminating against union activists.[4] In the 1950s, personnel experts promoted these practices outside the union sector as a system of modern personnel administration. Now they recast the programs again as antidiscrimination measures.

Today, chief executives and human resources managers mostly forget that their firms installed these programs in the 1970s and 1980s under the mantle of equal opportunity. New job descriptions and promotion rules didn't come with the label *equal opportunity*, and so a decade or so later there was nothing to signal that they had been part of a compliance strategy.

But the bureaucratization of hiring and promotion did change the face of equal opportunity, leaving Americans with an expanded sense of workplace fairness. Workers came to think that they had a right to throw their names in the hat when a job came open, a right to an objective performance evaluation, and a right to see job prerequisites in writing.

The last chapter documented personnel's creation of a system for managing civil rights compliance. Equal opportunity offices would track legal changes and implement compliance innovations; grievance procedures would intercept complaints en route to the government; performance evaluations would make line managers accountable. All three practices were widely popular among America's largest firms, and low-cost grievance procedures caught on even among smaller firms. This chapter documents personnel's concurrent promotion of a system that could both quash bias and increase efficiency by formalizing hiring and promotion decisions. Equal opportunity experts made that system wildly popular. My national workplace surveys show that 70 to 80 percent of employers had put in performance evaluations, job descriptions, and salary classification by the mid-1980s, and that job-posting systems and centralized hiring and firing were not far behind.

New Enforcement Powers and the "Best Practices" Model

In the early 1970s, judges and regulators endorsed equal opportunity practices that personnel experts had installed in leading firms. When executives asked Department of Labor regulators how to achieve new affirmative action goals, they pointed to the special recruitment and training programs that Plans for Progress firms created in the 1960s.[5] Plans for Progress personnel experts had implemented one bureaucratic technique, job test validation, at the end of the 1960s to ensure that tests didn't arbitrarily exclude minorities, and the Supreme Court endorsed that approach in its landmark 1971 decision in *Griggs v. Duke Power*. When the EEOC published a guidebook for employers in 1974, *Affirmative Action and Equal Employment*, it recommended a set of new bureaucratic hiring and promotion techniques that former Plans for Progress firms had recently put into place.[6]

From 1973, the year after Congress authorized it to sue employers, the EEOC brokered a series of high-profile consent decrees with leading employers. The decrees were widely reported in the press because of their price tags. In the 1973 and 1974 AT&T agreements, America's biggest private employer settled on back-pay awards and immediate raises for women and minorities with a price tag of $75 million. In 1974 the EEOC signed a consent decree with nine giant steelmakers and the steelworkers union, distributing $31 million in back pay. Leading banks (the Bank of California, the Bank of America, and Security Pacific National Bank), utilities (Pacific Gas and Electric, El Paso Natural Gas), and the major trucking firms were next to sign consent decrees.[7]

The remedies these consent decrees specified came right from the Plans for Progress manual, signaling that federal regulators would expect companies to embrace the "best practices" personnel experts had installed in leading firms. AT&T agreed to reexamine salary classification to guarantee equal wages to blacks and whites, men and women, and promised to use only validated job tests, following the advice of Plans for Progress leaders. It set up interdepartmental implementation committees, modeled on those of General Electric and other defense contractors. The steel and trucking industry decrees promised to replace departmental seniority, which was keeping blacks out of desirable jobs, with plant-level seniority, following on Lockheed's promise in 1961 to break down union barriers that had kept minorities in poor jobs.[8] The decrees established recruitment programs targeting women and minorities, and evaluated women and minorities already on the payroll for promotion—two strategies found in all of the PfP companies.[9] None of these things was required by federal statute, but their regular appearance in consent decrees produced a kind of "legislation of best practices."

In 1975 the Supreme Court, in *Albemarle Paper Company v. Moody*, signaled that employers found guilty of discrimination would routinely pay the kinds of mammoth back-pay awards seen in the consent decrees.[10] Personnel experts now advised all sorts of firms to put in equal opportunity "best practices" to inoculate themselves. At the same time, a change in the character of discrimination suits piqued executive interest in bureaucratizing promotion. The early onslaught of race discrimination charges based on failure to hire was giving way to sex discrimination charges based on failure to promote.[11] As equal opportunity consultant Barbara Boyle wrote in the *Harvard Business Review* in 1973, "Many large corporations . . . do have . . . a large percentage of women—all in low-level jobs—so development and upgrading objectives are of primary importance."[12] The mass of underemployed women constituted a huge potential class of litigants, and new formal promotion systems might ensure that these women would end up in management rather than in court. It was thus that local trucking firms, small assembly plants, and second-tier retailers put into place elements of the fancy personnel systems pioneered between the 1930s and the 1950s at DuPont, Proctor & Gamble, and Chase Manhattan Bank. Meanwhile those leading firms revamped their programs under the banner of equal opportunity.

Personnel Champions Bureaucracy

Bureaucratic personnel systems offered four distinct advantages, personnel experts argued. First, they could counter what sociologist Rosabeth Moss Kanter called "homosocial reproduction"—white men replicating themselves in positions of power—by ensuring that hiring and promotion decisions were based on ability.[13] Equal opportunity experts argued that line managers would inevitably discriminate, if only because of indelible cultural attitudes. Formal personnel systems were a tried-and-true method for undermining discrimination against unionists. All that was needed was to apply these principles to the task of eliminating discrimination by race, ethnicity, and sex.

Second, they left a paper trail that, in the event of lawsuit, could be used in a defense. "Keep Records" is a headline in Carey Thorp's 1973 article in *Personnel Journal*:

> The burden of proof rests with the employer. He must show that his personnel policies are not discriminatory. . . . Without written records to document his personnel actions, such proof may be very difficult to sustain. Many employers have been able to short circuit false or weak claims of discrimination quite easily by showing documentation of personnel actions (employment decisions, promotions, rewards, disciplinary steps, etc.) which clearly establish that valid reasons were behind the decision.[14]

Third, the EEOC now required employers to detail the gender, race, and ethnicity of workers. Personnel consultants advised employers to create job classification systems and job descriptions to line up with the nine job categories on the EEOC's reporting form. Big federal contractors also had to conduct "utilization" analyses comparing their workers to those in the local labor pool, and set hiring goals and timetables for each job category. Formal hiring and promotion systems would give employers what they needed for these reports.

The fourth reason personnel experts gave was mostly spoken of among themselves. In strengthening enforcement in the early 1970s, Washington gave personnel experts license to implement the sophisticated personnel programs they had always wanted. Many bemoaned the new regulations, but a growing number argued that the profession could now expand its numbers, put into place favored programs, and gain control over hiring and promotion decisions. These new programs were a boon for the personnel profession, and of course for consultants who had come out of the profession. Boyle advised companies to hire people like herself to revamp their personnel systems, creating modern bureaucratic systems that could stem bias: "Who should have responsibility at the coordination, design, and implementation level? . . . Some companies are now turning to experienced outside consultants. This approach shortens the start-up phase, demonstrates commitment, and minimizes the risk of initiating programs."[15]

Origins of Bureaucratic Personnel Systems

Bureaucratic personnel systems were the bread and butter of personnel management in the 1950s. Different elements of those systems had been pioneered in different sectors in the 1920s and 1930s. Henry Ford's first assembly line, opened in 1913, used Frederick Taylor's principles of scientific management to analyze the skills needed for each job. In banking, where customers were reassured by seeing the same faces day in and day out, personnel fashioned internal promotion systems, with job classification and formal job ladders, to stem turnover in the 1920s.[16] By 1924 railroad unions had won open job-posting systems and bidding procedures to protect union leaders from retribution.[17] The new industrial unions that grew after the Wagner Act of 1935 negotiated for formal job descriptions, job ladders, and rules governing promotions and seniority.[18] They did this to win job security and the promise of advancement for workers, and to protect the jobs of union activists.[19] And so, as MIT labor economist Thomas Kochan and colleagues conclude, "Collective bargaining contracts were gradually transformed from simple documents specifying the economic terms of the employment bargain to detailed and enforceable manuals guiding workplace practices."[20] As business historian Sanford Jacoby concludes, it was unions that pushed companies to formalize the employment relationship, and personnel experts who put into effect America's distinct system of "job control" unionism.[21]

Washington contributed directly to this trend, according to sociologist Michael Burawoy, by narrowing the scope of union bargaining in the 1930s and 1940s.[22] Unions bargained over the things Washington left on the table. Under the wartime wage freeze, for instance, unions could still negotiate over job duties, promotion rules, job ladders, job-bidding systems, seniority, and benefits. So they focused on these measures, to protect union leaders and also to secure jobs against recession. Even beyond the union sectors, bureaucratic personnel systems helped firms to provide the War Production Board, War Labor Board, and War Manpower Commission with the data and documents they needed to justify labor allotments and new hiring authority.[23]

In the 1950s and 1960s, personnel experts sold the elements of job control unionism—job-bidding systems, seniority systems, job ladders, job descriptions, salary classification, and merit ratings—to nonunion firms as components of modern personnel administration. These practices could check unionism, and guarantee that it was hard work and not cronyism that was rewarded with job security and advancement.[24] By the late 1960s, these practices were more common in firms with strong personnel departments than they were in firms with unions.[25]

From the late 1960s, equal opportunity experts argued that practices that had protected unionists could protect minorities and women. The Court's 1971 decision against Duke Power, questioning neutral personnel practices that kept blacks down, lit a fuse under these practices and sent them skyrocketing. Prima facie neutrality was no longer a defense. Firms would need personnel systems that made bias impossible.

Job Tests: The Supreme Court Endorses Personnel's Long-standing Advice

When the Supreme Court ruled in 1971 that Duke Power's job tests were discriminatory, many on the left championed a new, expanded, definition of discrimination. Many on the right decried the decision as judge-made law. In fact, the Court's landmark decision merely endorsed the long-standing view of industrial psychologists and vetted a practice—job test validation—that Plans for Progress firms had embraced years before. As in the case of the other Plans for Progress innovations, personnel experts at leading firms devised a compliance strategy, and Washington followed their lead.

The employment test dates back some two thousand years to the Han Dynasty, where emperors sought to break family strongholds by replacing inheritance of offices with tests for aspirants.[26] In the mid-1600s, Prussia established a competitive civil service for much the same reason, and France soon followed suit. New York City set up America's first exam-based city civil service system in 1877, to end cronyism and patronage, and in 1883 the Pendleton Act set up a permanent competitive federal civil service.[27] Before World War I, Frederick Taylor argued that tests could ensure that private-sector workers would be assigned to "the highest class of jobs" they were capable of performing, which would benefit both employee and employer.[28] Industrial psychologists who assigned recruits during the war further developed job testing, and their techniques spread after the war.[29] By the 1950s testing signaled that an employer was scientific and modern.[30]

By the early 1960s, some personnel experts argued that testing could put an end to discrimination. Hiring decisions and job assignments would be based on ability, untouched by racial prejudice. Test scores might even protect employers accused of discrimination in court. But others argued that in practice, firms used tests to justify discrimination. A Boston Edison executive on loan to a job bank for minorities argued in 1966 that "some companies have now resorted to testing as a rejection mechanism." They implemented tests "to protect themselves against possible discrimination accusations by rejected Negro applicants. These companies feel they have to have objective proof for their rejections."[31] The test helped to cool out rejected blacks: "any of the standard employment tests provide a subtle means of screening out undesirables since the personnel manager is under no compulsion to divulge to an applicant how or why he failed."[32]

Even when they were administered fairly, standardized tests might lead to discrimination. Experts since Frederick Taylor in 1911 had argued that job tests should be validated—proven to predict job performance. The tests that Han emperors used to select minions covered Chinese arts and letters, not the skills needed to administer the agricultural empire. Circa 1960, industrial psychologists argued, many modern employment tests suffered from the same weakness. If you were hiring a machine operator, a test of manual dexterity might be more relevant than a test covering division and spelling. Taylor had called for tests tailored to the job, but many companies used generic tests such as the General Aptitude Test Battery (GATBY) no matter what the job.[33]

Personnel Psychology devoted its first 1966 issue to the problem of testing and equal employment opportunity.[34] In that issue, experts from Litton Industries, Lockheed, IBM, the Peace Corps, the Port of New York, and the army sketched strategies for validating job tests that companies could build on. Howard Lockwood from the Plans for Progress pioneer Lockheed sketched a blueprint for how to ensure that testing would not impede progress on equal opportunity. More than the problem of requiring a high school diploma at a time when the average white worker had 12 years of education and the average black 9.5, "the use of various personnel tests . . . has presented a [great] source of concern to employers. . . . Companies have indicated that a much smaller percent of Negroes qualify on selection test batteries than do whites being considered for the same jobs." To remedy this, Lockwood advocated a return to the basics of testing:

> Some of the main actions which personnel psychologists can immediately take in regard to the testing of minority applicants are:
>
> 1. We should carefully examine job content before choosing tests for use and validation to see that test content is relevant to job requirements.
> 2. We should, whenever possible, be certain that the tests we are using have actually been validated for the specific use to which they are being put. Lacking specific validation, we should have evidence from other studies.[35]

Scores on standardized tests, Lockwood noted, may reflect neither native ability nor suitability for the job at hand, but differences in the quality of education. "Differences in test scores may very well point out the most critical problem of all in providing equal employment opportunity: the more complex social problem of providing equal educational opportunity. . . . Negro high school graduates may, on the average, be as much as two years behind their white counterparts in educational achievement."[36]

On August 24, 1966, the Equal Employment Opportunity Commission issued guidelines on employment testing, expanded on August 10, 1970, that echoed the advice personnel psychologists had offered since World War I, which Lockheed and other leading personnel departments had already embraced—tests should be tailored to the job and statistically proven to predict job performance. As the *Personnel Journal* later pointed out:

> Some employers are dismayed about the EEOC guidelines which require the validation of tests used in employment. But these guidelines ask no more than what industrial psychologists and authorities in the field of test administration have been advising for years: "Don't use a selection criterion unless you can show that it is valid." Invalid tests are not only unfair to the applicant, but they provide a disservice to the employer who uses them and mis-

takenly believes that such tests are providing him with a means of distinguishing the "good" from the "bad" applicants.[37]

Here Washington followed the advice personnel experts had proffered.

Experts continued to make substantive arguments about why conventional tests could be discriminatory. In 1967, *Nation's Business* wrote in "More Jobs for Negroes": "aptitude tests are out. With their background of slum upbringing [black] youngsters cannot show their real potential on the basis of most tests now in wide usage." One auto executive argued that GATBY "is a great test, if you read at the sixth grade level. But we have kids that can strip a car in 10 minutes but cannot pass the mechanics' aptitude test." A director of Chicago's Jobs Now, which found jobs for gang members, reported that they asked employers to "waive all normal standards that have been set up to sort out whom you hire and whom you don't hire, to forget the high school diploma."[38]

In 1968 the *Report of the National Commission on Civil Disorders* noted that employers establish "minimum qualifications for employment or promotion [that] often have . . . prejudicial" effects, when they require either a high school diploma or passage of an equivalent test.[39] In 1960, 35 percent of whites and 23 percent of blacks over the age of 25 had finished high school—the gap was even wider in the South.[40] Lewis Ferman found in his 1968 study of equal opportunity programs that common tests were often poor predictors of performance. In one plant he studied:

> Fifteen Negro workers were employed on a production line in assembly work. Due to production pressures, these workers were hired without the usual Wunderlicht battery of tests. After a six-month period, the workers were given the tests. In spite of the fact that each one of the workers had received a satisfactory supervisor rating on the job, not one of the fifteen received a passing test score.[41]

The popular Wunderlicht test was not assessing skills needed on the production line.

The call for test validation from Plans for Progress pioneers such as Lockheed had stimulated change in many leading firms and elicited support from the EEOC. By 1967 the Bureau of National Affairs found that, among 225 large firms—more than a quarter of them in Plans for Progress—69 percent of those using tests had reviewed them for validity. Some reported that tests "correlated with job success," or proved "valid and reliable in their application." Others who found that their generic tests did not tap job skills either discontinued them, "pending further studies," or replaced them with "specific skill tests."[42] Plans for Progress firms had helped to popularize the personnel profession's long-standing advice to validate tests.

The Supreme Court Accepts Personnel's Standard   In *Griggs v. Duke Power Company*[43] the Court endorsed personnel's view that seemingly neutral tests could be discriminatory. Duke Power had required job applicants for high-paying jobs to either produce a high school diploma or pass a standardized test. Blacks failed the test disproportionately, and plaintiff attorneys representing 13 blacks employed at Duke's 95-person Dan River steam station argued that the test was discriminatory because it did not test for skills needed on the job.

In the decision, the Court backed World War I era industrial psychologists, Plans for Progress leaders, and the EEOC guidelines that Plans employers had inspired.[44] It ruled that a test that measures abilities unrelated to job performance can have a "disparate impact," needlessly excluding minorities. When personnel practices arbitrarily exclude blacks, motive is not at issue: "good intent or absence of discriminatory intent does not redeem employment procedures or testing mechanisms that operate as 'built-in headwinds' for minority groups and are unrelated to measuring job capability."[45] Where the consequence of a practice is to exclude, the practice must be changed. In the court's words, under Title VII, "practices, procedures, or tests neutral on their face, and even neutral in terms of intent, cannot be maintained if they operate to 'freeze' the status quo of prior discriminatory employment practices." Congress had "directed the thrust of the Act to the *consequences* of employment practices, not simply the motivation," and so absence of malice was no defense.[46] Justice Burger took language from the act about "business necessity" and from personnel experts about relatedness to "job performance" to distinguish fair from unfair tests: "The touchstone is business necessity. If an employment practice which operates to exclude Negroes cannot be shown to be related to job performance, the practice is prohibited."[47]

The Court went beyond the narrow issue of test validation, to outlaw practices that had a "disparate impact" on minorities and to rule that proof of intention to discriminate was not necessary. Sociologist Daniel Sabbagh suggests that the Court chose to issue a ruling with wide scope, for there was plenty of evidence that Duke Power intended to discriminate.[48] The company had implemented the test after a long history of explicit discrimination, on the very day the Civil Rights Act came into effect, in a state (North Carolina) where a tradition of segregated schools left blacks with poor test-taking skills. In defining intent as immaterial, the Court chose to call into question not only testing, but all "practices" and "procedures" that might "freeze" the status quo.

Personnel Experts: Validate Tests, or Drop Them Personnel experts stepped up the advice they had been giving ever since the early 1960s: employers should either validate tests or get rid of them.[49] Boston attorney Antonia Chayes, in the *Harvard Business Review*, told employers to tread carefully.

> Many companies, under the cloud of testing practices that might be disallowed, have sought other selection procedures. A careful analysis of actual skills required for each job may in itself cause a shift or abandonment of tests used previously. However, if testing is to be used, it is advisable to secure the services of an industrial psychologist to ensure that job-relatedness can be established.[50]

Experts heralded the *Griggs* decision for promoting the kind of testing validation that industrial psychologists had always wanted. In articles such as Richard Arvey and Stephen Mussio's "Determining the Existence of Unfair Test Discrimination for Female Clerical Workers," published in *Personnel Psychology* in 1973, industrial psychologists argued that gender- and race-neutral tests could be designed to evaluate abilities relevant to the job, protecting employers against discrimination suits *and* better matching people to jobs.[51]

Some employers without the resources to pay industrial psychologists, or without enough employees to permit statistical validation, simply dropped tests.[52] *Personnel* reported that 15 percent of firms abandoned tests in the two years following *Griggs*.[53] In a study I conducted with colleagues in 1986, 15 percent of employers that used job tests before *Griggs* had dropped them, as had 11 percent of employers that had used promotion tests. Yet when we looked at more than two dozen other personnel practices, no more than 2 percent of users dropped any of them over the course of two decades.

Some personnel departments left tests in place and crossed their fingers. The human resources manager at a medium-sized New Jersey manufacturer told us in 1997: "We do a lot of testing . . . to see if the person is a high school graduate or equivalent, if they can add, subtract" for a job operating statistical processing controls. He didn't "have the time to babysit" workers who couldn't do the math. So the manager used an off-the-shelf test, and hoped to be able to "tie in" to other validity studies if dragged into court: "because we're a small employer we definitely cannot afford validation studies like a large employer would. So, we'll throw ourselves on the mercy of the court if anything happens." Even police and fire departments, which often faced court-ordered quotas, left unvalidated tests in place. In 1977 New York City was still using a 1970 test that had not been validated and that excluded 45 percent of blacks and only 18 percent of whites. In 1999, the city of Memphis was still using an IQ test that had been shown, in the 1980s, to exclude 3 percent of whites and 31 percent of blacks.[54]

Surveys have not successfully captured the diffusion of test validation, in part because validation can be a gray area. New York City redesigned its police test in 1970, but didn't actually validate the test. My data do suggest, however, that *Griggs* had a chilling effect on the adoption of new job tests. Initially promotion tests declined after the *Griggs* decision, and then spread slowly compared to other bureaucratic personnel practices. The prevalence of job tests rose from about 30 percent to 45 percent between 1970 and 1985, while salary classification and job descriptions rose from about 30 percent to 70 percent and 80 percent respectively (see figure 5.1).

Differences in test scores between groups became an active research area for psychologists in the coming decades. Many studies have now confirmed the findings of Claude Steele and colleagues, that "stereotype threat" can produce a kind of performance anxiety, and poor test scores, in stigmatized groups.[55] Under experimental conditions, where the race or gender of a person from a stigmatized group is made

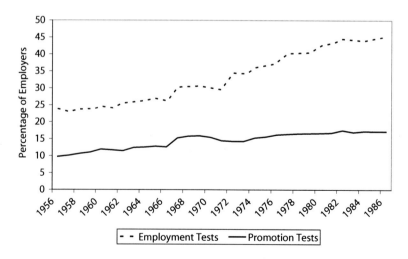

Figure 5.1. Employment and Promotion Tests (1956–86)

Source: Survey of 279 employers in 1986 (Dobbin et al. 1993).

salient, test performance declines. This may explain why tests have been shown to poorly assess the abilities of women and African-Americans. In keeping with the theory, in 1998 there were fewer than 20 blacks at the rank of captain and above in the New York Police Department, and evidence suggested that able blacks failed the captaincy test at an inexplicably high rate.[56]

Using Everything from the Bureaucratic Tool-Kit

By introducing the concept of "disparate impact," the *Griggs* decision lowered the bar for discrimination suits by putting employers on the defensive. Once a plaintiff showed that an employment practice excluded women or minorities, it was up to the employer to show a "manifest relationship" between the practice and "business necessity."[57] All kinds of employment practices could be challenged. In 1973, in *Meadows v. Ford Motor Co.*, the court nixed a policy requiring production workers to weigh at least 150 pounds that excluded 80 percent of young women and only 30 percent of young men.[58] In its 1974 guidelines the EEOC ruled that education and experience could not be used as selection criteria if they hadn't been shown to predict job performance.[59] It was not until 1991 that George H. W. Bush signed legislation endorsing the Supreme Court's idea of "disparate impact," but from 1971 the courts generally used the "disparate impact" standard.

Personnel experts warned that hiring and promotion traditions might pose two problems. They might sustain inequities without specifically excluding any group, as when, for instance, managers' jobs descriptions required experience in lower-level jobs that no women ever held. Or they might give supervisors the opportunity to exercise bias, as when informal systems for announcing new jobs permitted managers to handpick applicants.

The Business Case for Formal Personnel Systems

Personnel experts writing in the business press now argued that formal personnel systems could prevent discrimination by middle managers and improve efficiency by guaranteeing that each job would go to the best candidate. In a 1974 *Harvard Business Review* article titled "Make Your Equal Opportunity Program Court-Proof" Boston lawyer Antonia Chayes, who had helped to solve the construction industry's affirmative action compliance crisis, argued that formal personnel schemes could help to fill "the need for positive action against the risk of prolonged and serious litigation or crippling financial judgments."[60]

Herbert Froehlich and Dennis Hawver, consultants with PhDs in personnel management and management psychology respectively, wrote in "Compliance Spinoff: Better Personnel Systems" in 1974, "Viewing the [equal opportunity] guidelines in strictly negative terms, executives have failed to see that the government concern for programs of EEO compliance actually provides the impetus for developing a personnel system that has positive business implications."[61] Consultants made the case far and wide that equal opportunity law was improving personnel administration, through open bidding systems that undermined favoritism, through valid job tests, and through annual performance evaluations that tied promotions to proven abilities: "The employment system we suggest places emphasis on the validity of the decision-making process—that is, on ensuring that the most qualified person is recruited, selected, placed, trained, transferred, and promoted. And this is exactly the focus of the Civil Rights Act, the governmental enforcement agencies, and the Supreme Court."[62] Personnel experts now hawked virtually every element of conventional personnel administration, as it had been forged in the teens in assembly line manufacturing, in the twenties in banking, in the thirties in newly unionized manufacturing firms, and in the forties in the context of wartime labor regulations.[63]

Job Descriptions: Putting Prerequisites in Writing

In 1962, on the heels of Kennedy's affirmative action order, four oil refineries in Lake Charles, Louisiana, signed a consent decree with the attorney general. One problem was that supervisors told blacks, but not whites, that they needed high school diplomas to train for skilled jobs.[64] The refineries agreed to end that practice. Yet even in firms with public commitments to equal opportunity, managers continued to exclude blacks and women by using double standards. In 1970, General Electric found in a company survey that "black hourly employees tend to be somewhat better educated than their white counterparts" and discovered that managers steered blacks away from the best jobs they were qualified for. GE's personnel experts wrote job descriptions detailing prerequisites.[65] By posting job descriptions, firms could eliminate the double standard, as consultant Barbara Boyle argued in the *Harvard Business Review*.[66]

Soon after the *Griggs* decision, courts endorsed the advice that personnel experts had given to Plans for Progress firms for a decade—write job descriptions specifying prerequisites. In 1972 a federal court supported a plaintiff's claim that Savannah Sugar's lack of job descriptions invited discrimination: "There are no written instructions or guidelines for supervisors pertaining to qualifications necessary for promotions," with the result that "an individual supervisor could, if he were so inclined, exercise racial discrimination in his selection of candidates for promotion." Such a system is a "ready mechanism for discrimination which may be concealed from management."[67] The court went along with the plaintiff's proposal to require job postings that "contain a specific job description for each vacancy, the rate of pay, and information with respect to the qualifications required and how and where application can be made" so that blacks would know whether they were qualified, how to apply, and how much the job would pay.[68]

Prerequisites could still create needless barriers. Companies often required experience in feeder positions that had been segregated, making it impossible for women or minorities to move up. Edward Goldstein, president of Glass Containers Corporation, argued, "We're . . . searching for qualified women who have the talent and potential to advance in our company. I know their qualifications won't always be the same as the men's; in sales, for example, just add 'ten years of experience' as an important criterion and you've eliminated most women."[69] Thoughtful job descriptions could avoid the problem, and protect against Equal Pay Act suits, according to a *Harvard Business Review* piece in 1977. A system of job descriptions allowed one company to see that women were underpaid relative to men in similar jobs. Management rectified the pay disparity and instituted regular job audits.[70]

Personnel managers set up formal systems of job descriptions across the country. Among medium-sized and large employers in my 1986 survey, the use of job descriptions had risen gradually between 1956 and 1966, from 22 percent to 28 percent. But over the next 20 years, job

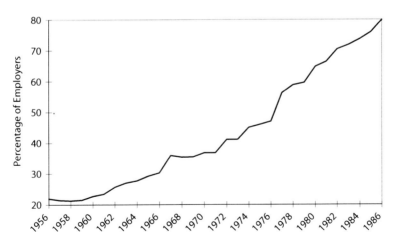

Figure 5.2. The Increased Use of Job Descriptions (1956–86)
Source: Survey of 279 employers in 1986 (Dobbin et al. 1993).

descriptions caught on. Eight out of 10 of these firms used written job descriptions by 1985.

Job Posting: Opening Promotion to Women and Minorities

In the 1970s, many companies heard that managers were not letting women and minorities know when there were promotions to apply for. In the 1940s, unions had tried to counter crony promotions by negotiating open job-bidding systems that would be managed by personnel departments. In the Department of Labor's 1970 survey of collective bargaining agreements, nearly half specified promotion procedures, and two-thirds of those stipulated job-posting systems.[71] Equal opportunity experts now proposed open job posting for all companies on the union model. Plaintiffs championed the idea. In 1962, GM's Atlanta Chevrolet plant opened all jobs to blacks, but began to post job openings only in 1968 on the eve of a discrimination trial. GM briefly promoted one of the three plaintiffs to foreman but backpedaled. The plaintiffs won on appeal and a new job-posting system was part of the bargain.[72] In the 1972 Savannah Sugar case, the U.S. District Court for Southern Georgia found that supervisors had kept news of openings from blacks, and, on personnel experts' advice, the court commanded Savannah Sugar to "post on bulletin boards in conspicuous places throughout all departments . . . notices of all job vacancies available for promotion or transfer of current employees."[73]

Articles in leading personnel and management journals recommended job-posting systems, which could stem bias and reduce training costs. University of South Carolina personnel managers Steve Garris and Ann Black wrote in *Personnel* in 1974, "The fact that it is cheaper and more efficient to promote employees than to hire them from the outside was a strong incentive" to adopt a system whereby all "transfer and promotional opportunities are advertised" internally. The system resulted in more blacks and women applying for jobs, and a higher proportion of those applicants being selected.[74] Business professors Robert Fulmer from Trinity University and William Fulmer from Harvard interviewed executives at six major corporations for a 1974 *Personnel Journal* article, "Providing Equal Opportunities for Promotion." One executive told them that job posting had become popular because it was "believed to prevent difficulties" with the EEOC. Another mentioned that "minorities seem to prefer the system," because they are "interested in maximizing job information." Others said that the main reason for using job posting was "fairness."[75]

In my 2002 survey, based on a national sample of more than 800 employers, about two in 10 companies had policies requiring posting of jobs as of 1971. By 2002, nine in 10 companies had such policies (see figure 5.3).

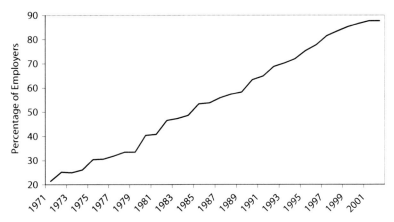

Figure 5.3. Rise of Required Job Postings (1971–2002)

Source: Survey of 829 firms in 2002 (Kalev, Dobbin, and Kelly 2006).

Salary Classification: Basing Pay on Duties

Job classification systems, in which each job is placed into a salary range based on the skills, education, and experience required, were common both in the civil service and in unionized manufacturing. All typists, across all departments, would be in the same wage band. Classification established the relative rank of all jobs, so that whether a particular job change represented promotion, demotion, or treading water would be known to all.

Personnel experts now argued that employers needed salary classification to comply with the Equal Pay and Civil Rights acts. It was the only way to make sure you weren't paying women less than men for the same work. Discrimination plaintiffs demanded the kinds of salary classification systems personnel managers had created in leading companies. In *Schultz v. Wheaton Glass Co.* in 1970, a federal appeals court ordered Wheaton to pay nearly $1 million in back pay to women inspectors, who had been paid less than men doing the same work under a different job title.[76] In *Corning Glass Works v. Brennan* in 1974,[77] the Supreme Court ruled that employers couldn't pay women less than men by assigning them different job titles "simply because men would not work at the low rates paid women."[78] *Business Week* reported in November 1972, "All told, some 400 equal pay cases have been filed by the U.S. Labor Department, and the results should gladden a feminist's heart."[79] The courts gradually came to side with employers in equal pay cases, but for the time being these decisions bolstered personnel experts' arguments for salary classification systems and job analysis—evaluation of job duties—to check unfair pay.

C. F. Fretz and Joanne Hayman reported in the *Harvard Business Review* in 1973 on a study of 20 leading companies in manufacturing and service: "In the majority of organizations in our study, 'equal pay for equal work' is always a policy but frequently not a practice." One problem was that without salary classification, a firm could pay a man and a woman doing the same work, in different departments, different wages.

A modern salary classification system could align wages of different jobs, though only with effective oversight personnel, experts warned.[80] Barbara Boyle tells of a service sector giant where women were consistently placed lower in the wage band than similar men. The president expressed surprise: "I knew most of the women were in lower levels than they deserved to be. But I'm really shocked to see that even within their level, when I know they're the best in that category, their salaries are less than that of the average man."[81] The Towers Perrin consultants warned that salary classification could also fail when managers circumvented it:

> In one service organization, for example, all authorized officers of a certain accountability and responsibility level were in the annual salary range of $14,000–$21,000. There were two exceptions—both females—who were placed in the $12,000–$18,000 range, and, to make matters worse, they were paid $10,600 and $10,900 respectively.[82]

The solution was to create salary classification systems, and routinely review compensation of all employees to make sure inequities had not emerged.[83]

Poorly designed salary and job classification systems could be a source of discrimination. When a woman with a decade of tenure at Phillips Petroleum lost her job to a man with fewer years during a layoff, Phillips argued that a neutral company policy gave seniority and bumping rights to certain jobs—"roustabouts" and "roughnecks."[84] Yet Phillips had created a special job title, which did not carry seniority protection, for women doing the same work as roustabouts or roughnecks. After the court cited Phillips for discrimination, the *Labor Law Journal* advised in 1973 that personnel departments would have to rethink existing classification systems.[85] In 1974, Antonia Chayes recommended reviewing current standards to "ensure that prescribed qualifications and pay scales can be justified on business grounds and that inadvertent barriers have not been erected against women and minorities."[86]

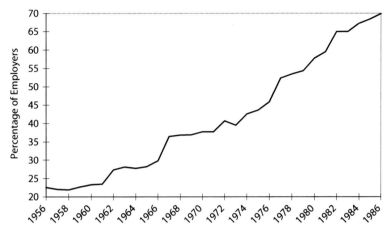

Figure 5.4. Growing Popularity of Salary Classification (1956–86)
Source: Survey of 279 employers in 1986 (Dobbin et al. 1993).

The growing popularity of salary classification systems can be seen in figure 5.4, based on my 1986 survey. By the early 1970s, about one-third of employers had salary classification systems. By the mid-1980s, some 70 percent had them. Employment tests were about equally popular in 1970, but only 45 percent of employers had them by the mid-1980s.

Job Ladders: Beware of Dead Ends

Personnel experts were less enthusiastic about job ladders as equal opportunity measures, even though they had been part of the modern personnel administration toolkit. Job ladders specified promotion trajectories from entry-level jobs upward. Sociologist Thomas DiPrete argues that the problem with job ladders was simple: women and blacks were often crowded in jobs with no rungs above them.[87] Boyle wrote that women have often been "protected" from dirty or stressful jobs.

> But this chivalry has worked more against than for them. Not only do these "unfeminine" jobs often pay well; they also can offer more upward mobility. Unless a woman has worked in the "dirty" areas of a plant, for instance, she can never be a plant manager. In many companies, unless she has aggressively knocked on doors as a sales representative, she cannot qualify for the more responsible and rewarding positions.[88]

In firms that created job ladders before the1960s, entry-level jobs dominated by women and minorities typically had no rungs above them.

Personnel experts advised firms to abolish or restructure such job ladders. Giblin and Ornati counseled firms to examine whether ladders "create unwarranted restrictions to minority mobility," and in particular whether "women or minorities are concentrated in certain jobs *outside* any line of progression or in jobs that dead-end."[89] An engineering firm, Boyle found, discovered that job ladders leading only from *engineering* jobs to management created a bottleneck for women. Supervisory jobs "could be filled by intelligent nonengineers," and there were plenty of women who were qualified, but few had engineering backgrounds. Personnel opened up the whole range of management jobs to women without engineering backgrounds.[90] A pharmaceutical giant found that, while the secretarial job ladder dead-ended, "more than 20 percent of the secretaries had college degrees that were appropriate to the business. So the company placed emphasis on upgrading and development."[91] A revision of the job ladder fixed the problem for future cohorts.

A common remedy was to replace job ladders with open bidding. A 1973 *Human Resource Management* article advocated "institution of a method of job posting so that all employees are aware of vacancies as they occur and that promotion into these vacancies is based on qualifications, not sex" or prior position.[92] Another remedy was to create job ladders with attention to guaranteeing that the lines of progression were open to lower-level jobs of all sorts. In the public sector, many organizations created bridges between different job ladders, so that clerical workers could move into management, for instance.[93]

In our 1986 survey, we found not that job ladders were being dismantled, but that personnel managers were not nearly as keen on them as they were on salary classification, job descriptions, and performance evaluations. Figure 5.5 shows that the use of job ladders doubled between the mid-1970s and the mid-1980s, to 30 percent of employers. By that time, job descriptions, salary classification, and performance evaluations could be found in 70 to 80 percent of firms.

Departmental Seniority Systems as Job Ladders   In unionized firms, departmental seniority systems created problematic de facto job ladders, because blacks hired into departments without promotion prospects lost their seniority if they transferred to departments with better prospects. In a downturn, they would be first to suffer layoffs. From the early 1960s, some Plans for Progress firms had replaced departmental seniority systems with plant-wide seniority rights that, as the Conference Board pointed out in 1975, "protect existing compensation and job rights of minorities and women while bringing them up to their 'rightful place' in the more desirable job-progression lines."[94] The steel

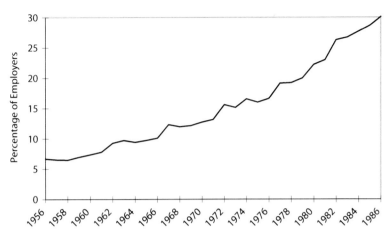

Figure 5.5. The Increased Use of Job Ladders (1956–86)
Source: Survey of 279 employers in 1986 (Dobbin et al. 1993).

industry consent decree of 1974 broke the system that segregated blacks in low-paying, dangerous, "Negro jobs" without promotion prospects, by creating plant-level seniority so that blacks could transfer to better departments without losing seniority.[95] Columbia Business School economist Casey Ichniowski found that, in its first four years, the consent decree helped significant numbers of minorities move into skilled jobs.[96]

A broader problem with seniority was that it protected the jobs of people who had been hired under a regime of discrimination. As Charlotte Hallam wrote in *Labor Law Journal* in 1973, "Seniority provisions of contracts, while providing great protection to employees . . . may operate in a manner contrary to an affirmative action plan."[97] If women and minorities were the last hired, they would be the first fired. But in 1977 the Supreme Court argued that to abolish seniority would punish existing union members for the past transgressions of their employers.[98]

Performance Evaluations: Evidence-Based Pay and Promotions

Since the 1930s, management and personnel journals had extolled annual, written evaluations for use in promotion, pay, and disciplinary decisions.[99] From the late 1960s, they argued that a good performance appraisal system could prevent prejudice from tainting promotion and pay decisions.[100] In its 1967 survey of 225 leading employers, the Bureau of National Affairs found that companies were beginning to use standard performance evaluations to that end.[101]

Judges reinforced the idea. At its Atlanta Chevrolet plant, GM would consider applicants for promotion only with the supervisor's recommendation on file. Supervisors had frozen blacks in their jobs by withholding recommendations. The Fifth Circuit Court faulted GM in 1972: "promotion/transfer procedures which depend almost entirely upon the subjective evaluation . . . of the immediate foreman are a ready mechanism for discrimination against Blacks much of which can be covertly concealed." In the 1972 Savannah Sugar decision, the court echoed the idea: such promotion procedures are "a ready mechanism for discrimination which may be concealed from management."[102]

These decisions gave personnel experts new ammunition. In 1974 Froehlich and Hawver, writing in *Personnel*, argued for objective metrics to improve efficiency and fairness: "Performance reviews should . . . be based on solid criteria available to all concerned parties." This would allow more efficient use of talent, which "coincidentally . . . ties in with the intent of [EEOC] guidelines."[103] Evaluations would also help management to spell out its priorities, whether customer service, on-time production, or units produced.

My 1986 survey shows that about 20 percent of firms had performance evaluations in 1956 and that by 1966, another 5 percent added them. If the pace of adoption between 1956 and 1966 had continued, perhaps 35 percent of firms would have installed performance evaluations by 1986. Instead, 80 percent of employers had installed them.

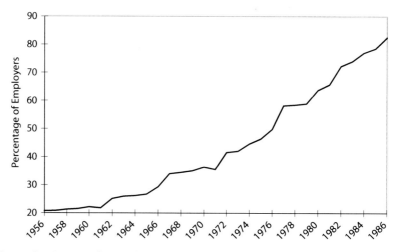

Figure 5.6. Increased Use of Performance Evaluations (1956–86)
Source: Survey of 279 employers in 1986 (Dobbin et al. 1993).

Personnel Takes Control of Hiring, Promotion, and Discharge

The problem of bias in manager's decisions about hiring and promotion was a thorny one. Frederick Taylor had argued in 1911 that line managers should not make placement decisions, but middle managers resisted ceding control to personnel departments. It was unions pursuing job control strategies in the 1940s that first convinced many firms to give the final say to personnel, as Fulmer and Fulmer argued in their 1974 how-to article on equal opportunity in promotion.[104] Job control unionism changed that in some firms.

From the early 1960s, consultants advised firms to write guidelines for hiring, promotion, and discharge, and give personnel departments final say on all decisions to stop managers from hiring their friends and firing minorities without cause.[105] According to a 1974 *Personnel* article, there was a long-standing business rationale for limiting supervisory discretion: "Astute executives have for some time seen the usefulness of the systems approach in reorganizing manpower practices along more business-oriented lines." Now executives faced "an unmistakable prod from various government regulations," and those who had resisted the business argument would "have to bring this functional area in line with its more advanced business counterparts. The result will be not only the significant benefit of meeting compliance standards, but also improved

Figure 5.7. Centralized Hiring, Promotion, and Discharge Practices (1956–86)
Source: Survey of 279 employers in 1986 (Dobbin et al. 1993).

manageability, efficiency, and economy."[106] Centralized control of decisions, and guidelines for decision making, were the solution.

In my 1986 employer survey, there was little change in the popularity of centralizing hiring, promotion, and discharge in the personnel office in the last half of the 1950s. Plans for Progress firms were the first to take control over placement and discharge from individual foremen and managers, and from the time of Kennedy's affirmative action orders of 1961, the popularity of centralization rises in the sampled firms. Centralized hiring rose from 16 percent in 1961 to 46 percent in 1986. Centralized promotion and discharge rose from 12 percent in 1961 to 39 percent.

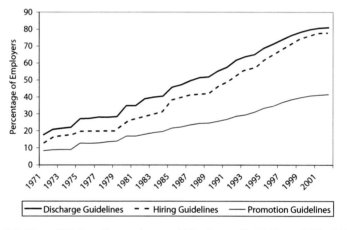

Figure 5.8. Use of Hiring, Promotion, and Discharge Guidelines (1971–2002)
Source: Survey of 829 firms in 2002 (Kalev, Dobbin, and Kelly 2006).

In our 2002 survey, my research team asked about the use of written hiring, promotion, and discharge guidelines. These typically required that decisions be approved by the human resources department. Eight in 10 firms had hiring and firing guidelines by 2002.

Quotas: The Bureaucratic Remedy That Wasn't

Quotas were one bureaucratic solution that never took off. Personnel experts argued that they were incompatible with merit-based systems, and quotas had never before been used by personnel experts. They had, by contrast, been part of the professional toolkit of university admissions officers, where schools had long used regional quotas, initially to check the incursion of Jews, according to sociologist Jerome Karabel.[107]

Congress and the courts repeatedly forbade quotas except where required, or approved, by a judge.[108] Neither Kennedy's nor Johnson's affirmative action orders condoned quotas, and by 1965 Secretary of Labor W. Willard Wirtz, who was vice chair of the President's Committee on Equal Employment Opportunity, insisted that the government would not countenance quota hiring. "There will be neither pressing nor acceptance of the idea of quotas as far as the Administration and government is concerned, and as far as the President's Committee is concerned."[109] Senator Hubert Humphrey insisted during the Senate debates over the Civil Rights Act that it would outlaw quotas: "Contrary to the allegations of some opponents . . . there is nothing in [Title VII] that will give any power to the [EEOC] or to any court to require hiring . . . or promotion of employees in order to meet a racial 'quota' or to achieve a certain racial balance."[110] The act's architects inserted a proviso that it should not be interpreted to "require any employer" to "grant preferential treatment to any individual or to any group because" of an imbalance in the "race, color, religion, sex, or national origin" of employees.[111] The Department of Labor's 1971 affirmative action guidelines explicitly forbade quotas.[112]

While Washington forbade quotas designed by employers, courts imposed quotas on recalcitrant municipal governments.[113] In 1974, Jackson, Mississippi, signed a consent decree with quotas designed to achieve a goal of 40 black municipal workers, and Columbus, Ohio, signed a decree in which 40 percent of each police academy class would be black until the force reached 18 percent.[114] Studies show that quotas like these led to significant increases in minority representation—they worked.[115]

Some criticized the 1971 requirement that contractors set goals and timetables for minority hires, based on Nixon's 1969 "Philadelphia Plan" for construction contractors, for encouraging quotas.[116] The guidelines stated, "Placement goals may not be rigid and inflexible quotas. . . . Quotas are expressly forbidden," but critics were skeptical.[117] Antonia Chayes, who had helped design the plan, argued: "Conceptually, there is a clear distinction between goals and quotas, one accepted for several years by the courts . . . [goals] establish a target set of figures to be obtained by good faith efforts," not a rigid requirement.[118]

Reverse discrimination suits helped to fuel the belief that employers used quotas. Figure 5.9 shows Title VII discrimination cases and reverse discrimination cases decided by appellate courts. Only three reverse discrimination cases reached appellate courts between 1965 and 1970, and just 24 reached appellate judges between 1971 and 1976.[119] Reverse discrimination suits represented a tiny fraction of all suits, but won wide media coverage in the middle to late 1970s (see figure 5.10).

Newspaper articles may have fueled the belief that employers had covert quotas in place, but they also reminded personnel experts that anything that looked like a quota could land them in court. Two Supreme

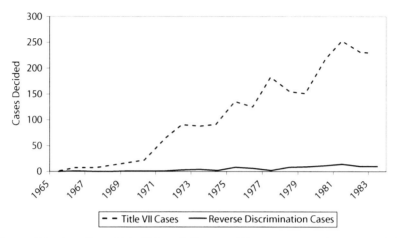

Figure 5.9. Appellate Title VII and Reverse Discrimination Cases Decided (1965–83)

Source: Burstein and Monahan 1986.

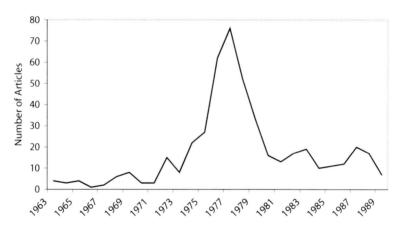

Figure 5.10. *New York Times* Articles Mentioning Reverse Discrimination (1963–89)

Source: Proquest Historical Files.

Court decisions at the end of the 1970s, one banning quotas in college admissions and one permitting them in job training, sent the same message. In the widely reported *Bakke* case, brought by a man who charged he'd been denied admission to the University of California–Davis medical school because of a quota, the Court struck admissions quotas.[120] College admissions officers devised a point system instead.[121] In *Brian Weber v. Kaiser Aluminum* in 1979, the Court allowed a quota devised by

Kaiser and the steelworkers' union of one black for every white admitted to a skill-training program. Kaiser had paid dearly in legal bills and bad press, and so experts like Kenneth Marino, writing in *Personnel*, counseled against quotas: "The quota strategy is a natural extension of the good-faith-effort strategy" of demonstrating the firm's commitment to nondiscrimination, yet companies should avoid them "for the present" in light of the *Weber* case.[122] In fact, well before the *Bakke* decision, Antonia Chayes and other experts advised companies that voluntary quotas could "render them liable to legal attack."[123] An explicit quota would invite reverse discrimination suits.[124]

Quotas never picked up much steam in part because they were not part of the Plans for Progress prescription, and were out of synch with the programs personnel experts were instituting. General Electric's VP of management development and employee relations wrote in 1965, "The establishment of some fixed ratio of Negro to white employees would conflict with the principle of hiring and advancement on the basis of qualifications. . . . What was needed . . . was affirmative action to make certain that numbers of qualified Negroes had the same opportunity to be considered as whites."[125] For Froehlich and Hawver, quotas were incompatible with Title VII and with merit-based hiring systems.[126] Some would reduce "standards for minorities and women . . . but we feel strongly that such a 'random selection' approach is not in agreement with the Civil Rights Act, is not 'affirmative action,' and is not a sound business decision." The General Accounting Office (GAO) ruled out quotas for federal workers as incompatible with the merit system.[127] How could personnel managers institute quotas, and at the same time put in validated job tests for hires and performance evaluations for promotions?

Were There Surreptitious Quotas?　Reverse discrimination suits had fueled the belief that firms used covert quotas. A Department of Labor official reported in the early 1990s that employers themselves sometimes perpetuated "the false notion" that hiring decisions were "being driven by quotas" when they explained to disappointed white male job applicants that they had had to give the job to a woman or minority.[128]

Of the dozens of surveys of equal opportunity practices I reviewed in writing this book, only two reported on the use of quotas. In 1983, the Ford Foundation surveyed 49 government contractors about quotas. None favored quotas, none used them, and none thought that affirmative action regulations required them.[129] The Department of Labor's internal study of its field offices in 1993 and 1994 found few contractors that had been cited for failing to reach goals—citations might have pressured firms to treat goals as quotas—and no contractors who used quotas.[130] Of course, it could be that no other surveys covered quotas because they were illegal, but in-depth interviews and quantitative analyses surfaced no evidence of explicit or implicit quotas. When Lauren Edelman and I interviewed 53 personnel managers in the San Francisco Bay Area in 1983, many had pointed complaints about affirmative action law, but none told us they had used quotas or, for that matter, reported strides in the hiring of women and minorities that might have indicated covert quotas.

Economist Jonathan Leonard tested the thesis that employers treated affirmative action goals as quotas in the 1970s. If employers met their goals, Leonard reasoned, it might suggest they were practicing quota hiring. Employers virtually never achieved more than a small fraction of their goals.[131] More generally, employers using surreptitious quotas should have been more likely to hire blacks than whites when faced with equal candidates.[132] A couple of early studies suggested that employers had a slight preference for blacks in jobs requiring advanced degrees.[133] But field experiments suggested that employers consistently preferred whites and men. When the Urban Institute sent black and white men with matched resumes to DC employers, blacks got further in the hiring process 7 percent of the time, while whites got further 25 percent of the time. Blacks got job offers over whites 5 percent of the time, while whites got job offers over blacks 15 percent of the time.[134] Sociologist Devah Pager later found in Milwaukee that blacks without criminal records had less success than matched whites *with felony convictions*.[135] Economists Marianne Bertrand and Sendhil Mullainathan found in a mailed resume study that applicants with typically white first names were twice as likely to be offered interviews as those with typically African-American names.[136] Economist David Neumark and colleagues found that among high-end Philadelphia eateries, men were twice as likely as women to be interviewed and five times as likely to be offered jobs.[137]

These studies do not rule out the possibility that the odd firm used covert hiring quotas, but they do suggest that hiring quotas for blacks and women never caught on.

Could Unions or Tight Labor Markets Have Driven Bureaucratization?

One question remains. Every survey confirms that the bureaucratic promotion systems discussed above and the grievance procedures discussed in chapter 4 spread rapidly in the 1970s and 1980s, but could something other than equal opportunity law have caused this? Scholars have long maintained that employers fight both labor turnover[138] and unionization[139] with formal personnel systems that promise stability and promotion opportunities,[140] and grievance systems to remedy complaints.[141] Could one of these things explain bureaucratization? Union drives could not have been the cause, for when these new programs were spreading in large numbers in the late 1970s, unions were not making inroads anywhere but in the public sector. Tight labor markets could not have been the cause, for the last half of the 1970s saw unemployment rates that the country had not seen since the 1930s, an issue I return to in chapter 7.

Were Human Resources Gurus behind Bureaucratization?

Could employers, instead, have bureaucratized hiring and promotion on the advice of new human resources gurus, who also flogged grievance procedures to foster feelings of corporate citizenship, quality of worklife programs, job enrichment, organizational development, and communications training? There was much talk about human resources management in the late 1970s and early 1980s. In 1981, Harvard Business School introduced a core course in Human Resources Management, the first major change to its curriculum in 20 years.[142] But the record suggests that grievance and promotion systems did not spread as part of the package hawked by HR advocates. First of all, those things began to spread in the early 1970s, well before HR gurus backed them. Second, new HR practices that weren't part of the equal opportunity portfolio—quality of worklife, job enrichment, and organizational development—either didn't spread at all or didn't spread until much later.[143] Columbia Business School professor Casey Ichniowski and colleagues questioned in 1989 whether the supposed HR innovations were even new, in an article titled "The New Resource Management in U.S. Workplaces: Is It Really New and Is It Only Nonunion"?[144] HR experts may have helped to fuel the spread of the bureaucratic practices in the 1980s, but as we have seen, performance evaluations, salary classification, job descriptions, and job posting were well on the way to saturating American employers by the time HR advocates began backing them.

Conclusion

The Supreme Court's 1971 "disparate impact" decision in the *Griggs* case is largely credited with causing a paradigm shift in how America thought about discrimination. From that point, discrimination meant not just "No Negroes Need Apply" signs, but the host of company traditions that maintained race and gender segregation, whether by design or not. The decision was monumental, to be sure, yet the idea that paper and pencil tests could be discriminatory did not come from the Court. It came from personnel psychologists at Plans for Progress firms who had introduced test validation in the 1960s. Test validation itself was as old as the field of industrial testing.

Personnel experts now championed every tool in their bureaucratic arsenal as an equal opportunity measure: validated job tests, job descriptions, job posting, job and salary classification, reengineered job ladders, and performance evaluations. Supervisors at the Lake Charles oil refineries had rebuffed blacks by fibbing about the educational prerequisites for skilled jobs. Personnel experts came to the rescue with formal job descriptions. Supervisors at GM's Atlanta Chevrolet plant had kept news of openings from blacks. Personnel experts came to the rescue with formal job-posting systems just as a discrimination suit was going to court. Supervisors at Savannah Sugar had nixed all blacks interested in advancing to skilled jobs. Personnel experts came to the rescue with objective performance evaluations. Managers at Phillips Petroleum gave women job titles that didn't qualify them for seniority protection. Personnel experts came to the rescue with a job classification system to ensure that women and men who did the same work would have the same pay and perquisites.

Personnel experts spread these new programs far and wide. Only the smallest firms were immune. Less than a third of employers had salary classification, performance evaluations, and job descriptions at the start of the 1970s, yet 70 to 80 percent had them 15 years later. Job-posting systems and centralized hiring and firing were just a few years behind. In statistical analyses, my colleagues and I have found that equal opportunity regulations drove firms to install these new bureaucratic personnel systems.[145] Employers also created maternity leave programs in this period, as we will see in chapter 7.

In the largest of firms, it was the new equal opportunity departments discussed in chapter 4 that put these practices into place, as well as equal opportunity grievance procedures and performance evaluations. In firms too small to have their own equal opportunity departments, it was personnel managers who bureaucratized hiring and promotion.

Personnel experts convinced executives that formal systems could stem discrimination and keep them out of court.[146] Executives were taken by the idea of quashing both prejudice and the kind of cronyism that demotivated workers and rewarded the incompetent. By 1979 some two-thirds of top corporate executives favored government affirmative action efforts, and the *Harvard Law Review* concluded a decade later that this was because they saw the law as promoting efficiency.[147] Robert J. Samuelson summarized the consequences of civil rights compliance in the *Washington Post* in 1984: "Many firms have overhauled personnel policies. . . . Promotions are less informal. When positions become open, they are posted so anyone (not just the boss's favorite) can apply. Formal evaluations have been strengthened so that, when a manager selects one candidate over another . . . there are objective criteria."[148] Econometric analyses later supported the idea that affirmative action increases corporate efficiency by leading managers to fill jobs on the basis of qualifications rather than connections.[149]

In promoting these solutions, personnel experts defined discrimination as the absence of formal systems for placing and evaluating workers. They had pushed for these systems since the 1930s to rationalize personnel decisions.[150] Bureaucratic measures must be carefully designed to work against bias, to be sure. Tests that excluded people from manual jobs on the basis of reading and math skills discriminated against blacks who had gone to inferior, segregated schools. Job ladders that created a path from stockboy to CEO, but a dead end for the gal Friday, prevented women from moving up. Such practices built discrimination into the bureaucracy, producing "institutional" racism and sexism. The absence of bureaucracy, however, was an invitation to discriminate. Subjective performance evaluations, unwritten job requirements, case-by-case salary setting, and hiring through the old-boy network permitted supervisors to exercise prejudice.

Now discrimination meant more than personal bias and Jim Crow rules. It also meant rules and practices that were unfair in their consequences. Sociologists Philippe Nonet and Philip Selznick (1978) termed the remedy "procedural justice"—just procedures for making decisions about hiring, promotion, pay, and discharge. Latent sources of discrimination could be found in the way firms did business. When they refashioned the traditional tools of personnel management as antidiscrimination devices, personnel managers helped to expand the definition of discrimination. Personnel psychologists had given the *Griggs* attorneys the idea that practices that appeared to be neutral could be discriminatory in effect. The personnel profession continued after the *Griggs* decision to build compliance measures on this principle.

It wasn't personnel managers alone who were promoting the idea that discrimination could be embedded in institutions. The civil rights activist Stokely Carmichael argued that institutional racism was the problem, not merely individual bigots. Sociologists made this point as well.[151] But the new idea of fighting discrimination by institutionalizing procedural justice was the brainchild of personnel experts. While Stokely Carmichael won a wide audience in the late 1960s and 1970s, personnel managers grabbed the attention of much of the American workforce by instituting new employment systems that symbolized fairness in hiring and promotion, and due process rights for employees through the grievance procedures discussed in chapter 4. People had found jobs through word of mouth. Now they were to find jobs through a neutral bureaucracy. *What* you know was to replace *who* you know.

What was surprising about the highly publicized handful of reverse discrimination suits of the early 1970s is that they were based on a principle that equal opportunity law had popularized, that of merit.

As we saw in chapter 3, in 1960 most employers used gender to place all women in one or two jobs—secretary or stenographer—and race to place African-American men in one or two jobs—janitor or washroom attendant. The idea of using merit and skill across the board was introduced by the Civil Rights Act, and in no time critics were using the idea to claim that equal opportunity programs created "reverse discrimination."

Why are these bureaucratic practices, which were the hot thing in equal opportunity compliance in the 1970s, so rarely described as equal opportunity measures today? When Ronald Reagan signaled that affirmative action would not be vigorously enforced, personnel revived the old efficiency rationale under the new rubric of human resources management, as we will see in chapter 6. For grievance procedures, they reiterated economists' arguments that due process protections could keep skilled workers with the firm.[152] For formal promotion systems, HR gurus argued that motivating employees was job one, and to motivate employees you have to guarantee them a fair shot at moving upward. Written performance evaluations and clear job descriptions could make career opportunities transparent and guarantee that workers would be treated fairly. The "civil rights" stamp also wore off these practices because it wasn't embossed on their permanent labels. It was easy to rewrite the motive for performance evaluations, job classifications, and grievance procedures. Before long human resources experts were emphasizing portable skills, careers that spanned multiple organizations, flexible benefits packages, and contract employment.[153] But firms stuck by the grievance mechanisms and bureaucratic personnel systems they had adopted in response to the second wave of equal opportunity regulations.

The new personnel system that spread in the 1970s symbolized not only fair treatment, but the ambitions of women, African-Americans, and Latinos. The various systems in place at the end of the 1950s had symbolized ambition as the province of white men in skilled and management jobs. Those in other jobs were excluded from career systems. Now women and African-Americans were in job ladders leading upward. Now Latinos received performance evaluations that served as the basis for promotions. Now everyone was eligible for training and upgrading, for educational reimbursements and career counseling. While the jury is still out on whether these programs did much to equalize opportunity, there is little doubt that they served to symbolize ambition as universal.

■   ■   ■   ■

THE REAGAN REVOLUTION
AND THE RISE OF
DIVERSITY MANAGEMENT

RONALD REAGAN RODE INTO OFFICE in 1981 waving the banner of small government. He blamed overregulation for the stagflation of the 1970s, and promised to rein in affirmative action and a range of other regulations. Personnel experts responded by rebranding equal opportunity programs in two ways. Some programs they folded into the new "human resources management," which in practice looked a lot like classical personnel administration. They grouped new performance evaluation and grievance mechanisms, for instance, with other human resources innovations. They rebranded other programs as part of their new diversity management efforts. Companies should adopt these not to comply with the law, they argued, but to gain a "strategic advantage by helping members of diverse groups perform to their potential."[1] Antidiscrimination policies, targeted recruitment, and a set of new initiatives became the core of the diversity management program, which itself was one component of the human resources approach.

It was no news to personnel experts that, as sociologist Robert Jackall found in his study of safety programs, "productive return is the only rationale that carries weight within the corporate hierarchy."[2] It was news that Washington might try to end affirmative action so soon, leaving them to define return not in terms of avoiding costly lawsuits, but in terms of improving productivity. It had been less than a decade since the Nixon administration had set the current affirmative action system up. Yet affirmative action had been a temporary expedient from the start, and Americans had long been averse to federal meddling in private business affairs. At the root of that aversion was a sense, dating back to the Revolution, that the country prospers when citizens are shielded from the sort of tyranny colonists felt under the British.[3] The Constitution's separation of powers, dispersion of political authority to communities, and limits on federal rule over enterprise sent the message that federal meddling in industry was politically dangerous and economically inefficient. Federal oversight of hiring and firing did not sit well with many Americans. Once discrimination had been rooted out, most expected, affirmative action regulations would be dismantled.

During the 1970s, the civil rights movement had faded into the background as personnel officers, the courts, federal bureaucrats, and Congress tried to work out how equal opportunity would function on the ground. During the 1980s, federal bureaucrats and Congress faded into the background, leaving it to personnel officers and the courts to work out new compliance measures. Congress was no longer trying to expand the scope of equal opportunity law, because new legislation faced a near certain veto at the pen of Ronald Reagan. Federal bureaucrats took a step backward, as their agencies came under the control of small government crusaders.

The new president could stifle congressional action and appoint bureaucrats who believed in small government, but the judiciary was a supertanker that could not reverse course so quickly. Judges who held life terms had to be replaced one by one, and judges appointed by Kennedy, Johnson, Nixon, and Carter continued to expand the reach of equal opportunity law in the 1980s. More class-action suits were certified, and in the 1990s settlements costing scores of millions of dollars were still making the papers. The courts also recognized new forms of discrimination. So while pundits remarked on the demise of affirmative action, executive, were ever more aware of the perils of ignoring discrimination.

Building on executives' dual worries about increasing efficiency and avoiding lawsuits, human resources consultants promoted a new wave of diversity measures even as they were rebranding the measures of the 1970s to remove the taint of affirmative action.[4] With the rhetoric of the human resources management and corporate culture fads, diversity consultants now promised to reengineer the culture to maximize the performance of diverse workers and, incidentally, to nip discrimination complaints before they turned into calamitous class-action suits. The centerpiece of diversity management was diversity training, the best hope for challenging ingrained biases and altering corporate culture. Personnel experts looked again to their professional playbook for solutions, basing diversity training on the sensitivity training seminars that management consultants popularized in the 1960s. Along with training, firms paid for "culture audits" modeled on old attitude surveys, and for two actual innovations, networking and mentoring programs designed to make the culture more inclusive. New diversity programs were popular among America's leading firms by the mid-1980s and continued to spread to smaller employers through the 1990s.

Equal opportunity experts seemed to be under attack, but they turned the challenge to their advantage, popularizing a host of new programs under a new rhetoric linking diversity to efficiency. On paper, firms were doing more than ever to promote equal opportunity. Yet econometric studies suggest that Reagan's regulatory pullback slowed progress for women and African-Americans. Companies were doing more to symbolize their commitment to diversity, but under executive branch regulators who had no passion for government oversight, they were making less progress. Studies show that firms and industries subject to affirmative action saw significant increases in black and female employment during the 1970s.[5] In the 1980s, change slowed to a standstill. Blacks no longer gained more ground in industries subject to affirmative action regulations.[6] Their gains slowed in other industries as well.[7]

Reagan's Deregulation Campaign

Reagan campaigned on the idea that the stagflation of the 1970s was the government's fault. Washington had introduced hundreds of new regulations, and was repaid with anemic growth. Most regulations backfired anyway—firms either opted out of compliance or focused on esoteric compliance goals rather than the big picture. The goals of improved safety, a cleaner environment, and reduced discrimination remained elusive. Reagan's predilection for deregulation was backed up by social scientists who added the idea of government failure to the concept of market failure. Market failure occurred when markets did not achieve desired outcomes. A new group argued that government regulations designed to fix this problem often failed themselves. Leading schools of social scientists embraced the idea, including new institutionalists and transaction cost theorists in economics and public choice theorists in political science.

The solution was a government that championed societal goals, such as equality, but left the specifics to firms. The idea had been inspired by Jeremy Bentham's *Principles of the Civil Code*, which was the basis of nineteenth-century British sunshine commissions that reported on railroad accidents, factory working conditions, and hospital deaths. The theory was that, if the government let the sun shine on enterprises, informed consumers and workers would vote with their feet, shunning the worst.[8] In the 1960s and 1970s economists at the Federal Communication Commission, the Civil Aeronautics Board, and the Interstate Commerce Commission championed deregulation under Bentham's theory.[9] Academics offered supporting arguments.[10] Bardach and Kagan's *The Problem of Regulatory Unreasonableness* charted the inefficiencies produced by excessive environmental regulation.[11] Kip Viscusi's *Risk by Choice* chronicled ludicrous micromanagement at the Occupational Safety and Health Administration (OSHA), which was fixated on such minutiae as the height of stair railings.[12] Viscusi's title captured the driving idea that an informed public will choose acceptable levels of risk.

Reagan's Attack on Affirmative Action

In running for office, Reagan had railed against affirmative action's "bureaucratic regulations which rely on quotas, ratios, and numerical requirements."[13] Once in office, he argued that Washington should leave it to employers to solve the problem of equal opportunity.[14] Reagan didn't single out affirmative action. He cut enforcement of the Pension Reform Act by the Pension Benefit Guarantee Corporation and Department of Labor. He directed the Department of Justice to cut back antitrust enforcement, allowing firms to acquire their competitors.[15] He told OSHA to curtail inspection of workplaces, to halt ongoing litigation, and to reduce the number of regulated toxins.[16]

Reagan's three attempts to cut affirmative action were not altogether successful, in part because of opposition from his administration and Congress, but those attempts signaled that affirmative action was under attack.[17] First, in 1981 labor secretary Raymond Donovan proposed that only the biggest federal contractors should have to write affirmative action plans. The threshold would rise from 50 employees and $50,000 in federal contracts to 250 employees and $1 million, reducing the number of companies covered from 16,767 to 4,143.[18] Reviews of contractors in advance of large awards would be cut. These changes would have dismantled Nixon's affirmative action system, but complaints from the EEOC and Congress led Reagan to scuttle the plan in 1983.[19]

Second, after the midterm elections of 1983, White House staffers proposed to close the Office of Federal Contract Compliance Programs (OFCCP), which monitored affirmative action compliance, and institute a National Self-Monitoring Reporting System. AT&T, Hewlett Packard, General Motors, and IBM signed self-monitoring agreements before opposition within the administration undermined the plan.[20]

Third, in 1985 the Department of Justice ordered public agencies in 56 cities to halt the use of goals and timetables in their affirmative action programs,[21] and Attorney General Edwin Meese proposed to end Nixon-era goals and timetables for private firms.[22] Secretary of State George Schultz, who as Nixon's secretary of labor had helped to craft the goals-and-timetables system, killed the plan with the help of William Brock at Labor, Howard Baker at the Treasury, and Elizabeth Dole at Transportation.[23]

Reagan did not get all he wished for, but he did succeed in curtailing enforcement. His new EEOC head, Clarence Thomas, directed the agency's general counsel not to approve conciliation agreements that included employment goals and timetables.[24] The EEOC sponsored fewer conciliation agreements and delayed decisions about pending cases.[25] EEOC funding and staffing were cut.[26]

The OFCCP wasn't closed, but its staff was cut in half. Meanwhile it initiated more compliance reviews under a streamlined review process, with the effect that many more firms were given clean bills of health.[27] The new chief, Ellen Shong, stopped targeting visible industries for reviews and lifted sanctions of all sorts.[28] Contractor debarments declined from 13 for 1977–80 to 4 for 1981–85. Workers receiving back pay fell from 4,336 in 1980 to 499 in 1986. Conciliation agreements were set up for 49 percent of violators in 1980 but only 33 percent in 1985—and violations themselves were down.[29] These changes led economist Jonathan Leonard to conclude at the end of Reagan's presidency that "an administration lacking the will to enforce affirmative action beyond rubber-stamped compliance reviews has resulted in an affirmative action program without practical effects since 1980."[30]

Under deregulation theory, by increasing the likelihood that discrimination would be caught, the increased number of compliance reviews could pressure firms to practice fair employment. Economist Ronald Edwards tested this idea against Gary Becker's theory of the deterrent effect of strong sanctions, based in research on crime.[31] His survey results challenged deregulation theory, finding that corporations were more influenced by the severity of punishment than by the likelihood of being caught.[32] Reagan's changes in theory had increased the likelihood of being caught by increasing compliance reviews, while reducing the severity and likelihood of sanctions.

Reagan also fought affirmative action in the courts. His Department of Justice filed amicus briefs supporting challengers of affirmative action, and, in key cases in 1984 and 1986, helped to win victories against affirmative action plans that suspended seniority rules during layoffs to retain minority workers.[33]

Reagan appointees also swung the Supreme Court to the right, sapping judicial support for affirmative action. Justice Sandra Day O'Connor insisted that affirmative action plans meet strict criteria for legality.[34] Then, in two 1989 rulings, in *Atonio v. Wards Cove Packing Co.* and *Lorance v. AT & T Technologies*, the Court made discrimination suits more difficult to win.[35] In *Wards Cove* the Court worried that the *Griggs* disparate impact ruling meant that any employer with a racially imbalanced workforce "could be hauled into court and forced to engage in the expensive and time-consuming task of defending the 'business necessity' of the methods used to select the other members of his work force. The only practicable option for many employers will be to adopt racial quotas."[36] The Court returned to plaintiffs the onus of proving discriminatory intent. Congress would reverse the Court two years later, but the ruling confirmed the view that Reagan's judicial appointees would undercut affirmative action.

On one front, Reagan did expand antidiscrimination law. As America's oldest president, elected at the age of 69, Reagan signed an amendment to the Age Discrimination in Employment Act to protect not only workers between 40 and 65, but workers over 70. Age discrimination and forced retirement were now illegal, with certain retirement exceptions for college professors, firefighters, and police officers.[37]

Executives Rally around Affirmative Action

Some of the opposition that Reagan faced came from a group he thought would be behind him, corporate executives. Executive support for affirmative action measures played a role not only in Reagan's difficulty carrying out the demolition of affirmative action, but also in the human resources profession's successful reframing of diversity as a business issue.[38]

Many leading executives had become cheerleaders for affirmative action by President Jimmy Carter's last days in office. Some thought the programs could inoculate against a reoccurrence of the race riots of the 1960s, while others made arguments about equality being the American way.[39] In 1979, a *Wall Street Journal* poll of top executives found that nearly two-thirds favored government programs to increase hiring of women and minorities.[40] Many executives now fought Reagan, filing amicus briefs supporting affirmative action, sending telegrams to the White House to protest plans to cut affirmative action orders, and testifying before Congress on the benefits of affirmative action.[41] A 1985 survey of 128 Fortune 500 companies found that over 95 percent intended to "continue to use numerical objectives to track the progress of women and minorities" even if Washington eliminated goals and timetables.[42] A 1986 survey of Fortune 500 companies found that despite enforcement cutbacks, nine out of 10 planned no changes to affirmative action programs and the tenth planned to expand them.[43]

Human Resources Experts Invent Diversity Management

Leading firms had installed their own equal opportunity departments and affirmative action officers in response to the regulatory expansion of the early 1970s. Experts now confirmed sociologist Philip Selznick's prophecy that when you hire someone to take charge of a new function, they cheerlead for that function.[44] Experts within firms championed equal opportunity, and dreamed up ways to keep their programs alive. John Field concluded in a 1984 study of leading federal contractors that "the affirmative action concept has become an integral part of today's corporate personnel management philosophy and practice . . .

[with] a highly professionalized specialty."[45] For Lauren Edelman and colleagues, equal opportunity programs developed "a life of their own" and evolved in ways that had little to do with legal requirements.[46]

Equal opportunity consultants, most drawn from the ranks of personnel, also pulled for affirmative action. They quickly regrouped as diversity consultants under the human resources management umbrella. In 1983 R. Roosevelt Thomas founded the American Institute for Managing Diversity at Morehouse College. Thomas was a Harvard MBA and former Harvard Business School professor who had previously developed a training program for supervisors of black managers. Kaleel Jamison's eponymous consulting group had its roots in the race relations workshops Jamison set up for Connecticut General Life Insurance in 1972. Frederick A. Miller was then Connecticut General's training director, and he joined Jamison's consultancy to become president in 1985. By the late 1980s the group focused on creating "High Performance Inclusive" organizations through expanded diversity programs, and listed Fortune 500 companies, national nonprofits, and federal agencies among its clients. Lewis Griggs and Lennie Copeland were Stanford MBAs who had developed the video *Going International* for executives doing business abroad. In 1988 they released the video series "Valuing Diversity." After Copeland published three articles in *Personnel* and *Personnel Administrator* in 1988, sales of the videos went through the roof as trainers integrated them into diversity workshops.[47]

Consultants now developed a new economic rationale. Many had argued all along that equal opportunity programs could save money by preventing social unrest, or by keeping companies out of court. In 1965 the Chicago Merit Employment Committee argued, "it's plainly good business to hire more Negroes" so as to prevent riots due to "the overwhelming sense of frustration of Negro youths who feel there are no opportunities for them in a dominant white society." The *Wall Street Journal* quoted University of Chicago sociologist Philip Houser as saying that riots "could potentially happen in almost every one of the central cities in the 215 metropolitan areas in which half of the Negro population of this nation is now concentrated."[48] Reducing the risk of riots was worth the cost of the programs. In his 1973 *Harvard Business Review* article, Ackerman wrote that firms pursued equal opportunity, not because doing so was efficient in and of itself, but because the government put a price on discrimination: "to the extent that governmental regulations exact penalties, a social issue is converted into an economic one and so can be managed just like any other business problem."[49] Reducing the risk of lawsuits compensated for the cost of affirmative action.

In the 1980s, experts rejected the argument that diversity programs could only be cost effective if they averted race riots or lawsuits. They argued that diversity programs could pay their own freight. Two arguments predominated. First, to tap women and minorities, make optimal use of their talents, and assure integration at work, employers would have to pay attention to diversity. Second, a workforce with more viewpoints and life experiences would be more creative, and would better design, produce, and market goods and services for a diverse clientele.

Using a Cornucopia of Talent

Some experts had argued from the start that formal hiring and promotion rules inspired by EEO law would not only help employers fight discrimination suits, but would help them put workers to better use. At the end of the 1950s economist Gary Becker argued that discrimination was inefficient.[50] Firms that abandoned it would get better workers, at lower wages, by broadening the pool they hired from. Uniroyal Tire's president argued in 1970, "In the decades ahead any organization which ignores or underestimates the potential of women—or overlooks any source of talent for that matter—will be making a fatal mistake." An internal 1970 study at one of America's largest firms anticipated changes in the 1970s: "It will be an increasingly female labor force. Women will account for more than half of the 15.5 million [person] growth in the labor force in the decade to 1979." America at present was not "making fully effective use of the aptitudes, intelligence, and education of many women in the labor force," and "this corporation could gain considerable competitive advantage by prompt and creative moves in this area."[51] Becker had argued that government intervention to equalize opportunity would be inefficient, and that market pressures would extinguish discrimination. Economist John Donohue argued in "Is Title VII Efficient?" that Becker likely had it wrong, and that by preventing price discrimination in employment, equal opportunity law might increase efficiency overall.[52]

Proponents of the business case for diversity management argued that, as society became more diverse, corporations that could not make use of the new talent would lose out. John Field, writing for the Conference Board in 1984, described positive programs to improve integration as an "essential management tool which reinforces accountability and maximizes the utilization of the talents of [a firm's] entire work force"—women, African-Americans, and Latinos included.[53] As an equal opportunity director explained in 1986, his company's "programs are now self-driven. Although we want to avoid EEO liability, we conduct affirmative action because we think it makes good sense to do so. We have no intention of abandoning the use of goals."[54]

The corporate culture fad helped diversity experts to build an organizational argument for a systemic approach. In 1983 McKinsey consultants Tom Peters and Robert Waterman published the first true blockbuster management book, *In Search of Excellence*, spelling out the recipe for a corporate culture that would breed business success. The book would sell more than 3 million copies, making corporate culture the management buzzword of the decade. Diversity consultants argued that managing different cultures within the firm was key to developing an effective and coherent organizational culture.

Others argued that, by bringing people with varied skills and perspectives to the table, an employer could improve design, production, and marketing. A personnel executive explained in 1986 that cultural diversity has positive consequences: "We have learned that cultivating differences in our work force is a key competitive advantage for our company. The differences among people of various racial, ethnic, and cultural backgrounds generate creativity and innovation as well as energy in our work force."[55] In a brief filed in the 1986 Sheet Metal Workers case, the National Association of Manufacturing described affirmative action as a "business policy which has allowed industry to benefit from new ideas, opinions and perspectives generated by greater workforce diversity."[56] Diversity management tracts increasingly mentioned the importance of diversity for achieving business success by developing new sales strategies and by developing products for new markets.

The Unintended Consequences of Labor's *Workforce 2000* Report

Proponents of the business case got an unexpected boost in 1987 from a report commissioned by the Reagan administration. The political sociologist Robin Stryker argues that the Reagan revolution was such a resounding success because, rather than choosing officials near the center of the political spectrum, Reagan chose ardent champions of his views.[57] Secretary of Labor William Brock was an exception. Appointed early in Reagan's second term, Brock questioned Reagan's efforts to curtail affirmative action enforcement and commissioned the Hudson Institute to write *Workforce 2000*. In the words of the report's authors, Brock "provided . . . valuable guidance as it progressed."[58]

Halfway through Reagan's second term, the report made headlines by claiming that most new workers would be immigrants, people of color, and women. Its impact, sociologists Judith Friedman and Nancy DiTomaso argue, was due to the fact that it left readers with an exaggerated sense of how quickly the workforce was changing.[59] According to the report, only 15 percent of the labor force's "new entrants" in coming years would be white men. By "new workers" the authors meant *net additional* workers, after discounting retirees, but if you didn't read the fine print, it seemed that nearly all of the people available for entry-level jobs would be women and minorities.

Journalists did not read the fine print. *Business Week* reported: "By the year 2000 . . . only 15% of the people entering the workforce would be American-born white males." In fact, 33 percent of the people entering the workforce for the first time between 1994 and 2005 were projected to be white men, and 33 percent were projected to be white women.[60] The misreading stuck. As Delores Wolf, vice president of personnel at American Airlines, recalled five years later: "in 1987 we found ourselves both riveted and skeptical in response to the Hudson Institute's ground-breaking study, *Workforce 2000*. . . . We read that between now and the year 2000 approximately 85 percent of all new workers entering the labor force will be women, minorities and immigrants."[61] Telecom U.S. West's CEO Richard McCormick told the Conference Board in 1992: "About 85 percent of people coming into the work force in this decade will not be white males. In a global competitive environment, we have to tap all the resources—both natural and human—that are available to us. Diversity is one of our six 'priority business strategies.'"[62] The report rallied support for corporate diversity programs. Just five years after *Workforce 2000* was published, 55 percent of the personnel executives surveyed by the consultancy Towers Perrin reported that they had a "Work Force 2000" program in place.[63] A 1995 study would find that human resources managers reported that their efforts to make the business case for diversity management were aided by projections from the report.[64]

The Spread of the Diversity Management Paradigm

Firms that had been affirmative action leaders now joined the diversity management bandwagon, including the Digital Equipment Corporation, where equal opportunity director Barbara Walker had developed a "Valuing Differences" training package in the early 1980s;[65] Avon, which brought in R. Roosevelt Thomas for a major overhaul of the corporate culture; Xerox, which had adopted aggressive affirmative action programs in the early 1970s and had a "Balanced Workforce" plan by 1985; and large defense contractors.[66] By the early 1990s, the American Society for Training and Development held an annual National Diversity Conference, the Society for Human Resource Management was offering a training and certification program for diversity specialists, and the Conference Board provided templates for diversity programs and ran national conferences and diversity roundtables.[67] Business school professors could choose from a host of diversity management textbooks and readers.[68] The human resources manager at a high-technology firm reported that she heard each week from 20 consultants who wanted to pitch diversity management services.[69]

Fueling the new fad, according to one critic, was an army of equal opportunity managers who had been victims of the downsizing fad of the 1980s: "The key personnel, ideas, and strategies driving this diversity machine come from preexisting, heavily female or minority networks . . . in affirmative action offices . . . linked up with an army of downsized colleagues-turned-consultants."[70] The new "human resources" paradigm had suggested that people could be managed like any other factor of production, and the new "diversity management" paradigm fit neatly into the human resources framework, suggesting that diversity was one aspect of the person to manage.

In many firms the equal opportunity office became the Office of Diversity Management.[71] A 1992 Conference Board survey found that three-quarters of America's biggest firms had a diversity manager. In two-thirds of these, the head of diversity was one and the same as the head of equal opportunity.[72] By 1994, more than two-thirds of Fortune 50 companies boasted of diversity initiatives.[73]

Rebranding Equal Opportunity as Diversity Management

By the mid-1990s, diversity managers were arguing that their programs had nothing to do with affirmative action or equal opportunity. Compliance was one thing, managing diversity was another. Yet core diversity programs were little more than rebranded equal opportunity programs.[74] The Conference Board's 1995 compendium of diversity practices drew every single element from the affirmative action stockpile of the late 1970s. Equal opportunity policies were rewritten as diversity mission statements. Race relations workshops became diversity training seminars. Equal opportunity committees became diversity task forces. Attitude surveys became culture audits. Equal opportunity experts had advised firms to rethink job ladders to allow women and minorities to move up, and now diversity consultants advised firms to study the "pathways to power."[75] Career planning to equalize opportunity became career planning to manage diversity.[76] Plans for Progress leaders touted informal mentoring in the 1960s, and now diversity consultants hawked formal mentoring programs to promote diversity.

As in the 1970s, America's biggest firms led the charge. All of the diversity innovations were widespread among Fortune 500 companies by the end of the 1980s, as surveys of industry leaders demonstrate. However, as my surveys covering a broader cross-section of industry show, most of the innovations spread to small to middling firms in the late 1980s and 1990s.

Equal Opportunity Policy 2.0, the Diversity Mission Statement

Firms that joined Plans for Progress, the private-sector arm of Kennedy's affirmative action program, had signed public commitments to equal opportunity in high-profile Oval Office ceremonies beginning in 1961. They inscribed their commitments in formal equal opportunity statements distributed to employees and job applicants. They reiterated their commitment in job ads with the tag line "an equal opportunity employer and member of Plans for Progress." By the end of the 1970s, half of medium-sized firms had an equal opportunity policy in place, according to my national surveys.

The diversity mission statements that consultants advocated from the early 1980s were mostly revamped equal opportunity policies. Equal opportunity policies typically promised equality for the categories protected by Title VII and amendments to it—race, color, religion, national origin, sex, pregnancy, age, disability, or covered veteran status. Diversity mission statements often left out mention of these categories, or added a bunch of others. First Citizen's Bank's 2007 mission statement mentioned business goals as motive and said nothing about legal categories.

First Citizens Bank remains committed to a culture of diversity that reflects the communities in which we live and do business. Our goal is to foster an environment that enables and encourages all members of a diverse workforce to contribute their full potential to help us achieve business goals and deliver customer service excellence.

We are focusing on the following areas:
- Leadership Commitment
- Workforce Representation
- Associate Awareness
- Targeted Business Development
- Supplier Diversity Program
- Corporate Citizenship
- Internal Associate Programs
- Customer Feedback[77]

More than half of the leading firms responding to a 1991 Conference Board survey had a diversity mission statement.[78] In my broader national sample, containing many smaller firms, mission statements had spread to 40 percent of medium and large firms by 2002. Figure 6.1 shows that firms did not replace their equal opportunity statements, but built on top of them.

Race Relations Workshops Modeled on Management Sensitivity Training

Early members of Plans for Progress had integrated race relations training into their management training curricula at the dawn of the 1960s.

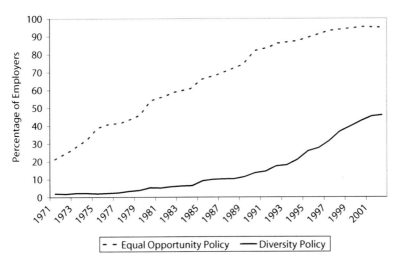

Figure 6.1. Employers with Equal Opportunity or Diversity Policies (1971–2002)
Source: Survey of 829 firms in 2002 (Kalev, Dobbin, and Kelly 2006).

Western Electric added a two-day module on prejudice in the early 1960s to its long-standing, six-month management training program. Lectures were given by Dr. Harold Lett of the National Conference of Christians and Jews, City College psychology professor Kenneth Clark, and the novelist James Baldwin. To train the old hands running Western Electric plants, in 1963 the company held the first in a series of national conferences for managers from every location, "from the largest plant to the smallest distribution center," with the hope that "once they returned to their home locations, they would be able to transmit the knowledge they gleaned to all their subordinates." After seeing a film featuring Martin Luther King Jr., James Baldwin, and Malcolm X, executives heard lectures by Clark, James Farmer from the Congress of Racial Equality, James Foreman of the Student Nonviolent Coordinating Committee, Roy Wilkins of the NAACP, and Whitney Young Jr. of the Urban League.[79]

The Plans for Progress training sessions of the early 1960s were big-hall, big-name-speaker affairs. But, by the late 1960s, personnel psychologists had begun to model race relations workshops on the small-group sensitivity training sessions that had become popular in management training.[80] The sensitivity training fad of the late 1960s drew on the human relations school of management, and its studies from the 1920s and 1930s at Western Electric's Hawthorne plant, which showed that managers could increase productivity by being sensitive to workers' feelings and motives.[81] In 1962, Chris Argyris's *Interpersonal Competence and Organizational Effectiveness* showed that managers exposed to a week of sensitivity training had better interpersonal skills, and were more aware of subordinates' needs. In 1963, Warren Bennis of MIT published an article in the leading academic management journal, *Administrative Science Quarterly*, which reviewed a host of studies showing how sensitivity training for managers could improve productivity. Robert Blake and Jayne Mouton argued in management texts from 1964 and 1968 that training could transform insensitive brutes into successful leaders.[82] Articles in *Administrative Science Quarterly*, *Academy of Management Review*, *Industrial and Labor Relations Review*, and the business press popularized the idea that sensitivity training could make firms happy and wealthy.[83] Leading firms embraced ideas from what had once been called "cow sociology," for the notion that contented cows produced more milk.[84]

Corporate race relations workshops of the late 1960s used sensitivity training as a model, and in the early 1970s federal agencies hired the same trainers to enlighten federal employees. When Richard Nixon charged the Civil Service Commission with implementing equal opportunity in federal agencies, the personnel psychologists it consulted advised "equal opportunity sensitivity training." James Frazier, the commission's equal opportunity officer, told the *New York Times* in 1971, "We encourage training in race relations. Most agencies are doing it." By the winter of 1970, Elliot Richardson, secretary of Health, Education and Welfare (HEW), had hired Curber Associates, led by an African-American man with a psychology PhD from Columbia, to run off-site equal opportunity training for 3,000. When Senator Sam Ervin called the sessions "brainwashing," Richardson countered with the language of personnel psychology: "You are aware that prejudice with respect to minorities is often a result of unconscious views. . . . Our Equal Employment Opportunity Training has been 'sensitive,' since it must deal with deeply held views which may unfairly discriminate against some employees." Fifty thousand Social Security Administration staffers had completed similar workshops by the end of 1971. Personnel consultants were running training sessions at a dozen federal agencies.[85]

Press coverage of this new personnel innovation fueled the trend in corporate America. Personnel experts set up training for the first firms that signed EEOC consent decrees, including AT&T and the big steelmakers.[86] A 1973, an article in the *Harvard Business Review* suggested, "In-house seminars give managers a chance to bring out and examine their attitudes and assumptions so that they can change their behavior." Sessions involved lectures, guided discussions, videotaped vignettes, and role-playing: "The sessions usually start with a discussion of typical remarks such as 'women can't travel with our salesmen,' 'they're

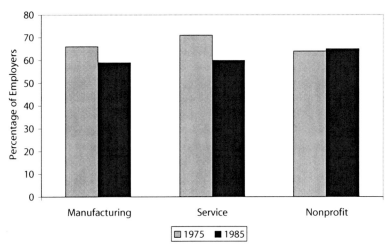

Figure 6.2. Equal Opportunity Training for Managers (1975 and 1985)

Note: The category of nonprofit includes some government agencies. The surveys covered 160 leading firms in 1975 and 114 in 1985.

Source: Bureau of National Affairs 1976, 9.

too emotional,' and 'they'll leave and get married.'"[87] By 1973 Barbara Boyle wrote that race relations training had become old hat at many companies.[88] By the end of the 1970s, women's groups were advocating additional training in sexual harassment sensitivity based on the same model.[89] I take that up two chapters hence.

When the Bureau of National Affairs in 1976 surveyed members of its Personnel Policies Forum—industry leaders for the most part—it found that over 60 percent offered equal opportunity training for managers.[90] More than three-quarters of BNA members were federal contractors, but that training was popular across sectors, and it declined only slightly after Reagan announced deregulation (figure 6.2).

From Race Relations Workshops to Diversity Training   Kaleel Jamison had developed race relations workshops for Connecticut General Insurance as of 1972. In the mid-1980s, his new, eponymous consulting group began offering diversity training. Lauren Edelman argues that consultants now distanced diversity training from the law and dropped language about protected categories.[91] By 2006, diversity trainers hired by a food-processing firm in North Carolina had all but eliminated mention of race and sex, the human resources manager told us: "Differences—that was the biggest thing that they taught. Not necessarily white/black, female/male. It was more about everybody is different. Tall, short, some people wear glasses. Some are bald."

Despite the new rhetoric, by the late 1990s HR managers responding to a survey overwhelmingly listed legal protection as the first reason for using diversity training.[92] The Conference Board's diversity management specialist concluded in 1994, "In its most narrow sense, diversity training is about compliance—equal employment opportunity, affirmative action and sexual harassment" compliance.[93] HR consultants brought in to design remedies in discrimination cases, in fact, gave diversity training a larger and larger role. In a 1995 Wal-Mart case on religious discrimination, diversity training was at the top of the list of remedies.[94] In its 1996 race discrimination settlement, for $176 million, Texaco agreed to spend $35 million on a task force that would redesign hiring and promotion and revamp diversity training.[95] In a 1999 race discrimination consent decree at Boeing, mandatory training was front and center.[96] The Coca-Cola task force overseeing its $192.5 million race discrimination settlement of 2001 set up a two-day Diversity Awareness Training workshop, a Coaching and Feedback Training module, and a Rater Accuracy Training module to ensure that bias did not tinge performance evaluations.[97]

The Black Jelly Bean Debacle

When a tape of two of its executives making racially coded jokes was leaked in 1996, Texaco reached a quick settlement of a race discrimination case that had been dragging on for years, agreeing to pay out a total of $176 million. The transcript reads:

ULRICH [*Texaco's treasurer*]: This diversity thing. You know how black jelly beans agree.

LUNDWALL [*Texaco's finance department manager*]: That's funny. All the black jelly beans seem to be glued to the bottom of the bag.

ULRICH: You can't have just we and them. You can't just have black jelly beans and other jelly beans. It doesn't work.

According to accounts in the press, Ulrich had lumped all blacks together, Lundwall (the leaker) had suggested that they could not move up at Texaco, and both had used the same racial image, "black jelly beans." Texaco commissioned an independent investigation of the tape by a former assistant U.S. attorney that concluded that Ulrich had picked up the phrase "black jelly bean" from the celebrity diversity consultant R. Roosevelt Thomas, who used it in written materials and in a diversity seminar Ulrich and Lundwall had attended.[98]

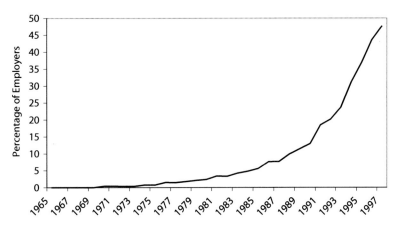

Figure 6.3. Employers Offering Diversity Training (1965–97)
Source: Survey of 389 employers in 1997 (Dobbin and Kelly 2007).

A Conference Board survey of 406 leading firms found that 63 percent offered training by 1991.[99] Surveys that included some smaller firms found that about 30 percent had diversity training by the early 1990s.[100] In our broad national survey, covering a wide range of employers, about one in five offered training by the end of the 1980s. Among smaller firms, the wave hit later, but, in that sample, nearly half of employers had training by 1997.

From Attitude Surveys to Diversity Culture Audits

Old-school personnel directors had been conducting attitude surveys for years. They were a mainstay of the "welfare capitalism" movement of the 1920s, led by Ford, Filene's Department Stores of Boston, and others.[101] Harvard Business School professor Elton Mayo had experimented with them in the 1920s at Western Electric's Hawthorne plant, as part of the inquiry that spawned the human relations school of management.[102] D. H. Ewing wrote in the *Harvard Business Review* in 1933 that the forward-thinking employer undertook a "systematic, organized program of interviewing for the purpose of discovering employee attitudes and grievances."[103] In the late 1940s, personnel experts used surveys to gauge potential support for unions, and to help engineer loyalty and increase satisfaction. When the Conference Board surveyed 3,498 large employers in 1946, 7 percent reported using attitude surveys. They were most popular in aircraft (23 percent) and retail (22 percent), which suffered from turnover due to wartime labor demand.[104]

In the 1960s, the industrial psychologists who championed sensitivity training also touted attitude surveys. In *The Social Psychology of*

Organizing, published in 1966, Daniel Katz and Robert Kahn argued that surveys could be used not only to judge employees' sentiments, but to give employees a sense that their opinions mattered.[105] Attitude surveys could improve communication between workers and management and make the firm more effective, Harold Guetzkow argued in a chapter from James March's 1965 bible of management knowledge.[106] By carefully deploying the feedback received in attitude surveys, firms could change managers' behavior for the better.[107] IBM conducted attitude surveys in its subsidiaries in 66 countries between 1967 and 1973, surveys that later became the data for Geert Hofstede's book, *Culture's Consequences*.[108]

In the 1970s the "quality of worklife" movement made another plug for surveys. Business professors Fred Foulkes and Henry Morgan argued in *Harvard Business Review* in 1977 that personnel should focus on worklife quality: "Currently, there is a great deal of interest in improving the quality of work life to fight boredom and decreased productivity in both blue collar and white collar jobs."[109] Attitude surveys were the first step. By the early 1980s, that movement had hit not only white-collar firms, but General Motors and other big industrials. Quality circles could improve morale and productivity, and communication programs such as "open door" policies and attitude surveys could identify areas of weakness.[110] Unionized firms were as progressive as nonunion firms in using information sharing, employee participation, and attitude surveys.[111]

Generic attitude surveys, then, got a second wind in the 1980s. They were popular, however, mostly among large firms. My 1986 survey showed less than 10 percent of a broad sample of employers with attitude surveys, and those with surveys were among the largest.

The race relations survey was first used in the early 1960s by Plans for Progress signatories seeking a sense of how blacks felt about their workplaces. From the early 1980s, equal opportunity experts revived race relation surveys, touting them alongside grievance procedures and "open door" policies as ways to take the pulse of disadvantaged groups and preclude lawsuits. MIT equal opportunity ombudsperson Mary P. Rowe and diversity consultant Michael Baker wrote in a 1984 *Harvard Business Review* piece titled "Are You Hearing Enough Employee Concerns?" that this was an important step for equal employment officers to take, and a way to prevent the firm from being blindsided by a lawsuit.[112]

After three federal district courts found sexual harassment to be covered by the Civil Rights Act in 1977, equal opportunity consultants began to use anonymous attitude surveys to gauge the prevalence of workplace harassment as well. Frederick Sullivan, a Massachusetts employment lawyer, argued in *Personnel* in 1986 that periodic attitude surveys were key to identifying harassment problems in the workplace.[113]

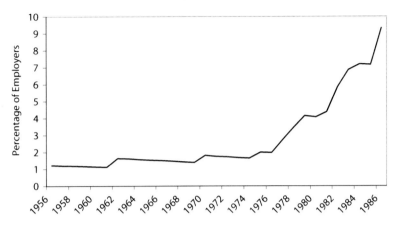

Figure 6.4. Employers Using Attitude Surveys (1956–86)
Source: Survey of 279 employers conducted in 1986 (Sutton et al. 1994).

Freada Klein, a Massachusetts consultant specializing in firms facing harassment, reported in 1989 that she had conducted such surveys in a number of firms. The *Wall Street Journal* reported in 1991 that the costs of preventing a sexual harassment lawsuit, which included diversity training and attitude surveys, were nothing compared to the cost of defending the company in court.[114]

In the 1980s, diversity consultants expanded the attitude survey, conducting comprehensive "culture audits" for their clients that sometimes included interviews with key personnel and focus groups.[115] Leading diversity consultants insisted on doing culture audits before designing a diversity training program, so that training could target the firm's problem areas. Allstate CEO Wayne Heiden reported in 1992, "To guide our communications efforts, we're now surveying about 5,000 of our employees to get a baseline idea of their understanding of diversity as a business issue."[116] Surveys often employed psychological tools to assess group conflict.[117]

Culture audits were never widely popular, in part because they could cost upwards of $100,000, even for a medium-sized firm. Among large firms, however, culture audits were common by the late 1990s. In my 2002 survey, they had reached nearly 20 percent of a broad sample of firms.

Mentoring and Networking: Challenging the "Old Boys' Club"

Like diversity mission statements, diversity training, and culture audits, new networking and mentoring programs built on the notion that executives could reengineer corporate culture. Personnel experts who

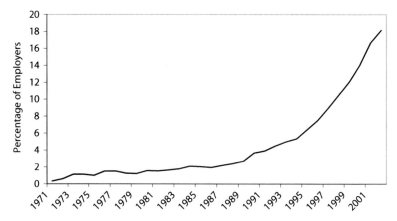

Figure 6.5. Employers Conducting "Culture Audits" (1971–2002)
Source: Survey of 829 firms in 2002 (Kalev, Dobbin, and Kelly 2006),

had encouraged mentoring in the 1970s to help aspiring managers learn the ropes now created mentoring programs and affiliation networks for underrepresented groups. They argued that women and minorities had been disadvantaged by social isolation, and would benefit from formal programs to make sure they were mentored, and an old girls' club alongside the old boys' club.

Network theorists in the social sciences began to argue in the early 1970s that credentials alone did not determine career success—networks mattered too. In his landmark 1972 study, sociologist Mark Granovetter showed that people use broad networks of weak contacts to find jobs.[118] Network contacts provide social support and informal coaching, and help to build trust.[119] White men typically have ties to other white men, who dominate the management ranks where hiring decisions are made.[120] Poor links to managers can hamper women and minorities.[121] Diversity consultants began to promote affiliation networks, with many reporting that demand came from below. The programs ranged in form and degree of intensity, from occasional brown-bag lunch meetings to regular on-site meetings and lavish annual conferences.[122] By 2006 the internet technology giant Cisco Systems had a Women's Action Network with 31 chapters; the Cisco Black Employee Network; Conexion, the Cisco Latino Network; the Gay Lesbian Bisexual Transgender Advocates; the Cisco Asian Affinity Network; and the Volunteers for India Development and Empowerment Network.[123]

By the late 1970s, management psychologists were promoting mentoring programs as well, spurred by a 1978 *Harvard Business Review* article titled "Everyone Who Makes It Has a Mentor."[124] The idea was that mentors can help novices to wend their way upward, and that women and minorities need help finding mentors. When Susan Vernon-Gerstonfield and Edmund Burke conducted an intensive study in the early 1980s of nine firms famed for their equal opportunity programs—Digital Equipment, General Electric, GTE, Hewlett-Packard, Johnson & Johnson, Kodak, Kraft Foods, Proctor and Gamble, and Xerox—they found that all nine actively promoted mentoring: "The companies deliberately encourage mentor relationships between seasoned managers and new minority and female managers."[125]

Diversity consultants suggested formal programs to match aspiring managers with senior mentors. Later studies showed that women who succeeded in business were more likely to have had mentors, and that mentees improved social networks and tactical knowledge.[126] Harvard Business School professor David Thomas found that mentoring is key to the success of minorities in large corporations.[127] As women and minority mentors may be ill-situated to sponsor and coach protégés, consultants advised against matching mentors by race and gender.[128]

Once again, industry leaders were the pioneers. By the early 1990s, two studies showed that 20 to 30 percent of America's biggest firms had formal mentoring programs.[129] In my broader sample of American firms, only 2 to 4 percent had networking and mentoring for women and minorities by 1990, but 6 percent had mentoring and 12 percent had networking by 2002.

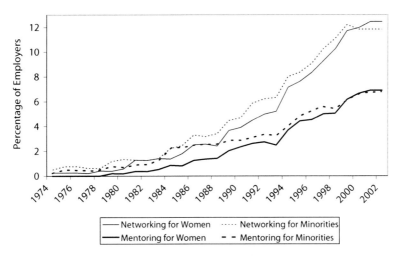

Figure 6.6. Mentoring and Networking Programs for Women and Minorities (1974–2002)

Source: Survey of 829 firms in 2002 (Kalev, Dobbin, and Kelly 2006).

From Equal Opportunity Task Forces to Diversity Task Forces

The diversity task force did not have the extensive lineage of the culture audit, which can be traced to attitude surveys of the 1920s, but it did have a precedent in the equal opportunity task forces of Plans for Progress innovators. As we saw in chapter 4, by the start of 1970, General Electric CEO Fred Borch had set up an Equal Opportunity/Minority Relations office under the leadership of Frank J. Toner, who created 27 different task forces to deal with workforce and community relations issues.[130] More recently the total quality management movement, which dates to the early 1960s in Japan, had encouraged American firms to create cross-functional quality teams to target specific areas in need of improvement.[131]

From the early 1980s, personnel consultants promoted diversity task forces, or councils, composed of department heads to identify problem areas—recruitment of minority nurses, or retention of female engineers—and brainstorm for solutions. The HR manager at a North Carolina food processor, where a third of workers are women and 80 percent are African-American or Latino, told us in 2006 that she chairs the task force. The VP of human resources at an insurance industry giant told us in the same year that he seeks volunteers from the lower ranks of the firm as well, so that all viewpoints will be represented. Those are the two membership models—department heads alone, and a more representative mix.

Some big companies followed General Electric's model of a task force for every problem. The accounting and consulting giant Deloitte & Touche created separate task forces at the end of the 1990s that analyzed the gender gap, recommended remedial steps, and established systems for monitoring results and ensuring accountability.[132] In smaller firms, task forces sometimes substitute for affirmative action officers, some actively developing new solutions and some playing a more symbolic role. At the North Carolina food processor, the task force identified retention and promotion of women and minorities as the key problem, and developed strategies for encouraging women to move out of unskilled production jobs into "high paying maintenance jobs." By contrast, the task force at another food processor sets up celebrations for Black History Month and Puerto Rico Day, but has nothing to do with hiring and promotion.

By the late 1980s, leading consultants were recommending task forces as a miracle drug. When Du Pont Merck Pharmaceutical faced reports of discrimination in 1988, division manager Kurt Landgraf set up a 10-member task force to look into the matter.[133] When Wall Street firms faced a series of discrimination lawsuits and a round of bad press

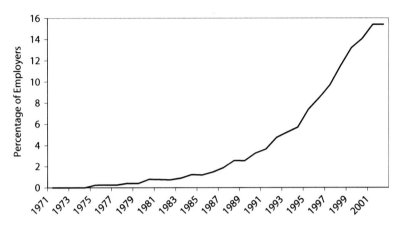

Figure 6.7. Employers with Diversity Task Forces (1971–2002)
Source: Survey of 389 employers in 1997 (Dobbin and Kelly 2007).

in the early 1990s, consultants again advised task forces. By 1994, only 57 women and 38 minorities could be found among Merrill Lynch's 546 directors. Goldman, Sachs counted only 7 women and one African-American among its 150 partners. Salomon Brothers had just one black trader. *Business Week*'s "Is Wall Street Finally Starting to Get It?" pointed to diversity task forces as the most promising remedy. Roger Vassey, a "heavy hitter" executive vice president formerly in charge of Merrill's fixed income department and now in charge of a new diversity task force with a $1 million annual budget, reported, "This program has teeth." Morgan Stanley hired a full-time diversity consultant, and put its new diversity task force under the charge of William M. Lewis Jr., an African-American managing director in investment banking.[134]

By 1991, a survey by the Conference Board showed that one-third of America's biggest firms had task forces.[135] My 1997 survey shows that task forces began to spread to the broader population of firms in the late 1980s, but really took off in the early 1990s. By 1997, 18 percent of the firms in that wider sample had task forces.

The Continuing Popularity of the Old Standards

The regulatory pullback of the 1980s might have led employers to cancel the equal opportunity programs they did not rebrand as diversity programs. Instead, all of the equal opportunity programs of the 1970s and 1980s continued to spread. While Reagan had curtailed executive branch oversight of firms, courts were certifying more and more class-action suits and were expanding the scope of equal opportunity law. In the Bureau of National Affairs studies from 1976 and 1985, firms with formal equal opportunity policies rose from 80 percent to 100 percent. Those with equal opportunity training for supervisors rose from 65 percent to 80 percent.[136] In the broader sample of large and small employers my colleagues and I surveyed in 1986, we found continued growth of the core programs. Those with policies protecting minorities grew from 45 percent at the end of 1981 to 60 percent at the end of 1986. Those with policies protecting women grew from 35 percent to 57 percent.[137] The constituency of equal opportunity experts within firms also grew. Equal opportunity departments spread from 15 percent of firms in 1981 to 19 percent in 1986.[138] Affirmative action officers spread from 21 percent to 27 percent. In our broad sample of firms contacted in 2002, we also found that targeted recruitment continued to spread, rising from 6 percent of firms in 1981 to 14 percent in 1990.[139] Affirmative action programs continued to spread, even to firms with federal contracts that were not required to have them.[140] We saw in chapter 5 that the new bureaucratic hiring and promotion systems continued to spread as well in the 1980s. Performance evaluations to rid decisions of bias, job descriptions to stop managers from inflating prerequisites for minorities, and salary classification to ensure equal pay for equal work reached 70 or 80 percent of firms in our broad sample by 1986.

Consolidating Diversity Management Rhetoric in the 1990s

In 1992 the Conference Board found that many executives had embraced the notion that diversity management was not just affirmative action in new clothing. The CEO of a top manufacturing firm claimed in 1993 that "the 1960s moral and social arguments [for diversity] have been replaced by tough business issues."[141] Big federal contractors still had offices devoted to legal compliance, and still paid close attention to shifting compliance standards, and some line managers resisted diversity initiatives as recycled affirmative action measures. As I have been arguing, many of the new programs were in fact relabeled affirmative action initiatives. As a Conference Board researcher argued: "Although there is a strong sentiment that diversity moves far beyond compliance, at this point, practices demonstrate a strong link between the two."[142] A 1992 survey of HR experts showed that "confusion between diversity and affirmative action" was a bigger barrier to diversity programs than cost, lack of executive support, or fear of backlash.[143]

Executives who supported diversity efforts now talked the new talk of diversity consultants, emphasizing pure business reasons for pursuing diversity. Richard McCormick of U.S. West reported, "I don't even think about equal employment or affirmative action any more. We think in terms of pluralism and diversity—creating a work force that reflects our customers and society." One driving idea was to better appeal to consumers: "We have other motives" than equity or legal compliance, such as "improving our business by understanding our customers."[144] Wayne Heiden, CEO of Allstate, argued that diversity was about remaining in the game: "It's obvious to us that managing diversity is not just a work force issue: it is a business issue . . . a competitive issue."[145] As the CEO of telecom giant U.S. West said, "In time, I hope the profile of our company will reflect society in general. We're going to be better team players and better listeners; we will communicate better with employees, customers, vendors and international suppliers. . . . I'm going to be stronger in terms of relating to women, blacks, and other minority members on my team." This would help to attract talent and investment: "To me, a company that can unleash that kind of human potential is a company where a young person would want to work and where an investor would want to invest."[146]

For Control Data's Lawrence Perlman, globalization made it imperative to have a diverse workforce: "We need the breadth of experience that comes from a diverse group of people to survive and prosper in an interconnected and rapidly changing world." Companies need to recognize "that people from diverse backgrounds are the helpers. Companies aren't helping them; they're helping companies to succeed." In sales, companies need to be represented "by women, by ethnic and racial minorities, and by people of different cultural legacies because that's who our customers are." Diversity at the top was key to getting the best talent: "To attract and retain the people we need to help us grow and prosper, management has to reflect the new demographics of the work force. . . . We won't get highly qualified, nonwhite, nonmale M.B.A.s or salespersons to join a company, department or division where every manager is a white male. They will not see opportunity but a glass ceiling."[147]

As star diversity consultant R. Roosevelt Thomas argued in a 1994 *Harvard Business Review* article, firms had come to promote diversity for business reasons: "Sooner or later, affirmative action will die a natural death. . . . If we look at the premises that underlie it, we find assumptions and priorities that look increasingly shopworn," such as the idea that firms should offer reparations for America's past discrimination. The central assumption is out of synch with the idea of true equality: "What affirmative action means in practice is an unnatural focus on one group, and what it means too often to too many employees is that someone is playing fast and loose with standards in order to favor [one] group."[148]

For the time being, federal officials began to look to new diversity programs for things to add to their list of best practices. When the Department of Labor circulated a draft of new affirmative action regulations in May 2000, it included on its list of recommendations not only things like special recruitment and equal opportunity performance evaluations that it had been suggesting for decades, but programs that had been popularized recently in the name of diversity, such as mentoring programs.[149]

Conclusion

When Congress, the administration, and the Supreme Court gave fair employment law a shot in the arm in the early 1970s, firms hired affirmative action officers and set up equal opportunity departments. Personnel managers shifted their focus from labor relations to equal opportunity, and the profession became increasingly feminized.[150] By the early 1980s, leading firms had troops on hand who were fighting for equal opportunity programs. They had internalized the civil rights movement. Reagan's well-publicized deregulation revolution had the unintended consequence of summoning those troops, who responded to Reagan's challenge by defending their activities with straight business arguments.

They recast many key equal opportunity innovations as part of the new "human resources management" paradigm. That paradigm then prospered as part of a rear-guard effort to defend equal opportunity programs when they came under attack. Management gurus hawked certain equal opportunity programs, mixed in with some new elements, as the main components of the HR paradigm. History, then, does not bear out the story that it was HR advocates who spearheaded things like performance evaluations and systems for airing complaints. They merely repurposed those things, and added to them some true innovations, such as teamwork and quality of worklife programs, which caught on later. The HR revolution was easily won because many of the innovations its proponents favored had already been put into place as equal opportunity measures.

Personnel experts pursued two different angles in reframing what they were doing. For one set of recent initiatives—grievance procedures, salary classification systems, performance evaluations, job descriptions, job posting—they revived straight business arguments under the rhetoric of human resources management. For the programs they could not so easily link to the HR paradigm, they developed a new language of diversity management, distancing their work from affirmative action. They recast race relations workshops as diversity training seminars, equal opportunity surveys as culture audits, and equal opportunity policies as diversity mission statements. They breathed new life into those programs with the language of diversity management. The diversity paradigm owed more than a little to a maverick in Reagan's cabinet. Labor secretary William Brock commissioned the Hudson Institute's 1987 report, *Workforce 2000*, which carried the message that white men would make up little of the twenty-first century workforce.[151] Corporate diversity experts found that they could win support for a set of new initiatives that came from the playbook of industrial psychology and sociology: diversity mentoring programs, networking programs, and task forces.

What they did conformed to an old sociological axiom, that people in organizations come to believe in the programs they administer and become ardent defenders of those programs (and their own offices) when they come under attack.[152] People defend entire organizations when they come under attack, for that matter.[153] What we saw in the 1980s and 1990s was a professional group that changed functions, as equal opportunity experts shifted from a focus on legal compliance to a focus on how diversity could increase productivity. Earlier the personnel profession had changed focus more generally. As its labor relations function faded, it found new life in managing equal opportunity, health and safety, and benefits regulations. Other expert groups have undergone similar changes after environmental shifts. Corporate accounting, for instance, was a back-office affair until the shareholder value paradigm offered accountants, in their CFO hats, the opportunity to manage the investor community.[154] One lesson is that professional groups, like organizations, can adapt when the environmental demand for their services dries up.

The literature on the professions has emphasized how different protoprofessional groups compete to gain control, and state licensure, in particular issue areas. I will argue in chapter 8 that in the case of sexual harassment policies, personnel experts and lawyers indeed competed for authority, but that the audience was not state regulators, it was CEOs who chose among alternative compliance solutions. Between the 1970s and the 1990s, however, the personnel profession was undergoing a more radical change. It had arisen to gain control of labor relations in firms. Now it won authority over a new realm. The profession was sustained by changing focus, and by claiming that its expertise was relevant to new problems. That claim was anything but obvious, for lawyers or general managers might just as well have staked their claims in the territory of affirmative action. The result was that in the end, personnel refashioned most of its professional tools as equal opportunity, and then diversity management, devices.

One-time Harvard Business School professor R. Roosevelt Thomas argued that diversity management was here to stay because there was a solid business rationale for it—it helped firms to manage a workforce that was becoming more diverse, and it helped them to design and market products for a customer base that was becoming more diverse. The business case for managing diversity was increasingly the only case heard in corporate America. Executives justified fair employment programs not with talk about slavery or social justice, but with business arguments. When the University of Michigan faced twin lawsuits challenging its admissions policies for undergraduates and law students in 2003, every amicus brief from the corporate world supported affirmative action with pure business arguments. General Motors' brief parroted diversity consultants: "cross-cultural competence" improves a firm's performance of "virtually all of its major tasks: (a) identifying and satisfying the needs of diverse customers; (b) recruiting and retaining a diverse work force, and inspiring that work force to work together to develop and implement innovative ideas; and (c) forming and fostering productive working relationships with business partners and subsidiaries around the globe." Sandra Day O'Connor's majority decision in one of those cases cited these business arguments liberally.[155]

Even if diversity experts were now making arguments about efficiency rather than about social justice, the new programs they sold still portrayed inequality as a consequence of organizational processes. By the early 1990s, diversity training programs, culture audits, mentoring programs, and networking programs signaled that bias could be embedded in organizational culture and tradition. Many expected that measures designed to prevent cultural bias would have a chilling effect on race relations in particular, leading whites to think that minorities were getting a free ride. That was not what happened. By the early 1990s, sociologist Marylee Taylor found, whites exposed to antidiscrimination programs at work were more likely to trace blacks' poor employment prospects to institutional discrimination than to individual failure. People working in firms with affirmative action programs were *more* likely to support it, *more* likely to believe that American institutions are biased against blacks, and *less* likely to believe that black disadvantage results from personal deficiencies.[156] On the whole the affirmative action and diversity programs of the 1980s led not to backlash, but to a more sociological understanding of discrimination among workers exposed to them.

■　■　■　■

THE FEMINIZATION OF HR AND WORK-FAMILY PROGRAMS

EARLY IN 1970, air force captain Susan R. Struck, a 28-year-old nurse serving at Camranh Bay in Vietnam, got pregnant. A devout Catholic, the unmarried Captain Struck decided to finish out the pregnancy and give the baby up for adoption. Captain Struck's plan was to continue her career in the air force. The air force had other plans. Under a policy of firing any employee who became pregnant, the air force discharged Captain Struck. Every year some 1,500 of the air force's 15,600 women got pregnant and had to leave.[1]

Many American companies had similar policies. Most had dropped their marriage bans for women by the end of the 1960s, on the theory that, because the Civil Rights Act required equal treatment of men and women, they would have to fire married men if they fired married women. But many executives reasoned that a policy requiring all pregnant workers to resign wouldn't affect men, and wouldn't contravene the principle of equal treatment.

When Captain Struck appealed to the Supreme Court, Solicitor General Erwin Griswold argued that "pregnancy diverts personnel from the primary function of fighting or support, and thereby impairs the readiness and effectiveness of the fighting force."[2] Facing Struck's appeal, the air force waived her discharge, allowing her to stay on. Yet the air force ban—with a new provision for waiver in individual cases—stayed in place, alongside bans at the army, navy, and marines.[3]

The armed forces, like corporate America, didn't fire just anyone who needed time off for medical reasons. Generals and CEOs had gotten accustomed to the idea that a worker who broke his arm had the right to take time off and to have his job waiting for him when he returned. Federal temporary disability insurance law was designed to give relief in exactly these situations, providing some pay while an injured or ill worker got well enough to return to his old job. Five states made temporary disability insurance mandatory; the other 45 required it for certain workplaces, often in the public sector. But for maternity, employers weren't offering disability pay and weren't guaranteeing that women could have their old jobs back. They were, by and large, requiring pregnant workers to resign.

In 1978, Congress required that companies with disability insurance offer coverage for maternity, and then in 1993, it required that all companies offer leaves, allowing new mothers and new fathers to take up to 12 weeks off and return to their old jobs. Yet by 1978, a majority of employers had maternity leave programs and, by 1993 nearly every large employer in the country had a program. Why did American employers create maternity leave programs before the law required them to? Some argue that companies were competing for women workers, yet firms put maternity leave programs in during the late 1970s, when it was a buyer's market for labor. Others credit the women's movement, yet the National Organization for Women (NOW) had picked other fights, particularly the Equal Rights Amendment and abortion rights.[4] While scholarship on maternity leave, like scholarship on corporate equal opportunity policies, has focused on the law or on social movements, the key agents of change were located in corporate personnel offices.[5]

Corporate maternity leave programs owe their existence to feminist activists, in government and in corporate personnel offices, and to the character of federal regulation. America's particular regulatory system helped activists in several ways. First, the common-law tradition created an opening for activists inside the government to define pregnancy bans as sex discrimination under the Civil Rights Act. The act didn't mention pregnancy, and the Supreme Court eventually rejected the claim that it outlawed pregnancy discrimination, but not before many leading firms replaced pregnancy bans with maternity leave policies. America's legal system thus made it possible for activists in government to change corporate behavior without changing the law.

Second, as we saw in chapter 6, by ramping up equal opportunity and affirmative action enforcement in the early 1970s without clarifying compliance criteria, Washington created an army of equal opportunity experts in personnel departments who became activists themselves. It was that increasingly feminized army that championed maternity leave programs long before Congress required them in 1993. Federalism had, moreover, made it possible for activists to win maternity leave laws in certain states, yet personnel managers put in maternity leave programs even in states without such laws. The burgeoning army of women in personnel advocated sexual harassment programs as well, as I discuss in the next chapter.

Third, politicians and corporate leaders had chosen, with little objection from unions, to create employer-based social insurance programs in the 1930s and 1940s.[6] Employers offered pension, disability, and health coverage, sometimes supplemented by public programs.

The employer-based social insurance model subsequently shaped what was imaginable and what was politically feasible. There was no serious discussion of a federal maternity leave program, or, when it came to later benefits, a federally mandated flexible work hours program or federal child care. Public policies encouraged private companies to do all of these things. Corporate personnel officers saw that it would be up to them to create work-family programs.

Once firms had maternity leave programs in place, personnel experts turned their attention to flexible work arrangements, which had recently spread from Europe as part of the quality of work-life movement and been given a boost by a federal demonstration project. They soon promoted child care benefits under the same umbrella, building on a new federal tax incentive, and then called for separate departments to manage work-family programs. By 2000, the typical Fortune 500 firm had a constellation of work-family programs in place. Personnel experts retheorized[7] flexible working arrangements and child care as components in the package of work-life programs, making arguments about both employee commitment and diversity. The high-minded language of equal opportunity had disappeared. The Civil Rights Act got the work-family ball rolling in the early 1970s, to be sure. Federal regulations encouraged various programs. Yet it was personnel managers committed to the cause who brought work-family programs to life.

From Pregnancy Bans to Maternity Leave

When the Civil Rights Act was passed, half of America's leading employers had formal policies requiring pregnant workers to resign (see figure 7.1).[8] Most allowed disability leaves for anything *but* pregnancy. Likewise, as Ruth Bader Ginsburg wrote in the *New York Times* in 1971, temporary disability insurance in most firms covered anything but pregnancy, that is, "all disabilities that both men and women incur, such as lung cancer, alcoholism, and skiing injuries, and all disabilities that only men incur, such as prostatectomies."[9] Some executives believed that pregnancy was different because it was voluntary, or because it was predictable in the lives of women.

The Women's Movement within Government

The women's movement was launched in 1966, with the formation of the National Organization for Women. Before that, women's rights advocates promoted their cause from federal offices. The Women's Bureau had been working in the Department of Labor since 1920 on protective legislation for women, and in the 1960s it expanded its mission by studying job segregation and wage discrimination and championing

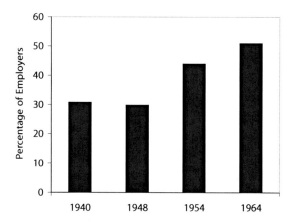

Figure 7.1. Employers Requiring Pregnant Workers to Resign (1940 through 1964)
Source: National Industrial Conference Board 1940, 1954, 1964.

equal pay legislation.[10] In 1961 Kennedy had created the 20-member President's Commission on the Status of Women, headed by Eleanor Roosevelt, which had spawned 48 state-level commissions by 1966. Beginning in 1964, the state commissions held an annual Conference of Commissions on the Status of Women. There were some women's rights advocates as well in the agencies charged with overseeing affirmative action edicts (the Office of Federal Contract Compliance) and the Civil Rights Act (the Equal Employment Opportunity Commission).

It was government officials—Richard Graham and Sonia Pressman from the EEOC; Mary Eastwood from Justice; Catherine East from the successor to the President's Commission on the Status of Women—who called for a grassroots women's movement that would promote the cause from outside of government. Like the OFCC, the EEOC focused on race, as Pressman, an attorney who joined the EEOC three months after its July 1965 founding, later recalled: "the overwhelming attitude at the commission was that they didn't want resources diverted to women's issues."[11] In 1966, at the third meeting of state commissions, the National Organization of Women was formed, electing Betty Friedan as its first president.[12] Historian Cynthia Harrison argues that the grassroots women's movement was a consequence, not a cause, of early activism within the government. Yet NOW wasn't credited with popularizing maternity leave even when it did take off, because it had bigger fish to fry, such as the Equal Rights Amendment, which passed the Senate in 1972. NOW raced to win passage in two-thirds of the states in the next decade.[13]

Federal Women's Advocates Define Pregnancy Bans as Illegal Advocates for women who had won positions in government could try to define pregnancy bans as illegal under the Civil Rights Act because the separation of powers allowed the executive and judicial branches to opine on what the law meant. The EEOC argued against corporate pregnancy bans in its 1966 annual report, claiming that providing "truly equal employment opportunities" meant protecting women's jobs during pregnancy and maternity.[14] Yet the EEOC did nothing to change employers' behavior, and allowed employers to exclude pregnancy from disability and health insurance programs.[15] In early 1966 the *New York Times* quoted a spokesman as saying that the commission was moving slowly on sex discrimination because "it did not want this area to interfere with its main concern, racial discrimination."[16] Aileen Hernandez, the lone woman among the five commissioners, reported that the mention of sex discrimination brought either "boredom" or "virulent hostility."[17] Only a handful of people at EEOC thought that the commission should be pursuing sex discrimination cases.[18] Executives detected waffling. A First National Bank of Cincinnati vice president noted that federal policy was unclear: "It is my understanding that while the EEOC favors the concept of maternity leaves, it has not agreed to a policy statement. Until such time, I shall follow my former policy"—of firing pregnant workers.[19] In 1967 a broad national survey suggested that few companies had put an end to pregnancy bans.[20]

While the EEOC waffled, the Citizen's Advisory Council on the Status of Women (CACSW), set up in 1963 to succeed the President's Commission on the Status of Women, recommended new rules on pregnancy.[21] Nixon had appointed a new slate of 20 members in 1969, made up of women from business and the professions, and headed by a World War II lieutenant colonel and volunteer for the March of Dimes, Jacqueline Goyette Gutwilling.[22] After consulting the Civil Service Commission, the OFCC, and Evangeline Swift of the EEOC, in 1971 the CACSW called for maternity to be treated like other disabilities. "Childbirth and complications of pregnancy are, for *all job-related purposes*, temporary disabilities and should be treated as such under any health insurance, temporary disability insurance, or sick leave plan of an employer, union, or fraternal society."[23]

In March 1972, the EEOC's new *Guidelines on Discrimination Because of Sex* took large chunks of the council report verbatim. Staffing and sentiments at the EEOC had changed. Employers committed discrimination when they required pregnant workers to resign and failed to offer maternity leaves with job guarantees. Neutral-sounding policies—"all pregnant workers must resign"—could be discriminatory if they targeted women. The guidelines made the front page of the *New York Times*:

> In the most sweeping revision of its guidelines on discrimination because of sex since they were first adopted in 1966, the employ-

ment commission now says that to deny a woman a job because she is pregnant is, on its face, a violation of the Civil Rights Act of 1964. . . . In addition, disabilities related to pregnancy, including recovery from childbirth, miscarriage and abortion, should be treated by employers the same as any other temporary disability in terms of leave time.[24]

EEOC's position was that employers could not refuse to hire, train, or promote a woman because of pregnancy.[25] If they provided leaves, health insurance, or income replacement for other temporary disabilities, they should do the same for maternity. Because the guidelines did not have the force of law, it was not clear that firms would follow them.

The Legal Battle Gives Personnel Experts Ammunition

The EEOC guidelines of 1972 came in the same year that the agency won the authority to initiate lawsuits. It was soon taking companies to court that did not abide by its guidelines. America's separation of powers had created an opening for the EEOC to rule that the Civil Rights Act covered pregnancy discrimination, and now the common-law tradition allowed lower courts to take sides. That was all the ammunition most personnel managers needed to fight for maternity leave programs. By the time the Supreme Court struck down lower-court rulings, leading firms had maternity leave programs in place. Then when Congress considered the Pregnancy Discrimination Act in 1978, CEOs who might have opposed the law a decade earlier, when they had pregnancy bans in place, didn't put up a fight because they were already in compliance.

To see how consequential American state structure was we need only engage in a thought experiment—what would have happened in France? Under France's civil law system, bureaucrats could not have ruled that an act outlawing sex discrimination in employment covered pregnancy discrimination, and judges could not have vetted the ruling.[26] Executives would not have read in *Le Monde* that pregnancy discrimination was illegal, and would not have been advised by consultants to offer maternity leaves and disability insurance. This was all immaterial by the time France got around to banning sex discrimination in employment, however, because France required employers to allow maternity leaves in 1913 and paid women during leaves through public sickness insurance as of 1946.[27]

How the Separation of Powers Promulgated Maternity Leave

General Electric had denied disability leaves and temporary disability insurance to pregnant workers on the theory that pregnancy is voluntary. In April 1974 Judge Robert Merhige of the District Court of Virginia found that, because GE covered voluntary disabilities such as sports injuries and cosmetic surgery, it could not exclude pregnancy alone: "That this is sex discrimination is self-evident."[28] The court of appeals upheld the decision in 1976.[29] Executives at other companies learned about the EEOC's position when they read in the papers of General Electric's legal fight.[30] If the separation of powers and the common-law tradition had allowed officials and judges to rethink what the Civil Rights Act covered, it was GE's challenge that promulgated the new interpretation through the press.

The GE case was the subject of 20 *New York Times* articles between 1972 and 1976 and was covered widely in the pages of *Business Week*, *Fortune*, and *Forbes*. In April 1974 the *Times* reported that, in the two years since the EEOC's guidelines were issued, the commission filed maternity leave suits against 11 big companies, hoping to maximize the impact of litigation by going after high-profile firms. In reporting on these suits, the *Times* warned: "Just as women have always known that it is impossible to be 'a little bit pregnant,' so the nation's employers are learning—from the Federal Government—that it is imprudent to be a little bit prejudiced against a pregnant employee."[31] *Business Week* reported in 1976 that, after the district court's 1974 decision, the EEOC filed more than 130 pregnancy discrimination suits and warned another 250 companies. The union that fought the case against GE soon brought charges against 73 other employers. According to *Business Week*, "Companies on the firing line include Westinghouse, RCA, Chrysler, Sperry Rand, Pennwalt, Honeywell, Philco-Ford, and Phelps Dodge."[32] Women's advocates within the EEOC, then, put some 400 big companies on notice even before the test case had run its course.

Figure 7.2 charts *New York Times* articles on maternity leave from 1970 to 1984, showing a spike in 1972 when the EEOC's guidelines came out, and then consistent coverage through 1977, the year after the Supreme Court ruling. EEOC's enthusiasm for the cause in the early 1970s can be seen in figure 7.3, which charts decisions in federal pregnancy discrimination decisions between 1965 and 1985, the bulk of which were pursued by the commission. Women's rights advocates in federal positions had successfully reinterpreted the Civil Rights Act to cover pregnancy discrimination, or so it seemed for a while.

The separation of powers and common-law tradition not only gave the EEOC and lower courts authority to propose their own definitions of the law. These state characteristics also meant that employers faced ongoing uncertainty and anxiety about just what Title VII would cover.

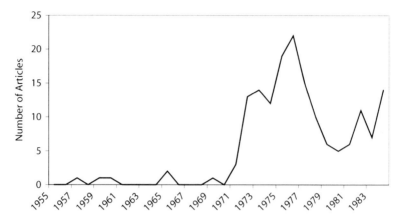

Figure 7.2. *New York Times* Articles on Maternity Leave (1966–83)

Source: Lexis-Nexis search of article titles and lead paragraphs for "maternity leave."

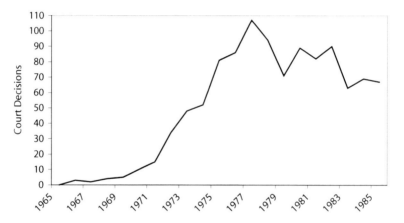

Figure 7.3. Federal Court Decisions in Maternity and Pregnancy Discrimination Cases (1965–85)

Source: Lexis-Nexis search of cases covering maternity or pregnancy discrimination.

The Women's Movement within Personnel Management

The champions of maternity protections in the federal government were joined by personnel experts in firms, who were increasingly attracted to the field by its new profile as protector of the disadvantaged. In 1960, personnel officers were white men who had trained in labor relations. From the early 1970s, when Congress, the president, and the

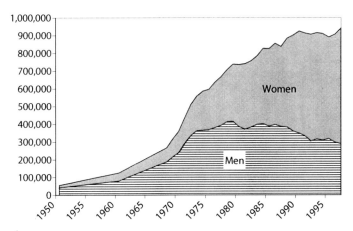

Figure 7.4. Increase in Women in Personnel Management (1950–95)

Note: Data on personnel specialists and managers, excluding clerical workers, from U.S. Decennial Census of Population and Current Population Survey of the Bureau of Labor Statistics.

Source: Annual data before 1968 are interpolated from the decennial census. http://factfinder.census.gov/ and http://www.census.gov/cps/, accessed November 1, 2006; Bureau of Labor Statistics 2006; U.S. Census Bureau 2006.

Supreme Court expanded the meaning of equal opportunity and the mechanisms to enforce it, women streamed into the profession. Census figures show that the number of personnel specialists and managers more than doubled between 1960 and 1970, and grew sixfold between 1960 and 1980.[33] That growth wasn't caused by growth in the workforce or in unions, for the workforce was up only 50 percent and unions were flat or down everywhere but in government.

By 1980 women made up half of personnel specialists and managers.[34] By the late 1990s, seven in 10 personnel specialists and managers were women. Personnel was no longer the dominion of white men trained to handle unions.[35] Women were more interested in personnel now, but personnel departments were also more interested in women, both because personnel managers practiced equal opportunity in hiring, and because they targeted women and minorities who could help them recruit. The percentage of personnel departments with blacks in clerical jobs nearly doubled between 1965 and 1967 alone, from 14 to 26 percent, according to one study.[36] Yet blacks and Hispanics gained ground much more slowly than did white women. While minorities held 10 percent of all personnel specialist and manager jobs by 1976, over the next 20 years they averaged only 12 percent.

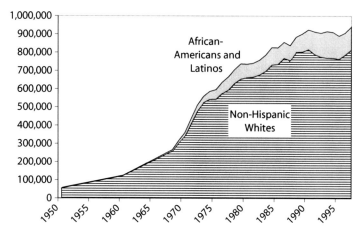

Figure 7.5. Increase in African-Americans and Latinos in Personnel Management (1950–95)

Source: See figure 7.4. Asians and others are grouped with whites.

Women's Advocates in Human Resources Promote Maternity Leave

Women in personnel led the charge to create maternity leave programs. Barbara Boyle, the IBM personnel executive turned consultant, reported in the *Harvard Business Review* in 1973 that leading firms had responded to the EEOC guidelines by adding pregnancy to their temporary disability insurance and leave plans: "IBM and Polaroid . . . have followed EEOC guidelines. . . . This helps reduce costly attrition and attracts feminine talent necessary to the business."[37] Articles in a wide range of venues offered advice on how to comply with the EEOC guidelines.[38] Many proclaimed that maternity leaves, with reinstatement rights, were now required under Title VII, despite the fact that the GE case was still wending its way through the courts. While the eventual disposition of the case was uncertain, Harry Edwards wrote in the *Labor Law Journal* that "reinstatements after childbirth will probably be required unless the employer can show that there is some compelling 'business necessity' which justifies a refusal to reinstate."[39]

The women executives Fretz and Hayman interviewed for the *Harvard Business Review* in the early 1970s argued that firms wasted women's talent by forcing them to resign when pregnant, or by assuming that their careers would come to an end when they gave birth: "Does it make good business sense to underutilize me during my employment based on the supposition that I will terminate for personal reasons sometime in the future? Why shouldn't my employer maximize my talents and contributions? Doesn't that make for a better investment in me as a human resource?"[40] Men's quit rates in management were not appreciably different from women's, Fretz and Hayman noted, and that fact tended to undermine the argument that women are a poor investment.

A Prentice Hall study of 108 employers in 1972 found that more than half were at least considering new maternity leave policies in the wake of the EEOC's guidelines.[41] One of America's 10 biggest industrial firms calculated that the new program would have cost it $12.7 million in 1971, based on 5,000 women collecting medical benefits for maternity.[42] EEOC commissioner Ethel Bent Walsh reported in 1974 in the *Labor Law Journal* that over three-fourths of banks and insurance companies had liberalized their maternity leave policies and benefits "as a direct result of [EEOC] Guidelines."[43] One study found that, between 1972 and 1975, two-fifths of employers made major changes in their maternity leave policies.[44] Another found that the number of firms offering maternity leave nearly tripled between 1969 and 1978.[45] With so many leading employers on board, the fate of maternity leave was all but sealed.

The Supreme Court Overrides the EEOC, Congress Overrides the Court

Late in 1976, the Supreme Court reversed the lower-court decisions in the GE case, relieving firms of the need to offer disability leaves for childbirth. Justice Rehnquist argued for the Court that excluding a condition from disability coverage as "a subterfuge to accomplish a forbidden discrimination" against women would be illegal if the condition were similar to covered conditions. But pregnancy is "not a 'disease' at all, and is often a voluntarily undertaken and desired condition."[46] Then, in 1978, Congress negated the Supreme Court's ruling with the Pregnancy Discrimination Act (PDA), which outlawed discrimination "on the basis of pregnancy, childbirth, or related medical conditions." The act required employers to treat women affected by these conditions "the same for all employment-related purposes," such as leaves and disability pay, as other persons "similar in their ability or inability to work."[47]

The Pregnancy Discrimination Act did not guarantee maternity leaves or disability pay. Employers that didn't offer these things for men with disabilities didn't have to offer them for pregnancy. It did affect the one-third of American workers with temporary disability insurance, under which jobs were guaranteed and compensation for lost wages was paid. One-third of workers are covered now, and one-third were covered then. Women, in fact, are less likely than men to be covered by disability insurance, in part because states encourage large employers to offer disability insurance, and women are more likely than men to work for small employers. Five states—California, Connecticut,

Hawaii, New Jersey, New York, and Rhode Island—make coverage mandatory but exempt small employers.[48]

The 1978 act faced little corporate opposition in part because equal opportunity managers had already created maternity leave programs and extended disability benefits in America's leading firms. Women's advocates in human resources kept up the pressure, and by the time of the Family and Medical Leave Act of 1993, three-quarters of America's medium-sized and large employers offered maternity leave.[49]

Some States Mandate Leaves: Employers Everywhere Install Them

Five states outlawed pregnancy discrimination between 1972 and 1981: Massachusetts, Connecticut, Montana, California, and Wisconsin. By 1993, another 20 had extended their disability leave laws to cover maternity or outlawed pregnancy disability for some groups, usually government workers.[50] But the diffusion of maternity leave continued apace. Women's advocates in personnel management put in maternity leave programs even in states that did nothing. We can see this by comparing California with a mandate, New Jersey with coverage under its disability law, and Virginia with no law. California's mandatory temporary disability insurance law was extended to include unusual pregnancies in 1973 and normal pregnancies in 1976.[51] In 1978 the state required all employers to offer pregnancy leaves of up to four months.[52] New Jersey was a first mover in 1961, covering eight weeks of maternity under its temporary disability program, and in 1980 it allowed doctors to determine the length of maternity disability.[53] Virginia provided no protection. Figure 7.6 charts the adoption of formal employer maternity leave programs in 279 workplaces in those states. After the 1960s, Virginia began to lag behind, but the rate of adoption increased in all three states. Moreover, thanks to a system of judicial enforcement of California's 1978 law, workers had to sue recalcitrant employers. Eight years after that law, more than a third of employers there had not put leave guarantees in writing.

Was Competition for Workers the Cause?

Some argued that companies put in maternity leaves voluntarily to compete for women workers, with no impetus from the law. In opposing a federal mandate, the United States Chamber of Commerce argued: "There is a growing sense, as the demographics of our work force change, that parental leave is a good benefit to have. . . . A recent Bureau of National Affairs survey showed that 90% of companies grant maternity leave. . . . We think that's terrific, so long as it's voluntary."[54] The Small Business Association wrote in 1991, "In the absence of any government mandate . . . between 74 and 90 percent of all businesses are

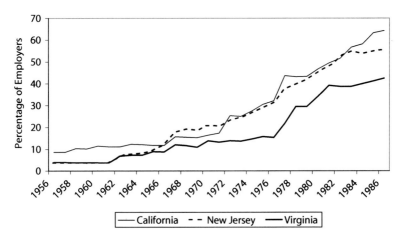

Figure 7.6. Adoption of Formal Protections for Maternity Leaves in Three States (1956–86)

Source: Survey of 279 employers in 1986 (Dobbin et al. 1993).

already addressing the problem."[55] After the Family and Medical Leave Act passed, presidential candidate Bob Dole argued in 1996 that Congress should not have used the "long arm of the federal government" to force employers to offer leaves, for "88 percent of the people" Clinton claimed credit for covering with the 1993 law "were already covered."[56] Companies had done this to win over women workers, Dole argued.

To suggest that employers offered maternity leave to attract workers was to forget the stagflation of the mid-1970s to the mid-1980s, which coincided with a doubling of the prevalence of leaves to 60 percent of employers.[57] As we see in figure 7.7, that period had the highest unemployment levels of any 10-year period between 1960 and 2006. Moreover, employers who offered maternity leave in the 1970s thought they were responding to a government mandate. The EEOC and two federal courts had found pregnancy discrimination to be illegal, and personnel experts argued that this was, or would soon be, black letter law.

Was Grassroots Activism the Cause?

Did the women's movement win corporate maternity leave programs? Historian Cynthia Harrison shows that the women's movement did little on this front. Women's groups had not fought for the Equal Pay or Civil Rights acts; in fact, in the early 1960s "the federal government experienced virtually no outside political pressure" for gender equality and faced no "extenuating circumstances that forced attention to programs for women."[58] Later, when women's advocates in Washington

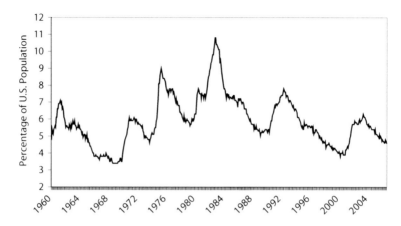

Figure 7.7. U.S. Unemployment Rates (1960–2006)

Source: Bureau of Labor Statistics 2006, Current Population Survey, at http://
data.bls.gov, accessed October 24, 2006.

were championing maternity leave, NOW focused its attention on abortion rights, the ERA, and hiring discrimination.[59] One reason was a split within the movement.[60] Groups such as NOW, the League of Women Voters, the National Women's Political Caucus, and the American Civil Liberties Union had opposed California's mandatory maternity leave law because, by singling out pregnancy, it seemed to be at odds with the Equal Rights Amendment.[61] In 1970 the Citizen's Advisory Council had warned against such special benefits for pregnancy.[62]

Some labor unions had also supported women's issues over the years, but unions did not lead the fight for maternity leave, even though some did join the battle.[63] At AFL-CIO biennial conventions, for instance, resolutions on family issues began to appear in the early 1970s, but there were never more than a couple in any year before 1984, when there were four of more per year for nine years in a row.[64]

The Family and Medical Leave Act of 1993

In 1993, Congress required employers to offer 12 weeks of unpaid leave to new mothers and fathers, allowing women who left to give birth to return to their jobs. That law had wide congressional support, in part because corporate America already had maternity leave programs in place. The idea of requiring companies to offer unpaid leaves had been kicking around Congress since 1985. After George H. W. Bush vetoed bills in 1991 and 1992, Bill Clinton campaigned on a promise to require employers to give leaves to new parents and workers with sick family members.[65] The Family and Medical Leave Act of 1993 requires leaves for men and women caring for a newborn, an adopted or foster child, or a sick family member, and for workers who themselves are ill or injured. If the very same job is not available when the leave is over, the employer must offer another with equal pay, benefits, and level of responsibility. Employee benefits are protected during the leave. The law covers employers with at least 50 workers within a 75-mile radius, and covers workers who have been on the job at least a year, and have worked at least 1,250 hours in that year.

Because personnel experts had already put maternity and medical leaves in place by 1993 (see figure 7.8), the main effect of the law was to popularize formal employer leave policies for paternity and for care of sick family members—the prevalence of each type doubled overnight. Maternity and medical leaves barely saw a bump in prevalence.

Corporate maternity leave had, in fact, already contributed to altering the behavior of young women. In 1975, 38 percent of women who became pregnant on the job returned to work after giving birth; by 1980, it was 51 percent, and by 1980, it was 68 percent. By the early 1990s, more than 75 percent of young women working full time were returning to work after childbirth. Economist Jane Waldfogel found that women who work for employers with guaranteed maternity leave have higher wages after childbirth than women who work for employers without such a policy—presumably because the former get their old jobs back.[66]

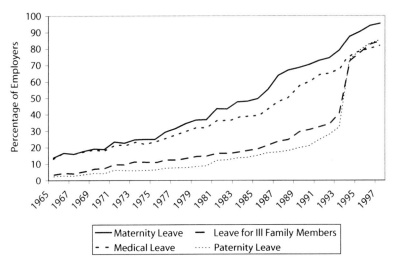

Figure 7.8. Employer Family and Medical Leave Programs (1965–97)
Source: Survey of 389 employers in 1997 (Dobbin and Kelly 2007).

The Crusade for Work-Family Programs

In most firms, maternity leave was the first battle work-family proponents won. The women who advocated work-family programs from their positions in human resources departments rarely claimed that they were required by the Civil Rights Act, for once the Supreme Court struck the idea that the act required maternity leave, there was little chance that the courts would find that it required flextime or child care assistance. If the Court had followed the lead of lower courts, deciding that the Civil Rights Act outlawed pregnancy discrimination, women's advocates might well have argued that it required other work-family benefits. Some did argue that those programs would help employers to show a "good faith" effort to end sex discrimination. As it was, flextime and compressed workweeks were framed instead as components of new "quality of work-life" programs, designed to increase employee commitment. Child care programs were heralded both for their capacity to allow workers to focus on their jobs, and for their capacity to keep women on the job.

Over time, human resources experts framed flextime and child care as part of a system of work-family programs, designed to help firms to attract and retain working parents, especially mothers. Ultimately, the rise of corporate work-family programs was a consequence of America's peculiar social insurance system, and tradition of using public incentives to shape corporate behavior. In other countries, parental leave, subsidized child care, and flexible working hours were implemented by states as social citizenship rights.[67] But the American way was to use federal incentives and demonstration projects to cajole private firms to offer these benefits. First, as we have seen, the EEOC tried to slip maternity leaves in under Title VII. Second, the General Accounting Office encouraged Congress to create flextime programs for federal workers, to reduce traffic congestion and improve morale, in the hope that private-sector employers would follow suit. Congress also created a part-time career program for federal workers, to help women juggling career and family, also with the idea that private firms would copy the program. Third, Congress encouraged worksite child care centers through tax incentives, and benefits experts invented the dependent care expense account to extend the tax benefit to workers in companies without on-site child care.[68] The result was a system of privately managed, work-based social benefits. That system was far from universal, though, for many employers opted out, and even employers with child care and flextime could select which employees could use the benefits.[69]

These new programs became popular only because the Civil Rights Act had created an advocacy group within the firm of human resources experts committed to the project of increasing opportunity for women.

Flexible Work Arrangements to Improve Efficiency

The German aerospace manufacturer Messerschmitt-Bolkow-Blohm (MBB) introduced flextime in 1967 to combat traffic congestion, tardiness, and absenteeism.[70] The idea was embraced by the "quality of work-life" movement whose leaders argued that flexibility increased job satisfaction and employee commitment. Thus, like everything from civil rights grievance procedures to performance evaluations, flextime was a part of the personnel arsenal before equal opportunity advocates embraced it and linked it to the work-family nexus of parental leave, family leave, child care, work-family workshops, and the rest of the flexible scheduling programs—job sharing, work-at-home arrangements, part-time career programs.[71] It became a measure to support gender diversity after the fact.

A German Hewlett-Packard plant followed MBB's example in 1967, and flextime spread from there to HP's U.S. plants in 1972. By 1977, HP had 22,000 workers using flextime.[72] Flextime programs typically establish a core set of hours and allow employees to select start and end times with their supervisors' approval. Related was the compressed workweek, in which full-time workers could complete 40 hours of work in four 10-hour shifts. Some entire plants shifted to compressed workweeks.[73]

HP's success had been widely linked to its founders' philosophy of demonstrating the company's commitment to its employees, and giving them both security and room to innovate. Flextime fit well with HP's anti-hierarchical philosophy, epitomized by its "open door" policy encouraging workers to share their concerns and ideas with their bosses and its famous participatory "Management by Walking Around" (MBWA).[74] The "HP Way" of doing things involved insurance benefits for all workers, profit sharing, a no-layoff commitment, and institutionalized corporate philanthropy.[75] William Hewlett described flextime as a way to make workers responsible for getting the job done, while allowing them to "plan their workday to gain more time for family leisure, [to] conduct personal business, avoid traffic jams, or satisfy other individual needs."[76] Flextime allowed workers to be on the job when they could do their best work. HP was soon experimenting with job sharing and with part-time career programs.[77]

At first flextime spread more rapidly in Europe, in part because U.S. overtime laws, union rules, and civil service regulations interfered with changes in the eight-hour day.[78] But HP was a model to many other firms, and others soon copied flextime. William Ouchi's 1981 best seller *Theory Z* lionized the company for its commitment to employees. In bad times HP had cut hiring, travel, and perquisites to keep employees on, and the result was "the lowest voluntary turnover rate, the most experienced workforce in the industry, and one of the highest rates of growth and profitability."[79] Personnel experts profiled the company in the business press, and when best-company lists proliferated in the 1980s and 1990s, HP was the one company nominated for every one of the 10 top lists.[80] Companies copied everything HP was doing, and flextime was no exception.

Personnel psychologists pointed to evidence that flextime improved job performance and attitudes, citing case studies done among European innovators.[81] When the Academy of Management published J. Carroll Swart's *A Flexible Approach to Working Hours* in 1978, it listed leading companies as participants in the flexible-hours movement: Occidental Insurance, Metropolitan Life, John Hancock, Northwestern Mutual, Eastern Airlines, Lufthansa North America, Sun Oil, Pacific Gas and Electric, Westinghouse, Scott Paper, Nestle, and Sandoz Pharmaceuticals.[82] Industrial psychologist Simcha Ronen argued in *Flexible Working Hours* that flexibility could reduce absenteeism and increase productivity.[83] Swart wrote in the *Harvard Business Review*, "Flexitime . . . is proving a big success in the vast majority of companies that have adopted it." Stanley Nollen reported that, in eight company studies using "hard data," productivity and morale were up, and reeled off a dozen side benefits, but nowhere mentioned work-family issues or gender equality.[84]

A Federal Demonstration Project for Flextime   Washington promoted flexible work arrangements in the 1970s under this efficiency rhetoric. Loath to dictate to industry, bureaucrats and legislators chose to create federal demonstration projects. The General Accounting Office (GAO) initiated experimental programs at the Bureau of Indian Affairs and at Social Security between 1972 and 1974, sparked by the same European experiments that had motivated HP. GAO hoped for improved morale and decreased commuting costs, and after the oil crisis of 1973 mentioned reducing oil use by alleviating traffic jams.[85] Congress extended the program in 1978 with legislation allowing federal agencies to implement voluntary flexible and compressed work arrangements. By 1985, 20 percent of federal workers used flexible or compressed work schedules, and Congress passed a permanent law.[86] The federal government became a demonstration project to show industry that these arrangements could work.

A Demonstration Project for Part-Time Careers   Congress also tried to set an example with a part-time career program, this time with the express goal of helping women with family demands. The House Civil Service Subcommittee, headed by Patricia Schroeder, wrote the

1978 act requiring agencies to allow federal workers to pursue careers working less than 40 hours a week when possible. The act mentioned the goal of providing "parents opportunities to balance family responsibilities with the need for additional income."[87] Schroeder was explicit about her desire to use the federal government as a model. "We made changes in the federal sector which we hope will serve as a model for employment policies in the private sector and in state and local government."[88]

HR Experts Redefine Flexibility as a Work-Family Issue Well into the 1980s flextime was being promoted with little or no mention of gender equality or work and family. In a 1981 report *Business Week* focused on productivity, tardiness, and absenteeism, and reported that 12 percent of companies had flextime, up from 5 percent in 1976.[89] Even the doyenne of corporate gender studies, *Men and Women of the Corporation* author Rosabeth Moss Kanter, described flextime in 1986 simply as part of the "quality of worklife" program designed to improve employee commitment.[90]

Personnel experts began to promote flextime in the business press as a strategy for gender equality. In 1980, Kenneth Marino advised in the journal *Personnel* that employers should pursue the "good-faith effort" strategy to show their commitment to equal opportunity for women, which included day care services and "flexible working hours for women with small children."[91] Merck personnel director Art Stratham put in flextime as part of a new portfolio of work-family practices, arguing, "If you help take away some of the stresses associated with family life, then when an employee comes to work, he or she will be able to put that much more attention to work."[92] A 1988 *New York Times* article cited Nestle's experience with a flextime program "developed to accommodate working mothers of small children." A MONY Financial Services HR director reported that flexible scheduling had helped her manage her own family duties, and that it was "one of MONY's most effective tools for recruiting and retaining good employees"—particularly women like herself.[93] When IBM expanded its flextime program that year as part of a new work-family package, a spokesman reported: "We're trying to deal with the whole concept of the balance between work and family life." IBM's VP of personnel reported, "IBM's work force mirrors changes in the national employment demographics, with more working women, dual-career couples, single parents." Women made up 30 percent of the firm's 228,000 workers, and "the trend is straight up."[94] In 1989, AT&T announced a new contract that included a host of work-family programs, including a new flextime policy that allowed employees to take two hours off at a time.[95]

In the early 1990s, human resources experts published a flurry of articles and books framing flextime, job sharing, work-at-home programs, and part-time career options as work-family programs designed to help women (and sometimes men) to balance career and family.[96] This was the best bet for increasing the number of women on the payroll, they suggested.

The Spread of Flextime   Human resources experts made flexible working arrangements widely popular among large firms. The Administrative Management Society found that flextime programs expanded from 15 percent of firms in 1977 to 29 percent in 1986.[97] A 1984 survey of industry leaders found that 32 percent had created flextime programs since 1980.[98] Sociologist Kathleen Christensen's study for the Conference Board found in 1987 that 46 percent of more than 500 large firms surveyed had flextime programs, and another 7 percent were looking into them.[99] When the consultancy Hewitt Associates surveyed benefits directors at 100 large industrial firms in 1988, 72 percent expected "major growth" in flextime, making it one of the top four areas of growth.[100]

Studies showed that flextime and part-time careers, the programs with federal demonstration projects, spread more quickly than programs without federal support, such as job sharing and work-at-home programs. A 1986 survey of 1,618 companies found that 35 percent had flextime, 34 percent had part-time career programs, 11 percent had job-sharing programs, and 10 percent had work-at-home programs.[101] In 1994 Joanne Miller found that 62 percent of 312 leading companies had flexible work hours, 44 percent had job-sharing or part-time programs, and 25 percent had work-at-home programs.[102]

Figure 7.9 presents results from my broad national surveys, and it suggests that even middling firms were jumping on the flexibility bandwagon. Here again, the programs with federal backing, flextime and part-time careers, come out ahead. About one-third of firms had a flextime policy, and only slightly fewer had a formal policy allowing part-time to full-time transitions, which are part and parcel of the part-time career system. About a quarter had a compressed workweek program by 2002, and one in five had a work-at-home program. Job sharing was still spreading as of 1997, when we last asked about it. All programs were becoming more popular, despite the fact that human resources managers were reluctant to put in some programs for fear that they would be overwhelmed by demand.[103]

Unlike grievance procedures, performance evaluations, or job posting, these programs were not universal within the firm that adopted them, as sociologists Erin Kelly and Alexandra Kalev found in their 2006 study. Every company they surveyed gave supervisors the final

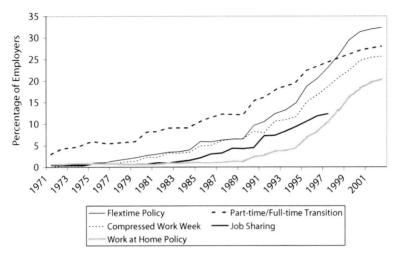

Figure 7.9. Employer Flexible Scheduling Policies (1971–2002)

Source: Surveys of 829 employers in 2002 and 389 employers in 1997 (Dobbin and Kelly 2007; Kalev, Dobbin, and Kelly 2006). Job-sharing data from the 1997 survey.

say in program use.[104] Employers might have left maternity leave to the discretion of supervisors as well, but maternity leave programs were designed in the 1970s to conform to civil rights law, which was framed around individual rights. Moreover, unlike programs such as temporary disability insurance, flexible work arrangements did not fall under fringe benefit regulations, which since 1974 had required employers to make benefits with tax-deductible costs universal. Flexible arrangements did not carry deductible costs.[105] If flexible work programs had been framed as Title VII accommodations, or if accountants had treated their costs as a tax deduction, personnel could have contended that the law required that they be offered universally.

Build It and They Will Come?   Do employees make use of flexible work arrangements that require supervisory approval, and that may contravene the "ideal worker" norm of unstinting commitment to the firm?[106] Kathleen Christensen's 1988 survey of 521 leading companies is telling.[107] The third column in table 7.1 shows the median number of workers using each policy among firms with the policy. The median number of flextime users by company was 250 to 300 depending on industry. But the median for work-at-home programs was from 3 to 5, and for job sharing it was from 2 to 3. Apart from flextime, workers appeared reluctant to use the new programs. Recall that by the late 1970s,

TABLE 7.1.
Prevalence and Utilization of Flexible Work Arrangements (1988)

	Employers Permitting	Company Policy	Median Number of Workers Using*	Percentage of Users Who Are Women
Flex-Time Compressed	50%	27%	250–300	63%
Work Week	36%	17%	30–71	40%
Job-Sharing	22%	6%	2–3	95%
Working at Home	7%	2%	3–5	60%

* The third column shows the range of medians across three industry categories.
Source: Christensen 1989. The sample is 521 leading firms.

22 percent of HP employees had signed on. The next most popular program, the compressed workweek, was used mostly by men, perhaps because women with children are reluctant to be on the job 10 hours a day or perhaps because the program is most often available in manufacturing firms with male workforces. Over 90 percent of the job-sharers were women, as were over 60 percent of those using flextime.[108]

The Economic Recovery Act of 1981 and Corporate Child Care

The women's movement does not take credit for workplace child care programs, for NOW and other groups did no more to promote child care than they had done to promote maternity leave. Dana Friedman, a researcher on women's issues at the Conference Board, complained in 1986 that activists neglected working women: "It's not that in the end they didn't sign off on child care initiatives, but they never put any real effort into this area."[109] As Albert Hunt wrote in the *Wall Street Journal* in 1986, "The highly visible and vocal National Organization for Women is curiously subdued" on the issue of child care: "In resolutions passed at last summer's convention, NOW devoted almost three times more attention to lesbian and gay parenting rights than to child-care issues."[110]

As in the case of flextime, federal initiative got the ball rolling. The Economic Recovery Act of 1981 encouraged workplace child care by making it tax deductible, as the sponsor explained: "dependent care provided by an employer is not taxed as income to the employee."[111] HR experts and consultants then led the charge, promoting on-site child care centers and child care vouchers under the new law. They argued that child care programs could pay for themselves in increased employee commitment and decreased turnover. Campbell Soup CEO

Gordon McGovern put in a child care center in the mid-1980s and found new applicants flocking to the company, "We started hiring people we couldn't hire before, because they were able to bring their children to the center. . . . I'm told people think we care about them for the first time. And people are telling me, 'This place is different now.'"[112] A 1992 study in *Personnel Psychology* found that on-site child care can "significantly affect employee attitudes and membership behaviors such as recruitment and retention."[113] Proponents in HR argued that company centers paid for themselves: "Fel-Pro and Johnson & Johnson, have conducted formal evaluations that link their company's child care center . . . with high levels of employee commitment and initiative. . . . Union Bank found a 2:1 return on its investment in terms of its annual savings from reduced turnover and absenteeism and free publicity."[114] The company without the demand or space to set up a center could offer child care vouchers, which allowed employees to use the company subsidy at nearby privately operated child care centers.

Human Resources Consultants Devise the Dependent Care Expense Account   Erin Kelly finds that the most popular child care benefit today, the dependent care expense account, was devised by personnel consultants in response to the 1981 act.[115] The legislation was set up to subsidize on-site child care, but leading personnel consultants—such as Hewitt Associates and Towers, Perrin, Forster, and Crosby—convinced the IRS to allow expense accounts under the law, funded with pretax income. This would permit workers who couldn't make use of on-site child care, or whose employers lacked the resources to offer it, to take the tax benefit.[116] The pitch to employers was that they could offer a tax benefit to workers for the cost of program management, a service that the consultancies offered. Employers escaped paying Social Security contributions for up to $5,000 in income diverted into expense accounts, and that could defray program management costs. The accounts benefited high-wage workers, saving a worker in the top tax bracket up to $1,980 as of 2000, but a single parent making $26,250 only $750. Low-wage workers benefited more from the Child and Dependent Care Credit.

Employers who couldn't afford on-site centers often settled for expense accounts. A corporate HR manager told us in 2001 that her female CEO wanted to buy a house to set up on-site child care but couldn't justify the cost. Then a consultant broached the expense account: "We have an insurance consultant and he does a fantastic job of keeping us up to date. . . . He came in and recommended it and said other people are doing this." A police department HR manager in 2001 told us that her chief of police wanted to build a center with a parking garage above so that "employees can park for free and drop their kids off." She judged this to be unaffordable: "And so we have a dependent care spending account program."

It was often the same vendors of benefits services that offered child care referral services. Work/Family Directions was created to help IBM provide referral services to its workers, starting in 1984. By 1997 it had more than 100 Fortune 500 clients and more than 500 employees, offering dependent care referral through local listings across the country.[117] Over time, child care referral services covered elder care referrals, and often counseling for a wide range of work-family issues, from addiction to marital strife. Stride Rite shoes was one of the first companies to open an elder care center, alongside its Cambridge child care center in 1989, nearly 20 years after it first built an on-site child care center.[118]

Dependent care expense accounts took off in the mid-1980s, and they were followed by referral services and on-site child care and vouchers, both of which helped to subsidize employee costs. In the 1988 Hewitt survey of 100 large industrial firms, 66 percent expected "major growth" in employer-sponsored day care in the near future.[119] Figure 7.10 shows that, by 2002, two-thirds of firms in our broad national sample offered dependent care expense accounts, about a quarter had child care referral services, and less than one in 10 offered on-site child care. Another broad survey of 1,059 employers in 1998 found a similar pattern, with 50 percent offering expense accounts and 9 percent offering on-site child care.[120] Large companies were more likely to have on-site child care, and this is borne out in our survey as well as in

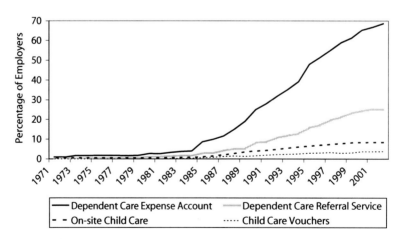

Figure 7.10. Employer Dependent Care Expense Accounts, Dependent Care Referral Services, and On-site Child Care and Child Care Vouchers (1971–2002)

Source: Survey of 829 employers in 2002 (Kalev, Dobbin, and Kelly 2006).

sociologist Joanne Miller's 1994 survey of 312 big firms, of which 19 percent had on-site child care.[121]

The Professionalization of Work and Family Management

As the issues of maternity leave, child care, and flexible working arrangements were promoted by the increasingly feminized human resources profession, work-family advocates won their own desks in human resources. Work-family positions began to take off only in the late 1980s, long after maternity leave, flextime, and dependent care programs were popular in America's biggest firms. A Conference Board survey from 1990, *The Emerging Role of the Work-Family Manager*, found that 60 percent of firms with the position had created it in the previous two years.[122] Deborah Shalowitz wrote in *Business Insurance* in 1992, "Although some benefits managers have a defined role in helping employees balance work and family responsibilities, employers increasingly are hiring or appointing special work and family managers to handle these issues."[123] These managers became internal champions for expanding work-family programs, just as equal opportunity officers became internal champions for diversity programs. In its 1990 survey of 68 work and family managers, the Conference Board found that companies appointed managers to signal their commitment to working families, and that managers became advocates for work-family issues, introducing new programs and educating executives about how leading companies were defining "best practices."[124] For sociologist Arlie Hochschild, these new work-family managers take on the role of social workers, and "Like many social workers, they [are] both part of the system and ideologically critical of it."[125]

Human resources experts had learned in the 1980s that the "business case" for diversity won them points with top management. As one newly appointed work-family manager reported in 1990, "They really want to be sure that if they've gone out on a limb to create my job, that there's going to be some benefit. Either it's going to save the company money or we're going to get a higher rating on my client survey—something tangible."[126] One study found that "defining and communicating the business case is the most important and pervasive part of the job," and quoted one work-family manager as saying: "I market 99 percent of the time."[127] In a book presenting model family-friendly organizations, Morgan and Tucker advise managers to "make the business case. Find out what the competition is doing. Cite the bottom line return in lower turnover and recruitment casts, improved morale, and increased productivity."[128] When Erin Kelly analyzed the rationales for work-family programs put forward in 130 articles in the management and mainstream press, she found that the vast majority made the business case, in one guise or another, and only 7 mentioned anything about women's employment opportunities.[129]

Many experts linked new work-family programs to the high-performance work systems movement of the 1980s and 1990s, which encouraged programs that demonstrated the employer's commitment to workers.[130] MIT labor economist Paul Osterman shows that companies that embraced high-performance work systems were most likely to install work-family programs.[131]

The popularization of work-family coordinators, and indeed of the specific programs, was fueled in part by the rise of company rankings that focused on work-family issues. With *Fortune's* "100 Best Companies to Work for in America" and *Working Mother's* "100 Best Companies for Working Mothers," firms began to compete in work and family benefits. *Fortune* ranks companies on pay, job growth, turnover, attention to work-family balance, women and minority workers, as well as on specific benefits, such as on-site child care (33 of 100 companies on the 2006 list had it).[132] While *Working Mother* relies on self-reports of programs, *Fortune* also tries to gauge workers' experience through a random-sample survey. The lists have stimulated articles proffering advice on how to get onto the lists, and one study found that listed companies get a stock price boost.[133]

In figure 7.11 we see that work-family workshops began to take off in the late 1980s, and work-family staff positions began to show up

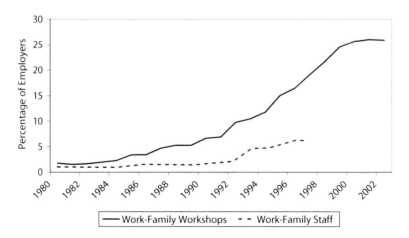

Figure 7.11. Work-Family Workshops and Staff (1980–2002)

Source: Surveys of 829 employers in 2002 and 389 employers in 1997 (Dobbin and Kelly 2007; Kalev, Dobbin, and Kelly 2006). Data on staffing is from the 1997 survey.

just a few years later. Workshops are often run by diversity managers in firms too small to have their own work-family, or work-life, managers. By 2002, more than a quarter of firms offered workshops. Our time line for staff positions ends in 1997, the year our survey covered that position.

Conclusion

The story people tell about corporate work-family programs is a market story about the growing number of working parents and steps firms had to take to compete for their services. Thus Bob Dole had argued on the presidential campaign trail that women's presence in the workforce drove firms to put in maternity leave. The reality is more complex, and more political. The federal government played a larger role in promoting maternity leave than Dole acknowledged. Women's rights advocates in the Citizen's Advisory Council and the Women's Bureau and then the EEOC pushed for it. Because of the separation of powers, these groups were able to expand the Civil Rights Act to cover pregnancy discrimination, at least until the Supreme Court overruled them. The stick they carried was the potential that courts would side with the EEOC, defining pregnancy discrimination as illegal. Maternity leaves became popular not despite the fact that the courts were still waffling, but because the waffling won news coverage. Executives were constantly reminded that firing a worker absent for childbirth might land them in court. Battles between the three branches of government, then, served to promulgate a regulation that, in the end, did not stand. Companies responded to this imbroglio because the Civil Rights Act had led to the feminization of personnel, and thereby created a group of champions of work-family programs within the firm. Those advocates would later promote flexible scheduling and child care programs with efficiency arguments, and would bring those programs together in the 1990s under new work-family coordinators.

It wasn't competition for workers that led companies to put new maternity leave programs in, because maternity leave spread when unemployment was setting postwar records. It wasn't the women's movement that spurred companies on, for NOW was focused on passage of the Equal Rights Amendment and on abortion rights.[134] Instead, uncertainty over the scope and requirements of civil rights and affirmative action law had spawned a cadre of equal opportunity experts within firms. Those experts developed work-family programs, beginning with maternity leave in the 1970s, which they installed in response to news accounts suggesting that the Civil Rights Act required it. When the Supreme Court ruled otherwise, they continued undeterred.

Once companies had installed maternity leave, Congress could out-law pregnancy discrimination because corporate opposition had been quelled. Thus as maternity leave became ubiquitous in America's big-gest corporations, Congress passed the Pregnancy Discrimination Act of 1978, requiring employers to treat maternity like any other disability. Then finally in 1993, when many medium-sized companies had mater-nity leave programs, Congress passed the more sweeping Family and Medical Leave Act. While government regulations got the ball rolling, the champions of women's rights in newly feminized personnel de-partments took the ball and ran with it. The personnel managers who advocated maternity leave, flextime, and child care made efficiency ar-guments about these programs from the start, although some added that these programs could demonstrate a good-faith effort to provide equal opportunity to women in the event of a sex discrimination charge.

Congress also pushed for flextime and workplace child care, though not as part of a systematic effort to expand equal opportunity. It cre-ated demonstration projects for flextime programs and part-time ca-reers, and then tax breaks for on-site child care, which consultants reinvented, with the IRS's blessing, creating tax-free dependent care ac-counts. In that case, the separation of powers enabled a federal agency to dramatically expand upon Congress's intent; in contrast to the case of maternity disability coverage, the expansion stuck. The whole menu of corporate work and family policies was promoted by Washington, but it was promoted piecemeal and indirectly.

Executives came to see a more tenuous connection between most work-family policies and fair employment law than they saw be-tween targeted recruitment, job posting, or equal opportunity griev-ance procedures and the law.[135] In fact, those general antidiscrimination measures had no more support in case law than did the work-family measures. The history of work-family policies thus underscores how law-like the other programs had become in the minds of executives as well as workers.

In other developed countries, maternity leave, flexible work hours, and child care are government programs. In France or Canada or Ger-many, the government chooses a level of benefits and that level becomes universal. Part of the reason for America's exceptionalism is that Con-gress was unsure of its own authority. The Constitution and its Tenth Amendment reserved some powers for the states. This kept alive the founders' concern that the government might descend into the sort of tyranny they had felt at the hands of the British. Even in the legislation it did pass, Congress signaled its uncertainty about its authority to dictate to firms. In the Civil Rights Act, it invoked its authority over interstate commerce. In the Pregnancy Discrimination Act, it invoked language of equal protection from the Fourteenth Amendment. By leaving it to employers to devise programs, Washington fueled the rise of work-family managers and departments that ran programs of their own making. Human resources consultants advised firms to create offices to manage parental leave, family leave, flextime, compressed workweeks, part-time career programs, job sharing, work-at-home programs, on-site child care, child care vouchers, dependent care expense accounts, dependent care referral services, and work-family workshops. Once they had a toehold, work-family managers championed new innovations. Now the movement for working women had a desk within the firm.

■   ■   ■   ■

SEXUAL HARASSMENT AS EMPLOYMENT DISCRIMINATION

THE CITY OF BOCA RATON sits on the Atlantic coast of Florida between West Palm Beach and Fort Lauderdale. In the spring of 1990 former city lifeguard Nancy Ewanchew wrote to the head of personnel
complaining of harassment. The city disciplined supervisors Bill Terry
and David Silverman. Two months later Beth Ann Faragher, who was
working her way through college as a lifeguard, quit when she tired
of the same two supervisors groping her, talking dirty, and simulat-
ing sex acts. Neither Faragher nor Ewanchew had filed formal complaints when they worked for the city, but they later sued under the
Civil Rights Act. The Supreme Court recognized that Boca Raton had
a sexual harassment grievance procedure, but faulted it for failing to
make it known to workers.[1]

In this and a companion case, the Court for the first time specified policies that could insulate employers from liability for sexual harassment.[2]
Justice Anthony M. Kennedy wrote that "Title VII is designed to encourage the creation of antiharassment policies and effective grievance
mechanisms."[3] Those words signaled just how successful feminists had
been in defining sexual harassment at work as employment discrimination, and how successful human resources experts had been in defining
the remedy. In 1964 it would have surprised backers of the Civil Rights
Act to hear that it was designed to outlaw sexual groping and dirty talk,
much less that it was designed to encourage harassment policies and
grievance procedures. Once again, the structure of federal authority had
enabled women's advocates in federal agencies to expand the definition
of sex discrimination, and this time, in contrast to the experience with
pregnancy discrimination, the Supreme Court went along.

As for a legal remedy to the problem of harassment, the Court found
that a proper, well-advertised grievance procedure could be used in a
defense where sexual comments and horseplay created a "hostile environment," but not in the quid pro quo cases that feminist legal theorist
Catharine MacKinnon had dubbed "put out or get out." Then, in 1999,
in *Kolstad v. American Dental Association*, the Court determined that

harassment prevention training could protect employers in these same cases.[4] The Court said that employers had a safe harbor from punitive damages if they "adopt anti-discrimination policies and . . . educate their personnel on Title VII's prohibitions."[5]

These cases might have led to an explosion in sexual harassment grievance procedures and training programs, but by then 95 percent of corporations had grievance procedures and 70 percent had training.[6] These provisions had spread despite the fact that, before 1998, courts had given little encouragement to employers with grievance procedures. By 1993, employers had only trotted out civil rights grievance procedures in a few dozen Title VII suits of any sort, and in only 16 had federal courts even hinted that they could help.[7] By that time, personnel experts had sold harassment grievance procedures to 60 percent of employers, according to my broad national survey. Meanwhile, a number of lawyers had been advising employers to avoid grievance procedures. Did the personnel profession beat lawyers at their own game by predicting the Supreme Court's position?

The case of sexual harassment illustrates what Lauren Edelman calls the endogeneity of the law.[8] Compliance standards were worked out by the regulated, through a national network of human resources specialists. The Supreme Court followed their lead, but not until most employers themselves had voted. The Court had declined entreaties to vet grievance procedures between 1986 and 1998. Harassment grievance procedures and training programs did not become popular because they were lawful, they became lawful because HR experts had made them popular.

While the women's movement secured the recognition of harassment as employment discrimination, it lost control of corporate remedies just as the civil rights movement lost control of corporate remedies to job discrimination. HR experts took over, modeling harassment grievance procedures on civil rights and union grievance procedures, and modeling harassment sensitivity training on race relations workshops and management sensitivity training.

Corporate attorneys weighed in on how firms should protect themselves, and the battle between HR and legal experts holds interesting lessons for the changing relations between corporations and the professions. Lawyers warned that grievance procedures would give employers notice of harassment, making them susceptible under the "knowledge" standard of liability. Or they suggested that, as procedures ran their course, complainants would sue, and judges would be skeptical of remedies adopted in the face of suit. The early legal wisdom was that harassment should be dealt with swiftly and decisively, with legal counsel on hand. Executives embraced grievance procedures nonetheless, for they preferred HR's promise of a bureaucratic vaccine to attorneys' case-by-case approach.

The case of harassment demonstrates the increasing importance of corporate executives in vetting professional groups, a task historically carried out by the state. The American state's reluctance to dictate the terms of compliance to firms put executives in a position to choose from compliance strategies offered by different professions. In choosing, they licensed one profession over another. Personnel won out because executives looked for a routinized solution, and personnel had one to offer. Lawyers, true to form, hesitated to prescribe a bureaucratic solution before the courts had ruled. Perhaps the lesson is that professions that best cater to executives' preferences prevail in such contests for jurisdictional authority. Groups that promise ways to reduce legal risk, whether in safety, accounting, corporate governance, antitrust, or civil rights, may win when executives are the ones choosing—even when that promise is empty. In this case, the promise proved to be self-fulfilling.

The stylized corporate response to the problem of harassment emerged in no small part because the law was a moving target. America's common-law system and separation of powers left the door open for the executive and judicial branches to recognize new forms of discrimination—both quid pro quo and hostile environment harassment—and also to select a compliance standard. HR could credibly claim that the courts would arrive at an expansive definition of harassment and would accept as a defense a two-pronged remedy based in the ideas that training could effect behavioral change, and that a grievance procedure constituted a fair hearing.

In the years since 1990, the feminization of the human resources profession contributed to a shift toward corporate equal *gender* opportunity programs. The profession became disproportionately female, but it never matched the population's percentages of African-Americans or Latinos. The EEOC continued to receive large numbers of race discrimination complaints, yet, in these years, much of the action in the workplace surrounded work-family and harassment issues. As the civil rights movement moved into the firm, then, the fact that it was now populated by white women shaped the issues the movement-within-the-firm would take up.

The Women's Movement Defines Harassment as Discrimination

The women's movement made harassment a public issue, and gained power for the cause by defining it as employment discrimination under the Civil Rights Act. Most countries in Europe treated harassment as individual, rather than organizational, wrongdoing. France defined it as an act of violence alongside assault. Throughout Europe, sanctions were weak and were rarely enforced, even after the EU required member states to outlaw it.[9] In the United States, once harassment was defined as employment discrimination, it gained a natural constituency among corporate personnel experts handling Title VII.

In the early 1970s Catharine MacKinnon had argued, from her pulpit on the Yale law faculty, that sexual harassment at work constitutes sex discrimination under Title VII.[10] In 1975 Susan Meyer and Karen Sauvigné from the Human Affairs Program at Cornell established the Working Women United Institute and held the first "Speak-Out on Sexual Harassment."[11] Feminists argued that harassment was on the rise as women moved into men's jobs. Gloria Steinem contended that it was about power, calling harassment "a reminder of powerlessness—a status reminder."[12] In 1976 National Organization for Women president Betty Friedan argued, "To every woman who has had it happen, the initial feeling is that there is something wrong with me. . . . Slowly people are becoming aware that it is a problem that is happening to other people."[13]

Unions quickly picked up the idea. Screen Actors Guild president Kathleen Nolan told the *Washington Post* in January 1976, "We are more than ever finding that the casting couch still exists." The Guild's new contract forbade harassment and all job interviews conducted outside of the office, and in October 1975 the Guild set up a "morals complaint bureau" to hear harassment grievances.[14] That same month, Washington, DC's police union set up a new harassment grievance procedure after the *Post* carried a series on harassment of policewomen.[15] These first grievance procedures were based directly on union grievance systems administered by personnel departments.

Employees soon demanded action. United Nations workers complained that bosses pressured subordinates for sex and asked the UN to do something about it. Business students at Boston's all-female Simmons College demanded that harassment be covered in their training. Program director Margaret Henning argued that corporations were ignoring the issue: "With any other business problem [corporations] would have had people hard at work researching and planning. But as far as we can tell, nobody is doing anything." The Human Rights Commission of the City of New York wrote restrictions on "the abuse of sexual privacy" for corporate affirmative action programs. The EEOC had been convinced by early feminist advocacy, and in a 1975 harassment case against Bausch and Lomb filed a friend-of-the-court brief backing the plaintiff.[16]

A score of books about harassment appeared, including Carroll Brodksy's *The Harassed Worker* in 1976; Lin Farley's *Sexual Shakedown: The Sexual Harassment of Women on the Job* in 1978; the Cambridge

Alliance Against Sexual Coercion's *Fighting Sexual Harassment* in 1979; and the Mao's-Little-Red-Book for the antiharassment movement, Mac-Kinnon's *Sexual Harassment of Working Women* in 1979.[17] The popular press joined the bandwagon with articles such as Margaret Mead's "A Proposal: We Need Taboos on Sex at Work" for *Redbook*.

The idea that harassment might be illegal was revolutionary in many quarters. A 1936 article in *Harvard Law Review* pointed out that while "women have occasionally sought damages for mental distress and humiliation on account of being addressed by a proposal of illicit intercourse" at work, courts took the view that without "incidental assault or battery, or perhaps trespass to land" no law had been broken. The *Review* concluded that "there is no harm in asking."[18] Even in the 1970s, Stop ERA founder Phyllis Schlafley rewrote the old saw, "Men never make passes . . . ," in her Senate testimony: "Sexual harassment on the job is not a problem for virtuous women, except in the rarest cases. Men hardly ever ask sexual favors of women from whom the certain answer is no. Virtuous women are seldom accosted."[19]

MacKinnon defined two kinds of harassment as sex discrimination under Title VII, quid pro quo harassment in which a job depends on succumbing to sex, and hostile environment harassment in which sexual language or groping taint the workplace. Courts accepted the first definition in 1977, but it was not until 1986 that the Supreme Court accepted the second, 14 years after courts had recognized racial epithets at work as Title VII discrimination.[20]

Three Courts Side with Feminists

Federal judges initially rejected the idea that quid pro quo harassment amounted to employment discrimination. The courts first saw a sexual harassment claim in March 1972. Diane Sanchez Heiman charged that Jack Scholl, a vice president of Dr. Scholl's shoe company, told her she must sleep with him to keep her job, and that "no such conditions were placed upon the employment" of men.[21] In 1974 a district court dismissed *Barnes v. Train*, a quid pro quo case brought by a federal worker, with the argument that harassment "does not evidence an arbitrary barrier to continued employment based on plaintiff's sex," and reasoned that Congress had not intended to cover harassment.[22] Another federal court sided with defendant Bausch and Lomb, arguing that discrimination cases typically target company policies, whereas the conduct in question "appears to be nothing more than a personal proclivity, peculiarity, or mannerism. By his alleged sexual advances, [the supervisor] was satisfying a personal urge" and concluded that "there is nothing in the Act (Title VII) which could reasonably be constructed to have it apply to verbal and physical sexual advances by another employee."[23] The

U.S. District Court for Northern California questioned "whether Title VII was intended to hold an employer liable for what is essentially the isolated and unauthorized sex misconduct of one employee" and judged that it was not.[24] And in *Tomkins v. Public Service Electric & Gas Co.*, the U.S. District Court of New Jersey in 1976 found that Title VII "is not intended to provide a federal tort remedy for what amounts to physical attacks motivated by sexual desire on the part of a supervisor and which happens to occur in a corporate corridor rather than a back alley."[25]

In 1976 and 1977, the tide turned. Diane Williams had rebuffed the advances of her Department of Justice supervisor, Harvey Brinson, who began to reprimand her without cause and withhold information she needed to do her job. After three months, he fired her. In 1976 a federal court backed Williams, finding, "Retaliatory actions of a male supervisor, taken because a female employee declined his sexual advances, constitutes sex discrimination within the definitional parameters of Title VII of the Civil Rights Act of 1964."[26] Then the District of Columbia Circuit Court of Appeals reversed the dismissal of Barnes's 1974 suit, establishing two important principles.[27] First, the lower court had found no evidence of sex discrimination in employment because Barnes was fired not for being a woman, but for refusing to have sex. The appeals court found it sufficient that "gender . . . was an indispensable factor in the job-retention condition."[28] Second, the court held the employer responsible for harassment, on the principle that courts held employers responsible for other acts of supervisory discrimination. A clear policy might protect an employer, however, "should a supervisor contravene" that policy "without the employer's knowledge" and should the employer make things right on discovering the abuse.[29] This suggested that employers should write anti-harassment policies.

In the same year another federal circuit court overturned the 1976 *Tomkins* decision, finding that Public Service Electric & Gas (PSE&G) acquiesced in the supervisor's conduct and thus could be held accountable.[30] PSE&G settled the case and agreed to Tomkins's request that it set up a panel to hear grievances and make an anti-harassment training video. These cases defined quid pro quo harassment as discriminatory, establishing that employers could be held accountable for the conduct of supervisors.[31] The *Barnes* decision made clear that employers should prohibit harassment by supervisors and take swift action to rectify harassment when they learned of it.

The Press Fans the Flames

Managers were disquieted by early press reports that harassment equaled discrimination. A *Business Week* article mentioned Judge Sherman Finesilver's 1978 Denver district court finding: "An employer is liable under Title VII when refusal of a supervisor's unsolicited sexual advances is the basis of the employee's termination."[32] The media emphasized that executives could not claim that they were unaware of harassment by supervisors, because courts used a "strict liability" standard in Title VII cases, meaning that employers were liable for discrimination by supervisors even if they did not know about it. Meanwhile, America was seeing a dramatic rise of women in jobs that had been dominated by men. The City of Madison had no women police officers or firefighters in 1970, and, by 1980, half of each new police academy class of 25 was female and the Fire Department was hiring 10 women firefighters a year. Not everyone was happy with the change, including male firefighters who sported T-shirts reading: "If God had intended for women to carry a hose, He would have equipped them with one."[33]

The press played up state rulings that harassment constituted discrimination, as well as these federal cases. In the earliest cases, states denied unemployment benefits to women who had quit their jobs to escape harassment. Michele Wells, a Western-Davis truck driver, complained to a foreman that her supervisor physically and verbally abused her: "He told me I shouldn't take it personally, that it was more or less of a big joke." Wells quit after her supervisor threw her down on a lunchroom table and climbed on top of her, but her claim for unemployment insurance was denied. By 1979 both California and Wisconsin passed laws to change that.[34]

Women's Advocates in Government Side with MacKinnon

In 1980, EEOC chief Eleanor Holmes Norton issued "Guidelines on Discrimination Because of Sex," in the last lame-duck months of Jimmy Carter's administration, defining hostile environment harassment following Catharine MacKinnon:[35]

> Unwelcome sexual advances, requests for sexual favors, and other verbal or physical conduct of a sexual nature constitute sexual harassment when . . . such conduct has the purpose or effect of unreasonably interfering with an individual's work performance or creating an intimidating, hostile, or offensive working environment.[36]

As when they had defined pregnancy discrimination as covered by Title VII, the influence of federal officials came from the separation of powers, which allowed agencies such as the EEOC to take a position on what Title VII covered. It was up to the courts to accept this definition, but, for all employers knew, the courts would do just that.

HR Reengineers the Union Grievance Procedure

Personnel experts argued that the 1977 judicial decisions left many employers open to lawsuit. They proposed grievance procedures for sexual harassment complaints, both to intercept complaints and to gain credit with judges. Experts and consultants raised an alarm, citing surveys by women's groups, *Redbook*, and the navy, reporting that between 70 and 92 percent of working women had been harassed on the job.[37] Because those surveys were magnets for victims, they later proved to exaggerate the incidence of harassment.[38] By 1979, two-thirds of nonunion companies had grievance procedures, most of them designed for civil rights complaints, but personnel experts argued for special harassment complaint systems.[39] The case of Justice Department employee Diane Williams illustrated the need for special grievance systems. After her supervisor fired her for rebuffing his advances, the EEO officer, the agency complaint examiner, and the complaint adjudication officer each concluded that Williams had not faced sex discrimination. Only then did she go to court.[40] If the Justice Department's elaborate grievance system couldn't get it right, how could a generic corporate grievance mechanism? In 1979 *Personnel Administrator* advised readers that, to reduce harassment, they should create a special procedure that would be well advertised "throughout the organization, ensure confidentiality, and be under the authority of a highly credible, powerful individual."[41]

While some argued that a procedure could intercept complaints, others argued that a procedure would protect employers in court. Several cited EEOC director Eleanor Holmes Norton's lame-duck call for "appropriate sanctions" for harassers, and echoed defense lawyers' failed argument that procedures should inoculate employers.[42] A pair of HR professors wrote in the two leading professional journals that grievance procedures provided protection. In one piece they begin: "Employers can protect themselves against liability for sexual harassment charges with a strong policy against such activity and a grievance procedure." They continue, "Several courts have suggested [that] . . . liability can be avoided if . . . the employer has a policy discouraging sexual harassment, and the employee failed to use an existing grievance procedure," but they do not cite any cases in support of the point.[43] In the other article they argue that "liability may be avoided if . . . the employee has failed to present the matter to a publicized grievance board," and that "to ensure compliance with Title VII" employers "must establish a written grievance procedure."[44] Here the authors cite *Miller v. Bank of America*, in which the employer's claim that a grievance procedure should protect him *had been rejected* by the appellate court in 1979. In fact, as of 1980, courts had not found that grievance procedures could insulate employers in a harassment suit or any other sort of discrimination suit.[45] Personnel experts exaggerated judicial support for grievance procedures in a way that lawyers had not done in the history of Title VII, but that was their professional modus operandi for any untested compliance strategy—to make arguments based on what they thought the courts should find, not what they had found.

Some articles played up Tomkins's 1977 out-of-court settlement with New Jersey's electric and gas utility, which stipulated a grievance system but which in no way bound future judges to give employers credit for grievance panels.[46] Others mentioned grievance procedures in the same breath as things judges deemed necessary, such as a speedy remedy, blurring the line between judges' and experts' recommendations.[47] Still others provided blueprints from prestigious sources. Mary P. Rowe provided MIT's special grievance system as an example in her 1981 *Harvard Business Review* article.[48] These articles helped personnel vice presidents overcome executive concern that sex was a private matter, or that harassment was a myth. Richard Barron, assistant vice president for personnel at Michigan Bell Telephone Co., told *Business Week* in the fall of 1979: "It can be very sensitive for an employer to intrude into relationships between male and female employees." Herman M. Mapelli, president of a Denver liquor distribution company facing harassment charges, told the magazine: "We don't have a policy because we don't have sexual harassment."[49]

Personnel experts recommended law-like grievance procedures designed to convince both executives and judges of their legal standing. Washington, DC, adopted a policy for its employees that carried a confidential investigative procedure and explicit penalties for harassers. Templates published in management journals covered (a) how to file a complaint, (b) the constitution of the grievance panel, (c) the complainant's and accused's right to counsel, (d) forms of discipline, and (e) channels of appeal. Many took their definitions of harassment from the EEOC guidelines, the only clear definition that seemed to have legal standing. Thus the 1979 City of Madison policy defined hostile environment harassment based on a draft of the 1980 EEOC guidelines, as including "unwelcome sexual advances, unwelcome physical conduct of a sexual nature, or verbal or physical conduct of a sexual nature which shall include but not be limited to, deliberate or repeated unsolicited gestures, graphic materials, verbal or written comments."[50]

Many firms learned about harassment grievance procedures from these articles. Others learned from their peers. The head of HR in a department store told us that, as a first mover, colleagues elsewhere came to him when caught unaware by complaints: "I would get calls from

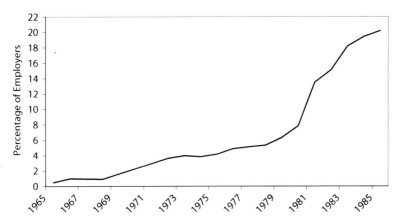

Figure 8.1. Rise in Sexual Harassment Grievance Procedures (1965–85)
Source: Survey of 389 employers in 1997 (Dobbin and Kelly 2007).

firms. . . . 'Harry over at [a competing retailer] said to give you a call because I got this situation, and he said you guys really have the setup [to handle a harassment complaint]. How do you do it?'"

Human resources experts sold some of the first grievance mechanisms to government officials. Washington mayor Marion Barry announced the city's 1979 grievance procedure himself because the city's Office of Personnel chief was on leave after being indicted for assaulting a staff aide/girlfriend.[51] In 1980 New York mayor Edward Koch ordered city agencies to create harassment grievance procedures and training systems to teach workers about the problem.[52] Figure 8.1 shows harassment grievance procedures in our broad national sample of employers. Before the district court decisions of 1977, fewer than one in 20 had harassment procedures, but eight years later one in five had them. Proponents found change too slow. Linenberger and Keaveny lamented in 1981, "Many companies have refused to consider sexual harassment a serious problem or to form policies to deal with sexual harassment."[53]

The Supreme Court Ratifies MacKinnon's Definition

The Supreme Court first spoke on hostile environment harassment in 1986.[54] Michelle Vinson had charged her former boss, a vice president at Meritor Savings, with fondling her in public, demanding sexual relations, exposing himself, and twice raping her. The district court originally denied Vinson's claim, which did not fit the quid pro quo profile because Vinson had succumbed to her boss's advances several dozen times, and had never lost a "tangible economic benefit" for refusing him. The Supreme Court supported Vinson's claim that she had faced an illegal, hostile environment and sexual harassment, and in so doing accepted the arguments of Catharine MacKinnon, who sat as co-counsel for Vinson.[55] Eleanor Holmes Norton had borrowed MacKinnon's 1979 definition of harassment for the 1980 EEOC guidelines, and now the Court borrowed it:[56]

> Unwelcome sexual advances, requests for sexual favors, and other verbal or physical conduct of a sexual nature constitute sexual harassment when . . . such conduct has the purpose or effect of unreasonably interfering with an individual's work performance or creating an intimidating, hostile, or offensive working environment.[57]

The decision piqued the interest of executives for two reasons. On the one hand, personnel experts had been teaching managers not to make jobs, promotions, or raises contingent on sexual acquiescence. Now the definition of harassment was much broader, and many employers realized that they might be susceptible to lawsuit.[58] On the other hand, the decision made clear that employers were responsible for harassment by their supervisors, just as they were responsible for other kinds of discrimination perpetrated by hired hands. You couldn't get off by saying the behavior was unauthorized.

The Court Hints That It Favors Personnel's Program

Both parties in the *Meritor* case explicitly asked the court to clarify how an employer might guard against liability, and whether a harassment grievance procedure might suffice. The EEOC's amicus brief took the personnel profession's side.

> If the employer has an expressed policy against sexual harassment and has implemented a procedure specifically designed to resolve sexual harassment claims, and if the victim does not take advantage of that procedure, the employer should be shielded from liability absent actual knowledge of the sexually hostile environment.[59]

The Court refused to set a standard: "We . . . decline the parties' invitation to issue a definitive rule on" what might protect an employer, and noted that the "mere existence of a grievance procedure and a policy against discrimination" would not insulate employers from liability.[60] But the ruling did mention that Meritor lacked a harassment procedure. Vinson objected to the bank's all-purpose grievance procedure, which would have required her to complain to her boss, the harasser. Following the personnel profession's preferred antidote, prescribed in articles such as Mary Rowe's 1981 *Harvard Business Review* piece, Vinson's lawyers had called for a complaint officer outside of the chain of command.[61]

Personnel Experts Champion the Grievance Procedure and Training for Managers

In quid pro quo cases, lower courts held that employers were liable regardless of the precautions they had taken. Given the chance, the Supreme Court had not said that grievance procedures could protect employers in hostile environment cases. Personnel experts might have taken the lesson that grievance procedures were a waste of time. Instead, they redoubled their efforts to promote grievance mechanism and training, arguing that the Court's broad definition of harassment made lawsuits more likely.[62] Many contended that a properly worded grievance procedure *would* protect employers. In *Personnel Administrator*, David Bradshaw counseled: "The key is to have a policy and a set of procedures that allow victims of sexual harassment to complain to appropriate employer officials . . . not . . . to the very person who is harassing them."[63]

HR experts noted that the Supreme Court had linked hostile environment harassment to racial harassment, and now recommended "general" anti-harassment procedures to cover all bets.[64] An article in *Public Personnel Management* held up Madison, Wisconsin's 1981 anti-harassment policy for city workers, which forbade harassment based on "race, sex, religion, color, national origin, handicap, and sexual orientation."[65] A computer manufacturer's HR director told us in 2000 that her 1994 "productive work environment" policy was designed to stop *"any sort of disruptive or harassing behavior."* Experts won converts to these general anti-harassment policies because the court had already expanded the meaning of discrimination, and ultimately because the court's authority to interpret legislation gave it power to go further. A public-sector HR manager told us in 2001 that the courts kept moving the target: "as years go by, the definition—what it is—gets a little bigger, a little bit broader . . . I think that really comes from the courts, as the courts keep interpreting and re-interpreting what constitutes . . . harassment." The general anti-harassment policy might cover activities not yet imagined by plaintiffs, but which would someday be forbidden by the courts.

The separation of powers was ultimately responsible for the rise of the harassment grievance procedure, as the same thought experiment we played in chapter 7 with pregnancy discrimination makes clear. Harassment would no more be folded into a sex discrimination law by the courts in France than pregnancy discrimination would be, because France's civil law system gives the courts little latitude in expanding the meaning of the law. In fact, in France, workplace harassment was covered by a separate statute defining it as violence, which treated harassment as an individual criminal violation rather than as a corporate civil violation.[66] In the United States, by contrast, women's rights advocates within the executive branch championed the cause of women who had been harassed at work. As in the case of pregnancy discrimination, those at the EEOC wrote guidelines in the absence of judicial action. And as in the case of pregnancy discrimination, the Supreme Court eventually ruled, but this time it recognized the new form of discrimination and a remedy for it in the grievance mechanism.

Personnel Underscores Costly Harassment Settlements

The *Meritor* case coincided with several costly, and widely reported, settlements. Early plaintiffs had been lucky to win $60,000 or $70,000, but shortly before the *Meritor* decision, a U.S. district court awarded Elizabeth Reece $250,000 for harassment suffered at a Washington architectural firm. Reece's boss had encouraged her to sleep with clients to win business. Shortly after *Meritor*, CBS settled a claim for $500,000. The press took note. *U.S. News & World Report* wrote: "Until recently, many corporate managers didn't take charges of sexual harassment seriously. Those days are over as a result of a Supreme Court decision . . . and big-dollar legal settlements."[67]

From the early 1980s, personnel experts had written that, while sex discrimination plaintiffs could not win punitive damages under Title VII, state civil suits and class actions could up the ante. In 1981 *Personnel Journal* described how a 1979 case against Western Electric had snowballed into a class action suit with nearly 2,000 plaintiffs that cost the company millions in back pay and legal fees.[68] Two years later the same journal reported on a harassment case against Loews l'Enfant Plaza Hotel, which had opened the floodgates for state tort suits for assault, invasion of privacy, and emotional distress, and warned that "employers may be on the verge of finding themselves exposed to a very serious new source of financial liability."[69] Big law firms, concerned about the financial exposure of partners, began to take personnel's advice. Los Angeles–based Gibson, Dunn, & Crutcher, with 500 attorneys, put in a harassment grievance procedure, and the firm's labor department began to report regularly at retreats on harassment case law.[70]

Harassment Sensitivity Training

From the late 1970s, personnel specialists had recommended harassment training modeled on race relations workshops.[71] If it was a short leap from management sensitivity training to race relations workshops, as we saw in chapter 6, it was an even shorter leap from those workshops to harassment training. In 1979 the Working Women's Institute told *Business Week* that there was widespread interest in the in-house workshops they were developing for supervisors and subordinates.[72] In January 1980, *Personnel Administrator* argued that training must get across the point that "any action which makes current/future employment contingent on acquiescence to sexual advances or demands is illegal."[73] That same year the Office of Personnel Management (OPM) developed a harassment training module for federal agencies.[74] *Public Personnel Management* suggested that training should "sensitize supervisors and employees to the problem."[75] The City of Madison enrolled its 1,800 workers in "intensive, on-going harassment prevention training" in 1980.[76] Like Madison, the army had adopted MacKinnon's broad definition; to illustrate, its 1982 training film included an unscripted scene in which a man yelled to an actress from a base window, "Hey baby! Why don't y'all come up here with me?" The major general who commissioned the film argued: "Our main mission in life is to fight as a team and to have cohesion and unit spirit. Anything that's divisive, such as racial disharmony or sexual harassment, has got to be faced and attacked."[77]

Personnel officers often had to counter executives' fears that training itself might open the tort floodgates. A pharmaceutical industry HR manager told us in 1997: "I think the concern was that if you enlighten people, then all of a sudden you're going to have many of these complaints and lawsuits." A human resources manager in publishing explained that executives first quashed his plans for training, arguing, "If [sexual harassment] goes on, and if they attend training, they're going to realize: 'My God I was being harassed.' And they'll sue us." To win executive backing, personnel experts often exaggerated federal support for training just as they had exaggerated support for grievance procedures. Some translated the EEOC's 1980 guidelines on sex discrimination, which mentioned "informing employees of their right to raise . . . the issue of harassment," into a training mandate.[78] A 1981 *Personnel Journal* article implied that the courts required training: "Prominent communication of corporate policy opposing harassment in the workplace, and the existence of in-house complaint procedures, *are mandatory since a number of judicial actions have placed strong reliance on such measures.*"[79] Up to 1981, the courts had not endorsed complaint procedures or training.[80]

Hostile Environment Training The *Meritor* decision created a huge gray area by vetting MacKinnon's definition of harassment, as *U.S. News and World Report* argued: "sexual harassment doesn't have to be linked to promises or threats about job advancement. A 'hostile or abusive work environment' is sufficient ground."[81] Quid pro quo harassment seemed relatively straightforward, but what was a hostile work environment? "Company confusion and concern have spurred a growth industry in training videos, seminars and consultants," reported *U.S. News* in 1986.[82] HR consultants such as Freada Klein touted omnibus training programs, covering behavior currently forbidden and behavior the courts might one day condemn.[83] They counseled executives to rewrite policies, forbidding behavior—a pat on the shoulder or romance between colleagues—that no court had questioned.[84] Firms began to update policies and training annually based, as one VP of human resources at a public utility told us in 1997, on bulletins in professional journals: "I read a lot about it in the general human resource literature." Indeed, with both state and federal courts debating the reasonable man, reasonable woman, and reasonable person standards for judging a hostile environment, and battling over whether employers were "strictly liable" for harassment, or might inoculate themselves in some way, well into the 1990s it was impossible to determine what the law implied.[85]

Trainers argued that they had a panacea, and many personnel experts joined the lucrative field of harassment training. In 2002, over 90 percent of firms with harassment and diversity training used live trainers, and most supplemented the live training with online courses or video vignettes.[86] Some trainers made their own videos, which typically last 30 minutes, run to $1,000, and require annual legal updates. One HR manager complained to us of the cost in 1997: "Do you watch *The Drew Carey Show*? . . . In one episode he made his own sexual harassment training video because he didn't have money to buy one."

Lawyers on Compliance: What You Don't Know . . .

Lawyers offered very different advice about compliance at first, advice drawn from case law. The upshot was that grievance procedures might backfire, and that employer policy should be to respond rapidly to notice of harassment. In hewing closely to case law, attorneys followed their professional modus operandi. That approach did not appeal to executives who wanted a vaccine against harassment lawsuits. Executives went along with personnel experts' advice to put in grievance mechanisms and training because personnel managers promised that these strategies would protect firms. In the process they gave the personnel profession unofficial license to manage compliance with harassment law—pending approval by the courts.

The early law review articles quoted the *Tomkins* district court case from 1977, advising managers to "take prompt and remedial action after acquiring . . . knowledge" of harassment.[87] An employer who immediately disciplines the harasser removes grounds for a lawsuit.

> Both the Constitution and Title VII relieve an employer of liability for the discrimination of its agents [supervisors, typically] if it takes corrective action. In constitutional terms, the principle that a plaintiff cannot continue to litigate once she has been afforded her requested relief is commonly called "mootness."[88]

Initiation of a grievance hearing could cause delay, permitting the complainant to sue. Once a lawsuit was under way, the chance for a grievance-system remedy had passed, for the Supreme Court viewed a remedy "in the face of litigation as equivocal in purpose, motive and permanence."[89] Moreover, as the *Meritor* court had found, an employer wouldn't get off the hook by claiming that it had a grievance procedure that the plaintiff had ignored.[90] In the final analysis, a grievance procedure seemed to have no merits, and might endanger the employer through delay.

The Danger of Grievance Procedures

Legal experts wrote that the courts had vacillated between two standards of liability, neither of which supported grievance procedures.[91] In quid pro quo cases, as in conventional discrimination cases, courts upheld "strict liability," meaning that employers got no credit for precautions like grievance procedures. In such cases, the editors of the *Harvard Law Review* noted in 1984, grievance procedures had not shielded employers: "The defendant in Miller was held strictly liable for harassment by all its employees, despite its express policy against sexual harassment and despite its creation of procedures for grievance resolution."[92] The *Miller* opinion cited four other federal appellate findings that employers are strictly liable for quid pro quo harassment, even when they are unaware of it and have a policy against it.

In early hostile environment cases courts had upheld a "knowledge" standard, meaning that employers were liable only if they knew of harassment. Those cases, wrote the *Harvard Law Review*, made grievance procedures dangerous. They gave employers "an incentive to remain ignorant" of harassment.[93] John Attanasio warned in the *University of Cincinnati Law Review*:

> Should courts continue to refuse to impute to unknowing employers the sexual [harassment] of their supervisors, the policy against sexual [harassment] could become see no evil, hear no

evil. . . . The employer has little incentive to encourage [complaints] because the fact remains that lack of knowledge equals lack of liability.[94]

A 1982 article in *Legal Economics* asked the question: "Is the employer liable for sexual harassment by its supervisors if it does not have 'notice' of the conduct?" In hostile environment cases, and in some quid pro quo cases, courts had "held that an employer is not liable for sexual harassment by its supervisory employees unless it has notice of the conduct."[95] A 1984 *North Carolina Law Review* article on the knowledge standard pointed out that in Tomkins's early quid pro quo case, the court wrote: "[We] conclude that Title VII is violated when a supervisor, *with the actual or Constructive knowledge of the employer*, makes sexual advances or demands toward a subordinate employee and conditions that employee's job status . . . on a favorable response."[96] These articles sent the message that a grievance procedure would probably not inoculate employers, and could prove dangerous, either when it delayed the remedy (permitting the harassee to sue), or when it gave the firm notice of the problem.

Ronald Turner's lead article in the *Howard Law Journal* argued explicitly that a grievance procedure could backfire because "an employer would not be held responsible for unlawful acts of supervisors that it neither knew of nor condoned" and took it one step further, arguing that a complaint that does not end the career of a harasser would make future incidents "foreseeable."[97] In the year after *Meritor*, the Sixth Circuit Court confirmed that a grievance procedure didn't protect the defendant from a harassment claim, but also faulted Avco Co. for failing to prevent "foreseeable" harassment by a man who had already been brought before the grievance panel once. For Turner, that decision made grievance procedures too risky.[98]

The *Harvard Law Review* noted that, while the EEOC had supported grievance procedures in its guidelines, whether these protected employers or endangered them wasn't the EEOC's call: "The EEOC does not have the statutory authority to issue regulations." The EEOC's guidelines on harassment "can acquire the force of law only through adoption by the Supreme Court."[99] Here the legal profession was true to form. Rather than concocting new compliance approaches based on old bureaucratic stand-bys, as the personnel profession had done, lawyers offered advice closely aligned with case law. Yet in the end personnel won this battle because executives were looking for a quick fix. The grievance procedure appeared to provide that, and lawyers could only counsel firms to hold off until the courts made a decisive ruling.

Lawyers as Antiharassment Trainers

While many lawyers contradicted the personnel profession's advice on grievance procedures, most agreed that harassment training could do no harm. Lawyers often played roles in training, either in developing materials or as trainers themselves, lecturing on the implications of the law.[100] A 1977 *Employee Relations Law Journal* article emphasized that managers must explicitly forbid harassment: "where no clearly articulated, known (to the employees) policy of discouraging sexual advances exists, direct suit" will be permitted by the courts.[101] In the year after *Meritor*, a *University of Cincinnati Law Review* article advised, "Employers should implement mandatory training sessions that teach supervisors to identify and alleviate sexual harassment," and a piece in *Tort and Insurance Law Journal* counseled, "all supervisory employees should be educated" and should be informed that "a 'boys will be boys' atmosphere will not be allowed and that severe disciplinary action will be taken against any supervisor who either participates in or condones . . . sexual harassment."[102] The *American Bar Association Journal* recommended educating non-managers as well: "All employees—whether in new-employee orientation or senior management retreats—should be made familiar with the definitions and ramifications of sexual harassment and its remedies."[103]

The Spread of Grievance Procedures and Training to 1990

Over the concerns of some lawyers that grievance procedures would backfire, and despite the fact that courts had given very little support to them, by 1990, 47 percent of the employers in our broad national sample had sexual harassment grievance procedures. Over a third had a general harassment procedure that covered racial and other forms of harassment, and a quarter had sexual harassment training. While both lawyers and personnel experts favored training, it was expensive compared to a grievance procedure. Advocacy from human resources experts had clearly worked.

In quantitative analyses of these data, Erin Kelly and I found that employers that relied on personnel experts for advice, either internal experts or HR consultants, were significantly more likely to create harassment grievance procedures and training programs. Employers who consulted with lawyers on HR matters were significantly *less* likely, all else being equal, to create grievance mechanisms, but no less likely to create training programs.[104] Those analyses confirm that employers were listening to the differential advice coming from personnel experts and lawyers—to embrace both grievance procedures and training, in

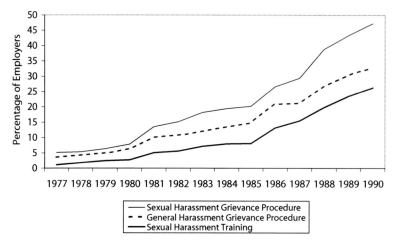

Figure 8.2. Growth in Harassment Grievance Procedures and Antiharassment Training (1977–90)

Source: National survey of 389 employers in 1997 (Dobbin and Kelly 2007).

the case of personnel experts, and to be wary of grievance procedures, in the case of lawyers.

The Civil Rights Act of 1991: A New Incentive

In 1989, in *Wards Cove v. Atonio*, the Supreme Court undermined its own 1971 "disparate impact" ruling. Future Title VII plaintiffs in all sorts of cases would have to prove intent to discriminate. In 1991, the Civil Rights Restoration Act undid *Wards Cove*, making disparate impact cases winnable again and extending compensatory and punitive damages from race cases to other sorts of cases. *Business Week* attributed the damage awards to the televised hearings on Clarence Thomas's nomination to the Supreme Court. The hearings riveted the nation when Anita Hill, a lawyer who worked for Thomas when he headed the EEOC, testified that he had made unwanted sexual remarks to her on the job: "The Thomas hearings are responsible for [a] civil rights breakthrough: a provision in the act giving the victims of sexual harassment the right to sue an employer for monetary damages."[105] The management journals remarked that the cost of discrimination had just risen sharply. *Industry Week's* headline was "Longer Dockets, Deep Pockets," and it led off with a discussion of costs: "The increased legal liability business will face from the enactment of the Civil Rights Act of 1991 is sobering indeed. The bill . . . opens the door—for the first time—for women, persons with disabilities, and those who are religious minorities to seek a jury trial and sue for punitive damages of up to $300,000."[106]

Before this, Title VII harassment plaintiffs could only recover lost income, as the head of the National Employment Lawyers Association reported: "I used to have to turn people away who had very legitimate claims. They had suffered outrageous sexual harassment on the job, but they did not have a wage loss; they quit the job and got another job." The new law created an incentive, argued a New York attorney: "Trial lawyers are entrepreneurs. . . . You give them a profit opportunity, and they're going to focus on it. Congress is giving a series of profit opportunities; these are not going to be ignored."[107] *Law Practice Management* predicted a rise in cases against law firms: "As the number of women denied partnership increases, so will the number of claims of sexual harassment."[108]

In 1991 a district court added a multiplier to the new damage limit by certifying the first class-action harassment suit. This opened the way to suits that could close down huge firms. Mitsubishi would settle suits in 1997 and 1998 for a total of $43.5 million. Meanwhile, state courts were becoming more aggressive. In 1994, a California state jury ordered the biggest law firm in the country, Baker and McKenzie, to pay $7.1 million—later reduced to $3.5 million—to a legal secretary who charged that a lawyer groped her breasts and pressed her from behind.[109]

The Thomas hearings had ramped up media coverage of harassment, and the press now turned to lawsuits. Figure 8.3 plots the number of *New York Times* articles about sexual harassment from 1970 through

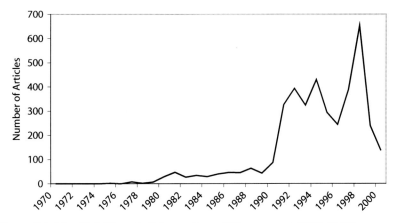

Figure 8.3. *New York Times* Articles on Sexual Harassment (1970–2000)

Source: Lexis-Nexis search of "sexual harassment" in article titles and lead paragraphs.

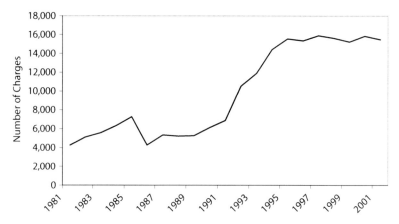

Figure 8.4. Sexual Harassment Charges to the EEOC (1981–2001)

Source: EEOC online database and published reports.

2000. In 1990 there were nearly 100 articles, but that number shot up to more than 400 in 1991 and remained high.

The sheer number of charges was one reason for the attention. Harassment charges now outpaced all other kinds of discrimination charges.[110] The *Detroit Free Press* analyzed the effect of the 1991 law on suits between 1991 and 1998. Using the best yardstick of viable claims—suits that the EEOC filed for plaintiffs—they found that race discrimination suits increased 16 percent, while sexual harassment suits increased by nearly 100 percent.[111] The February 1998 cover story of *Nation's Business*, "Lawsuits Gone Wild" (a play on the 1997 film *Girls Gone Wild*), argued that the 1991 act created a field day for employment lawyers: "Trial lawyers gained new financial incentives" to pursue discrimination cases.[112] Complaints to the EEOC rose sharply. They had ranged between 4,000 and 7,000, and rose to 10,000 in 1992 and 14,000 in 1994, where they stayed for the rest of the 1990s.[113] The field of employment law got a boost, as Chrys Martin, employment-law chair at the Defense Research Institute, would later write: "There used to be only a handful of employment attorneys. . . . Now there are hundreds of them in every major city."[114]

HR Experts Stand By Grievance Procedures and Sensitivity Training

For the human resources managers we interviewed between 1997 and 2001, the Clarence Thomas hearings and the new Civil Rights Act focused attention on harassment. In 1997 a liquor company HR executive linked the company's training program directly to the Thomas hearings: "We've had sexual harassment training. That goes back a little bit, three or four years ago. I think everybody jumped on that bandwagon—with

Clarence Thomas and Anita Hill scenarios—that made them say: 'We really ought to do something here.'" The introduction of punitive damages completed the one-two punch, allowing plaintiffs to find lawyers to represent them and walk away with large settlements even when their economic suffering had been minimal. A high-technology HR vice president told us in 2001 that the new threat of lawsuits had spurred his company to do something. You don't have to be "pulled into court by your earlobes and threatened with millions of dollars" in damages very often to address the problem. The HR director at a public utility told us she put in training in 1993 and was in the process of expanding it in 2001, "because we see and we read that that's been one of the fastest growing [areas of] litigation."

The Civil Rights Act of 1991
and Harassment Training
Wall Street Journal, December 2, 1991

BOYLSTON, Mass.—At Digital Equipment Corp.'s conference center here, nine men and women intently watch two colleagues act out a scene in which a woman fails to express her displeasure over sexual harassment. An executive strokes the woman's sweater as they pretend to ride an office elevator. "I've been meaning to tell you how fantastic you look today," he coos, and invites the assistant to dinner. "Maybe when we get together tonight, we can talk about you coming along on this [business] trip." Looking edgy, she bites her lip and spurns the offer. The scene ends. Their coworkers applaud the realism of the performance. Similar scenes are taking place across the country as employers rush to expand sexual harassment awareness training. The trend reflects both the furor surrounding the Supreme Court confirmation hearings for Justice Clarence Thomas and the new civil rights act. The law, which President Bush signed last month, lets sexual harassment victims receive jury awards for punitive damages for the first time.

"It's time for employers, whether large or small, to educate their employees about sexual harassment" and go beyond "just posting a sign on the wall," says Gloria Allred, a civil rights lawyer in Los Angeles. Some companies, including Digital and Du Pont Co., say sexual harassment suits against them have become less frequent since they initiated extensive training.

More than 90 percent of Fortune 500 companies will offer employees special training about sexual harassment within a year or two, predicts Freada Klein, a Cambridge, Mass., management consultant.[115]

HR consultants who offered training did much of the advocacy. They backed a Connecticut bill requiring employers with at least 50 workers to train their managers. As House sponsor Joseph Adamo noted: "it is the groups that are advocates for this particular legislation who do the training."[116] Insurance companies also promoted training and grievance procedures, requiring applicants for a new insurance product, Employment Practices Liability Insurance (EPLI) policies covering Title VII liability, to have them.[117]

By the late 1990s, the gargantuan Mitsubishi settlements and other big-ticket settlements gave HR executives new ammunition to push for grievance procedures and training. Shortly after the Texaco race discrimination suit was settled in 1997 for $176 million, an oil company HR executive told us he was rethinking harassment prevention:

> We do sexual harassment training. There's no question that the entire oil industry has kind of perked up its ears since this whole Texaco business. Sometimes new policies are initiated just because it's a good wake-up call, and sometime by shareholders writing letters, asking: "What are you doing in this area?"

Press coverage of these suits kept pressure on firms.

The Thomas hearings put firms on notice that harassment was an ongoing problem. The only antidotes were grievance procedures and train-

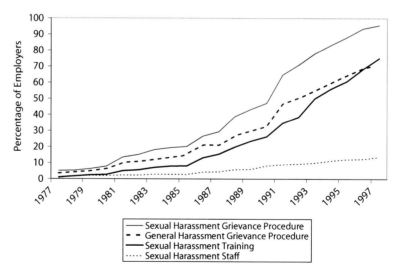

Figure 8.5. Employer Harassment Programs (1977–97)

Source: National survey of 389 employers in 1997 (Dobbin and Kelly 2007).

ing programs, even though neither had yet been vetted by the courts. No less an authority than *Glamour* magazine reported that 35 percent of Fortune 500 firms had training at the beginning of 1990, and 85 percent had it by late in 1992.[118] By 1993, the *Wall Street Journal* reported that harassment training had "moved from academia . . . to the general corporate world and beyond. The whole New York State Assembly got sensitized en masse a few weeks ago."[119] Even middling firms joined the bandwagon before the Supreme Court took a stand. In our broad national sample of 389 employers, a quarter had harassment training in 1990, but by 1997, 75 percent had it. Nearly half had a sexual harassment grievance procedure by 1990, but by 1997, 96 percent had one.

The Supreme Court Endorses Grievance Procedures and Training

The Supreme Court had offered little guidance. In the *Meritor* decision of 1986, Justice Rehnquist wrote for the Court that "debate over the appropriate standard for employer liability has a rather abstract quality about it" and demurred when both sides asked the court to settle that debate.[120] Lower-court rulings were all over the map. Finally in 1998 the Court took on four cases expected to be decisive. A front-page *New York Times* piece anticipated the decisions: "For a dozen years, the Supreme Court has skated above the complexities of sexual harassment law in a series of unanimous opinions that announced general principles while deferring the difficulties of practical application for another day. . . . That day has arrived."[121] On June 24, just weeks after Mitsubishi settled a class-action harassment suit for $34 million, the Supreme Court issued two rulings specifying what could protect employers in hostile-environment cases, and making it clear that nothing would protect them in quid pro quo cases. In hostile environment cases, the court reasoned, employers who had grievance procedures and training could expect workers to use the procedures before appealing to the courts. In these rulings the Court accepted the measures that personnel experts had made popular.

Kimberly Ellerth worked in sales in a two-person office in Chicago that was part of the 22,000-employee textile and clothing giant Burlington Industries. Ellerth complained that on a business trip her New York supervisor, Theodore Slowik, told her to "loosen up" when she gave no encouragement to his remarks about her breasts, and continued, "I could make your life very hard or very easy at Burlington." Slowik kept the behavior up, but never carried through on the threat to Ellerth's career.[122] The Court reaffirmed that when a supervisor takes a "tangible employment action" against an employee who has refused his advances, the company was responsible. As one attorney put it, "There is no escape.... The employer is dead meat."[123] No grievance system imaginable would provide protection. But absent retaliation, this was a hostile environment case. The Court held that the employer could mount an "affirmative defense," showing that Ellerth had failed to use its grievance procedure. The justices sent the case back to the lower court to decide whether the employer had an adequate procedure.

The Ellerth decision made clear that courts should take employer grievance procedures into account in hostile environment cases, ending the dithering of lower courts. Edelman and colleagues show that, up to 1980, corporate grievance procedures had not protected employers in discrimination cases of any sort.[124] Up to 1998, judges rarely cited grievance procedures in their decisions in discrimination cases, but defendants with procedures won cases at a greater rate (50 percent) than those without (30 percent).[125]

In Beth Ann Faragher's case, which led the chapter, the Court held the City of Boca Raton liable not because it lacked a policy against harassment or a grievance procedure, but because neither Faragher nor her harassers knew of them. In the following year, in *Kolstad v. American Dental Association*,[126] Justice O'Connor's opinion encouraged employers to "adopt anti-discrimination policies and to educate their personnel on Title VII's prohibitions."[127] In that case, three key purveyors of harassment prevention training, the Society for Human Resource Management, the Chamber of Commerce, and the Equal Employment Advisory Council, submitted amicus briefs arguing that employers offering training should escape liability.[128] The Court did not go that far, but it did allow that training plus a grievance procedure might be used in a defense.

Nation's Business reported "for the first time now employers can insulate themselves from many if not all harassment suits."[129] Attorney Walter Connolly Jr., who represented Mitsubishi in its class-action suit, applauded the fact that the rulings included a guide for employers: "The beauty of these rulings is that companies now know what they have to do: They have to advertise a no-harassment policy, run training programs and have a discipline-response mechanism. If the company does those things, they can defend against these cases."[130] Robin Conrad, the Chamber of Commerce's senior vice president for legal matters, applauded: "The Court responded to our cries in the wilderness for clear, bright-line standards so employers will know what to do."[131] A public-utility HR director we interviewed in 2001 told us the decision had set a standard: "The courts are saying to protect yourself. Whether you've had a complaint or not, you're going to get one. And if you do, you should have this and that and that in place." The new standard put laggards at risk, for, as attorney Richard Seymour of the U.S. Committee for Civil Rights Under Law said, "a lot of cases that would have been dismissed yesterday are good cases today."[132]

ACLU legal director Steven Shapiro told *Nation's Business*, "The Court's decisions will literally benefit millions of Americans."[133] In class actions, more and more money was at stake. Harassment plaintiffs netted $27.8 million in 1996 and $54.6 million in 2000.[134] The big judgments came in state courts without damage limits, for, as labor lawyer David Copus explained, a winning Title VII claim "will also, by definition, be a winning tort in any state in the country. . . . These torts are where the megabucks are coming, and they're all state-court common-law claims."[135]

Personnel Claims Vindication

Many observers claimed that the decisions moved the court into the territory of making law. Linda Greenhouse reported in the *New York Times*: "Taken together, the two decisions had an almost legislative sweep, establishing clearly defined rights and responsibilities for companies and their employees."[136] In their *Ellerth* dissent, justices Thomas and Scalia referred to the majority's principle of "affirmative defense" as a "whole-cloth creation that draws no support from the legal principles on which the Court claims it is based . . . although the Court implies that it has found guidance in both precedent and statute . . . its holding is a product of willful policymaking, pure and simple." In fact, the decision was based in precedent of another sort, a precedent of numbers. The Court accepted these procedures not because of their fit with abstract legal principles, but because they were ubiquitous in American firms. The Court had passed on the invitation to approve grievance procedures in 1986, and only changed course after employers had installed them.

Consultants now championed training with fresh enthusiasm. Trainer Sally Ford wrote in the *Business Journal* that employers should "Educate all employees about the nature and definition of sexual harassment, providing practical examples of prohibited conduct, including same-sex conduct. Training should be conducted and repeated on a periodic basis for both management and non-management employees."[137] HR consultant Marshall Colt recommended in the *Denver Business Journal* that companies review their policies, train employees periodically, and contract with an outside ombudsperson to hear and investigate complaints.[138]

The *Faragher* and *Ellerth* cases sent video producers back to the studios with new scripts. On the website for its video *Sex, Power, and the Workplace* ($249), Lumina Productions emphasized that the law was now crystal clear: "In the spring of 1998, the Supreme Court" elimi-nated "confusion surrounding sexual harassment suits" and endorsed training and grievance procedures. A new vignette underscored the Court's findings. TV production assistant Kelly faced dirty jokes and pornographic videos at work, but, because the station she worked for could prove that Kelly had been through training covering use of the harassment grievance procedure, it got off Scott free.[139]

Because Faragher and her harassers were unaware of city policy, consultants now advocated signature forms for every training session, and self-paced computer training with pop quizzes to document com-pletion and mastery of the material.[140] By 2001, one software engineer estimated that online legal compliance was a $150 million market that was growing by leaps and bounds among firms susceptible to class-action suits.[141]

Attorneys Back Grievance Procedures

After the 1998 decisions, lawyers of all stripes trumpeted the legal util-ity of training and grievance procedures. Attorneys for the two sides in the $34 million 1998 Mitsubishi case joined forces to send a message to employers. The *Minneapolis Star Tribune* wrote: "Both attorneys agree that companies can help avert legal action by forming and strictly en-forcing a sexual-harassment policy, and providing yearly training for supervisors and frequent companywide training. [Mitsubishi's lead attorney] said he counsels clients to get tough on front-line managers to avoid legal exposure. 'Fire supervisors who can't get ahold of the situation.'"[142]

Society for Human Resources Management senior VP Susan Meis-inger said that the rulings were a boon to law firms that did harassment training and consultation: "I'd bet the ranch that every law firm with an employment practice is working on the outline of a seminar on how to avoid sexual harassment lawsuits in the future . . . and our advice hot line will be ringing off the hook."[143] New York employment lawyer Michael Lee told the *Boston Globe*, "Every attorney in the field I know is sending out memos and flyers and notices to their clients telling them to get their act together . . . to have an employee grievance process and some sort of sexual harassment handbook."[144]

Attorneys now argued that firms without grievance mechanisms and training were in trouble. An attorney with the New York office of Lit-tler Mendelson told the *New York Times* that it expected two out of five managers at internet companies to face harassment complaints before long, twice the rate of managers at bricks-and-mortar firms, because internet companies don't have the "policies and procedures in place to handle employee complaints."[145]

In a 2001 decision, discussed in chapter 4, the Supreme Court vetted what HR experts had wanted from the start: harassment grievance procedures that would be binding, just like union procedures.[146] From the late 1980s experts had recommended having workers sign a pledge at the point of hire to use binding arbitration for all employment disputes. By 1994, the *Wall Street Journal* reported, 80 percent of securities industry workers were covered.[147] The results didn't always favor employers—Juno Online Services handled several complaints through arbitration but paid large settlements and won wide, negative, press attention.[148] But employers now had a way to make sure that workers would use their grievance systems to air claims of harassment, as personnel experts had wanted from the start.

Conclusion

Sexual harassment was not discussed in the debates over the Civil Rights Act of 1964, and it is unlikely that those who crafted the act ever considered the possibility that it outlawed harassment at work. The women's movement succeeded brilliantly in making the case that sexual harassment constituted sex discrimination. Catharine MacKinnon argued forcefully that women who lost their jobs for refusing to sleep with their bosses faced employment discrimination on the basis of sex. MacKinnon and her sisters in the women's movement eventually convinced America and the courts that women who faced abuse—dirty language, repeated come-ons, sexual horseplay—faced employment discrimination as well.

The courts played a key role in defining harassment as sex discrimination. Judges might have continued on the path of the first few cases, finding that harassment was caddish but did not contravene the Civil Rights Act. Or they might have sent the issue back to Congress, as they did with the issue of pregnancy discrimination, making Congress pass separate legislation to cover the issue. Instead, judges were convinced by arguments made by feminists. Americans came around to the view that sexual harassment on the job was discriminatory. This expansion of the purview of the Civil Rights Act could only occur because the Constitution permitted the executive and judicial branches to offer their own interpretations of legislation. Across Europe, in countries with civil-law rather than common-law systems, harassment has been outlawed with distinct legislation—neither public officials nor the courts expanded laws against employment discrimination to cover harassment.[149]

What neither Catharine MacKinnon and the women's movement nor William Rehnquist and the *Meritor* court decided was how employers should fight harassment. Personnel experts made that decision, trotting out the old union grievance procedure and its newer cousin, the civil rights grievance procedure, as models. With a grievance procedure, they argued, harassment complaints could be handled internally, without the involvement of the courts, and they could be handled discreetly. The grievance procedure would give harassed workers a venue for airing their complaints against bosses and coworkers, and would give the accused the chance to tell his or her side of the story. Personnel experts insisted that the courts would accept these grievance systems as substitutes for litigation. The precedent was union grievance procedures, which were binding because union contracts stipulated that they would be. Without a legal leg to stand on, personnel experts argued that the courts had required harassment grievance procedures, and that they would protect employers in court. They also argued far and wide that training could stop harassment, and ensure that grievance procedures were used.

Human resources experts had successfully defined what legal compliance would mean. Lawyers wrote of the potential danger of the grievance procedure, which could not protect employers in quid pro quo cases and which might render them liable in hostile environment cases by giving them notice of harassment. Executives adopted such procedures anyway, though those who consulted with lawyers held off. Corporate executives in search of an inoculation against calamitous lawsuits embraced the grievance procedure. It remained unproven in court in the period when most executives installed it, but employers preferred an untested inoculation to none at all.

While professional groups with expertise in new arenas had in past eras been licensed by the king, and in modern times by the state, the history of corporate harassment remedies highlights the growing role of executives in recognizing professional expertise. In new regulatory arenas with uncertain compliance criteria, executives must choose among solutions suggested by different groups. It is as true of corporate governance regulation, fringe benefits regulation, and environmental regulation as it is of equal opportunity regulation. New groups are knighted not by the king, but by the CEO, and CEOs have their own standards. In this case, they found a bureaucratic solution appealing. They ignored some of the advice coming from the sober profession with clear expertise, the bar, in favor of advice from the entrepreneurial profession with untested ideas. Their focus on legal risk led them to ignore the lack of evidence that grievance procedures actually reduce harassment, and so America institutionalized a compliance regime that has yet to be shown to alleviate harassment.

Perhaps most surprising about this episode in equal opportunity history is that it was personnel experts, not lawyers, who ended up changing the law. The popularity of grievance procedures and training was what led the Supreme Court to its 1998 decision that these programs could protect employers in certain hostile environment cases. Once these techniques were widespread, judges treated them as a litmus test of a company's sincerity. The public also came to believe that employers with training programs and grievance procedures were doing all they could to prevent harassment, despite the fact that, as legal scholar Susan Bisom-Rapp finds in a review of the scholarly studies, there is no evidence that harassment training actually reduces the incidence of harassment.[150] Lauren Edelman and colleagues find no evidence that grievance procedures reduce harassment lawsuits either.[151] The lack of positive evidence has deterred neither the human resources profession nor the courts from promoting training and grievance procedures.

HOW PERSONNEL DEFINED
EQUAL OPPORTUNITY

IT WAS CIVIL RIGHTS ACTIVISTS who fought for equal opportunity in employment, as well as in education, housing, and public accommodations. It was politicians who outlawed discrimination in private employment. But it was personnel managers who defined what job discrimination was and was not. Some of their experiments were rejected by Congress or the courts, but most everything companies did to promote equal opportunity was cooked up by personnel experts trying to guess how to comply with a law that was a moving target. And they did an astonishing number of things over the years, rethinking every step of the employment process, from recruitment to retirement.

In requiring equal treatment in private employment, Congress used grand language appropriate to the gravity of the project. The laws were mute on the nuts and bolts of compliance. Kennedy's 1961 executive order required federal contractors to take "affirmative action" to provide equal opportunity, and the Civil Rights Act of 1964 outlawed discrimination in general terms. It is not that these documents never got specific. They specified exactly which employers were covered and which groups were protected, but they left the terms of compliance open.

In the absence of clear government guidelines, personnel experts modeled compliance measures on classical personnel practices. What gave them clout with company executives was the American tradition of judicial interpretation of the law. It was anyone's guess how the courts would interpret the law next year. If the courts had not had the authority to reinterpret the law, personnel executives could not have sold wave after wave of equal opportunity measures, and the profession would not have grown as it did. If equal opportunity law had been as clear-cut as wages-and-hours laws, personnel would have had little work to do to comply. Instead, the employment rights revolution of the 1960s and 1970s proved a boon for personnel. The census shows that the personnel profession grew nearly tenfold in the 40 years after John F. Kennedy's affirmative action order of 1961 while the workforce as a whole barely doubled.

The Civil Rights Act and presidential affirmative action orders stimulated a national discussion about the character of discrimination, carried out in microcosm in every workplace. Executives, human resource managers, consultants, and workers debated what was fair—who should be eligible for special skill training and what sexual harassment policies should look like. In the national media, pundits debated quotas and reverse discrimination, blurring the line between higher education, where affirmative action sometimes meant quotas, and employment, where it rarely did. We have seen that employers subject to affirmative action regulations did almost exactly the things employers subject only to the Civil Rights Act did; they just did those things sooner. The one thing they all shied away from was quotas, for the high-pitched public debate over quotas sent the message that they were dangerous. Meanwhile ideas about institutional racism and cognitive bias that appeared in public discourse found their way into the equal opportunity programs human resources experts devised.

The story of equal opportunity at work holds lessons about the consequences of America's constitutional form for corporations and professions. Our common-law system and separated federal powers permitted the courts to reinterpret the Civil Rights Act as American views about discrimination changed. Each firm created its own legal code of behavior surrounding recruitment, hiring, promotion, and discipline. Personnel manuals came to resemble civil codes. Then when Ronald Reagan signaled that affirmative action's time was up, the constituency of equal opportunity experts that had grown within corporate personnel offices substituted a language of efficiency for the language of compliance to support the programs they had developed.

How a Weak State Created Legal Codes within the Firm

The rights language of the Wagner Act of 1935 had inspired the authors of the Civil Rights Act. The administrative model of the National Labor Relations Board had inspired them as well. As early as 1944, congressional Democrats from the North had proposed a sort of National Labor Relations Board for fair employment, with the power to halt discriminatory practices and to sanction companies that misbehaved.[1] Such a board might, like the NLRB, have established clear standards and simple compliance mandates. But Republicans and southern Democrats quashed the idea of another muscular administrative agency, and so the Civil Rights Act was enforced by hundreds of federal judges with their own understandings of the law and a federal agency without independent authority to sanction employers.

Judges were not empowered to invent new compliance standards from scratch, and they had little experience in regulating employment. So judges looked to leading employers when asked how firms should comply with fair employment laws. Employers frequently defended themselves by arguing that they had copied the best practices of their peers. The executive branch agencies charged with overseeing equal employment and affirmative action likewise looked to private employers to develop guidelines and their own best-practices lists. Lockheed's Georgia aircraft plant sent recruiters to historically black colleges in 1961, and Department of Labor officials recommended that approach in their guidelines. Big companies hired consultants to offer sexual harassment training in the 1990s, and the EEOC endorsed that approach. The personnel profession's favorite compliance strategies thus came to define equal opportunity and discrimination. Americans came to see a manager who hired his cronies without posting jobs, or repeatedly asked subordinates for dates, as practicing discrimination and contravening the Civil Rights Act. Nothing in the law suggested that these things constituted discrimination, yet companies adopted policies that forbade these practices and employees and the courts came to understand discrimination through job-posting policies and sexual harassment guidelines.

Judges and bureaucrats sometimes overturned the personnel profession's innovations, but in those cases they were usually adjudicating a debate between two groups of firms. In the *Griggs* case, for instance, the Supreme Court found in 1971 that the company seemed to be excluding blacks by testing for skills not needed on the job. In finding that Duke Power's test had a "disparate impact" on blacks, the Court supported another model, found among Plans for Progress firms that had validated employment tests to ensure that they were not screening out minorities. Thus the Court did not merely deny the specious, and probably insincere, argument of firms like Duke Power that generic job tests could prevent discrimination; it accepted an alternative argument and practice—test validation—embraced by another group of employers.

Judges in different courts often contradicted one another, but in the end they almost always backed the consensus view among human resources experts. At first the courts defined racial harassment as employment discrimination but treated sexual harassment as a private matter. By 1977, circuit courts had come to the view that sexual harassment on the job equaled employment discrimination, but as there was no reigning corporate standard, judges had divergent views on how employers might protect employees and avoid liability. Even after the Supreme Court nomination hearings for Clarence Thomas brought the issue of sexual harassment into the limelight in 1991, it was seven years before the Court supported the personnel profession's favorite remedies, harassment grievance procedures and sensitivity training. The Court backed personnel's standard, but only after employers had voted on it by institutionalizing it.

The personnel profession's advice, then, often became self-fulfilling. Any practice that personnel spread far and wide might be taken as evidence of good faith by the courts. As time went by, the legal test of whether an innovation advanced equality of opportunity was whether leading companies had adopted it. The courts looked to those companies. Judges rarely ruled that a practice would provide iron-clad protection against liability, but they did give employers that adopted innovations extra credit for effort. Human resources experts and corporate executives were often less concerned about whether new programs equalized opportunity than they were about whether those programs could help to protect them in court. Because the courts rarely rejected an emerging corporate standard when defense attorneys held it up, executives surmised that the best way to protect themselves was to follow the crowd.

Why Personnel Classics Became the Remedy

While personnel managers saw the Civil Rights Act as unwarranted federal meddling at first, many came to see opportunities for professional development in the law. They argued in the *New York Times* and *Harvard Business Review* that it would revitalize the profession. They crafted equal opportunity measures from the building blocks of the "industrial relations" system that had emerged between the 1930s and the 1950s, creating skill-training systems, job posting, job descriptions, performance evaluations, civil rights grievance procedures, and harassment grievance panels. Later personnel experts modeled "diversity management" measures on various and sundry personnel stand-bys. Almost everything they dreamed up had its origins in the personnel arsenal.

Rather than hiding their innovations from competing firms, personnel experts peddled them in the pages of *Fortune* and *Human Resources Management*. Some hoped that, by making new compliance strategies popular, they would win judicial support for them. They argued that employers needed specialists on their payrolls, and new regulatory uncertainty in the 1970s led executives to create offices to track compliance. This happened with regulatory expansion in other realms as well, from health and safety to fringe benefits.[2] Discussing health and safety, Burton Malkiel argued in 1980 in the *Harvard Business Review* that frequent regulatory changes undermine corporate planning: "It is not so much the direct cost of regulation that has inhibited investment and R & D but rather the unpredictability of regulatory changes."[3] Dedicated compliance offices could track administrative rulings, handle federal inspections, and monitor judicial decisions.[4] Not only personnel and equal opportunity experts, but benefits accountants, tax lawyers, safety engineers, and environmental specialists built careers on compliance in the 1970s.[5] In the case of equal opportunity, specialists exaggerated the risk of litigation to win executive attention, and argued that only dedicated offices could ensure legal compliance.[6]

Each time Congress strengthened the bite of equal opportunity law, as it did in the early 1970s and early 1990s, or its scope, as when it added older workers and the disabled, vice presidents of human resources called for new programs and additional staff. Each time judges or bureaucrats expanded the scope of the law, as when the EEOC defined pregnancy bans as discriminatory in 1972, personnel executives devoted more resources to figuring out how to comply. Each time the papers reported a multi-million-dollar civil rights settlement, human resources experts brought out new programs designed to inoculate against future lawsuits.[7]

These changes happened piecemeal, and by the beginning of the new century, they had revolutionized the employment relationship. This revolution was possible in part because personnel judiciously defined discrimination not as a consequence of managerial prejudice but as a consequence of antiquated management systems. All that was needed to end discrimination, they argued, was the application of modern, bureaucratic personnel methods. Each firm developed an elaborate legalistic code governing employment. Whereas the old personnel manual was a handbook, now personnel experts used loose-leaf binders so that they could swap out the old section on discipline or pregnancy when a new "best practices" list came out. Websites made this even easier, for HR experts could change policies with a mass e-mail message and a bit of new html code on the HR home page.

How Personnel Was Transformed

The personnel profession remade itself in response to the civil rights revolution. As the threat of unionization declined, the labor relations stalwarts who had defined the field in the wake of the Wagner Act gave way to women who championed equal opportunity. What it meant to be a personnel manager changed. Legal departments might just as well have taken responsibility for compliance, but some lawyers argued that the Civil Rights Act itself gave them too little direction to be of use in designing compliance strategies. That didn't stop personnel experts, whose professional modus operandi was not to hew closely to case law.

New recruits in the 1970s and 1980s argued that personnel's job was to make sure that the firm did not run afoul of federal regulations. Over time they redefined their function as integral to good management and embraced the new moniker of human resources management. The Civil Rights Act touched everything personnel departments did, so the new generalists in personnel had to understand fair employment law. Small firms, with only one or two people handling personnel, now hired women with backgrounds in equal opportunity rather than men trained in industrial relations.

Why Personnel Experts Defined Integration as Efficient

Perhaps it was because Americans have long conflated capitalism and democracy that personnel experts argued, from the very start, that true equality of opportunity would achieve both fairness and efficiency. The view that what is fair in the world must be efficient dates to the Utilitarian philosophers Jeremy Bentham and John Stuart Mill, who argued that freedom to participate in the economy and freedom to participate in the polity were two sides of the same coin. It was a short step to the idea that fair employment practices would improve efficiency. The idea found support in the work of economist Gary Becker, whose *Economics of Discrimination* of 1957 painted discrimination as inefficient. The American Constitution had created economic and political liberty in a single stroke, for white men at least. Its framers were convinced that by giving citizens freedom they would nurture prosperity. The idea that justice and efficiency are inextricably linked became embedded in American political institutions—perhaps most notably in antitrust law, adopted to prevent unfair business practices and soon recast as a way to create efficient market mechanisms.[8]

One legacy of a constitution that situated control over economic life squarely in civil society and a federal government confined to regulating interstate commerce was a firm belief that the state should not tell firms what to do. The Constitution portrayed government meddling with industry as illicit and inefficient. American personnel experts were thus predisposed by culture and by training to think of their activities in terms of efficiency rather than in terms of legal compliance. The fact that affirmative action was framed as a temporary expedient also encouraged personnel experts to frame their new programs as efficiency measures, which would not need to be dismantled when affirmative action regulations were taken down.

Because the Civil Rights Act did not specify what compliance should look like, personnel managers took credit for every last innovation. Because innovations were rarely mandated in subsequent legislation or case law, they remained the province of specialists, and many were never addressed in the public debate about affirmative action. Many of the innovations went by names that did not even identify them with equal opportunity, and once those were in place, most lost their connection to the law. HR managers could argue that performance evaluations guaranteed pay for performance, job descriptions increased the applicant pool, and salary classification linked pay to human capital requirements. These things spread like wildfire in the 1970s as equal opportunity measures. Then they were privatized—disconnected from the law—as they were folded back into a regime for the efficient management of personnel.

After Ronald Reagan floated the idea of ending affirmative action, personnel experts were loath to justify their programs in terms of compliance. It was no coincidence, then, that in the early 1980s personnel management underwent a paradigm shift. Everything personnel did was by that time colored by the law, but HR gurus argued that they were replacing the old "industrial relations" model with a new system designed to optimize the allocation of "human resources," foster employee commitment, and maximize productivity. Based loosely in ideas from sociology, economics, and psychology, the new portfolio struck like lightning—overnight, firms claimed to practice what HR proselytizers preached. That could only happen because personnel managers had already put many of the innovations into place under the cover of equal opportunity—annual evaluations, management training, job tests that mimicked real life. Human resources management did not offer a new set of practices so much as an efficiency rationale for measures already in place. The new HRM paradigm was not so much the cause of the revolution in practice as the result of it.

Personnel administration thus came full circle. Experts sold classical personnel programs as antidiscrimination measures in the early 1970s. A decade later, they were rebranding these measures as components of the new human resource management paradigm, designed to rationalize the allocation and development of human resources. Sociologist Philip Selznick found a similar process under way in the 1950s, in the wake of the "industrial relations" system spawned by the Wagner Act of 1935. By the 1950s, industrial relations practices were spreading to nonunion firms as components of a modern personnel system. They were described not in terms of containing labor strife or complying with contract provisions or National Labor Relations Board edicts, as they had been at first, but in terms of expanding efficiency by garnering commitment from workers through "industrial citizenship."[9] In this way, innovations that had been designed for compliance were recast as straight efficiency measures, reinforcing the American view that the firm is structured by the laws of the market, not the laws of the state.

In other arenas of regulation, this process of the privatization of legal compliance regimes has enabled Americans to sustain the faith that their state is weak and doesn't meddle in the affairs of business. When it comes to antitrust, or collective bargaining law, federal business regulations have been framed as supports for fair play in free markets rather than as government interventions—we now see antitrust not as an intervention to protect the small enterpriser, but as a market support, and we see collective bargaining legislation not as an intervention to protect workers, but as a way to level the playing field between labor and capital. As in those domains, we are coming to look on the Civil Rights Act not as an intervention to establish worker rights, but as a means of creating a free market for labor. It has opened job opportunities to all comers.

The strength of America's weak state, then, was twofold. On the one hand, the failure of Congress to create a muscular administrative agency, or to set the terms of compliance itself, led employers to create elaborate internal regulatory systems of their own and new departments to track the evolution of the law. On the other hand, the American belief in the laws of the market, and antipathy toward the laws of the state, led the corporate community to recast equal opportunity programs in terms of efficiency. This gave the programs a rationale outside of the law, bolstering them against the day affirmative action would be declared unnecessary.

Why Compliance Was a Moving Target

By creating openings for new interpretations of the Civil Rights Act, the regulatory system encouraged firms to heed new ideas about discrimination from social scientists and social movements.[10] When the idea of institutional racism was in the air, firms and then the courts reacted. When the idea of cognitive bias was in the air, firms and then the courts reacted. Americans were then exposed to new theories of discrimination on the job, through the programs their employers put into place. When the behemoth Kaiser Corporation took up the idea of institutional racism in the 1970s and created special skill-training tracks for blacks, line workers revised their understandings of discrimination. When General Electric took up the idea of cognitive bias in the 1980s and put in diversity training and mentoring programs, line workers revised their understandings of discrimination. There was backlash in some quarters, but surveys show that, in the main, Americans came to accept the programs their employers put into place. Workers in firms with affirmative action programs were more likely to believe in institutional racism than workers in firms without them.[11]

Studies of corporate equal opportunity measures have traced their inconstancy over time to the initial ambiguity of the law.[12] Erin Kelly, by contrast, argues that it is actually the separation of powers that led to changes in corporate practice and then the law, for it permitted groups to promote new interpretations of law.[13] In the case of federal child care support, the separation of powers allowed the meaning of a crystal clear statute to be altered by eager human resources consultants, who turned a tax break for workplace child care centers into dependent care expense accounts and won IRS approval. Political scientist Robert Lieberman has similarly argued that America's fragmented state led to much greater expansion of antidiscrimination law than did France's centralized state, because in America there were myriad openings for citizen input.[14] Taken together, these chapters in the history of equal opportunity show that, in the American context, professionals promoted new compliance programs by appealing to executive concern that the state could alter the terms of compliance overnight. It was executive anxiety over the future of the law that led to compliance innovations.

Why Social Science Revolutions Colored Equal Opportunity

New ideas about discrimination eventually shaped the law. Antidiscrimination measures of the early 1960s were crafted in a world of scholars and politicians and journalists influenced by behaviorism in the social sciences. Over the next several decades the social sciences underwent two revolutions that influenced those same groups. While human resources experts designed new antidiscrimination measures using spare parts from the personnel arsenal, the particular programs they concocted were shaped by the wider public discourse.

The Institutional Revolution and Discrimination

The behaviorism of the 1950s and 1960s depicted the actions of individuals as shaped by incentives, and collective social phenomena as reducible to the individual level. In political science, for instance, behaviorism was expressed in pluralist theory, which depicted individual self-interest as the driving force behind political affiliation. For behaviorists, individual bias was the problem behind employment discrimination, and to counteract bias, the state might create a disincentive to discriminate through lawsuits. That was the simple idea behind the Civil Rights Act.

In the 1970s, the institutional revolution brought new insights from labor economics and structural sociology to bear on the problem of employment discrimination.[15] These paradigms built on research on dual labor markets that began in the early 1960s.[16] They challenged the idea that inequality is the result of managerial prejudice alone, suggesting that social institutions may produce different opportunities for men and women, whites and blacks. Inertia may sustain employment institutions that are discriminatory even when they are also inefficient.

Institutionalists in labor economics found that national labor market institutions produced inequality by steering white men to entry-level jobs in stable industries with high wages and strong unions, and women and minorities to unstable industries with low wages and no unions.[17] Within the firm, labor market institutions affected career prospects by giving promotion opportunities to some groups and denying them to others.[18] Sociologists studying organizations and stratification were coming to similar conclusions. In 1965 Arthur Stinchcombe's "Social Structure and Organizations" pointed to how organizational and industrial practices become ossified. Sociologists who studied national labor markets and labor markets within firms found that traditions from another age excluded women and minorities from many careers.[19]

These two groups developed analyses of how employment traditions shape the life chances of different groups, tracing inequality to how firms sort employees at first and then structure their careers. As institutional ideas swept through sociology, economics, and political science, activists, journalists, and politicians embraced them. They talked of institutional racism and sexism. Employers came to see traditional hiring and promotion systems as discriminatory, and personnel experts advised them to redesign systems to eliminate obstacles to women and minorities.

The Supreme Court had sent a broad message in the *Griggs* decision in 1971, suggesting that employment practices that did not mention race, ethnicity, or gender could still exclude groups. The Court did not decree that employers should write job descriptions, create formal salary classification systems, set up annual performance evaluations, and reengineer their job ladders. The message was that the Court would sanction firms practicing de facto institutional discrimination even without evidence of malice aforethought. Social scientists shone a spotlight on institutional sources of discrimination, and personnel experts designed remedies.

The Cognitive Revolution and Discrimination

Whereas the institutional revolution in the social sciences was championed by economists, sociologists, and political scientists, the cognitive revolution of the 1980s and 1990s was championed by psychologists, anthropologists, and sociologists.[20] Its core insight is that people behave according to mental maps—to representations and customs they experience in the world.[21] In psychology this was an old insight, but the behaviorism of the 1950s and 1960s had focused the field on reward and punishment. In anthropology, the idea that mental maps of the world shape behavior was revived by Clifford Geertz and Mary Douglas.[22] In sociology, the importance of cognition had been recognized by constructionists such as Peter Berger and Thomas Luckmann and symbolic interactionists such as Erving Goffman, and the approach became central to the discipline with the rise of the sociology of culture in the 1980s.[23]

The cognitive revolution had two key implications for workplace inequality. One was that managers might discriminate not through prejudice or malice but through unconscious categorization. Sociologist Rosabeth Moss Kanter used the term "homosocial reproduction" to describe the tendency of white male managers to choose others like themselves for promotion.[24] Research suggested that the preference for members of one's own group is widespread, and that it can contaminate managerial judgment.[25] Stereotyping itself is part of a normal cognitive mechanism deriving from our efforts to link categories and concepts. Cognitive associations between female and secretary or between African-American and laborer can thus lead managers to place people in jobs traditionally held by others from the same group—and to appoint new managers who look like present managers.[26]

The second implication was that members of disadvantaged groups might face cognitive barriers to success. Studies found that students do better when teachers are led to expect they will do well.[27] In the 1980s, social psychologist Claude Steele found that blacks fare worse on standardized tests under conditions of stereotype "vulnerability" or "threat"—when they are sensitized to issues of race before the test.[28] Subsequent studies have reinforced the idea that "expectancy effects" extend to students themselves—that where race or gender is made salient to test-takers, performance is affected.[29] This reinforced Kanter's finding that women face particular status anxiety when they are in positions typically held by men.[30] Stereotypes thus may affect not only managers who make decisions about promotions, but underlings seeking promotions.

As the cognitive revolution swept the social sciences, journalists, politicians, and human resources managers embraced a cognitive view of discrimination. Managers could be unaware of their own bias, and training might remedy that. Managers might not realize that they were failing to hire women and minorities, and diversity performance evaluations might remedy that. Workers might suffer from seeing themselves as tokens and from lack of role models, and might not perform to their full potential or ask for the jobs they deserved. Mentoring and networking programs might help to provide models and methods of success.

It was thus that the insights of the cognitive revolution were put into practice in the workplace, and even those never exposed to the cognitive revolution itself were exposed to its prescriptions at work.

The Future of Equal Opportunity

The idea that the government could interfere with employers' decisions about whom to hire and fire took hold only gradually. When Robert Ackerman interviewed leading corporate executives in 1973, he found that each time public policy establishes a new arena of social responsibility and leaves it to business to work out the details, compliance is not really voluntary. It may seem so at first, but norms gradually develop that make compliance seem both right and inevitable. There is a fallacy in thinking that "corporate *action* on social issues is either voluntary or required. . . . For every issue there is a time period before it becomes a matter of social concern, and espousing the issue may even arouse economic and social sanctions. There is also a time when its acceptance is so widespread that adherence is an unquestioned part of doing business."[31] And so, child labor laws were contentious when they were first enacted, but restrictions on child labor were beyond debate when Ackerman was writing in 1973. Equal opportunity protections such as recruitment at historically black colleges or job-posting systems came to be accepted much as prohibitions against child labor were accepted.

Current diversity measures face little overt opposition in corporate America, in large part because the human resources profession has done such a good job of framing them as promoting efficiency, of depicting the problem as one of outdated personnel systems rather than as one of prejudice, and of making the case that the workforce is in the midst of becoming dramatically more diverse. These successes suggest that corporate diversity programs will continue to flourish even in the absence of new legislation.

Now it is easy for us to see diversity measures as increasing efficiency. How can employees facing harassment do their best work? How can a firm that kept Latinos out of management hope to attract the best talent? Solutions that opened up jobs to a wider pool of applicants, and assigned those jobs on the basis of merit, were compatible with management doctrine dating back to Frederick Taylor at the beginning of the twentieth century. Taylor assumed that some groups were naturally destined for drudgery at work. Equal opportunity experts started with a different assumption, and in short order, the idea that employers should select workers on the basis of ability alone seemed inevitable.[32] Opponents of affirmative action used that principle to argue against it, as when Harvard's Nathan Glazer argued in 1975 that civil rights law undermined the principle of equal treatment: "In effect, the EEOC is engaged in breaking the law under which it operates" by forcing firms to discriminate against white men.[33] It was only a dozen years earlier that virtually all leading firms excluded women and blacks from skilled and managerial jobs, and in that time America had accepted the principle that jobs should be assigned on the basis of merit, and that Washington had the authority to make sure that happened.

Bureaucratic remedies were made palatable by the fact that they depicted discrimination not as a problem of personal bias, but as one of antiquated hiring and promotion systems. The new diversity management programs that did address bias, such as diversity performance evaluations and diversity training, couched bias in terms of unwitting stereotypes rather than in terms of knowing prejudice. These programs whitewashed the problem of bias. And so we no longer hear the word "prejudice" on the lips of human resources managers.

Even though Congress has not expanded fair employment laws since the early 1990s, employers have stayed on the bandwagon. One reason may be that the courts have continued to enforce the law. Human resources managers are quick to remember that Texaco and Coca-Cola settled race discrimination suits in 1996 and 2001 for $176 million and $193 million respectively. Another reason may be that, as *Workforce 2000* predicted, many companies are becoming more and more diverse. Another still may be that federal regulators have kept up the pressure. A series of federal investigations and lawsuits led the major Wall Street firms to redouble their efforts to recruit and promote women, and now many are facing scrutiny for their treatment of minorities.[34] Executives and human resources managers from a wide range of industries report in our 2007 and 2008 interviews that they are in the midst of implementing new diversity measures. Firms are hiring chief diversity officers, rethinking their diversity training programs to eschew material on legal compliance, developing new systems for documenting diversity in real time with PeopleSoft and other human resources programs, building new diversity councils to advise managers on how to increase integration, and opening up networking programs to any group that wants to create a network. And so while equal employment and affirmative action have not gotten the press attention they got in the 1970s, many corporations have been doing more than ever.

Yet all of this activity still occurs in an evidentiary vacuum. The workplace has become markedly more diverse since the early 1960s, but how much of that is due to the particular programs that the human resources profession promulgated? We have little hard evidence that employer programs increase opportunity. When companies choose new diversity programs, they rely on "best practices" lists rather than on research findings. Perhaps that is not altogether by chance, for following "best practices" has often protected firms in court. If what matters is protecting yourself in court, and if the courts accept the argument that the defendant is doing what everyone else is doing, then the ultimate irony of the history of equal opportunity is that compliance is a self-fulfilling prophecy.

NOTES

Acknowledgments

1. For instance, Baron, Dobbin, and Jennings 1986; Dobbin et al. 1988; Dobbin and Kelly 2007; Dobbin et al. 1993; Kelly and Dobbin 1998, 1999.

Chapter 1
Regulating Discrimination

1. Quotas were sometimes imposed by courts, particularly on fire and police departments that resisted integration, but employer-initiated quotas were generally forbidden by courts and bureaucrats, the notable exception being a training quota permitted in *Brian Weber v. Kaiser Aluminum*. Blumrosen 1993, chap. 15; Shaeffer 1973, 90.

2. Graham 1990; MacLean 2006.

3. Harrison 1988.

4. Burstein 1985; Chen, forthcoming.

5. Lieberman 2005; Sabbagh 2007; Skrentny 1996.

6. Skrentny 1996, 2002.

7. Rosen 2006.

8. Quoted in *University of California Regents v. Bakke*, 438 U.S. 265 (1978); Sabbagh 2007, 142; Karabel 2005. (As Berkeley sociologist Jerome Karabel points out, those early "diversity" programs favoring rural areas and farflung states had originally been crafted to reduce the number of Jews.)

9. Edelman 2002; Edelman, Uggen, and Erlanger 1999.

10. Chen, forthcoming.

11. Bisom-Rapp 2001a; Edelman, Uggen, and Erlanger 1999; Krawiec 2003.

12. Chen, forthcoming.

13. Meyer and Scott 1983b.

14. Lieberman 2002b.

15. Kelly 2003.

16. Dobbin and Sutton 1998; Lieberman 2005; Lieberman 1998.

17. Ewick and Silbey (1998) find more generally that laymen think of their rights broadly, believing that the law protects rights they believe they should have.

18. Selznick 1969.

19. Vollmer and McGillivray 1960, 32.

20. Merton 1968.

21. See chapter 7.

22. Clemens 1997.

23. Skrentny 2002.

24. Harrison 1988; Vogel 1993.

25. Dobbin and Kelly 2007.

26. Dobbin, Simmons, and Garrett 2007.

27. Thelen 2004 describes how such gradual shifts can lead to momentous policy changes over time. See also Campbell 1997.

28. Bureau of Labor Statistics 2006; United States Census Bureau 2006.

29. Burstein and Monahan 1986; Petersen 1974; Skrentny 1996, 127.

30. Shaeffer 1975, 5.

31. Dobbin et al. 1993.

32. Edelman 1990; Sutton et al. 1994.

33. Dobbin and Sutton 1998; Kelly and Dobbin 1998.

34. Becker 1957.

35. Johnston and Packer 1987.

36. Bureau of National Affairs 1995; Lynch 1997.

37. Dobbin and Kelly 2007.

38. Bequai 1992.

39. For details about industries covered and sampling techniques see Dobbin et al. 1993; Dobbin and Kelly 2007; Kalev, Dobbin, and Kelly 2006.

40. De Schutter 2006.

41. Leonard 1990.

42. Dobbin, Kalev, and Kelly 2007; Kalev and Dobbin 2006; Kalev, Dobbin, and Kelly 2006.

CHAPTER 2
WASHINGTON OUTLAWS DISCRIMINATION WITH A BROAD BRUSH

1. Quoted in Brecher, Lombardi, and Stackhouse 1982, 136.

2. Purcell 1953, 111.

3. Purcell 1953, 31.

4. For instance, Leonard 1989, 1990 and Ashtenfelter and Heckman 1976 try to gauge the effects of affirmative action and by extension the prevalence of discrimination before affirmative action.

5. Purcell 1962, 5.

6. Quoted in "Anti-Negro Acts Are Laid to G.M.," *New York Times,* November 30, 1961, 31.

7. Bureau of the Census, 2000 U.S. Department of the Census Data Set: Census 2000 Summary File 3 (SF 3)—Sample Data, GCT-P13, "Occupation, Industry, and Class of Worker of Employed Civilians 16 Years and Over."

8. Perrow 2002, chap. 6. Quoted in Brecher, Lombardi, and Stackhouse 1982, 136. See also Dalzell's (1987) book on the Boston Associates, the group that developed the Massachusetts textile mills. Licht 1983, 222, presents figures for occupation segregation for 1860 through 1890 in Philadelphia railroading.

9. DiPrete's (1989) study of the Federal civil service describes missing rungs in the job ladders between entry-level posts, dominated by women and minorities, and upper-level posts, dominated by white men. In consequence, some women and minorities dominated lower-level jobs and found advancement to upper-level jobs to be blocked.

10. Seybold 1954, 15–16. The survey covered 515 factories and 501 offices.

11. The extent of segregation across industries is documented by Gordon, Edwards, and Reich 1982, and the extent of segmentation across jobs is documented in Baron and Bielby 1985.

12. Figures come from Reskin 1990, 191–93. Insurance firms also segregated men and women on the basis of the type of insurance they sold. The quote comes from an agent Robin Leidner interviewed, as quoted in Reskin 1990, 186.

13. Rennes 2007.

14. Slichter 1919.

15. Brandes 1976.

16. Taylor 1981, 41.

17. Stark 1980.

18. Bendix 1956, 308.

19. Taylor 1981, 39–73.

20. Gouldner 1954; Milkman 1997.

21. Hodson and Sullivan 1990, 163.

22. Brody 1989; Slichter, Healy, and Livernash 1960; Dimick 1978; Gouldner 1954.

23. Romm 1995.

24. Edwards 1979; Baron, Dobbin, and Jennings 1986; Burawoy 1985

25. Gouldner 1954, 64, 65, 64.

26. Milkman 1997, 28–30, 38, 37

27. Gouldner 1954; Halle 1984, 303

28. Bureau of the Census, 2000 U.S. Department of the Census Data Set: Census 2000 Summary File 3 (SF 3)—Sample Data, GCT-P13, "Occupation, Industry, and Class of Worker of Employed Civilians 16 Years and Over."

29. Tolbert and Zucker 1983; DiPrete 1989.

30. DiPrete 1989, 23–25.

31. Seybold 1954, 10.

32. Bureau of National Affairs 1967, 14.

33. Bureau of National Affairs 1967, 15.

34. Grove 1965, 32.

35. Bureau of National Affairs 1967, 16.

36. Braestrup 1961a.

37. *Rowe v. General Motors Corp.*, 457 F.2d 348 (5th Cir. 1972).

38. "U.S. Cites 2 Pacts to End Race Bias," *New York Times,* July 27, 1962, 9.

39. Bureau of National Affairs 1967, 16.

40. Grove 1965, 32.

41. Purcell 1962.

42. DuRivage 1985, 361.

43. DuRivage 1985.

44. Executive Order 10925, 26 Fed. Reg. 1977 (1961).

45. Graham 1990, 33.

46. Sabbagh 2002.

47. Graham 1990, 44.

48. Braestrup 1962d, 17.

49. Graham 1990, 33–59.

50. Boyle 1973, 86; Nelson and Bridges 1999.

51. Section 701b of the Civil Rights Act of 1964, Public Law 88-352, 241–68, July 2, 1964, 88th Congress H.R. 7152.
52. Title VII of the Civil Rights Act of 1964.
53. Lieberman 2002a.
54. Civil Rights Act of 1964, sec. 703 (j).
55. Stryker 1996, 5.
56. Eskridge 1994; Meltzer 1980.
57. Braestrup 1961d, 20.
58. Brauer 1983; Edwards 1973, 412.
59. Chen 2006, 2007, forthcoming; Rodriguez and Weingast 2003.
60. Chayes 1974, 82.
61. Shaeffer 1973, 7.
62. Skrentny 2002.
63. Gutman 1993, 194.
64. Gutman 1993, 289.
65. To which "Programs" was later added, making it the OFCCP. Burstein 1985; Edelman 1990; Hammerman 1984.
66. DuRivage 1985, 362.
67. Hammerman 1984, 12.
68. Ashenfelter and Heckman 1976, 46.
69. Edelman 1992; Lempert and Sanders 1986, 378–79.
70. Shaeffer 1973, 121.
71. Hammerman 1984, 11–12.
72. Shaeffer 1973, 12.

CHAPTER 3
THE END OF JIM CROW

1. Lipner 1965, 27.
2. Fretz and Hayman 1973, 134–35.
3. Jacoby 1985a; Baron, Dobbin, and Jennings 1986.
4. Braestrup 1961a.
5. Braestrup 1961a.
6. Graham 1990, 49; Sovern 1966, 109.
7. Gordon 2000.
8. Quoted in Sovern 1966, 109–0.
9. Braestrup 1961c.
10. Kenworthy 1963, 1.
11. Gordon 2000, 10.
12. Gordon 2000, 10.
13. Gordon 2000, 10.
14. Purcell 1962, 5.
15. Braestrup 1962b, 23.
16. Braestrup 1962d, 17.
17. Graham 1990, 56.

18. Kenworthy 1963, 1.

19. Sovern 1966.

20. Morse 1965, 128.

21. Baker 1965; Day 1965; Lawrence 1965; Mattison 1965; McFarland 1965; Morse 1965

22. Pomfret 1963, 15.

23. Quoted in Purcell 1962, 5.

24. Karmin 1966, 1.

25. "U.S. Laxity Charged in Making Firms Comply with Bias Laws," *Washington Post*, December 6, 1968, A2.

26. Graham 1990, 60.

27. Graham 1990, 52.

28. Prugh 1965, 10.

29. Grove 1965, 32.

30. "More Jobs for Negroes," *Nation's Business*, September 1967.

31. Prugh 1965, 10.

32. "More Jobs for Negroes," 36.

33. "More Jobs for Negroes," 36.

34. SHRM website: http://www.shrm.org/about/mission.asp, accessed January 16, 2008.

35. http://hrhouston.org/associations/1073/files/History-The1960s.pdf, accessed January 17, 2008.

36. "U.S. Cites 2 Pacts to End Race Bias," *New York Times*, July 27, 1962, 9.

37. Puma 1966, 45.

38. "U.S. Cites 2 Pacts," 9; "Anti-Bias Pledge Asked of Unions," *New York Times*, April 8, 1962, 53; Braestrup 1962c.

39. Bureau of National Affairs 1967, 8; see also Hallam 1973, 808.

40. Wehrwein 1962, 13; Braestrup 1962a, 20.

41. From the MIT electronic archives at http://www.tech.mit.edu/archives/VOL_085/TECH_V085_S0279_P015.txt, accessed December 19, 2006.

42. Stetson 1963, 1.

43. Bureau of National Affairs 1967, 10.

44. Details on the study can be found in Dobbin et al. 1993. We selected a random sample of American employers in three states representing different kinds of employment regulations (New Jersey, Virginia, and California) and representing a range of industrial, service, nonprofit, and government employers. Edelman 1990 finds that the percentage of employers with formal equal opportunity policies rose from 13 percent in 1980 to 47 percent in 1990.

45. Quoted in Shaeffer 1973, 12; emphasis added.

46. Jacoby 1997, 15.

47. National Industrial Conference Board 1940.

48. Milkman 1997.

49. Pedriana 2006.

50. Danovitch 1990.

51. Danovitch 1990.

52. Costain 1992; Harrison 1988; Pedriana 2004.

53. Danovitch 1990.

54. *Phillips v. Martin Marietta Corp.*, 400 U.S. 542, 542, 3 EPD 8088 (1971); see Edwards 1973, 415.

55. *Phillips v. Martin Marietta Corp.*, 542.

56. Peirce School 1935.

57. National Industrial Conference Board 1965.

58. Bureau of National Affairs 1967, 3.

59. Gocke and Weymar 1969.

60. Graham 1990, 421; Hobbs and Stoops 2002, 85.

61. Mays 1961, 9.

62. Raskin 1961, 1–50.

63. Gordon 2000, 7.

64. Mattison 1965, 151–52.

65. Gordon 2000, 10.

66. Baker 1965, 118.

67. Lawrence 1965, 143.

68. Braestrup 1961c.

69. Gordon 2000, 8.

70. "Desegregation Now in Effect at Lockheed," *New Pittsburgh Courier*, June 3, 1961, 31.

71. Stetson 1963, 1.

72. Lelyveld 1964, 41.

73. Braestrup 1961a; Lawrence 1965; Lipner 1965, 27;

74. Cray 1968, 43.

75. "More Jobs for Negroes," 32.

76. "More Jobs for Negroes," 32.

77. Grove 1965, 32.

78. McBee 1964, B2.

79. McBee 1964, B2.

80. Boyle 1973, 92.

81. Bureau of National Affairs 1967, 1.

82. Bureau of National Affairs 1967, 10.

83. Pomfret 1963, 21.

84. Quoted in Bureau of National Affairs 1967, 3.

85. National Industrial Conference Board 1965.

86. Halle 1984, 5.

87. Halle 1984, 303.

88. Braestrup 1961b.

89. McFarland 1965, 133.

90. Lawrence 1965, 142.

91. Peirce School 1935, 4.

92. "More Jobs for Negroes," 36.

93. Braestrup 1962a, 20.

94. "More Jobs for Negroes," 36.

95. Grove 1965, 32.

96. Grove 1965, 32.

97. "More Jobs for Negroes," 36.

98. Purcell 1960, 49–50.

99. Boyle 1973, 93.

100. Boyle 1973, 90.

101. Boyle 1973, 90.

102. Bureau of National Affairs 1967, 1976.

103. Bureau of National Affairs 1976, 8; 1986a, 13.

104. Anderson 1996.

105. Shaeffer 1973, 11.

106. Shaeffer 1973, 11.

107. Shaeffer 1973, 12.

108. *Leisner v. New York Telephone Company*, 5 EPD at 8498 S.D.N.Y. (1973).

109. Boyle 1973, 87.

110. Shaeffer 1973, 90–97.

111. Grove 1965, 32.

112. Chen, forthcoming.

113. Graham 1990, 46–59.

114. U.S. Department of Labor 2000. The latest version of the 1966 Affirmative Action Regulations can be seen at https://www.dol.gov/esa/regs/fedreg/proposed/2000010991.pdf, accessed August 12, 2008.

115. Puma 1966.

116. Gordon 2000, 17·

117. Day 1965, 157.

118. Baker 1965, 114.

119. Quoted in Shaeffer 1973, 8.

120. Shaeffer 1973, 10.

CHAPTER 4
WASHINGTON MEANS BUSINESS

1. Schofer 1971, 926.

2. Sloan 1963.

3. Schofer 1971, 926.

4. Jacoby 1985a.

5. Dobbin 1992.

6. Griggs v. Duke Power Company, 401 U.S. 424 (1971).

7. Edelman 1992, 1541.

8. DuRivage 1985, 362; Edelman 1992, 1537; Graham 1990; Leonard 1985; Shaeffer 1973, 11; Skrentny 1996.

9. Skrentny 1996, 142 A strict bottom-line approach was struck down in 1982 in *Connecticut v. Teal*; see Sabbagh 2008, 127–28.

10. U.S. Department of Labor 2000, 41 CFR 60-2.16, 26088.

11. Hammerman 1984, 13.

12. Boyle 1973, 92.

13. U.S. Department of Labor 2000, 41 CFR 60-2.16, 26107.

14. Hammerman 1984, 12.

15. Bradshaw 1987; Cabot 1987; Hallam 1973, 807; Skrentny 1996, 127

16. Edelman 1992, 1539–40; Lempert and Sanders 1986, 378–79.

17. Stryker 1996, 10.

18. 422 U.S. 405 (1975).

19. Burstein and Monahan 1986, 361.

20. Stryker 1996, 11.

21. Donohue and Siegelman 1991, 998; Siegelman and Donohue 1990, 1164; Stryker 2001.

22. Thorpe 1973, 645.

23. Chayes 1974, 81.

24. Karabel 2005, 214.

25. Boyle 1973, 86–87.

26. Burack and Smith 1977, 183.

27. Ropp 1987.

28. Fretz and Hayman 1973, 135.

29. Leonard 1985.

30. Bassford 1974; Bell 1971.

31. Dobbin et al. 1993.

32. Meyer and Scott 1992.

33. Kochan, Katz, and McKersie 1994, 45; Selznick 1969.

34. National Industrial Conference Board 1947, 16.

35. Lawrence and Lorsch 1967.

36. Thompson 1967.

37. Pfeffer and Salancik 1978, 273.

38. Meyer and Scott 1992, 275.

39. Kochan and Cappelli 1984, 146.

40. Foulkes and Morgan 1977, 171.

41. Edelman et al. 1991, 77.

42. Day 1965, 155.

43. Schofer 1971, 920.

44. Schofer 1971, 926.

45. Schofer 1971, 930.

46. Schofer 1971, 934.

47. Froehlich and Hawver 1974, 62.

48. Giblin and Ornati 1975, 37.

49. Boyle 1973, 88–89.

50. Giblin and Ornati 1975, 45.

51. Chayes 1974, 81.

52. Johns and Moser 1989, 56; Ropp 1987; Vernon-Gerstenfeld and Burke 1985, 59–60.

53. Marino 1980, 25.

54. Anderson 1975; Ewing 1983.

55. Mendeloff 1979, 92.

56. Ackerman 1975, 72.

57. Employee Retirement Income Security Act; Dobbin and Sutton 1998.

58. Foulkes and Morgan 1977, 160.

59. Foulkes and Morgan 1977, 160.

60. Ropp 1987.

61. Johns and Moser 1989.

62. Dobbin et al. 1993.

63. Edelman 1992, 1555.

64. Purcell 1974.

65. Schofer 1971, 969.

66. Purcell 1974, 99.

67. GE's July 1970 Equal Opportunity report to the U.S. Commission on Civil Rights, in Schofer 1971, 940.

68. Baron, Jennings, and Dobbin 1988; Jacoby 1985a.

69. Fligstein 1990.

70. Chandler 1977.

71. Ackerman 1973, 88.

72. Ackerman 1973, 91.

73. Boyle 1973, 90.

74. Boyle 1973, 90.

75. Fretz and Hayman 1973, 137.

76. Ackerman 1973, 89.

77. Quoted in Ackerman 1973, 94.

78. Vernon-Gerstenfeld and Burke 1985, 59–60.

79. Bureau of National Affairs 1976.

80. Spiro 1994.

81. Jacoby 1985a.

82. Cross 1938.

83. Ewing 1983; Selznick 1969, 91.

84. Berenbeim 1980, 5.

85. Selznick 1969.

86. Vollmer and McGillivray 1960.

87. Vollmer and McGillivray 1960, 32.

88. As quoted in McFarland 1965, 132.

89. "Anti-Negro Acts Are Laid to G.M.," *New York Times,* November 30, 1961, 31.

90. Hallam 1973, 808.

91. Order No. 420-69, 34 Fed. Reg. 12281, July 25, 1969.

92. *Williams v. Saxbe*, 413 F. Supp. 654 (1976).

93. Soutar 1981; Staudohar 1981.

94. Edelman 1990; Sutton and Dobbin 1996; Sutton et al. 1994.

95. Berenbeim 1980, 1.

96. Rowe and Baker 1984.

97. Reprinted in Rowe and Baker 1984, 14.

98. Marino 1980, 32.

99. Gery 1977, 203.

100. Youngblood and Tidwell 1981, 32.

101. Berenbeim 1980.

102. Donohue and Siegelman 1991, 1033.

103. Quoted in Berenbeim 1980, 12.

104. Reproduced in Berenbeim 1980, 20.

105. Rowe and Baker 1984, 10.

106. Berenbeim 1980.

107. Edelman, Uggen, and Erlanger 1999, 441.

108. Sutton and Dobbin 1996; Sutton et al. 1994.

109. Berenbeim 1980, 45.

110. Berenbeim 1980, 35.

111. Edelman, Uggen, and Erlanger 1999.

112. Edelman, Uggen, and Erlanger 1999.

113. Berenbeim 1980; Sutton et al. 1994.

114. Edelman, Uggen, and Erlanger 1999, 439.

115. Berenbeim 1980, 46.

116. Mills 1979, 154.

117. Jacobs 1994, B10.

118. Reed 2001.

119. *Circuit City Stores v. St. Clair Adams*, 121 S. Ct. 1302 (2001).

120. Dobbin and Sutton 1998.

121. Lawrence and Lorsch 1967; Meyer and Scott 1992, 275; Pfeffer and Salancik 1978.

122. Perrow 1986, chap. 1.

123. Kalev, Dobbin, and Kelly 2006.

124. Dobbin and Kelly 2007; Dobbin et al. 1993.

CHAPTER 5
FIGHTING BIAS WITH BUREAUCRACY

1. Boyle 1973, 88.

2. Cohen, March, and Olsen 1972.

3. Kingdon 1984.

4. Jacoby 1985a.

5. Feild 1984.

6. U.S. Equal Employment Opportunity Commission 1974, 4.

7. Shaeffer 1975.

8. In other industries, women had fought for plantwide seniority from the 1950s. Fehn 1993.

9. Shaeffer 1975.

10. 422 U.S. 405 1975; Wallace 1976.

11. Thorpe 1973, 646.

12. Boyle 1973, 87.

13. Kanter 1977.

14. Thorpe 1973, 49.

15. Boyle 1973, 88.

16. Baron, Jennings, and Dobbin 1988.

17. Fulmer and Fulmer 1974, 492; Baron 1984; Kahn 1976; Rubery 1978.

18. Kochan, Katz, and McKersie 1994, 88.

19. Elbaum 1984, 101.

20. Kochan, Katz, and McKersie 1994, 88.

21. Jacoby 1985a.
22. Burawoy 1985, 42.
23. Baron, Dobbin, and Jennings 1986.
24. Jacoby 1984; Selznick 1969; Stone 1974; Edwards 1979; Stark 1986; Kochan, Katz, and McKersie 1994, 88–89.
25. Cohen and Pfeffer 1986; Pfeffer and Cohen 1984.
26. Weber 1978.
27. DiPrete 1989; Tolbert and Zucker 1983.
28. Bendix 1956, 279; Guillén 1994; Stark 1986; Taylor 1911.
29. Baron, Dobbin, and Jennings 1986.
30. Bendix 1956, 308.
31. Puma 1966, 36.
32. Puma 1966, 154.
33. Bendix 1956, 279; Guillén 1994; Stark 1986; Taylor 1911.
34. See also Dugan 1966; Lopez 1966; Parrish 1966.
35. Lockwood 1966, 8–9; see also Bayroff 1966; Dugan 1966.
36. Lockwood 1966, 9–10; see also Peskin 1969, 137.
37. U.S. EEOC, 35 Fed. Reg. 12333; Thorpe 1973, 647.
38. "More Jobs for Negroes," *Nation's Business*, September 1967, 9.
39. Skrentny 1996, 97.
40. Bureau of the Census 1975, 380, Part I.
41. Ferman 1968.
42. Bureau of National Affairs 1967, 14.
43. 401 U.S. 424 (1971).
44. Thorpe 1973, 643.
45. *Griggs v. Duke Power Company*, 401 U.S. 424, 431–32 (1971).
46. *Griggs*, 432.
47. *Griggs*, 431; Thorpe 1973, 648.
48. Hammerman 1984; Sabbagh 2007, 121.
49. Campbell 1973; Gavin and Toole 1973; Gorham 1972; National Civil Service League 1973; Slevin 1973.
50. Chayes 1974, 86.
51. Arvey and Mussio 1973.
52. Walsh and Hess 1974.
53. Peterson 1974.
54. McCrary 2006, 6–7.
55. Spencer, Steele, and Quinn 1999; Steele and Aronson 1995.
56. Levitt 1998, A20.
57. *Griggs,* 432.
58. Edwards 1973, 414.
59. U.S. Equal Employment Opportunity Commission 1974, 35–40.
60. Kochan and Cappelli 1984, 147; Chayes 1974, 81.
61. Froehlich and Hawver 1974, 62.
62. Froehlich and Hawver 1974, 68; see also Bassford 1974; Bell 1971; Froehlich and Hawver 1974.
63. Baron, Jennings, and Dobbin 1988.

64. "U.S. Cites 2 Pacts to End Race Bias," *New York Times*, July 27, 1962, 9.

65. General Electric's 1970 report for the U.S. Commission on Civil Rights, reprinted in Schofer 1971, 949.

66. Boyle 1973, 94–95.

67. *Baxter v. Savannah Sugar Refining Corp.*, 350 F. Supp. 139, 145 (S.D. Ga. 1972).

68. *Baxter*, 147.

69. Boyle 1973, 92.

70. Foulkes and Morgan 1977.

71. Fulmer and Fulmer 1974, 493.

72. *Rowe v. General Motors Corp.*, 457 F.2d 348 (5th Cir. 1972).

73. *Baxter*, 147.

74. Garris and Black 1974, 57.

75. Fulmer and Fulmer 1974, 492.

76. *Schultz v. Wheaton Glass Co.*, 421 F.2d 259 (3rd Cir. 1970).

77. Corning Glass Works v. Brennan, 417 U.S. 188 (1974).

78. Edwards 1973, 423; Nelson and Bridges 1999.

79. Edwards 1973, 423.

80. Fretz and Hayman 1973, 137.

81. Boyle 1973, 89.

82. Fretz and Hayman 1973, 137.

83. Fretz and Hayman 1973, 137.

84. *Danner v. Phillips Petroleum Co.*, 447 F.2d 159 (5th Cir. 1971).

85. Edwards 1973, 413.

86. Chayes 1974, 81; Giblin and Ornati 1974.

87. DiPrete 1989, 197.

88. Boyle 1973, 90.

89. Giblin and Ornati 1974, 40.

90. Boyle 1973, 91.

91. Boyle 1973, 90.

92. Slevin 1973, 30.

93. DiPrete 1989.

94. Shaeffer 1973, 9.

95. Shaeffer 1973, 7.

96. Ichniowski 1983.

97. Hallam 1973, 808–9.

98. Gould 1977; Oelsner 1977.

99. Cunningham 1936; Drum 1960; Patton 1960; Rock and Grela 1960.

100. Peskin 1969, 130.

101. Bureau of National Affairs 1967, 16.

102. *Rowe v. General Motors Corp.*, 359.

103. Froehlich and Hawver 1974, 64.

104. Fulmer and Fulmer 1974, 492.

105. Garris and Black 1974.

106. Froehlich and Hawver 1974, 64.

107. Karabel 1984, 2005; see also Synnott 1979 and Oren 1985.

108. Pedriana and Stryker 1997; Stryker, Scarpellino, and Holtzman 1999.

109. Lockwood 1966.

110. 110 *Cong. Rec.* 6549 (1964).

111. SEC. 2000e-2. [Section 703] (j).

112. U.S. Department of Labor 2000, 41 CFR 60-2.16.

113. Chayes 1974, 88.

114. For quotas for municipal policeman see *Castro v. Beecher*, 4509 F.2d 725 (1st Cir. 1972), but see *Carter v. Gallagher*, 452 F.2d 315 (8th Cir. 1971).

115. Lundberg 1991; McCrary 2006.

116. Order 4 of 1970 and Revised Order 4 of December 1971. See *Contractors' Association of Eastern Pennsylvania v. Hodgson*, 442 F.2d 159 (3d Cir. 1971), cert. denied, 404 U.S. 854 (1971).

117. U.S. Department of Labor 2000, 41 CFR 60-2.16, 26099.

118. Chayes 1974, 87.

119. Burstein and Pitchford 1990; Burstein and Monahan 1986, 380.

120. *Bakke*, 438 U.S. 265 (1978).

121. Sabbagh 2007, 165.

122. Marino 1980, 26–27; Mintz 1978; Stryker 1996, 13.

123. Chayes 1974, 87.

124. Burstein and Monahan 1986; "Rethinking Weber: The Business Response to Affirmative Action," *Harvard Law Review* 102 (1989): 658–71; Leonard 1984a.

125. Day 1965.

126. Froehlich and Hawver 1974, 64.

127. DiPrete 1989, 199.

128. Stephanopoulous and Edley 1995, chap. 6.

129. Fisher 1985.

130. Stephanopoulous and Edley 1995, chap. 6.

131. Leonard 1985, 9.

132. Pager 2005; Stryker 2001, 31.

133. Jencks 1992; Sowell 1976.

134. Turner, Fix, and Struyk 1991.

135. Pager 2003a, b.

136. Bertrand and Mullainathan 2004.

137. Neumark, Blank, and Van Nort 1995.

138. Braverman 1974; Edwards 1979; Miller and Form 1964.

139. Gordon, Edwards, and Reich 1982; Marglin 1974.

140. Slichter 1919; Williamson 1985; Jacoby 1985b; Selznick 1969.

141. Edwards 1979, 21; Williamson 1985.

142. Beer et al. 1985.

143. Cole 1989; Storey 1992, 7.

144. Ichniowski, Delaney, and Lewin 1989.

145. Dobbin et al. 1993.

146. Becker 1957; Friedman 1962.

147. "Rethinking Weber," 669.

148. "Rethinking Weber," 668.

149. Donohue 1986; Lundberg 1991.

150. Stryker 2001.
151. Carmichael and Hamilton 1967; see also Stryker 2001, 16.
152. Williamson 1985; Edwards 1979.
153. Hirsch 1991; Pfeffer and Baron 1988.

CHAPTER 6
THE REAGAN REVOLUTION AND THE RISE OF DIVERSITY MANAGEMENT

1. Conference Boar 1992, 11; Kossek and Lobel 1995; Leach et al. 1995; Miller 1994.
2. Jackall 1983, 58.
3. Dobbin 1994.
4. Edelman, Fuller, and Mara-Drita 2001; Kelly and Dobbin 1998.
5. Ashtenfelter and Heckman 1976; Goldstein and Smith 1976; Heckman and Payner 1989; Heckman and Wolpin 1976; Leonard 1984b, 1984c.
6. Leonard 1990, 58; Rodgers and Spriggs 1996.
7. Kalev and Dobbin 2006; Kalev, Dobbin, and Kelly 2006.
8. Bentham 1840; Lubenow 1971; MacDonagh 1958.
9. See McCraw 1975.
10. Diver 1980; Mitnick 1978; Viscusi and Zeckhauser 1979.
11. Bardach and Kagan 1982.
12. Viscusi 1983.
13. Quoted in McDowell 1989, 34; see also Blumrosen 1993; Skrentny 1996.
14. Anderson 1996; Leonard 1990, 1996.
15. Achenbaum 1986, 155–56.
16. Ewing 1983; Hartnett 1996; Jackall 1983.
17. Edelman 1992, 1541.
18. 47 Fed. Reg. 17770 (April 23, 1982).
19. Bureau of National Affairs 1986b, A-9; Belz 1991, 193.
20. DuRivage 1985, 368.
21. DuRivage 1985, 366.
22. Detlefson 1991, 151; "Rethinking Weber: The Business Response to Affirmative Action," *Harvard Law Review* 102 (1989): 662; see also Belz 1991; McDowell 1989.
23. McDowell 1989.
24. Blumrosen 1993, 270; Skrentny 1996.
25. Blumrosen 1993; Yakura 1995.
26. Fox 1981; Mayer 1981.
27. OFCCP staffing never recovered. In 1996, it stood at 835, only about half of the 1978 peak of 1,700. Anderson 1996; DuRivage 1985; Edelman 1992, 301; Leonard 1989; Skrentny 1996.
28. DuRivage 1985, 363.
29. Anderson 1996, 274; Blumrosen 1993.
30. Leonard 1989, 74.
31. Becker 1968.
32. Edwards 1991.

33. *Firefighters Local Union No. 1784 v. Stotts* 467 U.S. 561 (1983); *Wygant v. Jackson Board of Education* 478 U.S. 1014 (1986), Bureau of National Affairs 1986b, 33.

34. *Local 28 (Sheet Metal Workers) v. EEOC* 478 U.S. 421(1986); *Johnson v. Transportation Agency* 480 U.S. 616(1987).

35. *Wards Cove Packing Co., Inc., et al. v. Atonio et al.,* 490 U.S. 642 (1989); *Lorance v. AT & T Technologies,* 109 S. Ct. 2261 (1989); see also *Price Waterhouse v. Hopkins,* 109 S. Ct. 1777 (1989).

36. *Wards Cove Packing Co., Inc., et al. v. Atonio et al.,* 642.

37. Cabot 1987.

38. "Rethinking Weber."

39. Fisher 1994, 271

40. "Rethinking Weber," 661.

41. "Rethinking Weber," 662.

42. Fisher 1994, 270.

43. Bureau of National Affairs 1986b, 90.

44. Selznick 1957.

45. Feild 1984.

46. Edelman et al. 1991, 74.

47. Thomas 2004; Bureau of National Affairs 1995; Lynch 1997.

48. Prugh 1965, 10.

49. Ackerman 1973, 92. See also Fretz and Hayman 1973, 135.

50. Becker 1957.

51. Quoted in Boyle 1973, 95.

52. Donohue 1986.

53. Feild 1984.

54. Bureau of National Affairs 1986b, 93.

55. Bureau of National Affairs 1986b, 93.

56. Quoted in "Rethinking Weber," 669.

57. Stryker 2001; see also DiTomaso 1985.

58. Johnston and Packer 1987, vi.

59. Friedman and DiTomaso 1996.

60. Friedman and DiTomaso 1996, 55.

61. Conference Board 1992, 9.

62. Conference Board 1992, 14.

63. Bequai 1992, 40.

64. Wheeler 1995, 7.

65. Walker later became Digital's, and apparently the nation's, first vice president of workforce diversity (Lynch 1997).

66. Thomas 2004; Bureau of National Affairs 1995; Lynch 1997.

67. Lynch 1997, 9, 176; Wheeler 1995; Wheeler 1994.

68. See Lynch 1997, 93; textbooks include Kossek and Lobel 1995; Leach et al. 1995.

69. Wheeler 1994, 15.

70. Lynch 1997, 8; on downsizing see Budros 1997; Kalev 2005.

71. Lynch 1997, 1.

72. Conference Board 1992, 23.

73. Wheeler 1994, 9.

74. Kelly and Dobbin 1998.

75. Thomas 1994.

76. Compare Wheeler 1995, 8, to Hall and Albrecht 1979, 28–29, 151, 162–64

77. http://www.firstcitizens.com/about_us/diversity_mission.html#, accessed September 20, 2007. The bank operated in Maryland, North Carolina, Tennessee, and the Virginias.

78. Conference Board 1992, 21.

79. Lawrence 1965, 139.

80. Barley and Kunda 1992.

81. Mayo 1933; Roethlisberger and Dickinson 1939.

82. Blake and Mouton 1964, 1968.

83. E.g., Lawrence and Lorsch 1967; Lowin, Hrapchak, and Kavanaugh 1969; Robin 1967; Scott 1968.

84. Bell 1947, 3288.

85. Robertson 1971.

86. Conference Board 1992, 13.

87. Boyle 1973, 93.

88. Boyle 1973, 87.

89. "Sexual Harassment Lands Companies in Court," *Business Week*, October 1, 1979, 120; Sawyer and Whatley 1980.

90. Bureau of National Affairs 1976, 9.

91. The published piece was retitled Edelman, Fuller, and Mara-Drita 2001.

92. Jordan 1998.

93. Wheeler 1994, 7.

94. *Hamby v. Wal-Mart Stores Inc.*, No. 93-3444-CV-S (W.D.Mo. July 28, 1995)

95. Bisom-Rapp 2001b, 26.

96. Bisom-Rapp 2001b.

97. *Ingram et al. v. The Coca-Cola Company* (2001); Herman et al. 2003.

98. The investigator's report was accessed October 12, 2006 at http://www.courttv.com/archive/legaldocs/business/texaco/report.html.

99. Winterle 1992, 21.

100. Rynes and Rosen 1994; Miller 1994.

101. Brandes 1976; Brody 1980.

102. Barley and Kunda 1992.

103. Ewing 1933, 106.

104. National Industrial Conference Board 1947, 32.

105. Katz and Kahn 1966.

106. Guetzkow 1965.

107. Klein, Kraut, and Wolfson 1971.

108. See Hofstede 1980; McSweeney 2002.

109. Foulkes and Morgan 1977, 149.

110. Kochan, Katz, and McKersie 1994.

111. Downie and Coates 1994, 28.

112. Rowe and Baker 1984.

113. Sullivan 1986, 44.

114. Lublin 1991.

115. Cross 1996; Lynch 1997; MacDonald 1993; Thomas and Ely 1996; Thomas 1991, 33, 47.

116. Conference Board 1992, 12.

117. Larkey 1996.

118. Granovetter 1974.

119. Baron and Pfeffer 1994; Castilla 2005; Kanter 1977.

120. Burt 1998; Reskin and McBrier 2000.

121. Blair-Loy 2001; Burt 1998; Ibarra 1992, 1995; McGuire 2000; Petersen, Saporta, and Seidelm 1998.

122. Crow 2003; Briscoe and Safford 2005.

123. Cisco Systems website accessed October 12, 2006 at http://www.cisco .com/web/about/ac49/ac55/about_cisco_employee_networks.html.

124. Lunding, Clements, and Perkins 1979; see also Roche 1979.

125. Vernon-Gerstenfeld and Burke 1985, 67.

126. E.g., Burke and McKeen 1997; Moore 2001.

127. Thomas 2001.

128. Burt 1998; Neumark and Gardecki 1996.

129. Conference Board 1992, 21; Miller 1994, 12.

130. Schofer 1971.

131. Cole 1989.

132. Sturm 2001, 492.

133. Gant and Gentile 1995.

134. Spiro 1994, 54.

135. Conference Board 1992, 21.

136. The studies covered 160 and 114 firms respectively and focused on large companies. Bureau of National Affairs 1976, 1986.

137. See also Edelman 1992.

138. Similarly, Edelman 1992 found that by 1990 18.5 percent of employers in a national sample had an equal opportunity office.

139. Kalev, Dobbin, and Kelly 2006.

140. Kalev, Dobbin, and Kelly 2006.

141. Wheeler 1995, 13.

142. Wheeler 1994, 7.

143. Conference Board 1992, 15.

144. Conference Board 1992, 17.

145. Conference Board 1992, 11.

146. Conference Board 1992, 14.

147. Conference Board 1992, 15.

148. Thomas 1994, 29.

149. U.S. Department of Labor 2000, 41 CFR 60-2.16.

150. I take up the feminization of the field in chapter 7.

151. Johnston and Packer 1987.

152. Selznick 1957.

153. Zald and Denton 1963.

154. Zorn 2004.

155. Wilkins 2004, 1576.
156. Taylor 1995.

CHAPTER 7
THE FEMINIZATION OF HR AND WORK-FAMILY PROGRAMS

1. Graham 1972, 8.
2. Graham 1972, 8.
3. "Pregnancy Discharges in the Military: The Air Force Experience," *Harvard Law Review* 86 (1973): 568–94.
4. Mansbridge 1986, 10.
5. Vogel 1993.
6. Dobbin 1992.
7. Strang and Meyer 1993.
8. National Industrial Conference Board 1964.
9. Ginsburg and Ross 1977, 33.
10. Goldin 1990; Pedriana 2004, 2006.
11. Danovitch 1990.
12. Costain 1992, 44–45; Harrison 1988, x, chap. 9; Skrentny 1996; Vogel 1993.
13. Mansbridge 1986.
14. Equal Employment Opportunity Commission 1966–97, 40.
15. Vogel 1993, 64–65.
16. Harrison 1988, 190.
17. Harrison 1988, 177.
18. Danovitch 1990.
19. Quoted in Bureau of National Affairs 1967, 20.
20. Bureau of National Affairs 1967, 20.
21. Harrison 1988, 174.
22. "Advisory Council of Women Named," *New York Times*, August 17, 1969, 41.
23. Citizens' Advisory Council on the Status of Women 1971, 4–7, 4, 20–22; Vogel 1993.
24. "Job Unit Widens Women's Rights," *New York Times*, March 31, 1972.
25. 37 Fed. Reg. 6835–37, 29 CFR 1604.10.
26. Bleich 2000; Lieberman 2002a.
27. Nord 1994.
28. Quoted in "Court Finds G.E. Guilty of Sex Bias in Denial of Disability Benefits," *National Underwriter*, April 20, 1974, 4.
29. Vogel 1993.
30. Fryburger 1975.
31. Dullea 1974, 41.
32. "A Pregnancy Ruling That Could Cost $1.6 Billion," *Business Week*, November 29, 1976, 41.
33. Jacoby 1985a.
34. See also Roos and Manley 1996.

35. Kochan, Katz, and McKersie 1994; Roos and Manley 1996; Selznick 1969.
36. Bureau of National Affairs 1967, 6.
37. Boyle 1973, 95.
38. Edwards 1973; Fryburger 1975; Sipser 1973.
39. Edwards 1973, 421.
40. Fretz and Hayman 1973, 134.
41. Hyatt 1972.
42. Fretz and Hayman 1973, 138.
43. Walsh 1974, 153–54.
44. Bureau of National Affairs 1975.
45. Kamerman, Kahn, and Kingston 1983, 56.
46. *General Electric v. Gilbert*, 49 U.S. 125, 136 (1976); Vogel 1993, 69.
47. United States Code Annotated 42 2000e (k).
48. Blau and Ferber 1992; Kamerman, Kahn, and Kingston 1983.
49. Kelly and Dobbin 1999.
50. Ruhm and Teague 1997, 136.
51. California Unemployment Insurance Code 2626, 1997.
52. California Government Code 12945.
53. New Jersey Statutes Annotated 43:21–29 (1997). LEXIS Law Publishing, 1997.
54. Quoted in Pear 1985, 16.
55. Jasinoski 1991, 3c.
56. "Campaign '96: Transcript of the Second Presidential Debate," *Washington Post*, October 17, 1996, A12.
57. Kelly and Dobbin 1999.
58. Harrison 1988, xii.
59. Mansbridge 1986.
60. Vogel 1993.
61. Mansbridge 1986; McCammon 1996; Vogel 1993, 78.
62. Vogel 1993, 74.
63. Schatz 1983.
64. Cornfield and Kane 1998.
65. Wisensale 1997.
66. Waldfogel 1997, 94–95.
67. Ruhm and Teague 1997.
68. Kelly 2003.
69. Kelly and Kalev 2006.
70. Avery and Zabel. 2000, 5.
71. Christensen 1989.
72. Didato 1977; Packard 1995, 137; Swart 1978, 120.
73. "Workplace Flexibility 2010 Legal Memo: The Federal Employees Flexible and Compressed Work Schedules Act (FEFCWA)," Georgetown University Law Center, Spring 2006; Swart 1978.
74. Baron and Kreps 1999.
75. Packard 1995.
76. Swart 1978, 129.

77. Ruby et al. 1976.

78. Ronen 1981.

79. Ouchi 1981, 218.

80. Fombrun 1998, 335.

81. Evans 1973; see also Golembiewski, Yeager, and Hilles 1975; see also Hartley 1976; "Summaries of Other Timely Articles, "*Management Review* 63, no. 4 (1974): 62.

82. Swart 1978, 103–65.

83. Ronen 1981, 1984; Ronen and Primps 1979.

84. Nollen 1979; Ralston 1989.

85. Ezra and Deckman 1996.

86. Public Law 99-196, signed on December 23, 1985; "The Bureaucracy; Giving New Meaning to Clock-Watchers," *New York Times*, October 22, 1985.

87. Federal Employees Part-time Career Employment Act of 1978, 5 U.S.C. 3401–8, Section 340.101 2a(1); Rosenberg 1980.

88. Rosenberg 1980.

89. "Why Flexitime Is Spreading," *Business Week*, February 23, 1981.

90. Kanter, Summers, and Stein 1986.

91. Marino 1980, 25.

92. Mayer 1984, H1–H8.

93. Singer 1988, WC1.

94. Swoboda 1988, A1, A17.

95. Swoboda 1989, A9.

96. Bailyn 1993; Bruce and Reed 1994; Hewlett 1991; Olmsted and Smith 1994; US Merit Systems Protection Board 1991; Walterscheid 1993.

97. Fenstein 1986.

98. Bureau of National Affairs 1986a.

99. Christensen 1989.

100. Solomon 1988.

101. Kanter, Summers, and Stein 1986.

102. Miller 1994.

103. Rapoport and Bailyn 1996.

104. Kelly and Kalev 2006.

105. Foulkes and Morgan 1977, 12.

106. J. Williams 2000.

107. Christensen 1988.

108. Christensen 1989.

109. Friedman 1986.

110. Hunt 1986, 24.

111. Kelly 2003, 619.

112. Hunt 1986, 24.

113. Kossek and Nichol 1992.

114. Bloomfield 1998.

115. Kelly 1999, 177.

116. Kamerman and Kahn 1987, 276–77.

117. Kelly 1999, 175.

118. Skrzycki 1989, 17.
119. Solomon 1988.
120. Galinsky and Bond 1998.
121. Miller 1994.
122. Johnson and Rose 1992.
123. Shalowitz 1992, 12.
124. Johnson and Rose 1992.
125. Hochschild 1997, 22.
126. Johnson and Rose 1992, 12.
127. Johnson and Rose 1992, 16.
128. Quoted in Kelly 1999, 181.
129. Kelly 1999, 184.
130. Selznick 1969.
131. Osterman 1995.
132. Filbeck and Preece 2003; http://money.cnn.com/magazines/fortune/bestcompanies/, accessed November 2, 2006.
133. Filbeck and Preece 2003.
134. Costain 1992; Harrison 1988; Pedriana 2004, 2006.
135. Kelly and Dobbin 1999.

CHAPTER 8
SEXUAL HARASSMENT AS EMPLOYMENT DISCRIMINATION

1. *Faragher v. City of Boca Raton*, 524 U.S. 775 (1998).
2. *Burlington Industries, Inc. v. Ellerth*, 524 U.S. 742.
3. *Burlington*, 764.
4. 527 U.S. 526, 545 (1999).
5. Quoted in Bisom-Rapp 2001b.
6. Dobbin and Kelly 2007.
7. Edelman, Uggen, and Erlanger 1999.
8. Edelman, Uggen, and Erlanger. 1999.
9. Saguy 2003; Zippel 2006.
10. Saguy 2003; Rochon 1998, 71; Farrell 1999, 17.
11. Crittenden 1977; Schultz 1998, 1771.
12. Dullea 1977, 1.
13. Bralove 1976, 1.
14. Bralove 1976, 1.
15. Jones 1975, A22.
16. Bralove 1976, 1.
17. Brodsky 1976; Farley 1978; MacKinnon 1979; Mead 1978; Sandport 1979.
18. Quoted in Linenberger and Keaveny 1981b, 11.
19. Quoted in Linenberger and Keaveny 1981a, 62; see Schlafly 1977.
20. *Rogers v. EEOC*, 454 F.2d 234 (5th Cir. 1972); Domenick 1999, 786.
21. Charlton 1972, 22; see Rochon 1998, 68.
22. 13 Fair Empl. Prac. Cas. (D.D.C. 1974) 124; see Saguy 1999, 71.

23. *Corne v. Bausch and Lomb, Inc.*, 390 F. Supp. 161, 163 (D. Ariz. 1975).

24. *Williams v. Saxbe*, 413 F. Supp. 654, 660–61; *Miller v. Bank of America*, 418 F. Supp. 233 (N.D. Cal. 1976); "Sexual Harassment and Title VII: The Foundation for the Elimination of Sexual Cooperation as an Employment Condition," *Michigan Law Review* 76 (1978): 1007-35.

25. Excerpted in Sawyer and Whatley 1980, 37.

26. *Williams v. Saxbe*, 657.

27. *Barnes v. Costle*, 561 F.2d 983 (D.C. Cir. 1977).

28. *Barnes v. Costle*, 990.

29. *Barnes v. Costle*, 993.

30. *Tomkins v. Public Service Electric and Gas Co.* (Tomkins II), 568 F.2d 1044 (3rd Cir. 1977).

31. Schultz 1998, 1776.

32. "Sexual Harassment Lands Companies in Court," *Business Week*, October 1, 1979, 120.

33. Spann 1990, 55.

34. "Sexual Harassment Lands Companies in Court," 120.

35. M. Williams 2000, 12.

36. 45 Fed. Reg. 74677, November 10, 1980; see Saguy 2003; Rochon 1998, 69.

37. "Sexual Harassment Lands Companies in Court," 120; Somers and Clementson-Mohr 1979, 23.

38. Spann 1990, 54; Gallup Organization 1991.

39. Berenbeim 1980, 4, 1.

40. *Williams v. Saxbe*.

41. Somers and Clementson-Mohr 1979, 26.

42. Hoyman and Robinson 1980.

43. Linenberger and Keaveny 1981a, 65–66.

44. Linenberger and Keaveny 1981b, 14–15.

45. Edelman, Uggen, and Erlanger 1999, 433.

46. See, for instance, Shah and Agrest 1979.

47. Sawyer and Whatley 1980, 37.

48. Rowe 1981, 46.

49. "Sexual Harassment Lands Companies in Court," 120.

50. Spann 1990, 57.

51. Coleman 1979, B1.

52. Haberman 1980.

53. Linenberger and Keaveny 1981b.

54. *Meritor Savings Bank v. Vinson*, 477 U.S. 57 (1986).

55. Farrell 1999, 17.

56. MacKinnon 1979.

57. *Meritor*, 72.

58. Kohler 1999, 117.

59. *Meritor*, 72.

60. *Meritor*, 72.

61. Rowe 1981; see also Berenbeim 1980.

62. Spann 1990, 58.

63. Bradshaw 1987, 52.

64. Domenick 1999, 786; Bradshaw 1987.
65. Spann 1990, 59.
66. Saguy 2003.
67. Brophy 1986, 8.
68. Kronenberger and Bourke 1981, 881.
69. Wymer 1983, 182.
70. Goldberg 1990.
71. Shaeffer 1980, 15.
72. "Sexual Harassment Lands Companies in Court," 120.
73. Sawyer and Whatley 1980, 38.
74. Renick 1980, 661.
75. McIntyre and Renick 1982, 289–91.
76. Spann 1990, 65.
77. Associated Press 1982, A12.
78. 45 Fed. Reg. 74677, November 10, 1980.
79. Kronenberger and Bourke 1981, 879; emphasis added.
80. Juliano and Schwab 2001.
81. Brophy 1986, 8.
82. Brophy 1986, 56; Machlowitz and Machlowitz 1987, 78.
83. Goldberg 1990, 34.
84. Schultz 2003.
85. *Harris v. Forklist Systems, Inc.*, 114 S. Ct. 367 (1993); *Bouton v. BMW of North America*, 29 F.3d 103 (3rd Cir. 1994); *Kelly-Zumari v. Wohl Shoe Co.*, 27 Cal. Rptr. 2d 457 (1994).
86. From our survey of employment practices, reported in Kalev, Dobbin, and Kelly 2006.
87. Burge 1984, 802.
88. Attanasio 1982, 32.
89. Attanasio 1982, 32 and 35.
90. Dolkart and Malchow 1987, 187.
91. Burge 1984.
92. "Sexual Harassment Claims of Abusive Work Environment under Title VII," *Harvard Law Review* 97 (1984): 1461.
93. "Sexual Harassment Claims," 1462.
94. Attanasio 1982, 32; emphasis added.
95. Baxter 1982, 20.
96. Burge 1984, 803.
97. Turner 1990, 10.
98. *Yates v. Avco Corp.*, 819 F.2d 630 (6th Cir. 1987); Turner 1990, 17.
99. "Sexual Harassment Claims," 1460.
100. Dobbin and Kelly 2007.
101. Ginsburg and Koreski 1977, 91; see also "Sexual Harassment and Title VII: The Foundation for the Elimination of Sexual Cooperation as an Employment Condition," *Michigan Law Review* 76 (1978): 1018.
102. Ecabert 1987, 1191; Dolkart and Malchow 1987, 181.
103. Machlowitz and Machlowitz 1987, 82.
104. Dobbin and Kelly 2007.

105. "Two Breakthroughs for Civil Rights," *Business Week*, November 11, 1991, 190.

106. Verespej 1991, 34.

107. Quoted in Barrier 1998, 14.

108. Wiley and Price 1992, 24.

109. Bingham and Gansler 2002.

110. Bingham and Gansler 2002, 240.

111. Daugherty 1998, A1.

112. Barrier 1998, 13.

113. The figures for 1981 through 1989 and for 1983 through 2001 come from the EEOC's website, http://www.eeoc.gov/stats/harass.html, which lists charge statistics. Figures for 1990 and 1991 come from Copus 1996, 128.

114. Barrier 1998, 15.

115. Lublin 1991, B1.

116. Olson 1993, A13.

117. See http://www.inscomp.net/sexual.html, accessed March 26, 2008; https://www.transact.aon.com/solutions/prod_serv/epli/eplinew.pdf and http://www.markelsocialservice.com/pdfs/ssappepli.pdf, accessed October 7, 2002.

118. Trost 1992, A1.

119. Olson 1993, A13.

120. Greenhouse 1998, A20.

121. Greenhouse 1998, A1.

122. *Burlington Industries v. Ellerth*, 118 S. Ct. 1998, 2263.

123. "The Supreme Court Issued Two Sexual-Harassment Rulings Last Summer That Should Both Worry and Hearten Employers," *Nation's Business*, December 1998, 15.

124. Edelman, Uggen, and Erlanger 1999.

125. Juliano and Schwab 2001.

126. *Kolstad*, 526.

127. *Kolstad*, 545.

128. Bisom-Rapp 2001a.

129. "Two Sexual-Harassment Rulings," 15.

130. Quoted in Daugherty 1998, A1; see Glater 2001, C8.

131. Quoted in Greenhouse 1998, A1.

132. Grimsley 1998, A10.

133. "Two Sexual-Harassment Rulings," 15.

134. Glater 2001, C8.

135. "Two Sexual-Harassment Rulings," 15.

136. Greenhouse 1998, A20.

137. Ford 1998.

138. Colt 1998.

139. http://www.sexualharass.com/, accessed October 8, 2002.

140. Glater 2001, C8.

141. Glater 2001, C8.

142. Tevlin 1999, 1D.

143. Grimsley 1998, A10.

144. Farrell 1999, 17.

145. Reed 2001, 11.

146. *Circuit City Stores v. St. Clair Adams*, 121 S. Ct. 1302 (2001).

147. Hauck 1998.

148. Reed 2001.

149. Zippel 2006.

150. Bisom-Rapp 2001a.

151. Edelman, Uggen, and Erlanger 1999.

CHAPTER 9
HOW PERSONNEL DEFINED EQUAL OPPORTUNITY

1. Chen 2006.

2. Abzug and Mezias 1993; Dobbin and Sutton 1998; Edelman 1992.

3. Malkiel 1979.

4. Meyer 1979.

5. Meyer and Scott 1992, 275; Lawrence and Lorsch 1967.

6. Edelman, Abraham, and Erlanger (1992) show that the personnel profession was much more likely to exaggerate the legal risk to employers than were lawyers.

7. Meyer and Rowan 1977; Pfeffer and Salancik 1978, 270.

8. Wilson 1980 made this argument, on the shoulders of economic historians.

9. Selznick 1969 found that the "industrial relations" system found in union firms spread to nonunion firms in the 1950s.

10. Meyer and Scott 1983a.

11. Taylor 1995; see also Steeh and Krysan 1996.

12. Dobbin et al. 1993; Edelman 1990.

13. Kelly 2002.

14. Lieberman 2002a.

15. Campbell 1998; Hall and Taylor 1996; Thelen and Steinmo 1992.

16. Doeringer 1967; Stiglitz 1973.

17. Bluestone 1970; Osterman 1975; Reich, Gordon, and Edwards 1973.

18. Doeringer and Piore 1971; Edwards 1979; Gordon 1972; Stone 1974; Williamson 1975.

19. Aiken and Hage 1968; Baron and Bielby 1980; Kalleberg and Sorensen 1979; Spilerman 1977; see Baron 1984 for a review.

20. Thagard 1996.

21. Chomsky 1957; March and Simon 1958.

22. Douglas 1986; Geertz 1983.

23. Berger and Luckmann 1966; Garfinkle 1987; Giddens 1984; Wuthnow 1987; DiMaggio 1997; Goffman 1959.

24. Kanter 1977.

25. Tajfel and Turner 1979; Baron and Pfeffer 1994; Reskin 2000.

26. For reviews see Gorman 2005; Heilman 1995; Lemm and Banaji 1999; Jost, Banaji, and Nosek 2004.

27. Rosenthal and Rubin 1978.

28. Steele 1992; Steele and Aronson 1995.

29. E.g., Lovaglia et al. 1998.

30. Kanter 1977.

31. Ackerman 1973.

32. Blumrosen 1993, ch 15.

33. Glazer 1975, 53 He later recanted (Glazer 1997), in *We Are All Multiculturalists Now*, which sings the praises of diversity in education.

34. Spiro 1994.

BIBLIOGRAPHY

Abzug, Rikki, and Stephen J. Mezias. 1993. The Fragmented State and Due Process Protections in Organizations: The Case of Comparable Worth. *Organization Science* 4:433–53.

Achenbaum, W. Andrew. 1986. *Social Security: Visions and Revisions. Cambridge.* Cambridge University Press.

Ackerman, Robert. 1973. How Companies Respond to Social Demands. *Harvard Business Review* 51 (1): 88–98.

———. 1975. *The Social Challenge to Business.* Cambridge: Harvard University Press.

Aiken, Michael, and Jerald Hage. 1968. Organizational Interdependence and Inter-organizational Structure. *American Sociological Review* 14:366–76.

Anderson, Bernard E. 1996. The Ebb and Flow of Enforcing Executive Order 11246. *American Economic Review* 86:298–301.

Anderson, C. Richard. 1975. *OSHA and Accident Control through Training.* New York: Industrial Press.

Arvey, Richard D., and Stephen Mussio. 1973. Determining the Existence of Unfair Test Discrimination for Female Clerical Workers. *Personnel Psychology* 26:559–68.

Ashenfelter, Orley, and James J. Heckman. 1976. Measuring the Effect of an Anti-discrimination Program. In *Evaluating the Labor-Market Effects of Social Programs*, ed. Orley Ashenfelter and James Blum, 46–89. Princeton, NJ: Industrial Relations Section, Department of Economics, Princeton University.

Associated Press. 1982. Army Presses a Wide Effort to Fight Sexual Harassment. *New York Times*, June 10.

Attanasio, John B. 1982. Equal Justice under Chaos: The Developing Law of Sexual Harassment. *University of Cincinnati Law Review* 51:1–41.

Avery, Christine, and Diane Zabel. 2000. *The Flexible Workplace: A Sourcebook of Information and Research.* Westport, CT: Quorum Books.

Bailyn, Lotte. 1993. *Breaking the Mold: Women, Men, and Time in the New Corporate World.* New York: Free Press.

Baker, Harry C. 1965. A Voluntary Approach to Equal Opportunity. In *The Negro and Employment Opportunity: Problems and Practices*, ed. Herbert R. Northrup and Richard L. Rowan, 111–21. Ann Arbor: Bureau of Industrial Relations, Graduate School of Business Administration, University of Michigan.

Bardach, Eugene, and Robert A. Kagan. 1982. *Going by the Book: The Problem of Regulatory Unreasonableness.* Philadelphia: Temple University Press.

Barley, Stephen R., and Gideon Kunda. 1992. Design and Devotion: Surges of Rational and Normative Ideologies of Control in Managerial Discourse. *Administrative Science Quarterly* 37:363–400.

Baron, James N. 1984. Organizational Perspectives on Stratification. *Annual Review of Sociology* 10:37–69.

Baron, James N. and William T. Bielby. 1980. Bringing the Firms Back In: Stratification, Segmentation, and the Organization of Work. *American Sociological Review* 45:737–65.

———. 1985. Organizational Barriers to Gender Equality: Sex Segregation of Jobs and Opportunities. In *Gender and the Life Course*, ed. Alice S. Rossi, 233–51. New York: Aldine de Gruyter.

Baron, James N., Frank Dobbin, and P. Devereaux Jennings. 1986. War and Peace: The Evolution of Modern Personnel Administration in U.S. Industry. *American Journal of Sociology* 92:350–83.

Baron, James N., P. Devereaux Jennings, and Frank Dobbin. 1988. Mission Control? The Development of Personnel Systems in U.S. Industry. *American Sociological Review* 53:497–514.

Baron, James N., and David M. Kreps. 1999. *Strategic Human Resources: Frameworks for General Managers*. New York: John Wiley and Sons.

Baron, James N., and Jeffrey Pfeffer. 1994. The Social Psychology of Organizations and Inequality. *Social Psychology Quarterly* 57 (3): 190–209.

Barrier, Michael. 1998. Lawsuits Gone Wild. *Nation's Business*, February.

Bassford, Gerald L. 1974. Job Testing—Alternative to Employment Quotas. *Business Horizons* 17:37–50.

Baxter, Ralph H., Jr. 1982. Sexual Harassment Claims: The Issues. *Legal Economics* 8 (6): 15–25.

Bayroff, A. G. 1966. Test Technology and Equal Employment Opportunity. *Personnel Psychology* 19:35–39.

Becker, Gary Stanley. 1957. *The Economics of Discrimination*. Chicago: University of Chicago Press.

———. 1968. Crime and Punishment: An Economic Approach. *Journal of Political Economy* 76 (2): 169–217.

Beer, Michael, Bert Spector, Paul R. Lawrence, D. Quinn Mills, and Richard E. Walton. 1985. *Human Resources Management: A General Manager's Perspective*. New York: Free Press.

Bell, Daniel. 1947. "Reflections on Jewish Identity." *Commentary*, April, 3279–88.

Bell, Duran, Jr. 1971. Bonuses, Quotas, and the Employment of Black Workers. *Journal of Human Resources* 6:309–20.

Belz, Herman. 1991. *Equality Transformed: A Quarter-Century of Affirmative Action*. New Brunswick, NJ: Transaction.

Bendix, Reinhard. 1956. *Work and Authority in Industry: Ideologies of Management in the Course of Industrialization*. New York: Wiley.

Bentham, Jeremy. 1840. *Principles of the Civil Code*. Boston: Weeks, Jordan.

Bequai, August. 1992. The New Office: Personnel Laws in the 1990s. *Risk Management* 39:40–44.

Berenbeim, Ronald. 1980. *Non-union Complaint Procedures*. New York: Conference Board.

Berger, Peter L., and Thomas Luckmann. 1966. *The Social Construction of Reality: A Treatise on the Sociology of Knowledge*. Garden City, NJ: Doubleday.

Bertrand, Marianne, and Sendhil Mullainathan. 2004. Are Emily and Greg More Employable Than Lakisha and Jamal? A Field Experiment on Labor Market Discrimination. *American Economic Review* 94:991–1013.

Bingham, Clara, and Laura Leedy Gansler. 2002. *Class Action: The Story of Lois Jenson and the Landmark Case That Changed Sexual Harassment Law.* New York: Doubleday.

Bisom-Rapp, Susan. 2001a. Fixing Watches with Sledgehammers: The Questionable Embrace of Employee Sexual Harassment Training by the Legal Profession. *University of Arkansas at Little Rock Law Review* 24:147–68.

———. 2001b. An Ounce of Prevention Is a Poor Substitute for a Pound of Cure: Confronting the Developing Jurisprudence of Education and Prevention in Employment Discrimination Law. *Berkeley Journal of Employment and Labor Law* 22:1–46.

Blair-Loy, Mary. 2001. It's Not Just What You Know, It's Who You Know: Technical Knowledge, Rainmaking, and Gender among Finance Executives. *Research in the Sociology of Work* 10:51–83.

Blake, Robert Rogers, and Jane Srygley Mouton. 1964. *The Managerial Grid: Key Orientations for Achieving Production through People.* Houston: Gulf.

———. 1968. *Corporate Excellence through Grid Organizational Development.* Houston: Gulf.

Blau, Francine, and Marianne Ferber. 1992. *The Economics of Women, Men and Work.* Englewood Cliffs, NJ: Prentice Hall.

Bleich, Erik. 2000. Antiracism without Races: Politics and Policy in a "Color-Blind" State. *French Politics and Society* 18:48–74.

Bloomfield, Judith David. 1998. Establishing Work-Site Child Care Centers: Basic Steps and Considerations. *Compensation and Benefits Management* 14 (3): 19–24.

Bluestone, Barry. 1970. The Tripartate Economy: Labor Markets and the Working Poor. *Poverty and Human Resources Abstracts* 5:15–35.

Blumrosen, Alfred W. 1993. *Modern Law: The Law Transmission System and Equal Employment Opportunity.* Madison: University of Wisconsin Press.

Boyle, M. Barbara. 1973. Equal Opportunity for Women Is Smart Business. *Harvard Business Review* 51 (3): 85–95.

Bradshaw, David. 1987. Sexual Harassment: Confronting the Troublesome Issues. *Personnel Administrator* 32:50–52.

Braestrup, Peter. 1961a. Lockheed Signs Equal-Jobs Pact. *New York Times,* May 26.

———. 1961b. U.S. Unit Presses for Job Equality. *New York Times,* June 5.

———. 1961c. 8 Companies Sign Negro Job Pledge. *New York Times,* July 13.

———. 1961d. 12 Concerns Sign Anti-bias Vows. *New York Times,* December 1.

———. 1962a. More Defense Concerns Sign Pact against Job Discrimination. *New York Times,* February 8.

———. 1962b. N.A.A.C.P. Accuses Kennedy on Jobs. *New York Times,* April 6.

———. 1962c. A.F.L.-C.I.O Chided over Negro Curbs. *New York Times,* June 1.

———. 1962d. U.S. Panel Split over Negro Jobs. *New York Times,* June 18.

Bralove, Mary. 1976. A Cold Shoulder. *Wall Street Journal,* January 29.

Brandes, Stuart D. 1976. *American Welfare Capitalism, 1880–1940.* Chicago: University of Chicago Press.

Brauer, Carl M. 1983. Women Activists, Southern Conservatives, and the Prohibition of Sex Discrimination in Title VII of the 1964 Civil Rights Act. *Journal of Southern History* 49 (1): 37–56.

Braverman, Harry. 1974. *Labor and Monopoly Capital*. New York: Monthly Review.

Brecher, Jeremy, Henry Lombardi, and Jan Stackhouse. 1982. *Brass Valley: The Stories of Working People's Lives and Struggles in an American Industrial Region*. Philadelphia: Temple University Press.

Briscoe, Forrest, and Sean Safford. 2005. Agency in Diffusion: Activism, Imitation and the Adoption of Domestic Partner Benefits Among the Fortune 500. Unpublished manuscript, Pennsylvania State University.

Brodsky, Carroll M. 1976. *The Harassed Worker*. Lexington, MA: Heath.

Brody, David. 1980. *Workers in Industrial America*. New York: Oxford University Press.

———. 1989. Workplace Contractualism in America: An Historical/Comparative Analysis. Unpublished manuscript, Department of History, University of California at Davis.

Brophy, Beth. 1986. Sexual Harassment: Crossing the Line into Verboten Territory. *U.S. News and World Report*, December 8, 8.

Brower, F. Beatrice. 1937. Personnel Practices Governing Factory and Office Administration. In *NICD Studies*. New York: National Industrial Conference Board.

Bruce, Willa, and Christine Reed. 1994. Preparing Supervisors for the Future Work Force: The Dual-Income Couple and the Work-Family Dichotomy. *Public Administration Review* 54 (1): 36–43.

Budros, Art. 1997. The New Capitalism and Organizational Rationality: The Adoption of Downsizing Programs, 1979–1994. *Social Forces* 76:229–49.

Burack, Elmer H., and Robert D. Smith. 1977. *Personnel Management: A Human Resource Systems Approach*. New York: West.

Burawoy, Michael. 1985. *The Politics of Production: Factory Regimes under Capitalism and Socialism*. London: Verso.

Bureau of Labor Statistics. 2006. Current Population Survey. October 24.

Bureau of National Affairs. 1967. A Current Look at: (1) The Negro and Title VII (2) Sex and Title VII. *PPF Surveys*. Washington, DC: Bureau of National Affairs.

———. 1975. *Paid Leave and Leave of Absence Policies*. Washington, DC: Bureau of National Affairs.

———. 1976. *Equal Employment Opportunity: Programs and Results*. Washington, DC: Bureau of National Affairs.

———. 1986a. *Work and Family: A Changing Agenda*. Washington, DC: Bureau of National Affairs.

———. 1986b. *Affirmative Action Today: A Legal and Practical Analysis*. Washington, DC: Bureau of National Affairs.

———. 1995. *Affirmative Action after Adarand*. Daily Labor Report series. 1–45. Washington, DC: Bureau of National Affairs.

Bureau of the Census. 1975. *Historical Statistics of the United States: Colonial Times to 1970*. Washington, DC: U.S. Government Printing Office.

———. 2000. *U.S. Department of the Census Data Set: Census 2000 Summary File 3 (SF 3)—Sample Data. GCT-P13. Occupation, Industry, and Class of Worker of Employed Civilians 16 Years and Over*. Washington, DC.

Burge, David J. 1984. Employment Discrimination—Defining an Employer's Liability under Title VII for On-the-Job Sexual Harassment: Adoption of a Bifurcated Standard. *North Carolina Law Review* 62:795–803.

Burke, Ronald J., and Carol A. McKeen. 1997. Not Every Managerial Woman Who Makes It Has a Mentor. *Women in Management Review* 12 (4): 136–39.

Burstein, Paul R. 1985. *Discrimination Jobs and Politics: The Struggle for Equal Employment Opportunity in the United States since the New Deal.* Chicago: University of Chicago Press.

Burstein, Paul R., and Kath Monahan. 1986. Equal Employment Opportunity and the Mobilization of Law. *Law and Society Review* 16:355–88.

Burstein, Paul R., and Susan Pitchford. 1990. Social-Scientific and Legal Challenges to Education and Test Requirements in Employment. *Social Problems* 37:243–57.

Burt, Ronald S. 1998. The Gender of Social Capital. *Rationality and Society* 10 (1): 5–46.

Cabot, Stephen J. 1987. Living with the New Amendments to the Age Discrimination in Employment Act. *Personnel* 32:53–55.

California Unemployment Insurance Code 2626. 1997. California Unemployment Insurance Code 2626. *Deering's California Codes Annotated.* LEXIS Law Publishing.

Campbell, Joel T. 1973. Tests Are Valid for Minority Groups Too. *Public Personnel Management* 2:70–73.

Campbell, John L. 1997. Mechanisms of Evolutionary Change in Economic Governance: Interaction, Interpretation and Bricolage. In *Evolutionary Economics and Path Dependence*, ed. Lars Magnusson and Jan Ottosson, 10–32. Cheltenham, UK: Edward Elgar.

———. 1998. Institutional Analysis and the Role of Ideas in Political Economy. *Theory and Society* 27:377–409.

Carmichael, Stokely, and Charles Hamilton. 1967. *Black Power: The Politics of Liberation in America.* New York: Vintage.

Castilla, Emilio J. 2005. Social Networks and Employee Performance in a Call Center. *American Journal of Sociology* 110:1243–84.

Chandler, Alfred D., Jr. 1977. *The Visible Hand: The Managerial Revolution in American Business.* Cambridge, MA: Belknap Press.

Charlton, Linda. 1972. Suit Contends Sex Was a Condition for Keeping Job. *New York Times*, March 30.

Chayes, Antonia. 1974. Make Your EEO Program Court-Proof. *Harvard Business Review* 52 (5): 81–89.

Chen, Anthony S. 2006. "The Hitlerian Rule of Quotas": Racial Conservatism and the Politics of Fair Employement Legislation in New York State, 1941–1945. *Journal of American History* 92 (4): 1–26.

———. 2007. The Party of Lincoln and the Politics of State Fair Employment Legislation in the North, 1945–1964. *American Journal of Sociology* 112 (6): 1713–74.

———. Forthcoming. *The Fifth Freedom: Jobs, Politics, and Civil Rights in the United States, 1941–72.* Princeton, NJ: Princeton University Press.

Chomsky, Noam. 1957. *Syntactic Structures.* The Hague: Mouton.

Christensen, Kathleen E. 1988. Introduction: White-Collar Home-Based Work: The Changing U.S. Economy and Family. In *The New Era of Home-Based Work: Directions and Policies*, ed. Kathleen E. Christensen, 1–11. Boulder, CO: Westview.

———. 1989. *Flexible Staffing and Scheduling in U.S. Corporations*. New York: Conference Board.

Citizens' Advisory Council on the Status of Women. 1971. *Women in 1970*. Washington, DC: U.S. Government Printing Office.

Clemens, Elisabeth S. 1997. *The People's Lobby: Organizational Innovation and the Rise of Interest Group Politics in the United States, 1890–1925*. Chicago: University of Chicago Press.

Cohen, Michael D., James G. March, and Johan P. Olsen. 1972. A Garbage Can Model of Organizational Choice. *Administrative Science Quarterly* 17:1–25.

Cohen, Yinon, and Jeffrey Pfeffer. 1986. Organizational Hiring Standards. *Administrative Science Quarterly* 31:1–24.

Cole, Robert E. 1989. *Strategies for Learning: Small-Group Activities in American, Japanese, and Swedish Industry*. Berkeley and Los Angeles: University of California Press.

Coleman, Milton. 1979. Barry Acts to Bar Sex Harassment in District Jobs. *Washington Post*, May 25.

Colt, Marshall. 1998. How Communication Can Prevent Lawsuits: Tips for Avoiding Expensive Legal Hassles. *Denver Business Journal*, August 7, http://denver.bizjournals.com/.

Conference Board. 1992. *In Diversity Is Strength: Capitalizing on the New Work Force. 75th Anniversary Symposia Series*. Report 994. New York: Conference Board.

Copus, David. 1996. *Employment Law 101 Deskbook: The Essential Foundation in the Law for Business Executives, Human Resource Professionals, and Employment Counsel*. Larkspur, CA: National Employment Law Institute.

Cornfield, Daniel B., and Melinda D. Kane. 1998. Gender Segmentation, Union Decline, and Women Workers: Changes in the AFL-CIO Policy Agenda, 1985–1993. Paper presented to the Annual Meeting of the American Sociological Association, San Francisco.

Costain, Anne N. 1992. *Inviting Women's Rebellion: A Political Process Interpretation of the Women's Movement*. Baltimore: Johns Hopkins University Press.

Cray, Douglas W. 1968. The Negro Emerges as Qualified Executive. *New York Times*, January 8.

Crittenden, Ann. 1977. Women Tell of Sexual Harassment at Work. *New York Times*, October 25.

Cross, Elsie Y. 1996. Managing Diversity. Letter to the editor. *Harvard Business Review* 74 (6): 77–78.

Cross, Ira. 1938. The Role of Grievance Machinery in Union-Management Relations. *Harvard Business Review* 17 (1): 105–16.

Crow, Kelly. 2003. Reaching Out—Staying Focused on Diversity Goals. *New York Times*, October 28.

Cunningham, Ross M. 1936. Some Problems in Measuring Performance of Industrial Salesmen. *Harvard Business Review* 14 (1): 98–113.

Dalzell, Robert F. 1987. *Enterprising Elite: The Boston Associates and the World They Made*. Cambridge: Harvard University Press.

Danovitch, Sylvia. 1990. Interview Conducted December 27, 1990 as Part of an Oral History Project to Commemorate the EEOC's 25th Anniversary. http://www.utoronto.ca/wjudaism/contemporary/articles/history_eeoc.htm. Accessed August 12, 2008.

Daugherty, Jane. 1998. Racial Discrimination Charges Rise in Michigan. *Detroit News*, July 15.

Day, Virgil B. 1965. Progress in Equal Employment Opportunity at General Electric. In *The Negro and Employment Opportunity: Problems and Practices*, ed. Herbert R. Northrup and Richard L. Rowan, 155–64. Ann Arbor: Bureau of Industrial Relations, Graduate School of Business Administration, University of Michigan.

De Schutter, Olivier. 2006. Three Models of Equality and European Antidiscrimination Law. *Northern Ireland Legal Quarterly* 57 (1): 1–56.

Detlefson, Robert R. 1991. *Civil Rights under Reagan*. San Francisco: ICS Press.

Didato, Salvatore. 1977. Problems Cut by Flexitime. *Washington Post*, May 22.

DiMaggio, Paul J. 1997. Culture and Cognition. *Annual Review of Sociology* 23:263–87.

Dimick, D. E. 1978. Employee Control and Discipline. *Relations Industrielles* 33:23–37.

DiPrete, Thomas. 1989. *The Bureaucratic Labor Market: The Case of the Federal Civil Service*. New York: Plenum.

DiTomaso, Nancy. 1985. The Managed State: Governmental Reorganization in the First Year of the Reagan Administration. *Research in Political Sociology* 1:141–66.

Diver, Collin S. 1980. A Theory of Regulatory Enforcement. *Public Policy* 28:257–99.

Dobbin, Frank. 1992. The Origins of Private Social Insurance: Public Policy and Fringe Benefits in America 1920–1950. *American Journal of Sociology* 97:1416–50.

———. 1994. *Forging Industrial Policy: The United States, Britain, and France in the Railway Age*. New York: Cambridge University Press.

Dobbin, Frank, Lauren B. Edelman, John W. Meyer, W. Richard Scott, and Ann Swidler. 1988. The Expansion of Due Process in Organizations. In *Institutional Patterns and Organizations: Culture and Environment*, ed. Lynne G. Zucker, 71–100. Cambridge, MA: Ballinger.

Dobbin, Frank, Alexandra Kalev, and Erin L. Kelly. 2007. Diversity Management in Corporate America. *Contexts* 6 (4): 21–28.

Dobbin, Frank, and Erin L. Kelly. 2007. How to Stop Harassment: The Professional Construction of Legal Compliance in Organizations. *American Journal of Sociology* 112:1203–43.

Dobbin, Frank, Beth Simmons, and Geoffrey Garrett. 2007. The Global Diffusion of Public Policies: Social Construction, Coercion, Competition, or Learning? *Annual Review of Sociology* 33:449–72.

Dobbin, Frank, and John R. Sutton. 1998. The Strength of a Weak State: The Employment Rights Revolution and the Rise of Human Resources Management Divisions. *American Journal of Sociology* 104:441–76.

Dobbin, Frank, John R. Sutton, John W. Meyer, and W. Richard Scott. 1993. Equal Opportunity Law and the Construction of Internal Labor Markets. *American Journal of Sociology* 99:396–427.

Doeringer, Peter B. 1967. Determinants of the Structure of Industrial Type Internal Labor Markets. *Industrial and Labor Relations Review* 20:206–20.

Doeringer, Peter B., and Michael J. Piore. 1971. *Internal Labor Markets and Manpower Analysis*. Lexington, MA: Heath.

Dolkart, Jane L., and E. Lynn Malchow. 1987. Sexual Harassment in the Workplace: Expanding Remedies. *Tort and Insurance Law Journal* 23:181.

Domenick, Debra. 1999. Title VII: How Recent Developments in the Law of Sexual Harassment Apply with Equal Force to Claims of Racial Harassment. *Dickinson Law Review* 103:765–801.

Donohue, John J., III. 1986. Is Title VII Efficient? *University of Pennsylvania Law Review* 134:1411–31.

Donohue, John J., III, and Peter Siegelman. 1991. The Changing Nature of Employment Discrimination Litigation. *Stanford Law Review* 43:983–1033.

Douglas, Mary. 1986. *How Institutions Think*. Syracuse, NY: Syracuse University Press.

Downie, Bryan M., and Mary Lou Coates. 1994. *Traditional and New Approaches to Human Resource Management*. Kingston, ON: Industrial Relations Centre.

Drum, Russell S. 1960. Performance Evaluation. *Personnel Journal* 38:338–40.

Dugan, Robert D. 1966. Current Problems in Test Performance of Job Applicants: II. *Personnel Psychology* 19:18–24.

Dullea, Georgia. 1974. Sick Leave Pay Still an Issue Where Pregnancy Is Concerned. *New York Times*, April 8.

———. 1977. Vast Changes in Society Traced to the Rise of Working Women. *New York Times*, November 29.

DuRivage, Virginia. 1985. The OFCCP under the Reagan Administration: Affirmative Action in Retreat. *Labor Law Journal* 36:360–68.

Earl, Elmer W., Jr. 1940. *Personnel Practices in Factory and Office II*. New York: National Industrial Conference Board.

Ecabert, Gayle. 1987. An Employer's Guide to Understanding Liability for Sexual Harassment under Title VII: *Meritor Savings Bank v. Vinson. University of Cincinnati Law Review* 55:1181–1206.

Edelman, Lauren B. 1990. Legal Environments and Organizational Governance: The Expansion of Due Process in the American Workplace. *American Journal of Sociology* 95:1401–40.

———. 1992. Legal Ambiguity and Symbolic Structures: Organizational Mediation of Civil Rights Law. *American Journal of Sociology* 97:1531–76.

———. 2002. Legality and the Endogeneity of Law. In *Legality and Community: On the Intellectual Legacy of Philip Selznick*. 187–203. Lanham, MD: Rowman and Littlefield.

Edelman, Lauren B., Steven E. Abraham, and Howard S. Erlanger. 1992. Professional Construction of the Law: The Inflated Threat of Wrongful Discharge. *Law and Society Review* 26:47–84.

Edelman, Lauren B., Sally Riggs Fuller, and Iona Mara-Drita. 2001. Diversity Rhetoric and the Managerialization of the Law. *American Journal of Sociology* 106:1589–1641.

Edelman, Lauren B., Stephen M. Petterson, Elizabeth Chambliss, and Howard S. Erlanger. 1991. Legal Ambiguity and the Politics of Compliance: Affirmative Action Officers' Dilemma. *Law and Policy* 13:173–97.

Edelman, Lauren B., Christopher Uggen, and Howard S. Erlanger. 1999. The Endogeneity of Legal Regulation: Grievance Procedures as Rational Myth. *American Journal of Sociology* 105:406–54.

Edwards, Harry T. 1973. Sex Discrimination under Title VII: Some Unresolved Issues. *Labor Law Journal* 24:411–23.

Edwards, Patrick Ronald. 1991. Choices That Increase Compliance. *Policy Studies Journal* 10 (4): 6–27.

Edwards, Richard. 1979. *Contested Terrain: The Transformation of the Workplace in the Twentieth Century.* New York: Basic Books.

Elbaum, Bernard. 1984. The Making and Shaping of Job and Pay Structures in the Iron and Steel Industry. In *Internal Labor Markets*, ed. Paul Osterman, 71–108. Cambridge: MIT Press.

Equal Employment Opportunity Commission. 1966–97. *Annual Report.* Washington, DC: U.S. Government Printing Office.

Eskridge, William, Jr. 1994. *Dynamic Statutory Interpretation.* Cambridge: Harvard University Press.

Evans, Martin G. 1973. Notes on the Impact of Flextime in a Large Insurance Company. *Occupational Psychology* 47:237–40.

Ewick, Patricia, and Susan S. Silbey. 1998. *The Common Place of Law: Stories from Everyday Life.* Chicago: University of Chicago Press.

Ewing, D. H. 1933. Employee-Attitude Interviews as a Tool of Personnel Management. *Harvard Business Review* 12 (1): 105–15.

Ewing, David W. 1983. Your Right to Fire. *Harvard Business Review* 61 (2): 32–52.

Ezra, Marni, and Melissa Deckman. 1996. Balancing Work and Family Responsibilities: Flextime and Child Care in the Federal Government. *Public Administration Review* 56 (2): 174–79.

Farley, Lin. 1978. *Sexual Shakedown: The Sexual Harassment of Women at Work.* New York: McGraw Hill.

Farrell, John Aloysius. 1999. Rewriting the Rules: For Decades American Society Has Grappled with Defining Sexual Harassment. *Boston Globe Magazine*, February 7.

Fehn, Bruce. 1993. "Chickens Come Home to Roost": Industrial Reorganization, Seniority, and Gender Conflict in the United Packinghouse Workers of America, 1956–1966. *Labor History* 34 (2–3): 324–41.

Feild, John. 1984. *Affirmative Action: A Fresh Look at the Record Twenty-two Years after the Beginning.* Washington, DC: Center for National Policy Review.

Fenstein, Selwin. 1986. Labor Letter. *Wall Street Journal*, June 10.

Ferman, Louis A. 1968. *The Negro and Equal Employment Opportunities: A Review of Management Experiences in Twenty Companies.* New York: Praeger

Filbeck, Greg, and Dianna Preece. 2003. Fortune's Best 100 Companies to Work for in America: Do They Work for Shareholders? *Journal of Business Finance and Accounting* 30:771–97.

Fisher, Anne B. 1985. Businessmen Like to Hire by the Numbers. *Fortune*, September 16.

———. 1994. Businessmen Like to Hire by the Numbers. In *Equal Employment Opportunity: Labor Market Discrimination and Public Policy*, ed. Paul Burstein, 269–73. New York: Aldine de Gruyter.

Fligstein, Neil. 1990. *The Transformation of Corporate Control*. Cambridge: Harvard University Press.

Fombrun, Charles J. 1998. Indices of Corporate Reputation: An Analysis of Media Rankings and Social Monitors' Ratings. *Corporate Reputation Review* 1:327–40.

Ford, Sally. 1998. Supreme Court Clarifies the Rules on Sexual Harassment. *Business Journal*, August 21.

Foulkes, Fred K., and Henry M. Morgan. 1977. Organizing and Staffing the Personnel Function. *Harvard Business Review* 55 (3): 142–77.

Fox, J. Ronald. 1981. Breaking the Regulatory Deadlock. *Harvard Business Review* 59 (5): 97–120.

Fretz, C. F., and Joanne Hayman. 1973. Progress for Women? Men Are Still More Equal. *Harvard Business Review* 51 (5): 133–42.

Friedman, Dana E. 1986. Child Care for Employees' Kids. *Harvard Business Review* 64 (2): 28–34.

Friedman, Judith J., and Nancy DiTomaso. 1996. Myths about Diversity: What Managers Need to Know about Changes in the U.S. Labor Force. *California Management Review* 38 (4): 54–77.

Friedman, Milton. 1962. *Capitalism and Freedom*. Chicago: University of Chicago Press.

Froehlich, Herbert, and Dennis Hawver. 1974. Compliance Spinoff: Better Personnel Systems. *Personnel* 51 (1): 62–69.

Fryburger, L. Bruce. 1975. Maternity Leave Policies under Title VII. *Labor Law Journal* 26:163–73.

Fulmer, Robert M., and William E. Fulmer. 1974. Providing Equal Opportunities for Promotion. *Personnel Journal* 53:491–97.

Galinsky, Ellen, and James T. Bond. 1998. *The 1998 Business Work-Life Study*. New York: Families and Work Institute.

Gallup Organization. 1991. *Gallup Monthly Poll No. 313*. Princeton, NJ: Gallup Organization.

Gant, Sarah B., and Mary C. Gentile. 1995. Kurt Landgraf and Du Pont Merck Pharmaceutical Company. *Harvard Business School Press*, March 13.

Garfinkle, Howard. 1987. Studies of the Routine Grounds of Everyday Activities. In *Studies in Ethnomethodology*, 35–75. Berkeley and Los Angeles: University of California Press.

Garris, Steve, and Ann Black. 1974. Revising Personnel Management Procedures. *Personnel* 51 (6): 50–58.

Gavin, James F., and David L. Toole. 1973. Validity of Aptitude Tests for the "Hardcore Unemployed." *Personnel Psychology* 26:139–46.

Geertz, Clifford. 1983. *Local Knowledge: Further Essays in Interpretive Anthropology*. New York: Basic Books.

Gery, Gloria J. 1977. Equal Opportunity: Planning and Managing the Process of Change. *Personnel Journal* 56:184–203.

Giblin, Edward, and Oscar Ornati. 1974. A Total Approach to EEO Compliance. *Personnel* 51 (5): 32–43.

———. 1975. Beyond Compliance: EEO and the Dynamics of Organizational Change. *Personnel* 52 (5): 38–50.

Giddens, Anthony. 1984. *The Constitution of Society: Outline of the Theory of Structuration*. Berkeley and Los Angeles: University of California Press.

Ginsburg, Gilbert J., and Jean Galloway Koreski. 1977. Sexual Advances by an Employee's Supervisor: A Sex-Discrimination Violation of Title VII? *Employee Relations Law Journal* 3 (1): 83–93.

Ginsburg, Ruth Bader, and Susan Deller Ross. 1977. Pregnancy and Discrimination. *New York Times*, January 25.

Glater, Jonathan D. 2001. New Guards to Lessen Liability: Software Trains Workers to Avoid Improper Behavior. *New York Times*, August 8.

Glazer, Nathan. 1975. *Affirmative Discrimination: Ethnic Inequality and Public Policy*. Cambridge: Harvard University Press.

———. 1997. *We Are All Multiculturalists Now*. Cambridge: Harvard University Press.

Gocke, Joseph R., and Caroline S. Weymar. 1969. Barriers to Hiring Blacks. *Harvard Business Review* 47 (2): 144–52.

Goffman, Erving. 1959. *The Presentation of Self in Everyday Life*. Garden City, NJ: Doubleday.

Goldberg, Stephanie Benson. 1990. Law's "Dirty Little Secret": Profession Must Confront Sexual Harassment, Panel Says. *American Bar Association Journal* 76:34.

Goldin, Claudia. 1990. *Understanding the Gender Gap: An Economic History of American Women*. New York: Oxford University Press.

Goldstein, Morris, and Robert Smith. 1976. The Estimated Impact of the Antidiscrimination Program Aimed at Federal Contractors. *Industrial and Labor Relations Review* 29:523–43.

Golembiewski, Robert T., Samuel Yeager, and Rick Hilles. 1975. Factor Analysis of Some Flexitime Effects: Attitudinal and Behavioral Consequences of a Structural Intervention. *Academy of Management Journal* 18:500–509.

Gordon, David. 1972. Taxation of the Poor and the Normative Theory of Tax Incidence. *American Economic Review* 62:319–28.

Gordon, David M., Richard Edwards, and Michael Reich. 1982. *Segmented Work, Divided Workers: The Historical Transformation of Labor in the United States*. Cambridge: Cambridge University Press.

Gordon, Hugh L. 2000. Interview by Joyce A. Patterson. Cobb County Oral History Series No. 75, Kennesaw State University.

Gorham, William A. 1972. New Answers on Employment Tests. *Civil Service Journal* 13:8–12.

Gorman, Elizabeth. 2005. Gender Stereotypes, Same-Gender Preferences, and Organizational Variation in the Hiring of Women: Evidence from Law Firms. *American Sociological Review* 70:702–28.

Gould, William B. 1977. The High Court Discriminates between Sex And Race. *New York Times*, June 12.

Gouldner, Alvin W. 1954. *Patterns of Industrial Democracy: A Case Study of Modern Factory Administration*. New York: Free Press.

Graham, Fred P. 1972. Justices to Weigh Pregnancy Issue. *New York Times*, October 25.

Graham, Hugh Davis. 1990. *The Civil Rights Era: Origins and Development of National Policy, 1960–1972*. New York: Oxford University Press.

Granovetter, Mark. 1974. *Getting a Job: A Study of Contracts and Careers*. Chicago: University of Chicago Press.

Greenhouse, Linda. 1998. Sex Harassment Seems to Puzzle Supreme Court. *New York Times*, April 23.

Grimsley, Kirsten Downey. 1998. For Employers, a Blunt Warning: Experts Call Strictly Enforced Policies a Must. *Washington Post*, June 27.

Grove, Gene. 1965. When a "No. 2" Applies for a Job. *New York Times*, September 18.

Guetzkow, Harold. 1965. Communications in Organizations. In *Handbook of Organizations*, ed. James G. March, 534–73. Chicago: Rand McNally.

Guillén, Mauro F. 1994. *Models of Management: Work, Authority, and Organization in a Comparative Perspective*. Chicago: University of Chicago Press.

Gutman, Arthur. 1993. *EEO Law and Personnel Practices*. Newbury Park, CA: Sage.

Haberman, Clyde. 1980. City Agencies to Set Up Policies on Sexual-Harassment Charges. *New York Times*, December 28.

Hall, Francine S., and Maryann H. Albrecht. 1979. *The Management of Affirmative Action*. Santa Monica, CA: Goodyear.

Hall, Peter A., and Rosemary C. R. Taylor. 1996. Political Science and the Three New Institutionalisms. *Political Studies* 44:936–58.

Hallam, Charlotte B. 1973. Legal Tools to Fight Sex Discrimination. *Labor Law Journal* 24:803–9.

Halle, David. 1984. *America's Working Man*. Chicago: University of Chicago Press.

Hammerman, Herbert. 1984. *A Decade of New Opportunity: Affirmative Action in the 1970s*. Washington, DC: Potomac Institute.

Harrison, Cynthia. 1988. *On Account of Sex: The Politics of Women's Issues, 1945–1968*. Berkeley and Los Angeles: University of California Press.

Hartley, Jo. 1976. Experience with Flexible Hours of Work. *Monthly Labor Review* 99 (5): 41–42.

Hartnett, John. 1996. *OSHA in the Real World: How to Maintain Workplace Safety While Keeping Your Competitive Edge*. Santa Monica, CA: Merritt.

Hauck, Vern E. 1998. *Arbitrating Sex Discrimination Grievances*. Westport, CT: Greenwood.

Heckman, James J., and Brook S. Payner. 1989. Determining the Impact of Federal Antidiscrimination Policy on the Economic Status of Blacks: A Study of South Carolina. *American Economic Review* 79:138–77.

Heckman, James, and Kenneth Wolpin. 1976. Does the Contract Compliance Program Work? An Analysis of Chicago Data. *Industrial and Labor Relations Review* 29:544–64.

Heilman, Madeline E. 1995. Sex Stereotypes and Their Effects in the Workplace: What We Know and What We Don't Know. *Journal of Social Behavior and Personality* 10 (6): 3–26.

Herman, Alexis M., M. Anthony Burns, Gilbert F. Casellas, Edmund D. Cooke Jr., Marjorie Fine Knowles, Bill Lann Lee, and Rene A. Redwood. 2003. *Second Annual Report of the Coca-Cola Task Force*. Prepared for the United States District Court for the Northern District of Georgia pursuant to a Settlement Agreement in Ingram, et al. v. The Coca-Cola Company (Case No. 1-98-CV-3679 (RWS)).

Hewlett, Sylvia Ann. 1991. *When the Bough Breaks: The Cost of Neglecting Our Children.* New York: Basic Books.

Hirsch, Paul M. 1991. Undoing the Managerial Revolution? Needed Research on the Decline of Middle Management and Internal Labor Markets. Paper presented to the Annual Meeting of the American Sociological Association, Cincinnati.

Hobbs, Frank, and Nicole Stoops. 2002. *Demographic Trends in the 20th Century.* Washington, DC: U.S. Government Printing Office.

Hochschild, Arlie Russell. 1997. *The Time Bind: When Work Becomes Home and Home Becomes Work.* New York: Metropolitan Books.

Hodson, Randy, and Teresa A. Sullivan. 1990. *Social Organization of Work.* Belmont, CA: Wadsworth.

Hofstede, Geert. 1980. *Culture's Consequences: International Differences in Work Values.* Beverly Hills, CA: Sage.

Hoyman, Michele, and Ronda Robinson. 1980. Interpreting the New Sexual Harassment Guidelines. *Personnel Journal* 43 (4): 996–1000.

Hunt, Albert. 1986. What Working Women Want. *Wall Street Journal,* June 6.

Hyatt, James C. 1972. Women Employees Seek Disability Coverage during Pregnancy Leave. *Wall Street Journal,* December 1.

Ibarra, Herminia. 1992. Homophily and Differential Returns: Sex Differences in Network Structure and Access in an Advertising Firm. *Administrative Science Quarterly* 34:422–47.

———. 1995. Race, Opportunity and Diversity of Social Circles in Managerial Networks. *Academy of Management Journal* 38:673–703.

Ichniowski, Casey. 1983. Have Angels Done More: The Steel-Industry Consent Decree. *Industrial and Labor Relations Review* 36:182–98.

Ichniowski, Casey, John T. Delaney, and David Lewin. 1989. The New Resource Management in U.S. Workplaces: Is It Really New and Is It Only Nonunion? *Relations Industrielles* 44:97–123.

Jackall, Robert. 1983. Moral Mazes: Bureaucracy and Managerial Work. *Harvard Business Review* 61 (6): 118–58.

Jacobs, Margaret A. 1994. Securities Firms Are Falling Short on Hiring Women and Minorities. *Wall Street Journal,* October 5.

Jacoby, Sanford. 1984. The Development of Internal Labor Markets in American Manufacturing Firms. In *Internal Labor Markets,* ed. Paul Osterman, 23–69. Cambridge: MIT Press.

———. 1985a. *Employing Bureaucracy: Managers, Unions, and the Transformation of Work in American Industry, 1900–1945.* New York: Columbia University Press.

———. 1985b. *Employing Bureaucracy: Managers, Unions, and the Transformation of Work in American Industry, 1900–1945.* New York: Columbia University Press.

———. 1997. *Modern Manors: Welfare Capitalism since the New Deal.* Princeton, NJ: Princeton University Press.

Jasinoski, Jerry J. 1991. Weighing the Merits of Family-Leave Act . . . Federal Mandate Is Not the Answer. *Post-Dispatch,* May 9.

Jencks, Christopher. 1992. *Rethinking Social Policy: Race, Poverty, and the Underclass.* Cambridge: Harvard University Press.

Johns, Horace, and H. Ronald Moser. 1989. Where Has EEO Taken Personnel Policies? *Personnel* 66 (9): 63–66.

Johnson, Arlene A., and Carol L. Rose. 1992. *The Emerging Role of the Work-Family Manager.* New York: Conference Board.

Johnston, William B., and Arnold Packer. 1987. *Workforce 2000: Work and Workers for the Twenty First Century.* Indianapolis: Hudson Institute; U.S. Department of Labor.

Jones, Linda Newton. 1975. D. C. Police Officers Fret over Sex-Story Damage. *Washington Post,* November 4.

Jordan, Katrina. 1998. Diversity Training in the Workplace Today: A Status Report. *Journal of Career Planning and Employment* 59:46–55.

Jost, John T., Mahzarin Banaji, and Brian A. Nosek. 2004. A Decade of System-Justification Theory: Accumulated Evidence of Conscious and Unconscious Bolstering of the Status Quo. *Political Psychology* 25:881–919.

Juliano, Ann, and Stewart J. Schwab. 2001. The Sweep of Sexual Harassment Cases. *Cornell Law Review* 86:548–93.

Kahn, Lawrence M. 1976. Internal Labor Markets: San Francisco Longshoremen. *Industrial Relations* 15:333–37.

Kalev, Alexandra. 2005. Gender and Racial Inequality at Work: Changing Organizational Structure and Managerial Diversity. Department of Sociology, Princeton University.

Kalev, Alexandra, and Frank Dobbin. 2006. Enforcement of Civil Rights Law in Private Workplaces: Compliance Reviews and Lawsuits before and after Reagan. *Law and Social Inquiry* 31 (4): 855–79.

Kalev, Alexandra, Frank Dobbin, and Erin Kelly. 2006. Best Practices or Best Guesses? Diversity Management and the Remediation of Inequality. *American Sociological Review* 71:589–617.

Kalleberg, Arne L., and Aage B. Sorensen. 1979. Sociology of Labor Markets. *Annual Review of Sociology* 5:351–379.

Kamerman, Sheila B., and Alfred J. Kahn. 1987. *The Responsive Workplace: Employers and a Changing Labor Force.* New York: Columbia University Press.

Kamerman, Sheila B., Alfred J. Kahn, and Paul Kingston. 1983. *Maternity Policies and Working Women.* New York: Columbia University Press.

Kanter, Rosabeth Moss. 1977. *Men and Women of the Corporation.* New York: Basic Books.

Kanter, Rosabeth Moss, David V. Summers, and Barry A. Stein. 1986. The Future of Workplace Alternatives. *Management Review* 75 (7): 30–34.

Karabel, Jerome. 1984. Status-Group Struggle, Organizational Interests, and the Limits of Institutional Autonomy: The Transformation of Harvard, Yale, and Princeton, 1918–1940. *Theory and Society* 13:1–40.

———. 2005. *The Chosen: The Hidden History of Admission and Exclusion at Harvard, Yale, and Princeton.* Boston: Houghton Mifflin.

Karmin, Monroe W. 1966. Job-Bias Showdown. *Wall Street Journal,* November 9.

Katz, Daniel, and Robert L. Kahn. 1966. *The Social Psychology of Organizations.* New York: John Wiley.

Kelly, Erin L. 1999. Theorizing Corporate Family Policies: How Advocates Built "The Business Case" for "Family-Friendly" Programs. *Research in the Sociology of Work* 7:169–202.

———. 2002. The Strange History of Employer-Sponsored Childcare: Ambiguity and the Transformation of Law in Organizational Fields. *Department of Sociology*, University of Minnesota Press.

———. 2003. The Strange History of Employer-Sponsored Child Care: Interested Actors, Uncertainty, and the Transformation of Law in Organizational Fields. *American Journal of Sociology* 109:606–49.

Kelly, Erin L., and Frank Dobbin. 1998. How Affirmative Action Became Diversity Management: Employer Response to Antidiscrimination Law, 1961–1996. *American Behavioral Scientist* 41:960–84.

———. 1999. Civil Rights Law at Work: Sex Discrimination and the Rise of Maternity Leave Policies. *American Journal of Sociology* 105:455–92.

Kelly, Erin L., and Alexandra Kalev. 2006. Managing Flexible Work Arrangements in U.S. Organizations: Formalized Discretion or "A Right to Ask." *Socio-Economic Review* 4 (3): 379–416.

Kenworthy, E. W. 1963. Rise in Negro Jobs Linked to Growth. *New York Times*, June 28.

Kingdon, John W. 1984. *Agendas, Alternatives, and Public Policies*. Boston: Little, Brown.

Klein, Stuart M., Allen I. Kraut, and Alan Wolfson. 1971. Employee Reactions to Attitude Survey Feedback: A Study of the Impact of Structure and Process. *Administrative Science Quarterly* 16 (4): 497–514.

Kochan, Thomas A., and Peter Cappelli. 1984. The Transformation of the Industrial Relations and Personnel Function. In *Internal Labor Markets*, ed. Paul Osterman, 133–62. Cambridge: MIT Press.

Kochan, Thomas A., Harry C. Katz, and Robert B. McKersie. 1994. *The Transformation of American Industrial Relations*. Ithaca, NY: ILR Press.

Kohler, Thomas C. 1999. The Employment Relation and Its Ordering at Century's End: Reflections on Emerging Trends in the United States. *Boston College Law Review* 41:103–24.

Kossek, Ellen Ernst, and Sharon A. Lobel, eds. 1995. *Managing Diversity: Human Resource Strategies for Transforming the Workplace*. Cambridge, MA: Blackwell.

Kossek, Ellen Ernst, and Victor Nichol. 1992. The Effects of On-Site Child Care on Employee Attitudes and Performance. *Personnel Psychology* 45:489–509.

Krawiec, Kimberly D. 2003. Cosmetic Compliance and the Failure of Negotiated Governance. *Washington University Law Quarterly* 81:487–544.

Kronenberger, George K., and David L. Bourke. 1981. Effective Training and the Elimination of Sexual Harassment. *Personnel Journal* 60:879–82.

Larkey, Linda Kathryn. 1996. The Development and Validation of the Workforce Diversity Questionnaire: An Instrument to Assess Interactions in Diverse Workgroups. *Management Communication Quarterly* 9 (3): 296–337.

Lawrence, Paul, and Jay W. Lorsch. 1967. *Organization and Environment: Managing Differentiation and Integration*. Boston: Harvard Graduate School of Business Administration.

Lawrence, R. G. 1965. Western Electric's Commitment to Fair Employment. In *The Negro and Employment Opportunity: Problems and Practices*, ed. Herbert R. Northrup and Richard L. Rown, 137–45. Ann Arbor: Bureau of Industrial Relations, Graduate School of Business Administration, University of Michigan.

Leach, Joy, Bette George, Tina Jackson, and Arleen LaBella. 1995. *A Practical Guide to Working with Diversity: The Process, the Tools, the Resources.* New York: AMACOM.

Lelyveld, Joseph. 1964. Kodak Says Rochester Offers Few Skilled Negroes. *New York Times,* July 29.

Lemm, Kristi, and Mahzarin R. Banaji. 1999. Unconscious Attitudes and Beliefs about Men and Women. In *Perceiving and Performing Gender,* ed. Ursula Pasero and Friederike Braun, 215–35. Opladen, Germany: Westdutscher Verlag.

Lempert, Richard, and Joseph Sanders. 1986. *An Invitation to Law and Social Science: Desert, Disputes, and Distribution.* New York: Longman.

Leonard, Jonathan S. 1984a. Antidiscrimination or Reverse Discrimination: The Impact of Changing Demographics, Title VII, and Affirmative Action on Productivity. *Journal of Human Resources* 19:145–74.

———. 1984b. Employment and Occupational Advance under Affirmative Action. *Review of Economics and Statistics* 66:377–85.

———. 1984c. The Impact of Affirmative Action on Employment. *Journal of Labor Economics* 2:439–63.

———. 1985. What Promises Are Worth: The Impact of Affirmative Action Goals. *Journal of Human Resources* 20 (1): 3–20.

———. 1989. Women and Affirmative Action. *Journal of Economic Perspectives* 3 (1): 61–75.

———. 1990. The Impact of Affirmative Action Regulation and Equal Employment Opportunity Law on Black Employment. *Journal of Economic Perspectives* 4 (4): 47–63.

———. 1996. Wage Disparities and Affirmative Action in the late 1980's. *American Economic Association Papers and Proceedings* 86 (2): 285–89.

Levitt, Leonard. 1998. One Police Plaza: Confidential: 1 Promotion, Long Way to Go. *Newsday,* June 15.

LEXIS Law Publishing. 1997. *Statutes and Regulations.*

Licht, Walter. 1983. *Working for the Railroad: The Organization of Work in the Nineteenth Century.* Princeton, NJ: Princeton University Press.

Lieberman, Robert C. 1998. Race and State in the United States, Great Britain, and France: Employment Discrimination Policy in Comparative Perspective. Paper presented to the Annual Meeting of the American Political Science Association, Boston.

———. 2002a. Weak State, Strong Policy: Paradoxes of Race Policy in the United States Great Britain, and France. Paper presented to the Thirteenth Biennial Conference of Europeanists, Council of European Studies, Chicago.

———. 2002b. Weak State, Strong Policy: Paradoxes of Race Policy in the United States, Great Britain, and France. *Studies in American Political Development* 16:138–61.

———. 2005. *Shaping Race Policy: The United States in Comparative Perspective.* Princeton, NJ: Princeton University Press.

Linenberger, Patricia, and Timothy J. Keaveny. 1981a. Sexual Harassment: The Employer's Legal Obligations. *Personnel* 58 (6): 60–68.

———. 1981b. Sexual Harassment in Employment. *Human Resource Management* 20 (1): 11–17.

Lipner, Irving. 1965. 3 Negroes Find "Equal Opportunity" Is Real. *New York Times*, February 13.

Lockwood, Howard C. 1966. Critical Problems in Achieving Equal Employment Opportunity. *Personnel Psychology* 19 (1): 3–10.

Lopez, Felix M., Jr. 1966. Current Problems in Test Performance of Job Applicants; I. *Personnel Psychology* 19:10–18.

Lovaglia, Michael J., Jeffrey W. Lucas, Jeffrey A. Houser, Shane R. Thye, and Barry Markovsky. 1998. Status Processes and Mental Ability Test Scores. *American Journal of Sociology* 104:195–228.

Lowin, Aaron, William J. Hrapchak, and Michael J. Kavanaugh. 1969. Consideration and Initiating Structure: An Experimental Investigation of Leadership Traits. *Administrative Science Quarterly* 14 (2): 238–53.

Lubenow, William C. 1971. *The Politics of Government Growth: Early Victorian Attitudes toward State Intervention, 1833–1848*. Hamden, CT: Archon.

Lublin, Joann S. 1991. Sexual Harassment Is Topping Agenda in Many Executive Education Programs. *Wall Street Journal*, December 2.

Lundberg, Shelly J. 1991. The Enforcement of Equal Opportunity Laws under Imperfect Information: Affirmative Action and Alternatives. *Quarterly Journal of Economics* 106:309–26.

Lunding, F. S., C. E. Clements, and D. S. Perkins. 1979. Everyone Who Makes It Has a Mentor. *Harvard Business Review* 56 (3): 89–101.

Lynch, Frederick R. 1997. *The Diversity Machine: The Drive to Change the White Male Workplace*. New York: Free Press.

MacDonagh, Oliver. 1958. The Nineteenth-Century Revolution in Government: A Reappraisal. *Historical Journal* 1 (1): 52–67.

MacDonald, Heather. 1993. Cashing in on Affirmative Action: The Diversity Industry. *New Republic*, July 5.

Machlowitz, David S., and Marilyn M. Machlowitz. 1987. Preventing Sexual Harassment. *American Bar Association Journal* 73:78.

MacKinnon, Catharine A. 1979. *Sexual Harassment of Working Women*. New Haven: Yale University Press.

MacLean, Nancy. 2006. *Freedom Is Not Enough: The Opening of the American Workplace*. Cambridge: Harvard University Press.

Malkiel, Burton. 1979. Productivity: The Problem behind the Headlines. *Harvard Business Review* 57 (3): 81–111.

Mansbridge, Jane J. 1986. *Why We Lost the ERA*. Chicago: University of Chicago Press.

March, James G., and Herbert A. Simon. 1958. *Organizations*. New York: Wiley.

Marglin, Stephen A. 1974. What Do Bosses Do? The Origins and Functions of Hierarchy in Capitalist Production. *Review of Radical Political Economics* 6:60–112.

Marino, Kenneth. 1980. Conducting an Internal Compliance Review of Affirmative Action. *Personnel* 57 (2): 24–34.

Mattison, E. G. 1965. Integrating the Work Force in Southern Industry. In *The Negro and Employment Opportunity: Problems and Practices*, ed. Herbert R. Northrup and Richard L. Rowan, 147–54. Ann Arbor: Bureau of Industrial Relations, Graduate School of Business Administration, University of Michigan.

Mayer, Caroline E. 1981. U.S. Relaxing Enforcement of Regulations. *Washington Post*, November 15.

———. 1984. Merck Blends Family Life with Work. *Washington Post*, October 14.

Mayo, Elton. 1933. *The Human Problems of an Industrial Civilization*. Boston: Graduate School of Business Administration, Harvard University.

Mays, Benjamin E. 1961. My View: We Will Watch Lockheed. *New Pittsburgh Courier*, July 8.

McBee, Susanna. 1964. Negro Universities Caught Off Base by Business Demand for Graduates. *Washington Post*, July 21.

McCammon, Holly. 1996. Protection for Whom? Maximum Hours Laws and Women's Employment in the United States, 1880–1920. *Work and Occupations* 23:132–64.

McCrary, Justin. 2006. The Effect of Court-Ordered Hiring Quotas on the Composition and Quality of Police. NBER Working Paper No. W12368.

McCraw, Thomas K. 1975. Regulation in America: A Review Article. *Business History Review* 49:159–83.

McDowell, Gary L. 1989. Affirmative Inaction: The Brock-Meese Standoff on Federal Racial Quotas. *Policy Review* 48:32–50.

McFarland, Harold S. 1965. Minority Group Employment at General Motors. In *The Negro and Employment Opportunity: Problems and Practices*, ed. Herbert R. Northrup and Richard L. Rowan, 131–36. Ann Arbor: Bureau of Industrial Relations, Graduate School of Business Administration, University of Michigan.

McGuire, G. M. 2000. Gender, Race, Ethnicity, and Networks: The Factors Affecting the Status of Employees' Network Members. *Work and Occupations* 27:500–523.

McIntyre, Douglas I., and James C. Renick. 1982. Protecting Public Employees from Sexual Harassment. *Public Personnel Management Journal* 11 (4): 282–92.

McSweeney, Brendan. 2002. Hofstede's Model of National Cultural Differences and Their Consequences: A Triumph of Faith—a Failure of Analysis. *Human Relations* 55 (1): 89–118.

Mead, Margaret. 1978. A Proposal: We Need Taboos on Sex at Work. *Redbook*, April.

Meltzer, Bernard. 1980. The Weber Case: The Judicial Abrogation of the Antidiscrimination Standard in Employment. *University of Chicago Law Review* 47:423–66.

Mendeloff, John. 1979. *Regulating Safety*. Cambridge: MIT Press.

Merton, Robert K. 1968. *Social Theory and Social Structure*. New York: Free Press.

Meyer, John W., and Brian Rowan. 1977. Institutionalized Organizations: Formal Structure as Myth and Ceremony. *American Journal of Sociology* 83:340–63.

Meyer, John, and W. Richard Scott. 1983a. Centralization and the Legitimacy Problems of Local Government. In *Organizational Environments: Ritual and Rationality*. 199–217. Beverly Hills, CA: Sage.

———. 1983b. *Organizational Environments: Ritual and Rationality*. Beverly Hills, CA: Sage.

———. 1992. *Organizational Environments: Ritual and Rationality*. Updated ed. Beverly Hills, CA: Sage.

Meyer, Marshall W. 1979. Organizational Structure as Signaling. *Pacific Sociological Review* 22:481–500.

Milkman, Ruth. 1997. *Farewell to the Factory: Auto Workers in the Late Twentieth Century*. Berkeley and Los Angeles: University of California Press.

Miller, Delberg, and William Form. 1964. *Industrial Sociology*. New York: Harper and Row.

Miller, Joanne. 1994. Corporate Responses to Diversity. Center for the New American Workforce, Queens College.

Mills, D. Quinn. 1979. Human Resources in the 1980's. *Harvard Business Review* 57 (4): 154–62.

Mintz, Morton. 1978. High Court Cases of Great Importance to Business, Labor. *Washington Post*, October 2.

Mitnick, Barry M. 1978. Deregulation as a Process of Organizational Reduction. *Public Administration Review* 38 (4): 350–57.

Moore, Paul Cameron. 2001. The Transfer of Human and Social Capital: Employee Development through Assigned Peer Mentoring. Graduate School of Business, Stanford University.

Morse, Gerry E. 1965. Equal Employment Opportunity at Honeywell, Inc. In *The Negro and Employment Opportunity: Problems and Practices*, ed. Herbert R. Northrup and Richard L. Rowan, 123–30: Ann Arbor: Bureau of Industrial Relations, Graduate School of Business Administration, University of Michigan.

National Civil Service League. 1973. *Training and Testing the Disadvantaged*. Washington, DC: Consortium.

National Industrial Conference Board. 1929. *Industrial Relations Programs in Small Plants*. New York: NICD.

———. 1936. *What Employers Are Doing for Employees: A Survey of Voluntary Activities for Improvement of Working Conditions in American Business Concerns*. New York: NICD.

———. 1940. *Studies in Personnel Policy: Supplement to the Conference Board Management Record*. New York: NICD.

———. 1947. *Personnel Activities in American Business (Revised)*. New York: NICD.

———. 1964. *Personnel Practices in Factory and Office: Manufacturing*. New York: NICD.

———. 1965. Office Personnel Practices: Nonmanufacturing. New York.

Nelson, Robert L., and William P. Bridges. 1999. *Legalizing Gender Inequality: Courts, Markets, and Unequal Pay for Women in America*. New York: Cambridge University Press.

Neumark, David, Roy Blank, and Kyle Van Nort. 1995. Sex Discrimination in Restaurant Hiring: An Audit Study. NBER Working Paper No. 5024.

Neumark, David, and Rosella Gardecki. 1996. Women Helping Women? Role-Model and Mentoring Effects on Female Ph.D. Student in Economics. NBER Working Paper No. W5733.

Nollen, Stanley D. 1979. Does Flexitime Improve Productivity? *Harvard Business Review* 57 (5): 12–22.

Nord, Philip. 1994. The Welfare State in France, 1870–1914. *French Historical Studies* 18 (3): 821–38.

Oelsner, Lesley. 1977. Supreme Court Backs Seniority Work Rules That May Discriminate. *New York Times*, June 1.

Olmsted, Barney, and Suzanne Smith. 1994. *Creating a Flexible Workplace: How to Select and Manage Alternative Work Options*. New York: AMACOM.

Olson, Walter. 1993. When Sensitivity Training is the Law. *Wall Street Journal*, January 20.

Oren, Dan. 1985. *Joining the Club: A History of Jews and Yale*. New Haven: Yale University Press.

Osterman, Paul. 1975. An Empirical Study of Labor Market Segmentation. *Industrial and Labor Relations Review* 28:508–23.

———. 1995. Work/Family Programs and the Employment Relationship. *Administrative Science Quarterly* 40:681–700.

Ouchi, William G. 1981. *Theory Z: How American Business Can Meet the Japanese Challenge*. Reading, MA: Addison-Wesley.

Packard, David. 1995. *The HP Way: How Bill Hewlett and I Built Our Company*. New York: HarperBusiness.

Pager, Devah. 2003a. Blacks and Ex-Cons Need Not Apply. *Contexts* 2 (4): 58–59.

———. 2003b. The Mark of a Criminal Record. *American Journal of Sociology* 108:937–75.

———. 2005. Walking the Talk: What Employers Say versus What They Do. *American Sociological Review* 70:355–80.

Parrish, Jack A. 1966. The Industrial Psychologist: Selection and Equal Employment Opportunity (a Symposium). *Personnel Psychology* 19:1–2.

Patton, Archibald. 1960. How to Appraise Executive Performance. *Harvard Business Review* 38 (1): 63–70.

Pear, Robert. 1985. Should Leaves for New Parents be Mandatory? Mr. Klein: No Concern of Government. *New York Times*, December 29.

Pedriana, Nicholas. 2004. Help Wanted NOW: Legal Resources, the Women's Movement, and the Battle over Sex-Segregated Job Advertisements. *Social Problems* 51 (2): 182–201.

———. 2006. From Protective to Equal Treatment: Legal Framing Processes and Transformation of the Women's Movement in the 1960s. *American Journal of Sociology* 111:1718–61.

Pedriana, Nicholas, and Robin Stryker. 1997. Political-Culture Wars 1960s Style: Equal Employment Opportunity–Affirmative Action Law and the Philadelphia Plan. *American Journal of Sociology* 103:633–91.

Peirce School. 1935. *Current Personnel Practices*. Philadelphia: Peirce School of Business Administration.

Perrow, Charles. 1986. *Complex Organizations: A Critical Essay*. New York: Random House.

———. 2002. *Organizing America: Wealth, Power, and the Origins of Corporate Capitalism*. Princeton, NJ: Princeton University Press.

Peskin, Dean B. 1969. Building Groundwork for Affirmative Action EEO Program. *Personnel Journal* 48:130–49.

Petersen, Donald J. 1974. The Impact of Duke Power on Testing. *Personnel* 51:31–37.

Petersen, Trond, Ishak Saporta, and Marc David Seidelm. 1998. Offering a Job: Meritocracy and Social Networks. *American Journal of Sociology* 106:763–816.

Pfeffer, Jeffrey, and James N. Baron. 1988. Taking the Workers Back Out: Recent Trends in the Structuring of Employment. *Research in Organizational Behavior* 10:257–303.

Pfeffer, Jeffrey, and Yinon Cohen. 1984. Labor Markets in Organizations. *Administrative Science Quarterly* 29:550–72.

Pfeffer, Jeffrey, and Gerald R. Salancik. 1978. *The External Control of Organizations: A Resource Dependence Perspective*. New York: Harper and Row.

Pomfret, John D. 1963. Negro-Job Pledge Is Found Flouted. *New York Times*, April 17.

Prugh, Peter H. 1965. Business & Race: Chicago Executives Press Campaign to Hire More Negros. *Wall Street Journal*, August 19.

Puma, John J. 1966. Improving Negro Employment in Boston. *Industrial Management Review* 8 (1): 37–45.

Purcell, Theodore. 1953. *The Worker Speaks His Mind on Union and Company*. Cambridge: Harvard University Press.

———. 1960. *Blue Collar Man*. Cambridge: Harvard University Press.

———. 1962. Management versus Jim Crow. *Management of Personnel Quarterly* 1 (4): 2–6.

———. 1974. How G.E. Measures Managers on Fair Employment. *Harvard Business Review* 52 (6): 99–104.

Ralston, David A. 1989. The Benefits of Flextime: Real or Imagined? *Journal of Organizational Behavior* 10 (4): 369–73.

Rapoport, Rhona, and Lotte Bailyn. 1996. *Relinking Life and Work: Toward a Better Future*. New York: Ford Foundation.

Raskin, A. H. 1961. Negro Makes Job Gain in South under Initial Drive at Lockheed. *New York Times*, June 18.

Reed, Susan E. 2001. New Economy, Same Harassment Problems. *New York Times*, August 12.

Reich, Michael, David M. Gordon, and Richard C. Edwards. 1973. A Theory of Labor Market Segmentation. *American Economic Review* 63:359–65.

Renick, James C. 1980. Sexual Harassment at Work: Why It Happens, What to Do about It. *Personnel Journal* 59:658–63.

Rennes, Juliette. 2007. *Le Mérite et la nature. Une controverse républicaine: L'accès des femmes aux professions de prestige, 1840–1940*. Paris: Fayard.

Reskin, Barbara J. 1990. Women's Gains in Insurance Sales: Increased Supply, Uncertain Demand. In *Job Queues, Gender Queues: Explaining Women's Inroads into Male Occupations*, by Barbara J. Reskin and Patricia A. Roos, 183–204. Philadelphia: Temple University Press.

———. 2000. The Proximate Causes of Employment Discrimination. *Contemporary Sociology* 29 (2): 319–28.

Reskin, Barbara F., and Debra B. McBrier. 2000. Why Not Ascription? Organizations' Employment of Male and Female Managers. *American Sociological Review* 65:210–33.

Robertson, Nan. 1971. "Race Awareness" Drive Stirs Capital Dispute. *New York Times*, November 29.

Robin, Donald P. 1967. An Input-Output Model of Employee Behavior. *Academy of Management Journal* 10:257–68.

Roche, Gerard R. 1979. Much Ado about Mentors. *Harvard Business Review* 57 (1): 14.

Rochon, Thomas R. 1998. *Culture Moves: Ideas, Activism, and Changing Values.* Princeton, NJ: Princeton University Press.

Rock, Milton L., and John J. Grela. 1960. Basing Bonus Payments on Opportunity and Performance. *Personnel Journal* 38:330–40.

Rodgers, William, and William Spriggs. 1996. The Effect of Federal Contractor Status on Racial Differences in Establishment-Level Employment Shares: 1979–1992. *American Economic Review* 86:290–93.

Rodriguez, Daniel B., and Barry R. Weingast. 2003. The Positive Political Theory of Legislative History: New Perspectives on the 1964 Civil Rights Act and Its Interpretation. *University of Pennsylvania Law Review* 151:1417–1542.

Roethlisberger, Fritz J., and William Dickinson. 1939. *Management and the Worker.* Cambridge: Harvard University Press.

Romm, Stuart. 1995. Layoffs: Principles and Practices. In *Local Justice in America*, ed. Jon Elster, 153–226. New York: Russell Sage Foundation.

Ronen, Simcha. 1981. *Flexible Working Hours: An Innovation in the Quality of Work Life.* New York: McGraw-Hill.

———. 1984. *Alternative Work Schedules: Selecting, Implementing, and Evaluating.* Homewood, IL: Dow Jones–Irwin.

Ronen, Simcha, and Sophia B. Primps. 1979. The Impact of Flextime on Performance and Attitudes in 25 Public Agencies. Graduate School of Business Administration, New York University

Roos, Patricia, and Joan E. Manley. 1996. Staffing Personnel: Feminization and Change in Human Resource Management. *Sociological Focus* 99 (3): 245–61.

Ropp, Kirland. 1987. How the Courts Affect Management Policy. *Personnel Administrator* 32:45–50, 100.

Rosen, Jeffrey. 2006. *The Most Democratic Branch: How the Courts Serve America.* New York: New York University Press.

Rosenberg, Gail S. 1980. When Less Is More . . . *Washington Post*, February 13, F1.

Rosenthal, Robert, and D. B. Rubin. 1978. Interpersonal Expectancy Effects: The First 345 Studies. *Behavioral and Brain Sciences* 3:377–86.

Rowe, Mary P. 1981. Dealing with Sexual Harassment. *Harvard Business Review* 59 (3): 42–45.

Rowe, Mary P., and Michael Baker. 1984. Are You Hearing Enough Employee Concerns? *Harvard Business Review* 62 (3): 127–38.

Rubery, Jill. 1978. Structured Labor Markets Worker Organization and Low Pay. *Cambridge Journal of Economics* 2:17–36.

Ruby, Michael, Tom Joyce, Barbara Graustark, and Elaine Sciolino. 1976. Women at Work. *Newsweek*, December 6.

Ruhm, Christopher J., and Jackqueline L. Teague. 1997. Parental Leave Policies in Europe and North America. In *Gender and Family Issues in the Workplace*, ed. Francine D. Blau and Ronald G. Ehrenberg, 133–56. New York: Russell Sage Foundation.

Rynes, Sara, and Benson Rosen. 1994. What Makes Diversity Programs Work? *HR Magazine* 39 (10): 67.

Sabbagh, Daniel. 2002. Affirmative Action at Sciences Po. *French Politics Culture Society* 20 (3): 52–64.

———. 2007. *Equality and Transparency: A Strategic Perspective on Affirmative Action in American Law.* New York: Palgrave Macmillan.

Saguy, Abigail. 1999. Sexual Harassment in France and the United States: Rethinking the Meaning of the Workplace. Paper presented to the Annual Meeting of the American Sociological Association, Chicago.

———. 2003. *What Is Sexual Harassment? From Capitol Hill to the Sorbonne.* Berkeley and Los Angeles: University of California Press.

Sandport, Wendy. 1979. *Fighting Sexual Harassment: An Advocacy Handbook.* Boston: Alliance Against Sexual Coercion.

Sawyer, Sandra, and Arthur A. Whatley. 1980. Sexual Harassment: A Form of Sex Discrimination. *Personnel Administrator* 25:36–39.

Schatz, Ronald W. 1983. *The Electrical Workers: A History of Labor at General Electric and Westinghouse, 1923–1960.* Urbana: University of Illinois Press.

Schlafly, Phyllis. 1977. *The Power of a Positive Woman.* New Rochelle, NY: Arlington House.

Schofer, August. 1971. General Electric's 1970 Report for the US Commission on Civil Rights. Exhibit No. 2U before the United States Commission on Civil Rights. *Clarification and Rebuttal of Staff Report: The Civil Rights Implications of Suburban Freeway Construction.* Baltimore: Regional Federal Highway Administration, Region 2. http://www.law.umaryland.edu/marshall/usccr/documents/cr12h8112_C.pdf. Accessed August 11, 2006.

Schultz, Vicki. 1998. Reconceptualizing Sexual Harassment. *Yale Law Journal* 107:1755–1878.

———. 2003. The Sanitized Workplace. *Yale Law Journal* 112:2061–2193.

Scott, William G. 1968. Technology and Organization Government: A Speculative Inquiry into the Functionality of Management Creeds. *Academy of Management Journal* 11:301–13.

Selznick, Philip. 1957. *Leadership in Administration: A Sociological Interpretation.* New York: Harper and Row.

———. 1969. *Law, Society, and Industrial Justice.* New York: Russell Sage.

Seybold, Geneva. 1948. *Personnel Practices in Factory and Office.* Studies in Personnel Policy, No. 88. New York: National Industrial Conference Board.

———. 1954. *Personnel Practices in Factory and Office.* 5th ed. New York: National Industrial Conference Board.

Shaeffer, Ruth G. 1973. *Nondiscrimination in Employment: Changing Perspectives, 1963–1972.* New York: Conference Board.

———. 1975. *Nondiscrimination in Employment, 1973–1975: A Broadening and Deepening National Effort.* New York: Conference Board.

———. 1980. *Nondiscrimination in Employment—and Beyond.* New York: Conference Board.

Shah, Diane K., and Susan Agrest. 1979. A Steno Who Said 'NO!' *Newsweek,* April 30, 72.

Shalowitz, Deborah. 1992. Managers Named for Work-Family Issues. *Business Insurance,* April 27, 12.

Siegelman, Peter, and John J. Donohue, III. 1990. Studying the Iceberg from Its Tip: A Comparison of Published and Unpublished Employment Discrimination Cases. *Law and Society Review* 24:1133–70.

Singer, Penny. 1988. Flexible Work Hours Grow More Popular. *New York Times*, September 25.

Sipser, Margaret Ann. 1973. Maternity Leave: Judicial and Arbitral Interpretation, 1970–1972. *Labor Law Journal* 24:173–90.

Skrentny, John D. 1996. *The Ironies of Affirmative Action: Politics, Culture, and Justice in America*. Chicago: University of Chicago Press.

———. 2002. *The Minority Rights Revolution*. Cambridge: Harvard University Press.

Skrzycki, Cindy. 1989. Family Concerns Spark Changes at Work. *Washington Post*, September 3.

Slevin, Dennis. 1973. Full Utilization of Women in Employment: The Problem and an Action Program. *Human Resource Management* 12:25–32.

Slichter, Sumner. 1919. *The Turnover of Factory Labor*. New York: Appleton.

Slichter, Sumner, John Joseph Healy, and Edward Robert Livernash. 1960. *The Impact of Collective Bargaining on Management*. Washington, DC: Brookings.

Sloan, Alfred P. 1963. *My Years with General Motors*. Garden City, NJ: Doubleday.

Solomon, Jolie. 1988. The Future Look of Employee Benefits. *Wall Street Journal*, September 7.

Somers, Patricia A., and Judith Clementson-Mohr. 1979. Sexual Extortion in the Workplace. *Personnel Administrator* 24:23–28.

Soutar, Douglas. 1981. Preempting Governmental Regulation of the Work Place through Self-Enlightened Policy Planning. *Employee Relations Law Journal* 7:67–76.

Sovern, Michael I. 1966. *Legal Restraints on Racial Discrimination in Employment*. New York: Twentieth Century Fund.

Sowell, Thomas. 1976. "Affirmative Action" Reconsidered. *Public Interest* 42:47–65.

Spann, Jeri. 1990. Dealing Effectively with Sexual Harassment: Some Practical Lessons from One City's Experience. *Public Personnel Management* 19 (1): 53–82.

Spencer, Steven J., Claude M. Steele, and Diane M. Quinn. 1999. Stereotype Threat and Women's Math Performance. *Journal of Experimental Social Psychology* 35:4–28.

Spilerman, Seymour. 1977. Careers, Labor Market Structure, and Socioeconomic Achievement. *American Journal of Sociology* 83:551–93.

Spiro, Leah Nathans. 1994. Is Wall Street Finally Starting to Get It? *Business Week*, September 26.

Stark, David. 1980. Class Struggle and the Transformation of the Labor Process: A Relational Approach. *Theory and Society* 9:89–130.

———. 1986. Rethinking Internal Labor Markets: New Insights from a Comparative Perspective. *American Sociological Review* 51:492–504.

Staudohar, Paul D. 1981. Exhaustion of Remedies in Private Industry Grievance Procedures. *Employee Relations Law Journal* 7:454–65.

Steeh, Charlotte, and Maria Krysan. 1996. The Polls—Trends: Affirmative Action and the Public, 1970–1995. *Public Opinion Quarterly* 60:128–58.

Steele, Claude M. 1992. Race and the Schooling of Black Americans. *The Atlantic* 269:68–78.

Steele, Claude M., and Joshua Aronson. 1995. Stereotype Threat and the Intellectual Test Performance of African-Americans. *Journal of Personality and Social Psychology* 69:797–811.

Stephanopoulous, George, and Christopher Edley. 1995. *Affirmative Action Review: Report to the President*. Washington, DC: U.S. Government Printing Office.

Stetson, Damon. 1963. More Salaried Positions Are Opening to Negroes. *New York Times*, November 12.

Stiglitz, Joseph E. 1973. Approaches to the Economics of Discrimination. *American Economic Review* 63:287–95.

Stone, Katherine. 1974. The Origins of Job Structures in the Steel Industry. *Review of Radical Politics and Economics* 6:113–73.

Storey, John. 1992. *Developments in the Management of Human Resources*. Oxford: Basil Blackwell.

Strang, David, and John W. Meyer. 1993. Institutional Conditions for Diffusion. *Theory and Society* 22:487–511.

Stryker, Robin. 1996. Law, Sociology, and Public Policy Issues in Equal Employment Opportunity. Paper presented to the Annual Meeting of the American Sociological Association, New York.

———. 2001. Disparate Impact and the Quota Debates: Law, Labor Market, Sociology, and Equal Employment Policies. *Sociology Quarterly* 42 (1): 13–46.

Stryker, Robin, Martha Scarpellino, and Mellisa Holtzman. 1999. Political Culture Wars 1990s Style: The Drum Beat of Quotas in Media Framing of the Civil Rights Act of 1991. *Research in Social Stratification and Mobility* 17:33–106.

Sturm, Susan. 2001. Second Generation Employment Discrimination: A Structural Approach. *Columbia Law Review* 101:459–568.

Sullivan, Frederick L. 1986. Sexual Harassment: The Supreme Court's Ruling. *Personnel* 12:37–44.

Sutton, John R., and Frank Dobbin. 1996. The Two Faces of Governance: Responses to Legal Uncertainty in American Firms, 1955–1985. *American Sociological Review* 61:794–811.

Sutton, John R., Frank Dobbin, John W. Meyer, and W. Richard Scott. 1994. The Legalization of the Workplace. *American Journal of Sociology* 99:944–71.

Swart, J. Carroll. 1978. *A Flexible Approach to Working Hours*. New York: AMACOM.

Swoboda, Frank. 1988. IBM Sets Flexible Work Rules to Ease Home, Office Strains. *Washington Post*, October 19.

———. 1989. AT&T Pact in Vanguard on Family-Care Benefits. *Washington Post*, May 29.

Synnott, Marcia Graham. 1979. *The Half-Opened Door: Discrimination and Admissions at Harvard, Yale and Princeton, 1900-1970*. Westport, CT: Greenwood.

Tajfel, Henri, and John C. Turner. 1979. An Integrative Theory of Intergroup Conflict. In *The Social Psychology of Intergroup Relations*, ed. William G. Austin and Stephen Worchel, 33–47. Monterey, CA: Brooks/Cole.

Taylor, Frederick W. 1911. *Scientific Management*. New York: Harper.

———. 1981. Scientific Management. In *The Sociology of Organizations: Basic Studies*, ed. Oscar Grusky and George A. Miller, 54–66. New York: Free Press.

Taylor, Marylee. 1995. White Backlash to Workplace Affirmative Action: Peril or Myth? *Social Forces* 73:1385–1414.

Tevlin, Jon. 1999. Two Sides of Harassment Case: Attorneys in Mitsubishi Suit Warn Companies to Take Action. *Star Tribune*, February 20.

Thagard, Paul. 1996. *Mind: An Introduction to Cognitive Science*. Cambridge: MIT Press.

Thelen, Kathleen. 2004. *How Institutions Evolve: The Political Economy of Skills in Germany, Britain, the United States, and Japan*. New York: Cambridge University Press.

Thelen, Kathleen, and Svein Steinmo. 1992. Historical Institutionalism in Comparative Politics. *Structuring Politics: Historical Institutionalism in Comparative Politics*, ed. Sven Steinmo, Kathleen Thelen, and Frank Longstreth, 1–32. New York: Cambridge University Press.

Thomas, David A. 2001. The Truth about Mentoring Minorities: Race Matters. *Harvard Business Review* 79 (4): 99–107.

———. 2004. Diversity as Strategy. *Harvard Business Review* 82 (9): 98–108.

Thomas, David A., and Robin J. Ely. 1996. Making Differences Matter: A New Paradigm for Managing Diversity. *Harvard Business Review* 74 (5): 79–90.

Thomas, R. Roosevelt, Jr. 1991. *Beyond Race and Gender: Unleashing the Power of Your Total Work Force by Managing Diversity*. New York: AMACOM.

———. 1994. From Affirmative Action to Affirming Diversity. In *Differences That Work: Organizational Excellence through Diversity*, ed. Mary C. Gentile, 27–46. Cambridge: Harvard Business Review Books.

Thompson, James D. 1967. *Organizations in Action*. New York: McGraw-Hill.

Thorpe, Carey D., Jr. 1973. Fair Employment Practices: The Compliance Jungle. *Personnel Journal* 52:642–49.

Tolbert, Pamela S., and Lynne G. Zucker. 1983. Institutional Sources of Change in the Formal-Structure of Organizations—the Diffusion of Civil-Service Reform, 1880–1935. *Administrative Science Quarterly* 28 (1): 22–39.

Trost, Cathy. 1992. Labor Letter. *Wall Street Journal*, October 13.

Turner, Margery Austin, Michael Fix, and Raymond J. Struyk. 1991. *Opportunities Denied, Opportunities Diminished: Racial Discrimination in Hiring*. Washington, DC: Urban Institute.

Turner, Ronald. 1990. Employer Liability under Title VII for Hostile Environment Sexual Harassment by Supervisory Personnel: The Impact and Aftermath of Meritor Savings Bank. *Howard Law Journal* 33:1–52.

U.S. Census Bureau. 2006. U.S. Decennial Census of Population. United States Census Bureau.

U.S. Department of Labor. Office of Federal Contract Compliance Programs. 2000. Government Contractors, Affirmative Action Requirements, Proposed Rule. 41 CFR Parts 60-1 and 60-2, 65 Fed. Reg. 26088–26109, May 4.

U.S. Equal Employment Opportunity Commission. 1974. *Affirmative Action and Equal Employment: A Guidebook for Employers*. Washington, DC: USEEOC.

U.S. Merit Systems Protection Board. 1991. *Balancing Work Responsibilities and Family Needs: The Federal Civil Service Response*. Washington, DC: U.S. Government Printing Office.

Verespej, Michael A. 1991. Longer Dockets, Deep Pockets: A Political Retreat on Civil Rights Will Make Business Sitting Ducks for More Lawsuits. *Industry Week*, November 18, 64.

Vernon-Gerstenfeld, Susan, and Edmund Burke. 1985. Affirmative Action in Nine Large Companies: A Field Study. *Personnel* 62 (4): 54–60.

Viscusi, W. Kip. 1983. *Risk by Choice: Regulating Health and Safety in the Workplace*. Cambridge: Harvard University Press.

Viscusi, W. Kip, and Richard Zeckhauser. 1979. Optimal Standards with Incomplete Enforcement. *Public Policy* 27:437–56.

Vogel, Lise. 1993. *Mothers on the Job: Maternity Policy in the U.S. Workplace*. New Brunswick, NJ: Rutgers University Press.

Vollmer, Howard V., and Patrick J. McGillivray. 1960. Personnel Offices and the Institutionalization of Employee Rights. *Pacific Sociological Review* 3 (1): 29–34.

Waldfogel, Jane. 1997. Working Mothers Then and Now: A Cross-Cohort Analysis of the Effects of Maternity Leave on Women's Pay. In *Gender and Family Issues in the Workplace*, ed. Francine D. Blau and Ronald G. Ehrenberg, 92–126. New York: Russell Sage Foundation.

Wallace, Phyllis A. 1976. *Equal Employment Opportunity and the A.T.&T. Case*. Cambridge: MIT Press.

Walsh, Ethel Bent. 1974. Sex Discrimination and the Impact of Title VII. *Labor Law Journal* 25:150–54.

Walsh, Richard J., and Lee R. Hess. 1974. The Small Company, EEOC, and Test Validation Alternatives: Do You Know Your Options? *Personnel Journal* 53:840–45.

Walterscheid, Ellen. 1993. Family-Friendly Work Policies. *Women in Business*, 45 (6): 30–31.

Weber, Max. 1978. *Economy and Society*. Berkeley and Los Angeles: University of California Press.

Wehrwein, Austin C. 1962. Job Bias Is Laid to Chicago Banks. *New York Times*, November 3.

Wheeler, Michael L. 1994. *Diversity Training*. New York: Conference Board.

———. 1995. *Diversity: Business Rationale and Strategies*. New York: Conference Board.

Wiley, Joseph E., and Suzanne I. Price. 1992. Ripe for Challenges: Employment Discrimination Claims. *Law Practice Management* 18 (2): 24.

Wilkins, David B. 2004. Symposium: Brown at Fifty: From "Separate Is Inherently Unequal" to "Diversity Is Good for Business": The Rise of Market-Based Diversity Arguments and the Fate of the Black Corporate Bar. *Harvard Law Review* 117 (1548):

Williams, Joan. 2000. *Unbending Gender: Why Family and Work Conflict and What to Do about It*. New York: Oxford University Press.

Williams, Melissa S. 2000. The Deliberative Transformation of Social Meanings: The Case of Sexual Harassment. Paper presented to the Annual Meeting of the American Political Science Association, Washington, DC.

Williamson, Oliver E. 1975. *Markets and Hierarchies: Analysis and Antitrust Implications*. New York: Free Press.

———. 1985. *The Economic Institutions of Capitalism*. New York: Free Press.

Wilson, James Q. 1980. *The Politics of Regulation*. New York: Basic.

Winterle, Mary J. 1992. *Workforce Diversity: Corporate Challenges, Corporate Responses*. New York: Conference Board.

Wisensale, Steven K. 1997. The White House and Congress on Child Care and Family Leave Policy: From Carter to Clinton. *Policy Studies Journal* 25 (10): 75–86.

Wuthnow, Robert. 1987. *Meaning and Moral Order: Explorations in Cultural Analysis*. Berkeley and Los Angeles: University of California Press.

Wymer, John F., III. 1983. Compensatory and Punitive Damages for Sexual Harassment. *Personnel Journal* 62:181–84.

Yakura, Elaine K. 1995. EEO Law and Managing Diversity. In *Managing Diversity: Human Resource Strategies for Transforming the Workplace*, ed. Ellen Ernst Kossek and Sharon A. Lobel, 16–29. Cambridge, MA: Blackwell.

Youngblood, Stuart A., and Gary L. Tidwell. 1981. Employment-at-Will: Some Changes in the Wind. *Personnel* 58 (3): 22–33.

Zald, Mayer N., and Patricia Denton. 1963. From Evangelism to General Service: The Transformation of the YMCA. *Administrative Science Quarterly* 8:214–34.

Zippel, Kathrin S. 2006. *The Politics of Sexual Harassment: A Comparative Study of the United States, the European Union, and Germany*. Cambridge: Cambridge University Press.

Zorn, Dirk. 2004. Here a Chief, There a Chief: The Rise of the CFO in the American Firm. *American Sociological Review* 69:345–64.

Lightning Source UK Ltd.
Milton Keynes UK
UKOW03f2309291116
288804UK00003B/282/P